Manager's Guide to Distributed Environments

From Legacy to Living Systems

Advance Praise for
Manager's Guide to Distributed Environments

In an era of global markets and rapid change, our IT infrastructure must be the "living system" described here—distributed, adaptable and manageable. IT professionals seeking to achieve this vision will find this book of interest.

—Ann Livermore
Vice President, Hewlett-Packard Company
General Manager, Software and Services Group

This book is a significant contribution for those struggling with the issues of deploying distributed network services of acceptable quality, at acceptable costs. The discussions of architecture coupled with the practicalities of managing these complex environments provides the kind of quality information and insight that professionals need today.

—John McConnell
President
McConnell Associates, Inc.
Boulder, Colorado

Ptak, Morgenthal, and Forge have created a book that provides an excellent introduction to the world of distributed computing and its new paradigms. It is a solid reference that belongs on the bookshelf of any serious IT manager.

—Rick Sturm
Principal
Enterprise Management Associates

Manager's Guide to Distributed Environments

From Legacy to Living Systems

Richard L. Ptak

JP Morgenthal

Simon Forge

WILEY COMPUTER PUBLISHING

John Wiley & Sons, Inc.

New York • Chichester • Weinheim • Brisbane • Singapore • Toronto

Publisher: Robert Ipsen

Editor: Marjorie Spencer

Assistant Editor: Margaret Hendrey

Managing Editor: Micheline Frederick

Text Design & Composition: SunCliff Graphic Productions

Designations used by companies to distinguish their products are often claimed as trademarks. In all instances where John Wiley & Sons, Inc. is aware of a claim, the product names appear in initial capital or ALL CAPITAL LETTERS. Readers, however, should contact the appropriate companies for more complete information regarding trademarks and registration.

This text is printed on acid-free paper. ∞

This publication is designed to provide accurate and authoritative information in regard to the subject matter covered. It is sold with the understanding that the publisher is not engaged in professional services. If professional advice or other expert assistance is required, the services of a competent professional person should be sought.

Library of Congress Cataloging-in-Publication Data

Ptak, Richard L. 1946–
    Manager's guide to distributed environments / Richard L. Ptak,
JP Morgenthal, Simon Forge.
        p.   cm.
    Includes bibliographical references (p.) and index.
    ISBN: 0-471-19712-2 (alk. paper)
    1. Client/server computing.   2. Electronic data processing-
-Distributed processing.   I. Morgenthal, JP, 1966–   .
II. Forge, Simon, 1946–   .   III. Title.
QA76.9.C55P83   1998
658.4'038'011--dc21   98-8275
                                                        CIP

Printed in the United States of America
10 9 8 7 6 5 4 3 2 1

To the memory of my father, Louis R. Ptak, whose heroism was never sufficiently acknowledged but was amply displayed as he and my mother raised their five children.

—Richard L. Ptak

I wish to thank my loving wife Amy Lynn, for all her support in my endeavors, and to my children Amanda and Daniel who inspire me to be my best in all I do.

—JP Morgenthal

I wish to acknowledge all those who have shown me a little of what writing can be, from the master, Raymond Chandler (for the little sister), to Martin Mayer (for Madison Avenue USA), Michael Dibden (for Aurelio Zen) and last but not leased, Kinky Friedman (for being basically killer bee).

—SCF

CONTENTS

CHAPTER 2

Using Objects   51

CHAPTER 3

Building Distributed Applications   81

Part two
Managing Distributed Systems 93

CHAPTER 4
Executive Management Roles 95

CHAPTER 5
Choosing the Architecture 115

CHAPTER 10

Outsourcing 257

CHAPTER 11

Building Extensible Systems 275

CHAPTER 12

Delivering Enterprisewide Network Services   317

GLOSSARY   329

INDEX   337

ACKNOWLEDGMENTS

The people one should really acknowledge, especially when doing RAD in a Web-based distributed system environment are one's team. So, to the greatest team in the world, for their amazing, outstanding creativity, dedication, energy, and sense of fun, including: Giovanni, Martin, Erik, Roberto, Susanna, Adriano and Silvia; and Franco, for enabling it. Also: Paolo B, Massimo S, Giacomo, Enzo, Massimo F, Maurizio C, Franco, Maurizio L and Paolo T, for aiding and abetting the struggle.

—Simon Forge
Paris 1998

First, I would like to thank my wife Amy, and my children, Amanda and Daniel, for providing me with the motivation to sit down and write. Their love and faith in me keeps me going. Secondly, I would like to thank my co-authors, Richard and Simon, for realizing the contribution I had to make and inviting me to participate in this venture. Finally, I would like to thank our editors, Margaret, Marjorie, and Micheline for providing us the time to earn a living and still become published authors.

—JP Morgenthal
Long Island 1998

First and foremost, I have to acknowledge the patience and understanding exhibited by my wife Diana and my children Jennifer, Justin, Todd, and Colin during the entire cycle of effort and activity that laid the foundations upon which this work is built. I extend my sincere appreciation to Margaret, Marjorie, and Micheline for their editorial guidance. And I owe my deepest gratitude to the clients and colleagues, who provided the challenges and opportunities that enabled us to develop and test the knowledge shared in the following pages.

—Richard L. Ptak
Amherst 1998

INTRODUCTION

Life has not been easy for the people in management who are charged with setting strategy and direction for enterprise information systems (IS) and information technology (IT) departments. Challenges they face include an explosion in distributed computing, pressure to adopt new technologies quickly, and end-user demands for enhanced information services. The complexity of the corporate computing environment has made quality network services dramatically more difficult to deliver and manage. In addition, end users are now sophisticated consumers who will not accept anything less than custom-tailored information and services delivered in an efficient and timely manner. Factors such as dramatic organizational changes driven by global competition and increasingly reliable remote communications and services combine with shrinking budgets and profit margins to mandate that IT and IS departments redefine the way they function within their parent organization.

> **NOTE:**
>
> It is important to point out the distinqtion between *information technology* (IT)organizations and *information systems* (IS). IT refers to the world of activity and equipment used for distributed desktop and client/server computing. IS refers to the world of mainframe and very large system computing. However, for the sake of simplicity in the balance of this book, we use the term IS to refer to all aspects of corporate computing.

To add to the confusion IS faces, vendors and integrators continue to assert confidently that their tools and techniques will allow the IS manager to satisfy any and all demands. Who should you believe when articles and anecdotes in the press and exchanged among peers clearly dispute the vendor claims of all-in-one solutions?

This book is intended for managers responsible for planning, designing, and implementing reorganized IS departments. We will help you understand the rapidly changing information technology environment and give you strategies to cope with this change effectively. You will see how existing and emerging technologies you choose will affect organizational operations, structure, roles, and activities. We will also recommend appropriate responses to changes caused by the solutions you have chosen to implement.

Though the right IS management solution is unique to your organization, the basic technology context and steps involved in defining the solution are common and consistent among all organizations. When you finish this book, you will understand common IS developmental and organizational problems, be able to identify and discuss critical management issues, as well as have a framework for developing the IS management solution that is right for your business.

This book is not a step-by-step implementation guide to specific products that resolve management problems. It is a pragmatic discussion of the distributed systems and client/server environments, as well as the technologies, tools, and end-user demands that affect that environment. After reading this book, you will have the knowledge you need to decide the correct path for your organization.

As authors, our combined backgrounds bring to these topics a complementary blend of experience, knowledge, and abilities. They cover a broad range of practical experience in a variety of industries and markets as a result of our work with clients in the United States, Europe, and Asia. Our practical experience in implementation is balanced by in-depth research and technology analysis. Our exposure to a wide variety of clients and industries enables us to identify common challenges, while understanding individual requirements unique to each business.

Overview of the Book and Technology

After reading this book, you, as the IS manager or other corporate decision maker, will be better skilled to:

- Understand the unique challenges and technologies of distributed computing.
- Structure an effective decision-making process to address IS issues.
- Understand and deal with the emerging challenges for IS management, ranging from staffing requirements to design philosophy.
- Understand and evaluate services and solutions in the management of distributed environments.
- Take steps to assure that when you do use outside services, lasting benefits will accrue, not disappear out the door with the hired experts.
- Make the right decisions for the delivery of enterprisewide network-based, distributed business services.

The underlying assumption in this book is that managers can and want to make informed decisions on a range of issues involved in information and technology systems, ranging from deciding whether IS service outsourcing makes sense to defining application development strategies and organizational and reporting structure. This book provides a basic context and language so that managers can begin to craft their solutions.

How This Book Is Organized

The book is divided into three parts. The first three chapters make up "Introducing Distributed Systems"; the next five are Part 2, "Managing Distributed Systems"; and the final four are "The New Shape of Distributed Systems." These groupings lead you from the present to the future. We start with a general overview of today's reality in IS, with its unique problems and approach. Then we move to a discussion of the specific tasks, functions, and issues as they relate to the management of enterprise systems, networks, and applications. The final chapters of the book are devoted to developing guidelines for defining a plan to deal with the future.

Part I. "Introducing Distributed Systems" offers an overview of today's computing environment and technologies, and describes conventional wisdom for building distributed application solutions. The overview will help you understand how and why elements of distributed sytems work the way they do today. Part I also provides a common ground for later sections, when we introduce new technologies and concepts that are transforming the traditional structure. Finally, Part I establishes a justification for the radical changes needed to meet increasing user demands while providing new capabilities.

Chapter 1, "Distributed System Environments,"is an overview of the client/server environment and distributed computing. It identifies and explains the role played by the three logical layers that constitute the system. The chapter then offers a look at the possibilities and construct of today's distributed computing environment. This chapter provides, using a combination of text and examples, gives a view of the architectural framework and underpinnings of the client/server model. It describes not only the pieces, terms, interfaces, and functions but explains how these interact to provide a powerful, functional, flexible solutions approach. If you are already familiar with the concepts of distributed computing and the client/server and OSI reference model, you can skip these descriptive sections.

Chapter 2, "Using Objects," explains how and why object technology provides a solid foundation for modeling and delivering automated business services and processes. It demonstrates the unique strengths of objects to represent business processes, using a combination of narrative and example. The chapter also reviews developing processes, the confluence of specific technologies (such as the Web), and standards that support object modeling. The discussion concludes with a road map to the successful use of the technology.

Chapter 3, "Building Distributed Applications," is an insight into the how-to of delivering solutions. The chapter is not meant to be a programmers guide, but an explanation of why and what special care is needed to successfully develop distributed solutions. The chapter includes the most important issues to keep in mind when developing a distributed application and describes why the client/server model of computing alone is insufficient to define the needs of a distributed application.

Part II. "Managing Distributed Systems" discusses the methods, challenges, tasks, tools, and theory of service management in the distributed environment. It reviews the early forces driving distributed management, and describes the evolving alternative solution structures, from management suites to enterprise platforms. It covers issues central to determining needs and evaluating products; where and when to use feature/function comparisons; and when to consider broader issues like organizational culture and work habits. Part II ends with a process for evaluating management solutions.

Chapter 4, "Executive Management Roles," examines how the role of the executive changes as the role of IS evolves in the face of new technologies and an emerging focus on business responsibilities and contribution. The chapter looks at how management roles must accommodate these new systems. It also examines some of the technologies that will help you compete in a global market.

Chapter 5, "Choosing the Architecture," examines influences and critical decisions the CIO must make to address the future. The chapter starts with a discussion of the events driving the need for redefinition of the IS organization, then reviews the alternative roles open to IS in relation to the business, and finally suggests a new IS department structure. The chapter also explores alternative end-user relationships and mechanisms for IS service delivery as it defines the appropriate place of information systems in the company operations today and tomorrow. Finally, it provides a review at both the macro level of the relationship with the user departments and at a micro level, suggesting new approaches for managing end-user relationships.

Chapter 6, "The Management Landscape," introduces a new focus, away from IS organizational, architectural, and delivery mechanisms to the task of distributed systems and network management. This chapter traces the development of standard models for distributed management, laying the groundwork for treatment in later chapters to help the decision maker understand requirements and evaluate the various solutions available. Chapter 6 fosters an understanding of the network and management functions to help the decision maker position vendors, evaluate alternative solutions, and discuss the underlying solution technologies.

Chapter 7, "Understanding the Management Toolbox," covers the evolution of the distributed network management toolbox. It describes the how and why of the evolution of distributed building management tools, from unsophisticated monitors of tool state to the current management "grail" of fully integrated, proactive, end-to-end service-level management. It concludes with a review and commentary on the alternative approaches to solution packaging, ranging from often self-described best-of-breed point solutions to fully integrated management platforms. The chapter includes a template for assuring that solutions you select match the problem you need solved.

Chapter 8, "Evaluating Management Solutions" provides a road map for comparing and judging management solutions. The goal of this chapter is to instill a sense that intelligent business practices go a long way toward creating the best management toolbox for an IS organization. The corporate view of IS must move beyond that of a mere infrastructure provider to that of an active partner, with powerful tools and the capability to creatively address business problems.

Part III. "The New Shape of Distributed Systems" makes specific recommendations for organizing the IS function to better face the future. It discusses requirements and guidelines for addressing personnel issues, reporting relationships, and management styles. Part III also considers outsourcing as a solution, using specific examples. It introduces a new definition and philosophy of systems development: *extensible systems*. The book ends with a description of how to organize to deliver networked services to the enterprise.

Chapter 9, "Reskilling for Tomorrow," introduces the challenges IS faces as the skills necessary for success undergo radical change in a period marked by a shortage of capable staff. It includes a discussion of alternative solutions, as well as a description of the newly emerging IS development environment. The chapter develops a strategy for introducing distributed systems to the enterprise, and shows how end-user involvement is an integral part of the distributed environment strategy.

Chapter 10, "Outsourcing," suggests considering this option when you lack the internal resources needed to build and manage all or parts of a distributed system. Also considered are some planning and contract negotiation concerns, and an examination of what can happen when an outsourcing arrangement is not properly planned.

Chapter 11, "Building Extensible Systems," examines some theories about the future of distributed systems and how to build them as "living systems" that will grow and change with your company. This chapter documents the importance of designing for extensibility through data reuse, in contrast to process reuse. It proposes a new model for designing distributed systems that separates the application from the partitioning methodology. Finally, it discusses a methodology for designing naturally interoperable applications.

Chapter 12, "Enterprisewide Network Services," explains how to deliver enterprisewide network services using data-centric computing. It introduces the infrastructure requirements for delivering support to that model throughout the enterprise. The also describes how to deliver generally available network services to the enterprise by combining data-centric computing requirements with distributed computing technologies.

Who Should Read this Book

This book is intended for managers with a pragmatic bent, who need to understand (at least on a basic level) the workings of the operating environment as they mold it to meet the future. It will also prove useful to business managers who are asking IS organizations to deliver new services. It provides a context in which all levels of managers can understand the IS environment and how to develop strategies for coping with change. It can also be used to provide the advanced manager or technical student with a view of the operational and organizational challenges to be faced in the successful delivery of computing-based services.

Summary

Most people have experience with computers and their interfaces. This democratization of the computing environment has created a legion of end users with frequently uninformed yet strongly held opinions. Unfortunately for IS, those end users include business managers who control budgets and exert considerable influence over the future of IS operations.

This book is intended to guide decision makers, those affected by their decisions, and those wrestling with the challenge of understanding and identifying the critical issues facing IS. For the more technically sophisticated, it offers insight to the business-based influences that will increasingly impact what initially appear to be technology-based decisions. For the business sophisticate, it provides information on the details of operation, implementation, and important technical issues, which will enable them to be more effective in making decisions and more realistic in their service demands and expectations from their IS staff.

Part one

Introducing Distributed Systems

1 DISTRIBUTED SYSTEM ENVIRONMENTS: A MANAGEMENT PRIMER

We propose to consider first the single elements of our subject, then each branch and then last of all the whole ... and so advance from the simple to the complex ... but everything takes a different shape when we pass from abstractions to reality.

On War, Carl Von Clauswitz, 1780–1831

This chapter:

Introduces the architecture of client/server systems and identifies the basic building blocks.

Looks inside the building blocks: what they achieve, how they work together.

Discusses relevant standards and the state of the technology.

Examines future developments.

Presents examples of what you can do with client/server systems.

To build a distributed environment of networked computers and their users, we need to fit together many pieces, somewhat like a puzzle. This chapter covers the main distributed system components, their functions, and assembly. Most distributed processing is based on the client/server model, so we will begin with a description of client/server systems.

Overview of Client/Server Systems

Distributed computing refers to linking computers across a network so they can work together to accomplish a common task. In contrast to centralized computing, where a system at the hub does everything, a distributed system enables separate

---

Distributed Computing and Client/Server Systems

An example of distributed computing is an automotive factory system where a number of separate computers control various stages on a production line; they act in synchronization to build cars; and though they must pass messages to each other, they are otherwise autonomous. Certainly, the production system could be run by one central computer, but that would be risky because if that one processor breaks down, the whole line would stop. With a distributed computing system it is possible to build in much more resilience to failure, and perhaps make each stage independent of the reliability of the computers in other stages.

A client/server system in an automotive factory would provide some service, which several of the computers along the production line could share. The shared service could, for instance, be the clients for a print service on a print server that outputs the details of each stage when completed for each car on the production line. The production computers and the print server would be a form of distributed computing: In the working implementation, there would be a number of requesting computers (clients) to a dedicated server.

So, the client/server model means that one entity in the network, the client, makes a service request to another remote entity, a server. By supplying a set of common services delivered by servers dedicated to that specific service, client/server systems provide a powerful paradigm for breaking up complex tasks into smaller chunks that are easier to solve. The traditional alternative has been to load everything onto one computer, which means that the total processing load is far heavier and that the processor cannot be customized for a specific task.

More on Client/Server Systems

The essential client/server model is made up of a set of services from servers and client applications that direct tasks. The client and server could reside on the same machine, but act as separate processes. While accomplishing any task, both the client and the server can make requests of one another. For instance, the print server could ask the client word processing program to perform a management task such as, "Please supply your identity for usage statistics."

Most commonly, the client is a PC or other end-user machine, like a network computer (NC), while the big processing load, requiring more computer power, resides in a larger machine, a server. This is not always the case, however. A print server, for example, might use an even smaller and simpler machine than a PC, say a processor card inside the printer with some software providing simple print server functions.

computers to interact and share the work. They are connected via a network to pass data and commands, and each processor on the network has an address. Thus, distributed systems allow companies to put processing power wherever the business needs it—in the factory, down the hall, in the warehouse. A client/server arrangement is one way of implementing a distributed system. In this arrangement, one processor (the server) provides a service to its client computer(s) over a network, be it a local area network (LAN) and/or a wide area network (WAN).

To further explain client/server computing, consider your PC: It has a word processing program and is connected to a network, a LAN; when you need to print, the word processing program is the client requesting a print service. An *intelligent* print server, shared on your network by many users, translates the output from the word processing program and takes care of page layout and the entire printing process. It may have a specialized processor for the page description language and for the graphics processing.

The client/server model is a powerful concept for distributed processing, but it also represents a continually evolving technology. Case in point: Just a few years ago, when we talked about distributed and client/server technology, it would not have included Internet technologies, today it does.

Logical Layers of Client/Server Systems

Client/server systems have three distinct logical layers, as illustrated in Figure 1.1:

- Applications, user-interface terminals, and data distributed across several remote machines.

- Middleware, which provides the interfaces or "glue" to enable remote machines to work together. Middleware hides details of the underlying systems software and hardware of particular computer platforms and networks from the applications, so that applications can converse in standard ways across a network.

- The basic platforms, systems, and networking software and hardware, which support communications among the different parts of the application.

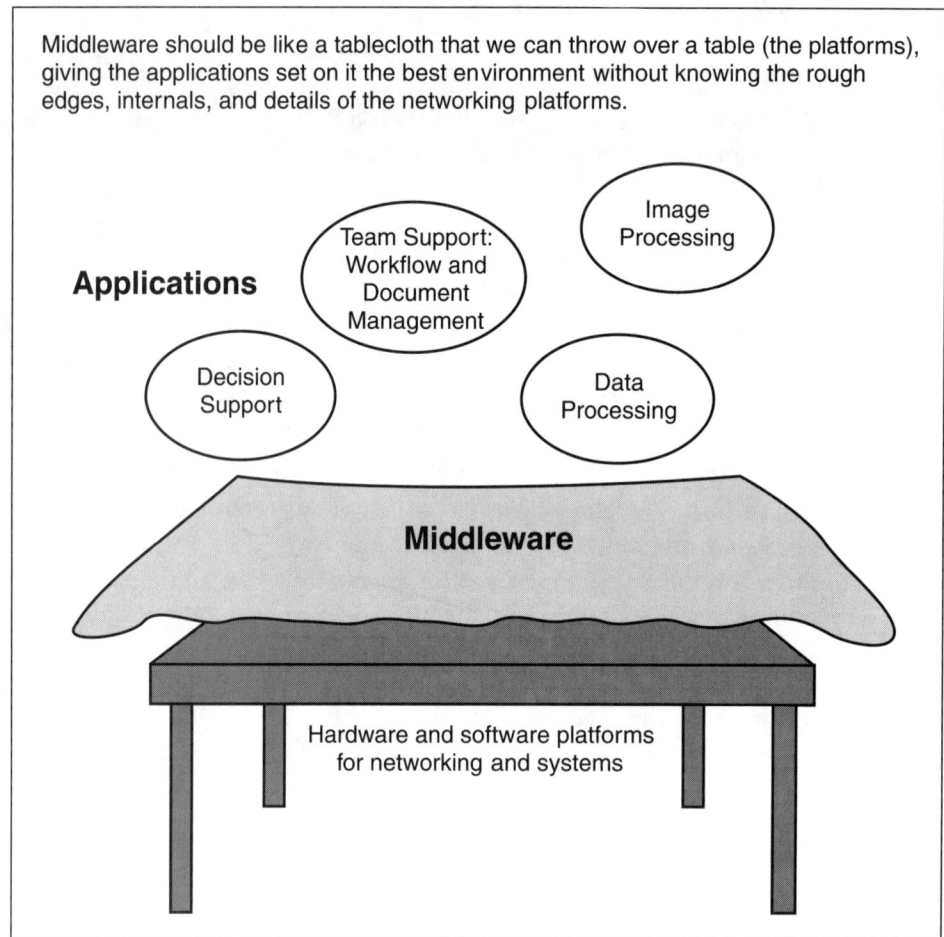

Figure 1.1 Distributed systems are held together by middleware.

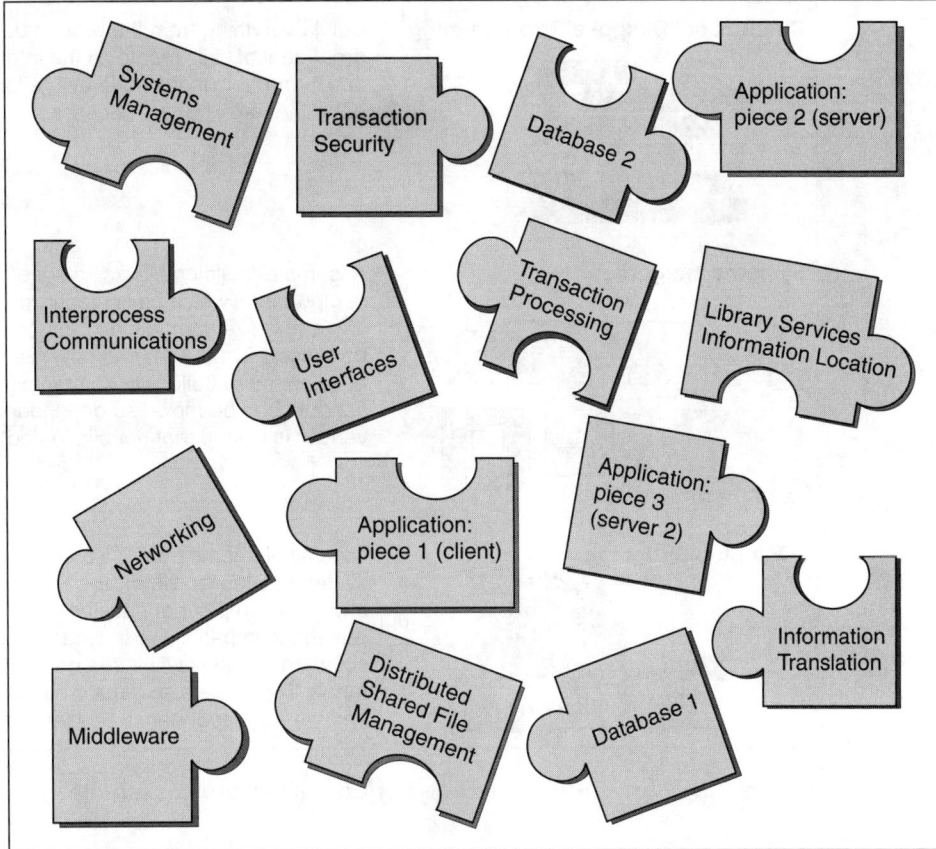

Figure 1.2 *Client/server and distributed systems in general are like a puzzle whose pieces we must fit together.*

Building Client/Server Systems

Recall the analogy at the beginning of the chapter comparing client/server systems to a puzzle of basic functions (see Figure 1.2). In this section, we approach the major technical aspects of the pieces of the puzzle at a systems level to see how they fit together.

First, we need a plan for assembling the pieces. Most of your design decisions will involve selecting software and the interfaces between software components. We will examine three ways to solve interfacing problems and to build client/server systems: *custom* or *"bespoke"* programming, *"one-stop shopping,"* and systems integration, as illustrated in Figure 1.3.

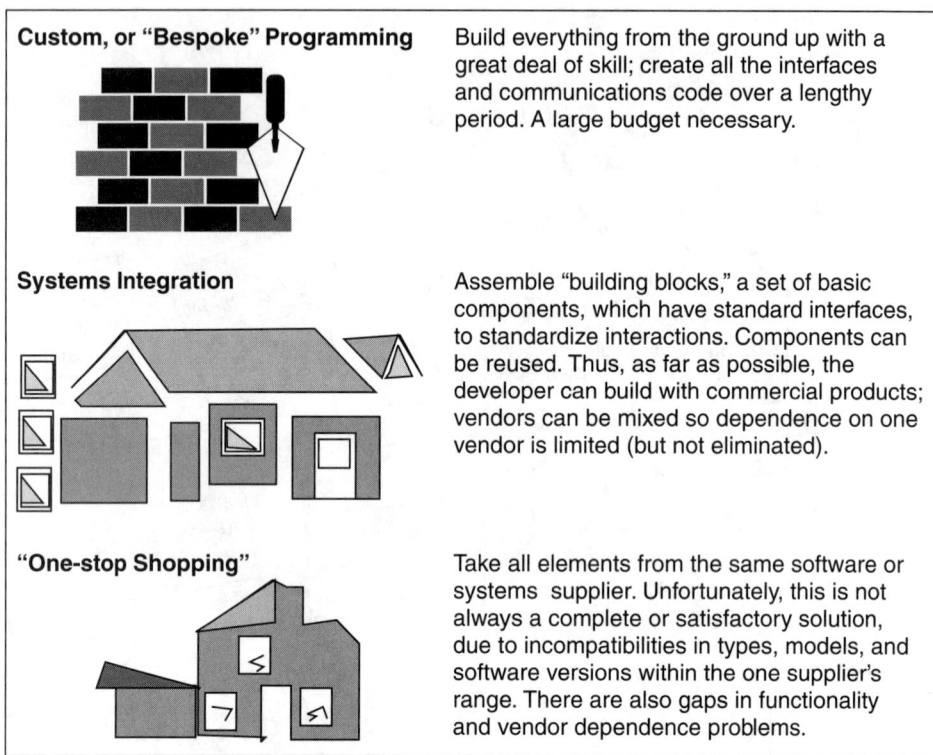

Custom, or "Bespoke" Programming — Build everything from the ground up with a great deal of skill; create all the interfaces and communications code over a lengthy period. A large budget necessary.

Systems Integration — Assemble "building blocks," a set of basic components, which have standard interfaces, to standardize interactions. Components can be reused. Thus, as far as possible, the developer can build with commercial products; vendors can be mixed so dependence on one vendor is limited (but not eliminated).

"One-stop Shopping" — Take all elements from the same software or systems supplier. Unfortunately, this is not always a complete or satisfactory solution, due to incompatibilities in types, models, and software versions within the one supplier's range. There are also gaps in functionality and vendor dependence problems.

Figure 1.3 Three approaches to building distributed systems.

Custom, or Bespoke, Programming

In the early days of distributed computing, because the building block approach was not widely known, some system builders were driven to try custom or bespoke programming, which is characterized by 1) building a system from the ground up, and 2) a lack of general standards. As you might expect, because everything has to be built from scratch, essentially handcrafted every time, the custom approach is lengthy, expensive, and requires highly skilled technicians. It also incurs major cost

---

NOTE

There exists a pressing need for universal public standards. The goal of distributed computing is so-called transparent communication, the ability to transmit information to any remote computer no matter what equipment is used to send and receive data.

penalties when interfacing to other systems, or when returning five years later to fix something (such as Year 2000 problems). This is true because probably anyone who knew the original system moved on long ago.

One-Stop Shopping

The second approach, one-stop shopping, entails buying all components of the system from a single vendor or systems supplier. Unfortunately, doing so rarely gives you a good solution. Far too often, integration and interoperability, even in products from a single vendor, are less than optimal, and developers are reduced to using the lowest common denominator in protocols to achieve compatibility, thus limiting both performance and user-friendliness. In one case, a large Australian transport organization was forced to use minimal screen protocols (IBM type LU2) as the common denominator for all the mainframe software to be integrated with the current system, even though all hardware and software came from the same vendor. This made the system very difficult to use because the latest in GUIs could not be implemented.

Systems Integration Approach

The third approach, systems integration, or building blocks, enjoys near universal acceptance today in client/server systems, and in distributed systems in general. As its alternate name implies, it uses standard components, or blocks, with industry interfaces and component standards.

De Facto Standards

De facto standards have become so because standards initiatives such as OSI (Open Systems Interconnection) and OSF (Open Software Foundation) have done little to change the computer industry except at lower levels of communications protocols, whereas Internet technologies have grown as publicly declared and available de facto standards, and often as free implementations in software.

Other de facto standards have grown up around operating systems, utilities, and networks—appearing in Windows on the client or on Unix servers for communications, or building on Novell NetWare as the basis for middleware. Currently, Windows NT is gaining market share from various Unix versions and is replacing Novell as middleware.

Today's hot contenders for distributed computing standards are the common standards developed for the Internet. They have a significant advantage: free distribution of many core utilities, such as Web browsers for the client machine. However, improvements are needed before robust distributed computing can be achieved using Web and Internet technology standards.

Building Blocks of a Client/Server System

The building block approach provides a logical and pragmatic way to build distributed systems, and this section describes standard components that are available and usable, along with other elements still in their infancy—emerging components with great promise.

Middleware

The first building block we examine is middleware, as it provides essential services to link clients, servers, data, and networks, as depicted in Figure 1.4. The layers of application, middleware, and the hardware/software/network platform are treated as the basic blocks, and they are supported by common services, as shown in the lower half of the figure.

The front end, or application-level user interface, handles presentation to the user, application information display format, and possibly some part of the application logic. It usually, though not necessarily, resides on the client; a *dumb* or *thin* client can have all the display sent to it from the server. Thin clients have greater communications dependency and increase network load. In an Internet technology-based system, the client front end is a browser, which is simply a platform for the presentation screens. Examples of browsers include Netscape Navigator and Internet Explorer from Microsoft.

At the application level, the back end on the server handles the rest of the application logic and database management. The server replaces the earlier general machines (mainframes or minis) by dedicating computing resources to one service or to a limited range of services. Servers can offer a wide range of services: complete applications, simple file storage, a printing service, a complicated database with its own data sorting, or a document search engine. Servers provide shared network resources to any client; therefore, server hardware and systems architecture should be optimized to handle several network requests simultaneously.

The client/server model requires an operating system for multitasking, a file storage system, and networking utilities, forming part of what is generically termed middleware:

- Middleware joins the client to the server and interfaces with the application fragments; it sits on top of the communications protocols.

- Communications over the network support middleware; it incorporates the underlying protocols and physical links between the various parts of the system.

When running an application, the division of labor between the client and the server depends on the application and the networking environment. If the balance

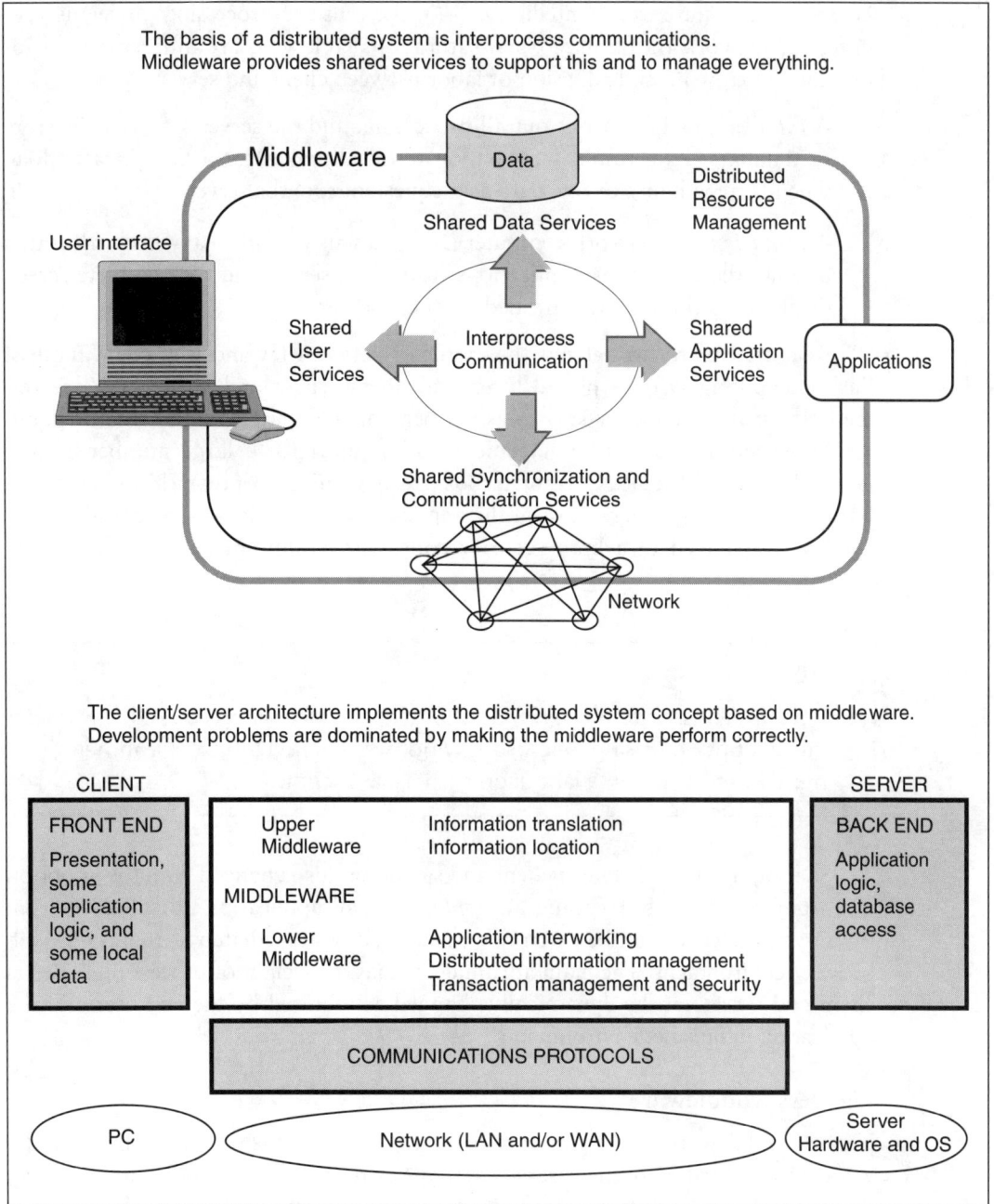

The basis of a distributed system is interprocess communications.
Middleware provides shared services to support this and to manage everything.

Middleware — Data

Distributed Resource Management

Shared Data Services

User interface

Shared User Services — Interprocess Communication — Shared Application Services — Applications

Shared Synchronization and Communication Services

Network

The client/server architecture implements the distributed system concept based on middleware.
Development problems are dominated by making the middleware perform correctly.

CLIENT

SERVER

FRONT END	Upper Middleware	Information translation Information location	BACK END
Presentation, some application logic, and some local data	MIDDLEWARE		Application logic, database access
	Lower Middleware	Application Interworking Distributed information management Transaction management and security	

COMMUNICATIONS PROTOCOLS

PC   Network (LAN and/or WAN)   Server Hardware and OS

Figure 1.4 *Client/server systems are made up of the logical parts of any distributed system.*

between client and server "intelligence" (in the sense of processing power) is very different, network traffic may reach saturation. Following are different scenarios that illustrate the possible division of labor between client and server:

A *fat client,* or PC, carries out all processing, and the server acts as a file store or database. As a result, information retrieval makes for a heavy traffic load when large volumes of raw data are requested from the server.

A *thin client,* or network computer (NC), can also create heavy network traffic because the client runs applications from a fat server and the complete screen displays are continually refreshed from the server.

Real systems try to balance the extremes between fat and thin client models. Early computing systems placed little load on the client and most on the server; then fat clients, commonly known as the personal computer, or PC, became popular. However, application management and support for a large number of networked PCs is difficult. Current trends are beginning to favor thin clients and intranet computing, where most of the application logic resides on a centrally managed server placed in a high security zone with comprehensive, sophisticated backup.

> **NOTE**
>
> If an applet is written in Java, a 32-bit client machine is required, so organizations still using Microsoft Windows 3.1 (a 16-bit environment) must write applets in a language such as JavaScript.

Sharing functions between client and server has also changed with the adoption of corporate intranets. By using an *applet,* a small application downloaded from the server, the client can be given new functionality immediately through the Web browser environment. The main advantage is that the weight of processing between client and server can be dynamically changed as required by the end user and the application in intranet environments.

Flawless Middleware

Because middleware is so essential to network functions, the primary concern of developers of distributed client/server systems is to make the middleware perform flawlessly. Many functions are grouped under the term middleware, the software "glue" for connection of applications, databases, user interfaces, and shared services, all of which sit on top of the basic communications. Middleware is the crucial part of any client/server system because it:

- Isolates applications from the network details and from all the mechanics of cross-platform transaction management.

- Locates remote resources, like applications, databases, printers, or specific data and documents, with directory services to process names and addresses.

- Handles the problems of interfacing, including any changes in application-level formats and presentations (the functions sometimes attributed to *upper middleware*).

- Manages the interactions and transactions between applications on the different machines, including low-level shared services at the application level, such as printing and filing, and functions such as security and recovery (the basic functions, sometimes attributed to *lower middleware*).

- Provides distributed environment management functions for the system manager, such as server naming, file access control, network resource addition and deletion, and often the functions of user addition, authorization, and password management.

Operational Models

Together, the client/server building blocks support the two most common types of working interaction:

- The linked interoperation of two applications across a network. One application requests processing from another application to complete its own task; results are then passed back. Note that the calling application must wait on the called application to hand back its results.

- A client application requests information from a database on a network, and the data is returned to the client for processing and display.

Client/Server Components in the Near Future

We can expect to see standard middleware environments for distributed processing that come preassembled, with many of the individual components already in place. However, for the next three to five years, the use of several discrete components of middleware will prevail as the primary way to build distributed and client/server systems. For maximum flexibility, all the components should be dynamically linkable, allowing you to choose a different database or server without interrupting the running application, for example. A new server or database can be chosen only if your choice has not been fixed by existent programming. Figure 1.5 shows components of client/server systems in detail.

The main software components in a distributed system, from a bottom-up point of view, are largely middleware, and include the following:

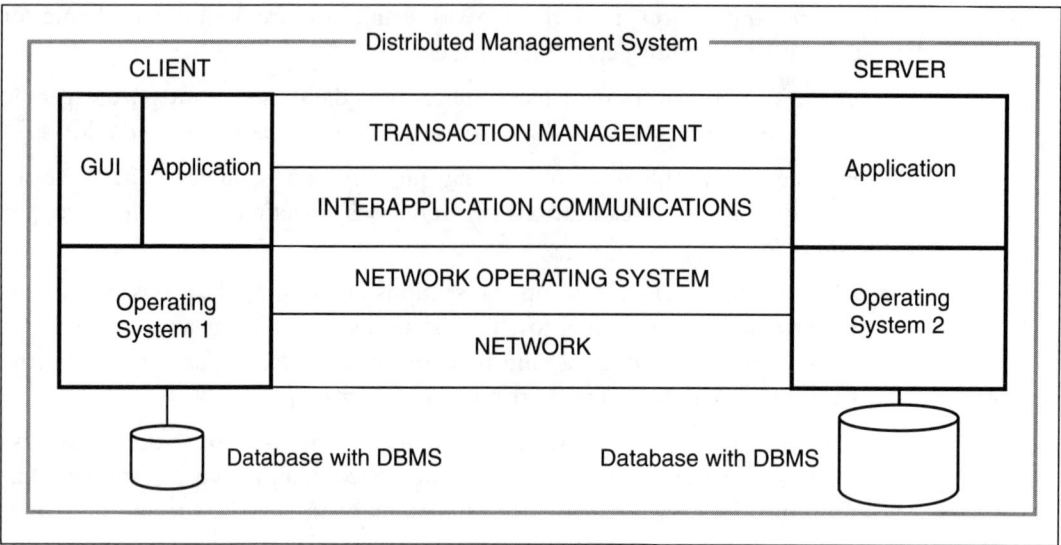

Figure 1.5 *Main working components of a client/server system.*

- Communications protocols (and the basic physical network).

- Network operating systems (separate software modules, Novell, incorporated in the server and client operating system, Microsoft NT).

- Interapplication communications.

- Standard interfacing for applications and services with application programming interfaces (APIs) and PC package interfaces.

- Databases and database management systems.

- Transaction managers, to handle transactions across several platforms.

- Utilities to locate resources, data, and documents across the system, and to change data formats to suit the client or server (often associated with components for interapplication communications, transaction managers, database managers, or network operating system—NOS—filing systems).

- GUIs (graphical user interfaces).

- Distributed management systems to administer everything.

Next we will explore the major components in greater detail and examine how they are used in common operational situations.

Application Communications: The Basic Network Protocols

Slowly, over the last 25 years, we have broken away from the computer network architectures of the major computer suppliers like IBM and Digital Equipment Corporation (DEC). Network protocols are now largely de facto standards for data communications that meld publicly available standards for the Internet, agreements in the world of telecommunications from the International Telecommunications Union (ITU), and to some extent, help from a model designed in the ISO public standards committees: the seven-layer OSI Reference Model of open networked communications. The latter, sometimes called the eight-layer model, with level zero being the hole in the ground for the cables, is explained in some detail next because it is useful for understanding networking between clients, servers, routers, hub switches, or any device that can interoperate through standard protocols.

The OSI Reference Model

The OSI model is based on a distributed system management principle:

1. Each layer must provide a set of functional services.

2. Operations within each layer depend on using common services.

3. Each layer is served by the layer immediately below, which provides all the required services needed by the layer above.

In top-down order, the model for networking communications is as follows:

7. **Application.** Includes all parts of the application that communicate across the network, and network and systems management functions.

6. **Presentation.** Provides information to application programs (and to human users) with the correct syntax, including the translation of data if required—that is, file format conversion. File transfer protocols and terminal access protocols are defined at this level.

5. **Session.** Coordinates and synchronizes dialogue during a communications session and manages interactions between the entities at the presentation level with security functions such as passwords or other measures.

4. **Transport.** Sets up the connection, using the underlying layers, to form a set of transport services for application sessions, the most important of which are transport addressing, class (or quality) of service, error detection, and flow control.

3. **Network.** Handles the way information is transferred through the network via control of the network elements: packet- or circuit-switched mode, network address processing, routing, primary security services (packet tracking, address verification).

2. **Data link.** Sets up data transfer across a network link. At a bit level this includes such things as determining packet structure, synchronization, implementation of error detection, and flow control.

1. **Physical.** Identifies mechanical and electrical specifications for the network and its connections right down to the plugs and power supplies, as well as its physical configuration, geography, and topology.

An example of the seven-layer OSI model at work is a Web server system, communicating with perhaps many thousands of end users, each using a browser on his or her PC-based client. The application is the Web server, containing additional programming to handle user requests, the Web database, and to create the HTML Web pages. The lower part of the application layer in a Web-based system would include the API for invoking the Web server application. The API may be custom, based on a de facto standard such as the Common Gateway Interface (CGI), or supplied by an Internet service provider (ISP), for example Netscape, which offers the NSAPI.

The presentation includes the tools, services, icons, buttons, and screens seen by the end users, as well as the browser itself (the HTML interpreter) on the client PC, the platform for the presentation.

The session handles all interactive dialogue during an online session, starting with the passwords and login, as well as the encryption in the Secure Sockets Layer (SSL), a de facto standard from Netscape. An unfortunate feature of Web server software is that most Web servers have no concept of state, which is why, when you click impatiently on a hyperlink three times, the page is loaded three times, instead of just once. When a transaction has been requested by a particular client, a repeat of the request should be ignored until the first request has been serviced. To fix the problem you would need to add a *state machine* to the browser of your intranet application and a small agent (called a *cookie*) to track the session events. The cookie can be either downloaded or preactivated.

A set of transport services for the Web application sends the HTML pages using the HyperText Transfer Protocol (HTTP) on top of the Transmission Control Protocol/Internet Protocol (TCP/IP) with Internet Protocol (IP) addressing and directories. For Internet applications, a domain name server (DNS) would translate an alpha Internet address like richjeffsimon.com to a physical Internet address, which is numerical.

At a lower level are networking protocols that define the other three layers partially or completely. In our Web application, for example, we have the following:

Network	SLIP (Serial Line Internet protocol) for slow modems, PPP (Point-to-Point Protocol) for fast point to point
Data Link	Computer connection, based on a simple voice circuit, X25, Frame Relay, ATM, ISDN, FDDI, or LANs
Physical	Via telephone networks, CATV, LAN, or wireless

Now let's take a closer look at application programming interfaces.

Application Programming Interfaces

Applications need standard ways to communicate with all components of a network. To meet this need, the networking industry has published service interfaces called Application Programming Interfaces (APIs). Their uses are shown in Figure 1.6.

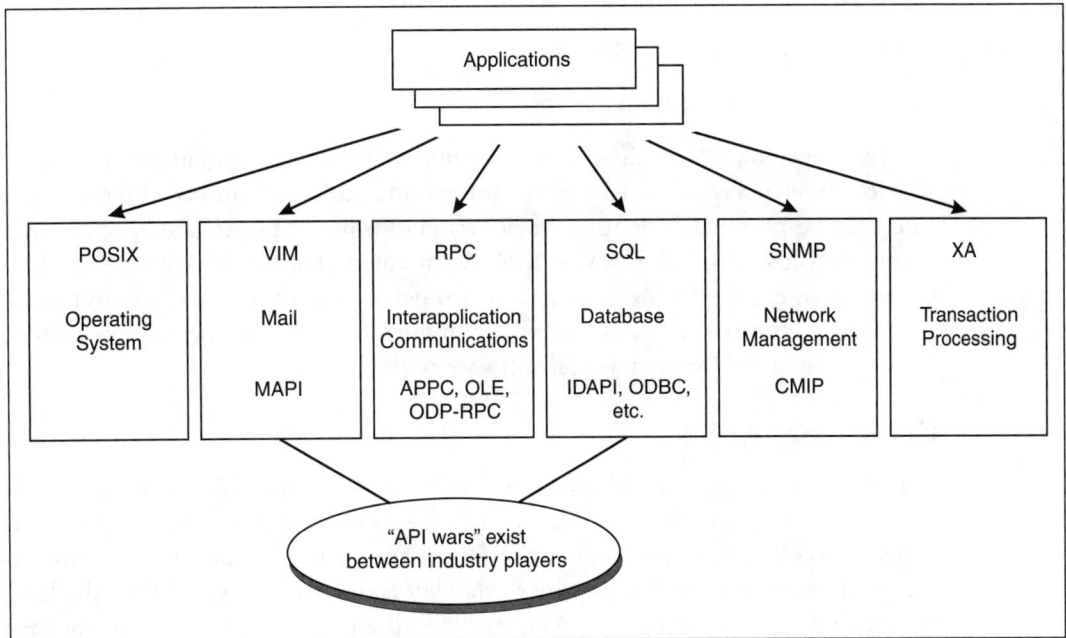

Figure 1.6 *APIs provide the glue that joins applications and building blocks.*

> **NOTE**
>
> APIs provide common doorways to all components at the application level. A future goal in distributed computing is a complete set of APIs.

APIs allow programmers to link information and services required by the application. APIs are modular, enable standardized access to any service a user requests, and ensure the service behaves as expected. APIs alleviate problems of building distributed systems, and separate application components in standard, easy-to-understand ways. Ideally an API will be supported by many vendors and be portable across programming languages. The holy grail for developers is a complete set of commonly adopted APIs.

APIs exist for

- User interfaces.

- Databases.

- Information representations such as graphics.

- Network and security management services.

- Data communications services.

- Operating systems interactions.

Two types of APIs include *high-level interfaces* for application programming, and *low-level interfaces* used for vendor-specific communications programming. APIs may be portable (able to move across platforms) or targeted at specific environments (Unix with C, or MVS/CICS). Most communications APIs are operating system specific. APIs are made public in two parts: as a set of functions, and as instructions on how to access them via a set of *language bindings*. Bespoke or custom APIs may be useful for commercial software packages.

Choosing APIs

APIs are most useful in giving *black box* qualities to services like printing; that is, users do not have to know what goes on inside—how it works—they only need to know the results, and how to interface. Black box qualities hide service complexities from programmers. The quality of the API is important, as it defines the level of service delivered through the API. And because no development team can support all the APIs available, you should limit the number of APIs you use, and reuse them whenever possible. The following subsections break out low- and higher-level APIs.

DISTRIBUTED SYSTEM ENVIRONMENTS: A MANAGEMENT PRIMER

An API Case Study

A major national U.S. automobile importer required transactions to be run from dealers to its own mainframe and to a mainframe for orders located in the production factory in Europe. The national dealers all had a package for their IBM AS/400 local servers for national parts location, inventory, and ordering. IBM APPC was chosen as the method of communication with the package—the API basis. However, APPC design concepts were felt to be the hardest to learn and use, and doing them only once was important to meet time and reliability goals. The importer worked with the package vendor to add an APPC-based API to the package as part of development of a multitransaction application. This application ran from the dealers into the importer's mainframe for national parts location and sales, and then on to car production for direct ordering, with full customer specification if the vehicle is not in stock. The API simplified the development of the distributed system, combining AS/400 servers with the two mainframe databases for parts location and for ordering and manufacturing of cars and parts as needed.

Low-level APIs

Low-level APIs include the following:

APPC. Application Program-to-Program Communications is the original IBM SNA interfacing protocol for peer-to-peer operations.

HLLAPI. This is the IBM High-Level Language API for 3270 datastream applications.

CPI-C. IBM's Common Programming Interface Communications for LU 6.2 SAA communications.

Higher-level APIs

Some of this category include major sets of standards:

NSAPI. This API connects an application to a Netscape Web server.

ISAPI. A Microsoft Internet server API that connects an application to the Microsoft Web server.

XA. The X/Open interface for TP monitor to DB communications.

VIM. Provides vendor-independent messaging—an e-mail API.

IDAPI. An integrated database API.

MAPI. A Microsoft e-mail API.

XFTAM. The X/Open API for FTAM, file transfer, and management.

XTI. The X/Open transport interface for communications.

ODBC. Microsoft's Open Database Connectivity API for connecting SQL databases with Windows applications.

SNMP. The simple network management protocol for TCP/IP network management.

CMIP. The Common Management Information Protocol from ISO.

SQL. Standard Query Language for database services access.

Novell Appear. API libraries for the Novell Netware NOS for networking applications.

POSIX operating system API. Standard call set for applications.

X.400 e-mail API. An API specification (and OSI application service) for message handling in "store-and-forward" electronic mail systems.

X.500 Directory services. An API for directory services which support name-to-address resolution for directories in distributed environments.

Berkeley sockets. Communications for the Unix world (and OS/) for TCP/IP and XNS.

APIs also offer help in dealing with a fundamental issue of distributed systems: network and systems management. Of the APIs listed, CMIP and SNMP offer the most promise for integrating management data from a range of vendors.

Managing Interapplication Communications

Understanding the NOS, an operating system that works across a network, will help to explain distributed processing software. The NOS may be an explicit separate entity, part of a server operating system, or even a part of a Web server and browser software. In all cases, it provides the most important support functions for managing a distributed computing environment. The NOS sits on top of the communications protocols running on the physical media. Its primary function is to handle the multiple control tasks across a network, so that all the computers and network elements can interwork, or cooperate, to process the application. Multiple control tasks link and manage the different operating systems, services, workstations, applications, LANs, and servers via a set of de facto standards. The configuration of an NOS for a PC-based LAN server (client/server model) and layers of its operation are detailed in Figure 1.7.

An NOS comes in several varieties, a fact that is not explicit in some NOS technical documentation. It may be part of the server operating system. Microsoft's Windows NT in its server version, for example, has growing market share with its effective NOS utilities, which are part of a multitasking server operating system. The NOS may be part of Web technology, which is inherently client/server in nature, and wraps the client communications in HTML and some management functions from the Web server with a very light application piece on the client machine, the PC browser. Or it may be an explicit piece of utility software, common in older PC LAN environments, such as Novell's Netware 4 (now "intranetware"), currently shrinking in market share.

An NOS may be distributed over several network nodes (such as Novell NetWare Lite) or reside on one central node. The latter is typical with Windows NT server-based LAN PC systems, when the server operating system (OS) is closely linked into the NOS, in which case, the NOS is effectively a set of OS utilities. In contrast, vendors such as Novell offer their own basic local operating system for a PC server to control services like filing and printing or to support a package like a database manager. A *Network Loadable Module* (NLM), as it is called, is dedicated to the server support function, and so has fewer capabilities, in comparison with a full operating system such as Unix or Windows NT. An NLM economizes on memory and disk space and is usually faster for its restricted operations, since it is a stripped-down OS. It is normally available at lower cost than a full-blown OS license for the server, and comes with development tools.

The current trend in corporate networking is to use a more simple client/server technology that scales to thousands of users in corporate intranets or private internets. Software comes from the same public Internet environment and is widely implemented based on simpler cheap Web software featuring a thin client, the browser, for search and display on a PC; a Web server platform from Netscape, Oracle, Lotus/IBM, or Microsoft (on top of Unix, or Microsoft Windows NT servers); and HTML, HTTP, and TCP/IP protocols for LAN and WAN operation over private virtual networks with frame relay, ATM, X25, or even SNA (which is rather inefficient).

The naming and addressing standards, essential to successful distributed systems, are moving to align with the public X.500 set of standards. The rise of Web technology has pushed IP addressing, a pure number system that theoretically covers every IP-connected device in the world. Its potential has been reinforced in its version 6, which has 64-bit addressing and DNS as the directory service. Organizations have to register IP addresses for external Internet communications.

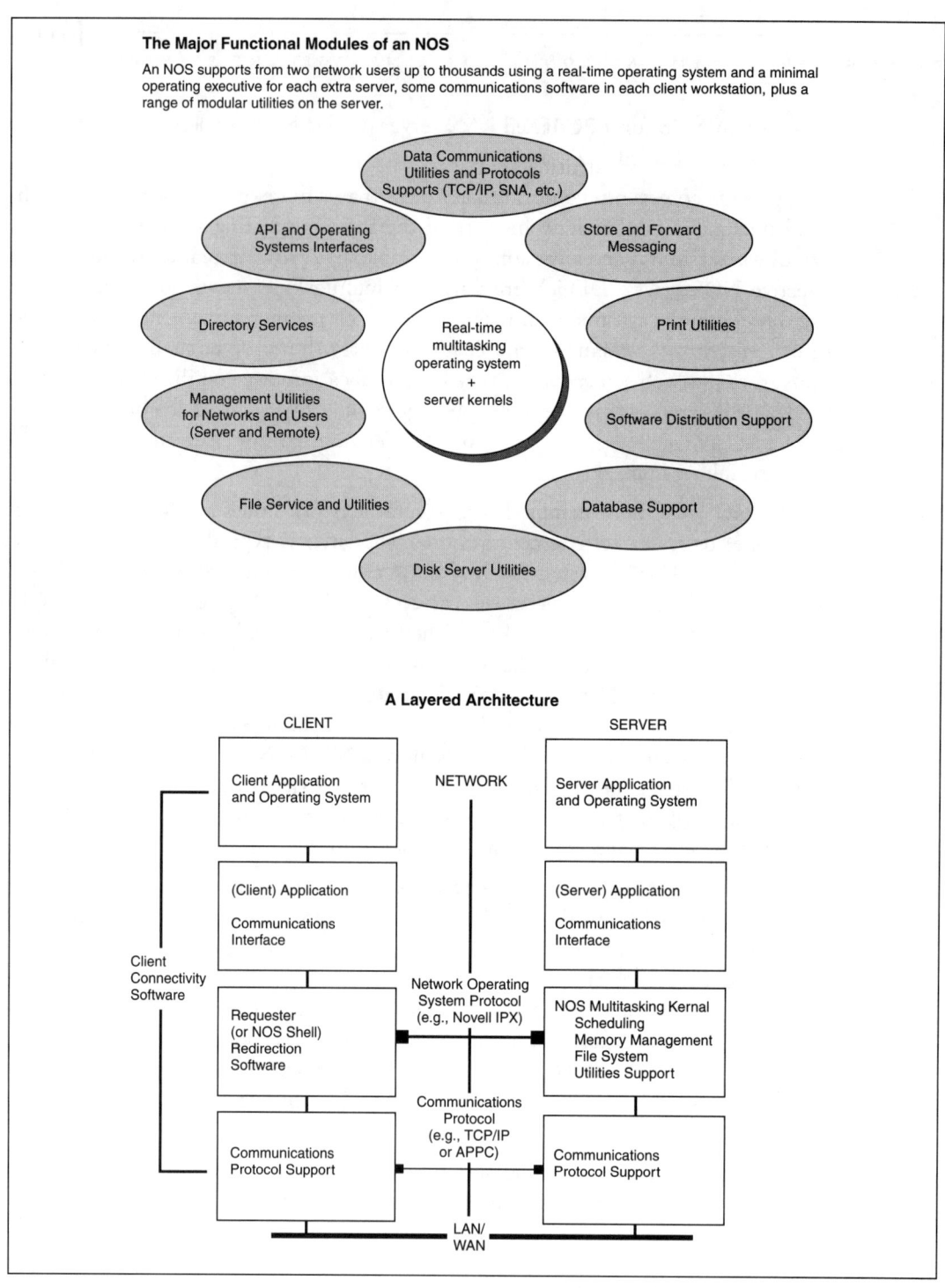

The Major Functional Modules of an NOS

An NOS supports from two network users up to thousands using a real-time operating system and a minimal operating executive for each extra server, some communications software in each client workstation, plus a range of modular utilities on the server.

- Data Communications Utilities and Protocols Supports (TCP/IP, SNA, etc.)
- API and Operating Systems Interfaces
- Store and Forward Messaging
- Directory Services
- Real-time multitasking operating system + server kernels
- Print Utilities
- Management Utilities for Networks and Users (Server and Remote)
- Software Distribution Support
- File Service and Utilities
- Database Support
- Disk Server Utilities

A Layered Architecture

CLIENT

NETWORK

SERVER

Client Application and Operating System

Server Application and Operating System

(Client) Application Communications Interface

(Server) Application Communications Interface

Client Connectivity Software

Requester (or NOS Shell) Redirection Software

Network Operating System Protocol (e.g., Novell IPX)

NOS Multitasking Kernal Scheduling Memory Management File System Utilities Support

Communications Protocol Support

Communications Protocol (e.g., TCP/IP or APPC)

Communications Protocol Support

LAN/WAN

Figure 1.7 The NOS carries out distributed interworking in the client/server model.

Distributed Programming Utilities

To date, middleware platforms are still limited, but market leaders, defined by the amount of interfacing software, are appearing. For distributed programming utilities, there are market leaders, and it pays to follow them. For instance, previously, server operating systems were dominated by both Unix and proprietary offerings from systems vendors (DEC, VMS, IBM, OS/400, etc.), whereas currently the market resides mostly on Unix. Microsoft Windows NT Server is making great inroads, though not as fast as many expected, especially in high-end systems. On the client, we see Microsoft Windows (3.1 and 95) and sometimes even MS-DOS as the leading PC client operating systems.

The middleware options just mentioned are considered market leaders by virtue of support from vendors of networked application software or PC packages, plus utilities like RDBMS and systems management. These applications and utilities are specifically designed to mesh with the market leaders in distributed systems environments. Nevertheless, network managers often complain that current distributed processing environments do not give them the true all-encompassing platform they need. They cite these significant shortcomings:

- Network management down to the workstation level remains weak, although tools are beginning to appear.

- The network operating systems and applications are highly sensitive to version changes. For example, if you change one of the NOS utilities or the application package, you may have to update the whole system, and deal with attendant new bugs. Avoiding version conflicts across a large organization requires strong configuration management. The same is true for Web-based software.

- Some distributed utilities targeted at LAN-based computing do not extend easily to wide area networks (WANs).

- Standards, where they exist, remain de facto, and thus liable to change under the influence of market forces.

Interapplication Communications: Hiding the Complexities

To enable two applications to communicate, or to gain access to a database, you need an interworking mechanism that can cope with separation in time and space (delays and communications breaks). A range of common interapplication mechanisms are available, identified in Figure 1.8, some of which are preprogrammed and some which can make links on the fly. However, some work only between applications in the same machine.

	STATIC: fixed, preprogrammed	DYNAMIC: change while running
SAME MACHINE	Preprogrammed custom links DDE, Dynamic Data Exchange DLL, Dynamic Link Libraries OLE, Object Linking and Embedding	DDE, Dynamic Data Exchange DLL, Dynamic Link Libraries OLE, Object Linking and Embedding ORB, Object Request Broker
REMOTE MACHINES	Named Pipes (Berkely sockets)	RPC, Remote Procedure Call Named Pipes (Berkely sockets) Message passing with queueing ORB, Object Request Broker Electronic mail (store and forward)

Figure 1.8 Interapplication communications can be static or dynamic for applications in the same machine or for applications interacting over a network.

Distributed systems often need to have new dialogues set up while the application is working, driven by real-time events. These interapplication dialogues must be ad hoc calls, with random destinations and timings of calls.

> **NOTE**
> All interworking mechanisms face the challenge of coordinating two processes not running synchronously across a network, which are often in different computing environments; they also must cope with network delays that are variable with traffic levels, protocol translation, and so on.

Applications and middleware components must be closely synchronized and carefully managed as to delays, retries, and failures. Therefore, the dialogue mechanism must cope with the notorious problems of distributed systems, including duplicated requests, partial transaction failures, transmission errors, time-outs, and random timing. These problems can make the correct interworking of applications next to impossible. Moreover, each application may be in a different environment, which means having different operating systems, hardware, and utilities. Two solutions are available: the older remote procedure call (RPC) and the newer message-queuing algorithm. These are discussed in the following subsections.

Remote Procedure Calls

To overcome synchronization problems while avoiding low-level custom programming, the separate applications on the client and server may cooperate through a standard remote procedure call. The RPC allows an application to be shared across several environments while shielding the developer from network details and differences in machines, data representations, and protocols. Think of this as hiding the nasty innards (or at least making them transparent). The RPC is the interprocess communications service that formalizes the way two or more applications interact across a network, as outlined in Figure 1.9. The RPC allows a program on one machine to call a procedure or program on a remote (and different type of) machine with the assurance that the expected behavior and reaction will result. The call runs over *interprocess communications channels* and distributed management set up by the NOS, or its equivalents in networking utilities, as a set of interprocess messages between clients and servers at the applications level.

In a client/server framework, the RPC becomes the core controlling mechanism, initiating remote execution on the server (or on a remote client from a

---

RPC and Distributed Systems

On some distributed systems projects, learning and coding for communications protocols can account for 25 percent of the effort. For example, IBM's earlier interprocess communications procedures (IBM LU6.2/APPC):

- Have a long learning curve.

- Take care of underlying technical differences, like different word lengths or byte ordering.

- Handle the location problem for the communicating entities.

- Set up and initiates the interprocess dialogue, termed the process binding.

- Formalize what happens in a failure by either caller or called entity, thereby reducing problems of additional unreliability introduced by networks.

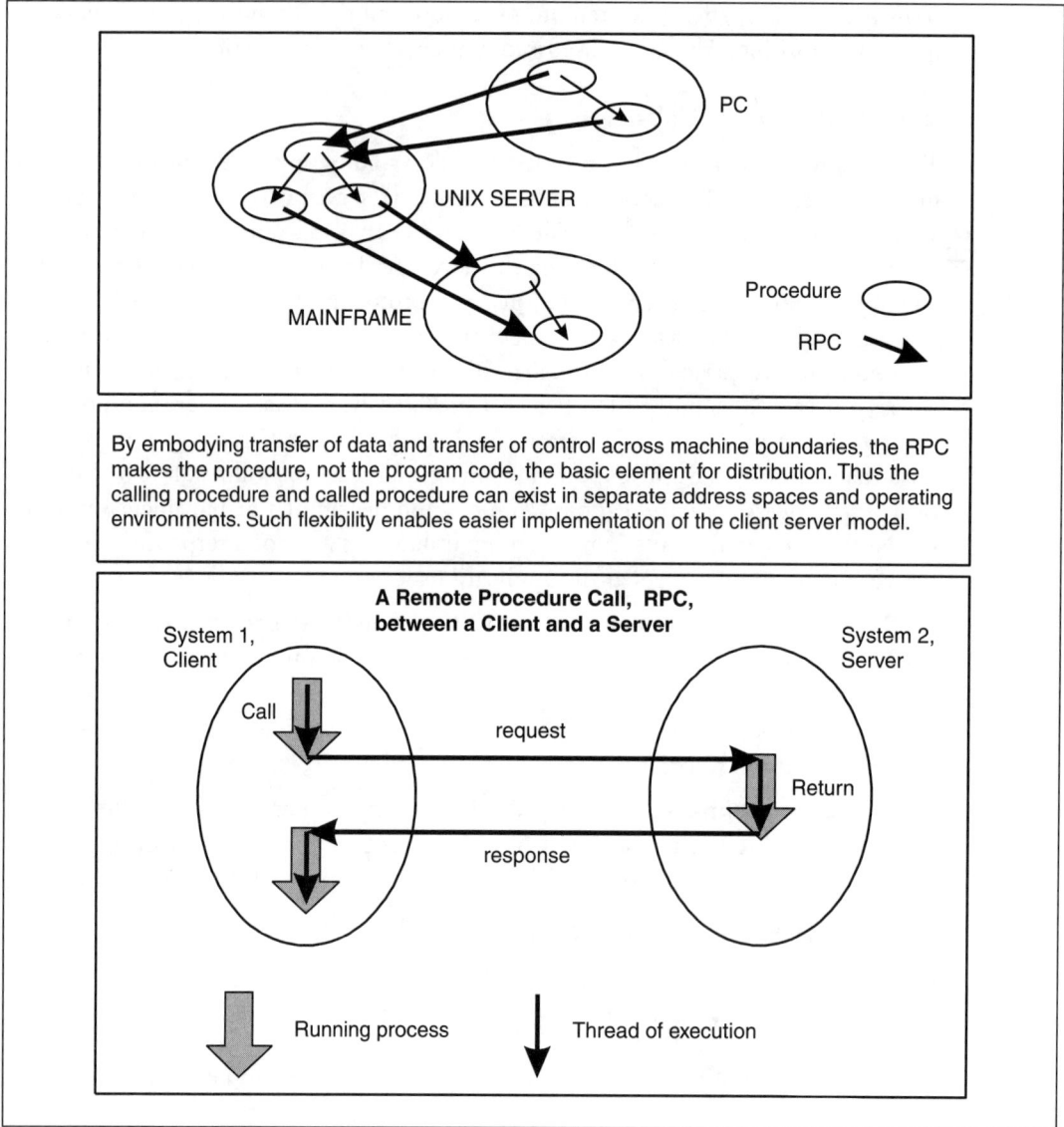

Figure 1.9 The RPC allows an application to be shared across several environments.

server). By acting in the same way as would internal calls among procedures inside each of the applications, it offers a simple and major step forward in the distributed control of execution and for accessing remote data in a multivendor, distributed environment.

The RPC code may come from a library of standard procedures, with appropriate adjustments for the operating system, NOS, and communications protocol. The network communications that set up and carry the call below the interapplication level are managed by the NOS. Server applications receive the call via *stubs* of code created by the RPC compiler, as do the client applications.

> **NOTE**
>
> The RPC hides complexity and standardizes communications.

> **TIP**
>
> Use RPC libraries and stubs to interface the various portions of the application that must be linked across the network.

To call an RPC, the application stub, a standard piece of calling code, is usually written as the first part of the "limb" that the application extends across the network to its cooperating procedure. Standardization allows you to reuse the stub, with reliable, tested behavior. Programming tools for writing RPCs across several environments generate the RPC code easily and simply for both client and server machines. Alternatively, libraries of prewritten, complete calls for the majority of environments can be purchased from vendors (Netwise and others) for common programming languages.

> **NOTE**
>
> Because there are too many RPC standards, no one prevails, although this may be addressed in the future by vendor consortiums. Currently, de facto standards include SunSoft's Open Network Computing (ONC) in the Unix world, NobelNet EZ-RPC for the C language, as well as offerings from vendors like Hewlett-Packard.

Message Queuing and Middleware

RPC was state of the art some years ago for interprocess communication services. Since then, newer mechanisms have overcome the central problem of the RPC, which is that in some situations, the calling process must wait for the called process to return before continuing. This provokes delays, and demands that delays be relatively short. If the called process takes hours, the whole system could be shut down during that time. If the called process then fails, the system may be halted for some indeterminate period. Instead, passing a message to request processing, and then sending back an alert, an *event*, when the results are ready, provides a more robust approach. This is referred to as *message queuing*, and represents the new direction in interprocess communication. *Message passing* occurs between two *application fragments* on the client and the server, as outlined in Figure 1.10, with queues of processing requests at the called resource.

If the called resource fails, on recovery it picks up its list of messages and continues processing. This interprocess mechanism follows the trend of object-oriented systems using *asynchronous message passing*. A standard message-queuing algorithm has been promoted by the Message-Oriented Middleware (MOM) Consortium, a vendor group that includes IBM (with its Message Queue Interface, MQI, mechanism).

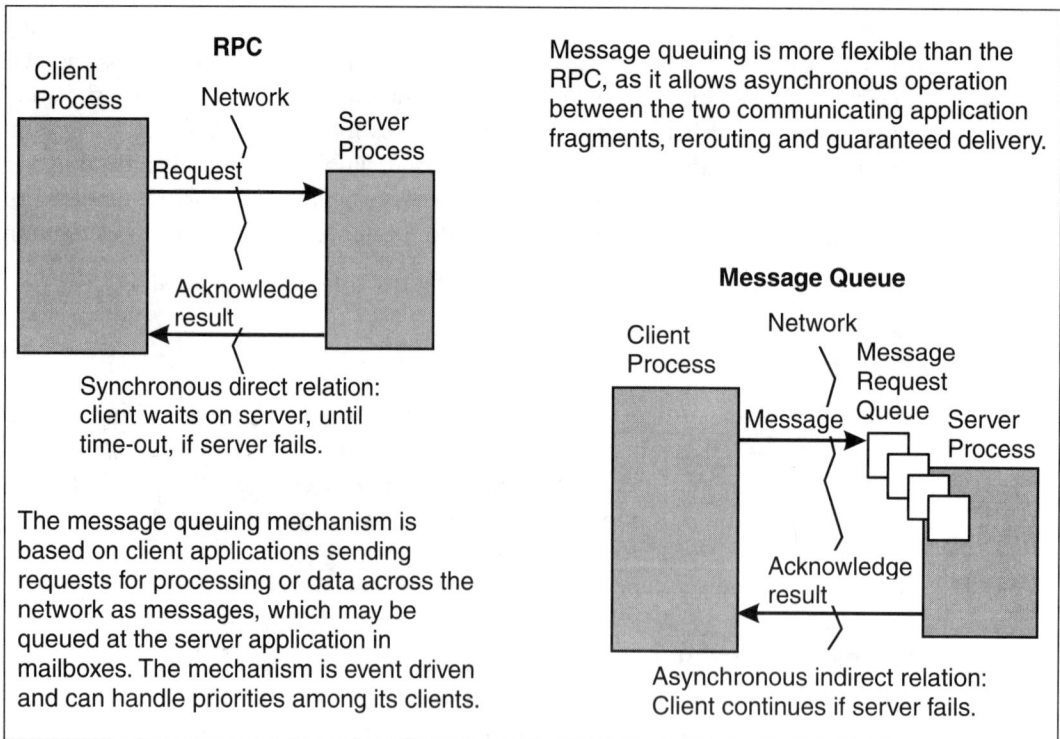

Figure 1.10 Message-passing middleware enables efficient distributed systems.

OLE for Linking PC Packages

Increasingly, users are developing applications in which a PC package can provide calculation, presentation, and data management capabilities. The user interfaces of PC packages—spreadsheets especially—are finding their way into bespoke development, where a PC client serves as part of the configuration. This approach allows you to use the available power and range of PC packages, along with any existing data and document files. Moreover, since most users are already trained in PC package interfaces, their training requirements are reduced, if not eliminated entirely. Incorporating existing PCs, however, means the new package must provide hotlink interfaces between the documents of the two PC packages. Object Linking and Embedding (OLE), from Microsoft Corporation, is the major PC package interface today (see Figure 1.11), and is oriented toward C++ and C development.

> **TIP**
>
> To link PC packages, use OLE, an API-like interface, for data passing between PC packages.

Other interfaces for package interfacing include OpenDoc (supported by Apple, IBM, Sun, Claris, Novell, and WordPerfect) and Lotus Embedding and Linking (LEL), from Lotus Development Corporation and IBM. OpenDoc is language-neu-

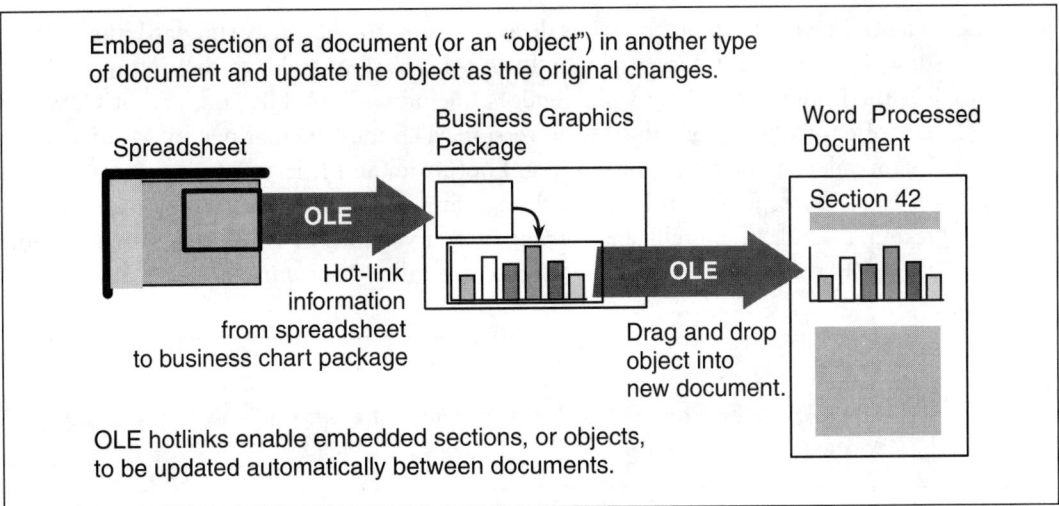

Figure 1.11 *Object linking and embedding with Microsoft OLE.*

tral, although its scripting language is modeled on AppleScript (from Apple Computer). All these interfaces allow PC packages to exchange data and, to some extent, to embed *document objects* in other documents. OpenDoc is aimed at multiple environments—Macintosh, OS/2, Windows95, and Unix—while LEL is an OLE-compatible way to link to Unix from PC applications.

Choosing a GUI

Three de facto standards exist in graphical user interfaces (GUIs), and there are GUIs for each major operating system. The universal adoption of more powerful PCs and workstations with full graphics at low cost has made the GUI on a client system the application user interface of choice. Developers can use GUIs to build custom user interfaces.

Various GUIs are available according to operating system for PCs, Unix workstations, and others (see Figure 1.12); they differ in style, especially in icon use and *intuitiveness*, and ease of use. A forerunner of many standards was the public X-Windows interface, favored by Unix suppliers. One traditional style is IBM's Common User Interface (CUA in various versions, such as CUA-91 and later), which is implemented by Microsoft Windows 3.1; and since 1984, Apple Computer has had its own sophisticated and highly intuitive Macintosh interface. Elements of all types of GUIs are present in window managers from Microsoft, and in the Unix workstations from HP, Sun, IBM, and others.

X-Windows and Motif for Unix

The Unix world still incorporates developments from an early standard: the X-Windows GUI (Figure 1.13), originally from MIT. Various styles of X-Windows still exist, the leading ones from Unix vendors, including IBM, HP, Sun, and SCO, which are often evolved from the Motif version. The implementations of Motif vary in quality, depending on supplier. Open Look from Sun Microsystems is close to Motif in user acceptance and sales, although Sun supports Motif. Some of the diskless terminals and "nonintelligent" terminals run versions of X-Windows that support the GUI favored by their supplier and so are called *X-terminals*.

> **NOTE**
> The GUI determines which tools, applications, and utilities are available to the user.

When choosing a GUI for an application under development, it pays to remember that market position is central, since the tool and package vendors follow the

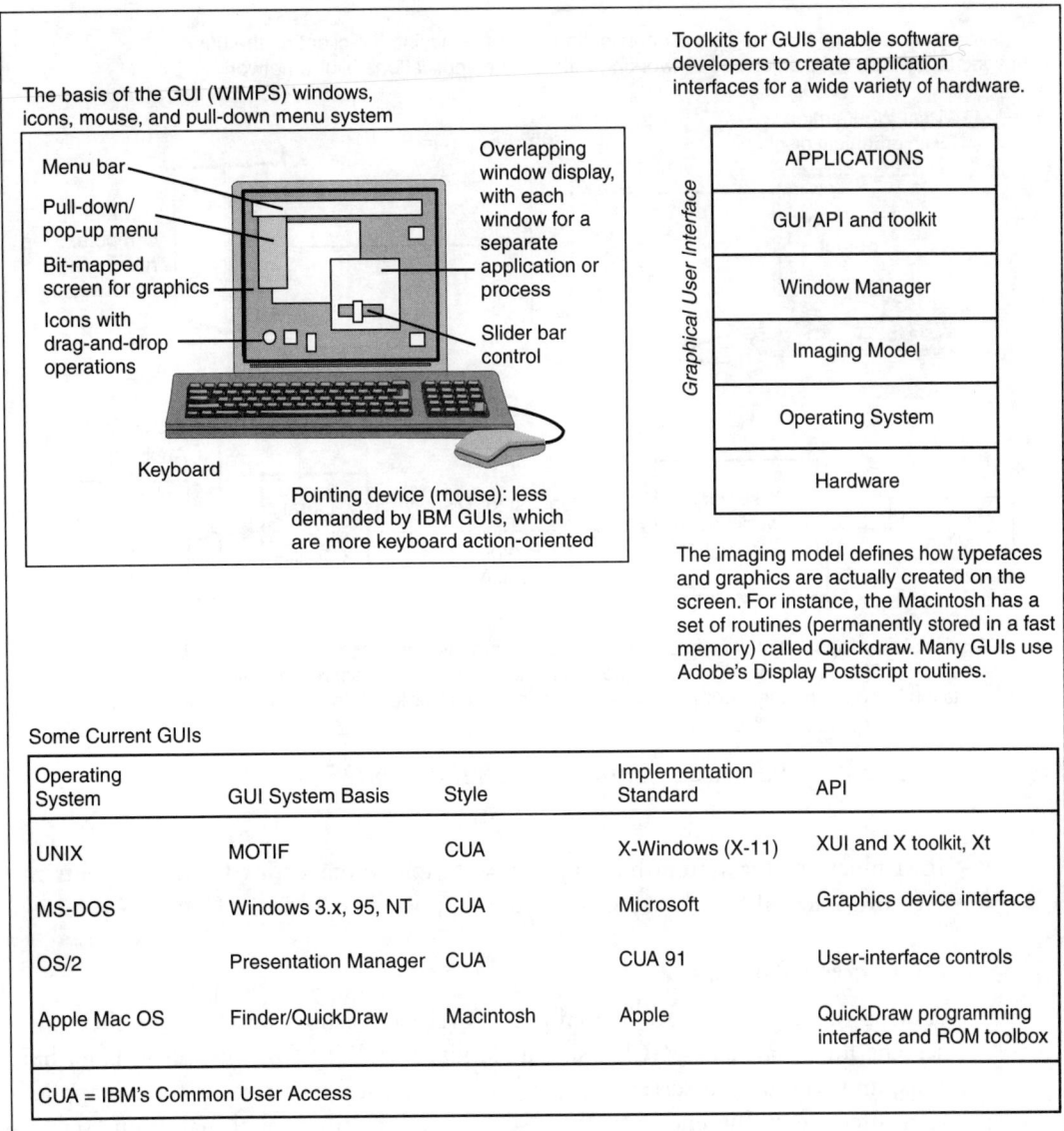

The basis of the GUI (WIMPS) windows, icons, mouse, and pull-down menu system

Menu bar

Pull-down/ pop-up menu

Bit-mapped screen for graphics

Icons with drag-and-drop operations

Keyboard

Overlapping window display, with each window for a separate application or process

Slider bar control

Pointing device (mouse): less demanded by IBM GUIs, which are more keyboard action-oriented

Toolkits for GUIs enable software developers to create application interfaces for a wide variety of hardware.

Graphical User Interface

| APPLICATIONS |
| GUI API and toolkit |
| Window Manager |
| Imaging Model |
| Operating System |
| Hardware |

The imaging model defines how typefaces and graphics are actually created on the screen. For instance, the Macintosh has a set of routines (permanently stored in a fast memory) called Quickdraw. Many GUIs use Adobe's Display Postscript routines.

Some Current GUIs

Operating System	GUI System Basis	Style	Implementation Standard	API
UNIX	MOTIF	CUA	X-Windows (X-11)	XUI and X toolkit, Xt
MS-DOS	Windows 3.x, 95, NT	CUA	Microsoft	Graphics device interface
OS/2	Presentation Manager	CUA	CUA 91	User-interface controls
Apple Mac OS	Finder/QuickDraw	Macintosh	Apple	QuickDraw programming interface and ROM toolbox
CUA = IBM's Common User Access				

Figure 1.12 *A GUI uses a window manager, and provides an API for programming.*

market. The most common GUI sold today is for the most common workstation, the PC. No surprise, this is the Microsoft Windows series, with tens of millions sold. The Windows95 GUI has its own toolkit (Windows Software Developers Kit, SDK), and the majority of application tools for GUI screen painting are designed for Windows and Windows NT. For developers who wish to follow the traditional

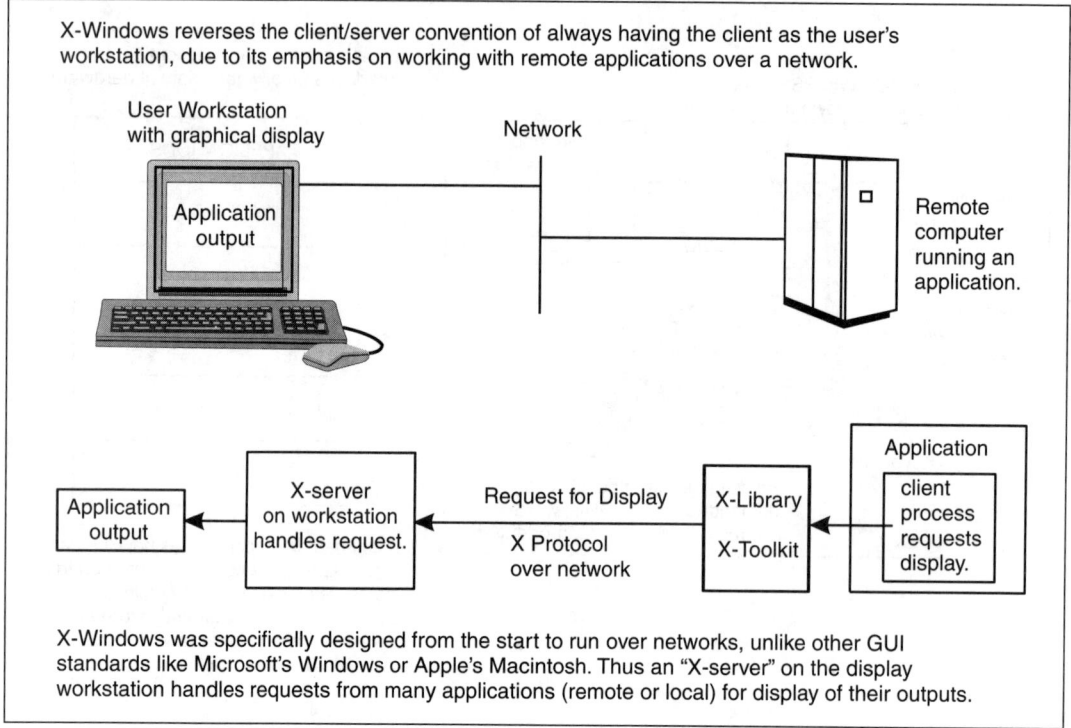

Figure 1.13 The X-Windows standard: Where's the client?

IBM blueprint for system building, Presentation Manager for OS/2 represents the GUI of choice, although Motif is still the supported GUI for the Unix AIX offering.

GUI Screen Painters

A wide range of tools are available to developers who want to paint their own screens for a particular GUI. Using a standard toolkit of menus, scroll bars, buttons, and windows, a screen designer can build a series of screens for the application interface to the end user. With such a toolkit, traditional mainframe screens can also be updated to the newer Windows-Icon-Pull-down (or Pop-up)-Menu System (WIMPS) style of interaction, using a PC to present the GUI. Although we refer to WIMPS as "new," the interface was first introduced by Xerox in the late 1970s and became wildly available and popular when Apple Computers shipped it as the default interface on their Macintosh systems in the 1980s.

Be aware, however, that by introducing a pointing device, movement, and menus, you may have to rethink the entire user interface, not merely new styles of visual presentation. How users interact with the application must be studied to understand the optimal representations for work sequences and responses; this is not straightforward. Few PC package vendors (and even fewer development departments) have really mastered this art because it demands understanding the part human intuition plays in interactions. One way to approach this challenge is to work with the end users to get a better understanding of their requirements.

> **NOTE**
>
> Screen painters are basic; user intuition is not.

In the intranet world, HTML pages sit on top of the window manager screens and can be painted using special tools, some of which come with the Web server (Microsoft Front Page) or with the browser (Netscape Navigator Gold), or can be bought separately (Adobe PageMill) for creative graphics. But remember that HTML browsers remain somewhat limited in their display capabilities, as well as their range of possible user interactions.

For the near future at least, the best advice is to follow the market leaders in GUIs, that is, Microsoft Windows and Windows NT; if you are using a Unix workstation, you will have to use the window manager packaged with the OS.

Different GUIs and Soft PCs

An alternative is to bring together different GUIs on the same screen as outlined in Figure 1.14. This allows use of the applications linked to the different windows in their native mode. In this way, different application environments, or "personalities," can be integrated on the desktop, and used in the same session.

Soft PCs, built to run Windows or DOS applications, are available from independent software suppliers for Unix environments and from the main Unix workstation suppliers. For instance, Wabi (Windows application binary interface) from SunSelect and Insignia Solutions' SoftWindows run Microsoft Windows PC applications with the GUI as a window of an X-Windows-style Unix workstation. Other soft PCs can run Apple Macintosh applications. Environments for the reverse situation also have begun to appear (a Windows GUI hosting a window for Unix X-Window applications), together with support for various nonintelligent terminals, such as the IBM 3270 screens or DEC VTxxx series as one of the windows. For instance, the Wintif Developer's Kit from IXI/SCO allows PCs with Microsoft Windows to act as a front end to Unix applications usually accessed from Motif-style workstations.

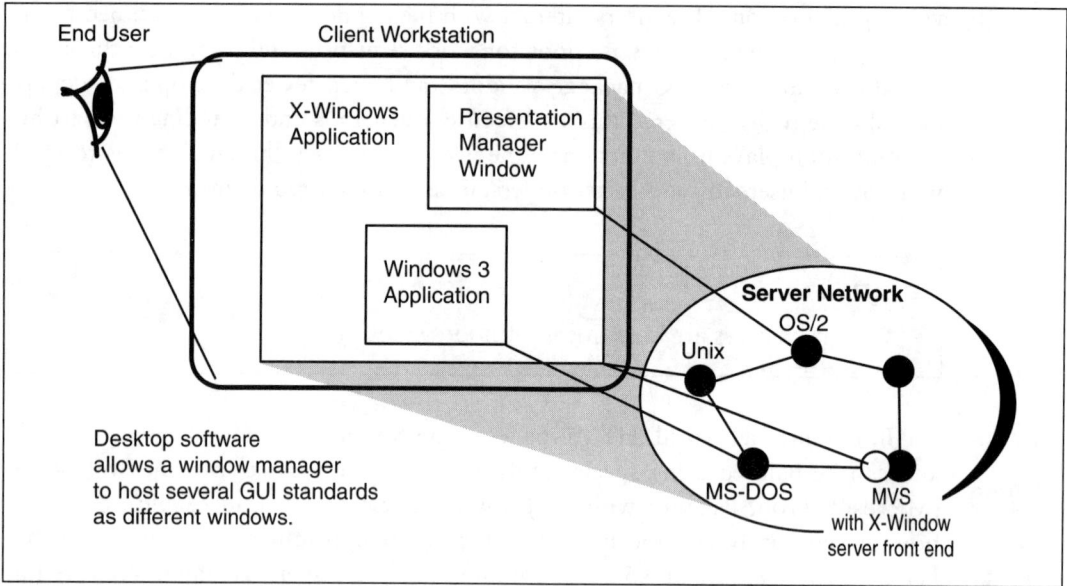

Figure 1.14 A GUI can be used to integrate sessions with multiple servers.

The Future of GUIs

Choosing one type of workstation does not necessarily preclude use of another GUI, either now or in the future, nor the application packages using that GUI. However, few standards exist to enable integration of actions between the different GUIs within each window and to increase desktop management interoperability. The integration task is complex; it involves session management, control of the various files, remote processes, workspaces, and icon usage.

> **NOTE**
>
> GUIs in the future will bring together session management and more intuitive graphics and icon usage.

Interfacing with Database Management Systems

Since the 1960s, database management systems (DBMS) have handled such functions as human-interface support, transactions, and database support in one program on one machine with nonintelligent terminals. Although fairly easy to implement, such systems do not enable easy distribution of the database across several machines on the network or straightforward distribution of functions such as user interface; nor do they encourage distribution of the application logic across the network.

> **NOTE**
>
> The client/server model is ideal for shared databases.

For a distributed environment, usually with a single database and many remote users, the client/server model is particularly useful for database access. When using multiple, interacting databases, the various databases may be complete entities handling a whole function such as customer records; or the information requested may be shared across several machines, environments, and database types: For example, bills due, credit history, accounts, and demographic data all maintained as separate, independent databases can be integrated into one customer profile.

Usually the distributed processing model involves separation of the user-interface support, such as GUI screen handling on a workstation, from the database storage and retrieval functions on the database server. Most vendors of relational databases support the client/server database model as a requester/server architecture, which has now been extended for multiple distributed databases, and is particularly useful for distributed processing.

The benefits of multiple distributed databases are numerous:

- Robustness and security with use of mirrored replication of databases as backup.

- Modularity, which enables cost-efficient increase in capacity of client/server databases; users add servers only as needed.

- Use of low-cost platforms, such as PC-LAN servers where possible, with extracts from more expensive databases.

- The ability to replicate remote data centers on multiple, local access databases to move data closer to the user reduces telecommunications charges and network traffic saturation while increasing performance.

- Federation of a number of disparate databases to build a logical, single composite information picture for the user at the client workstation.

- Placement of databases nearer to the users and owners of data to increase their control over their own data.

- Specific security requirements for physical separation of sensitive parts of the total database, and remote disaster center duplication of crucial parts.

- Flexibility to cope with new market directions in information access and storage, such as radio-linked hand-held client terminals for blue-collar and sales staff, Web server pages for the whole corporation, perhaps with multimedia information from video streaming servers.

SQL

The client/server model for database interaction is based on a public standard for database access with a query language, the Standard Query Language (SQL, often pronounced "sequel"). As outlined in Figure 1.15, SQL queries attach the application to the database(s). Unfortunately, success in imposing an industry standard SQL on database vendors has been limited thus far. Due to extensions, the flavors of SQL outnumber those of Unix, even though all relational database vendors "support" SQL.

> **NOTE**
>
> SQL sets the database interface standard, but there are many SQL choices, making it difficult to choose.

SQL allows just the dataset to be described, while the form of access is left to the DBMS. Some would class SQL as a form of database access programming

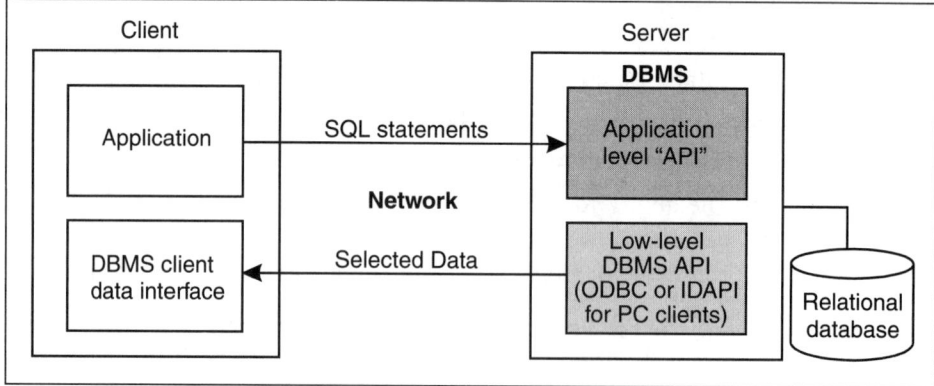

Figure 1.15 Database access in a client/server architecture.

rather than as an API (because it is done on the fly, often by end users), but it performs a similar role. Although there are variations in the features offered by the relational database vendors, several are common.

Relational Database Features

To support the creation of client/server and distributed system configurations, modern DBMSs offer *stored procedures,* which allow some of the data preparation to be done on the DBMS server by selection of processing from a standard set of procedures when programming. This can significantly reduce the number and size of transactions across the network, since only the results need to be communicated. Moreover, stored procedures can be used as the basis for the entire business logic for the application, and they provide a very simple development approach which is extremely fast. Note, however, that some RDBMS vendors do not offer stored procedures.

The RPC as described previously is not the only mechanism in use today that enables an application to communicate with database managers. Many tool and database vendors use an earlier from of interprocess communication, called *named pipes,* originally a Unix term. It is found in many operating systems (OS/2), in NOSs (Novell Netware and Microsoft LAN Manager), and in library constructs for programming languages (C and even Java). The mechanism enables the various applications to implement a client/server configuration between SQL databases and applications across a network.

The most common database APIs are for Microsoft Windows clients. Microsoft's Open Database Connectivity (ODBC) API for the DBMS allows PC users to access a range of relational databases, including those from Oracle, Informix, CA Ingres, Microsoft, Progress, Sybase, IBM, Hewlett-Packard, and DEC. An alternative API which encompasses ODBC is Integrated Database API (IDAPI), supported by Oracle, Informix, IBM, Sybase, and other software suppliers.

Finding and Using Information

In distributed systems, data and documents must be located by names, indexes, or contents, unless the locations are preset inside the applications. The structuring of information across a wide area network is still a largely unresolved problem for most distributed systems. In contrast, Web-based systems don't have the information-structuring problem, which is one of the reasons for their success. What is required is an open information architecture using a library tool to enable the sharing of documents, as well as data in files and databases. Another problem is translation of information from different databases and filestores into the form required by the client application. For example, in a major logistics system, the basic warehouse stock information was held on distributed systems with modern relational databases in each warehouse (there were eight) in a strange record format that differed for each warehouse! But orders were held in a legacy system running on a 15-year-old mainframe in flat files; and current deliveries were in a fourth minisystem, with a proprietary attached database. Finally, there was no way of identifying where all this information was, let alone of bringing it together in a common format at regular intervals for the decision support system required by management.

The location and translation function (or service) forms the core part of upper middleware, but no universally accepted scheme currently exists outside Web technology; there are only several proprietary approaches and tools. Developments in vendor groups and the public standards on directories for naming and addressing—X.500—have produced a partial solution for a directory. A different type of support, but proprietary, is from the library suppliers (for instance, Saros with Mezzanine), who attempt to keep track of all known information and documents across the enterprise with a *dedicated relational database*. Generally, such library products are PC LAN-oriented. The new tools take into account documents and data, not just data, as products from the RDBMS suppliers tend to. Among proprietary approaches is the Information Warehouse, from IBM, which integrates different data formats and databases through a single manager, and allows access via an SQL tool, EDA/SQL. It is part of IBM's proprietary Distributed Data Management (DDM) architecture for distributed databases; a subcomponent of that is the relational DBMS architecture, Distributed Relational Database Architecture (DRDA). Such approaches sometimes complement and sometimes rival the efforts of the vendor group, SQL Applications Group (SAG), to come up with an industry standard for distributed database management and access.

Transaction Processing

Management of online transaction processing (OLTP) with a database is performed by an OLTP or TP monitor. Traditionally, these have been mainframe utilities, sitting on top of the database management system. The best known is IBM's Customer Information Control System (CICS). OLTP monitors designed for Unix servers are also commonly used, especially Tuxedo, with the X/Open XA API for interfacing. Other new products are Top End (NCR), Encina (Enterprise computing in a new age) from Transarc and Hewlett-Packard, based on the DCE (discussed below), and IBM's CICS/6000 for its AIX Unix. The Tuxedo OLTP monitor specifically includes a three-layer model for distributed and client/server systems having PCs, Unix servers, and mainframes (which might host a TP monitor like CICS) to build layers of networked OLTP servers and distributed databases. Such monitors all work with a wide variety of databases through the standard API, the X/Open XA database interface. Choosing an OLTP monitor should be based on two major criteria: performance, and capability to ensure integrity across a distributed environment.

TIP

OLTP, from the mainframe to low-cost Unix servers with new TP monitors, is cost effective and gives robust transaction processing with good performance, plus easy connectivity for PC clients.

Handling Database Transactions

You must be prepared to handle database transactions across several platforms: transaction managers, two-phase commits, and other measures. With distributed systems, major technical problems are present around distributed database operation. Many of the issues of multiple, physically dispersed databases remain largely unresolved, specifically transaction integrity and the database design, as highlighted in Figure 1.16.

Transaction Systems Performance

The prime issue for transaction processing (TP) systems in general remains performance—the time it takes to process a transaction, which gives the maximum load it can handle. Another issue for distributed TP systems is transactions that do not complete successfully, leaving the database(s) and application(s) in an unknown state because an access or update was left in midair. Most RDBMS vendors now offer a protective mechanism for this event, termed the two-phase commit.

The two-phase commit makes database interactions more reliable, by ensuring a known transaction state. The first phase calls for a run-through of the transaction, checking that all participants are ready and data is complete. The second phase is to verify completion, by collecting acknowledgments from the subtransaction successes. If any participant in the transaction fails to complete successfully, the database manager(s) and transaction processing monitor can then always roll back to a known position at any point. Either the OLTP monitor, the DBMS manager, and/or an added transaction server must manage this whole process. As mentioned earlier, Web technology has not yet answered this need for a state machine; various extra mechanisms also must be added, for example, a cookie in the browser and an extra Web server routine.

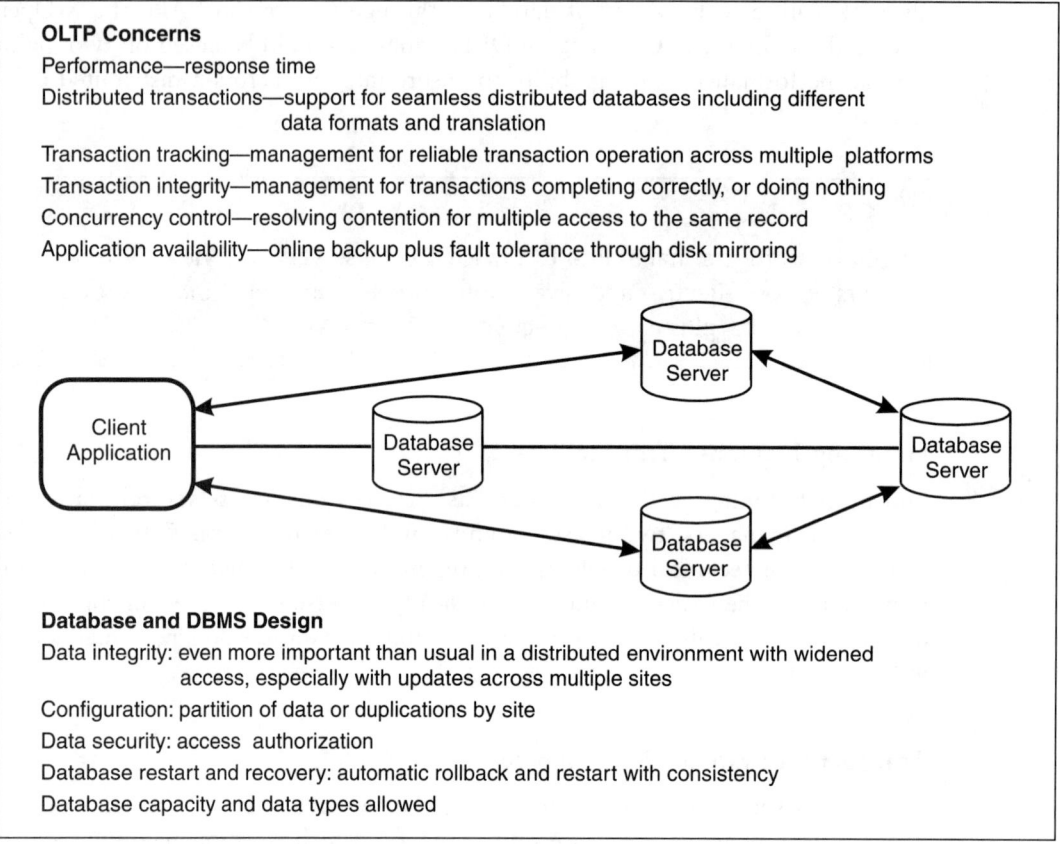

OLTP Concerns

Performance—response time

Distributed transactions—support for seamless distributed databases including different
data formats and translation

Transaction tracking—management for reliable transaction operation across multiple platforms

Transaction integrity—management for transactions completing correctly, or doing nothing

Concurrency control—resolving contention for multiple access to the same record

Application availability—online backup plus fault tolerance through disk mirroring

Database and DBMS Design

Data integrity: even more important than usual in a distributed environment with widened
access, especially with updates across multiple sites

Configuration: partition of data or duplications by site

Data security: access authorization

Database restart and recovery: automatic rollback and restart with consistency

Database capacity and data types allowed

Figure 1.16 In a distributed environment, most database concerns are related to on-line transaction processing and database server design.

Multilevel Client/Server and Transaction Servers

For multilevel client/server systems, the control of transactions across multiple machines is more complex and requires greater processing effort. Transaction servers or transaction managers, shown in Figure 1.17, were developed for this reason.

Transaction server managers may be separate from the OLTP monitor and specifically designed to compensate for cases where the OLTP monitor considers only two entities: the requester and the called database. They handle all the intermediate transaction stages and platforms. As they deal with overheads such as request preparation, acknowledgment of ready, and subsequent record closing, transaction servers can speed up the total transaction time and reduce network traf-

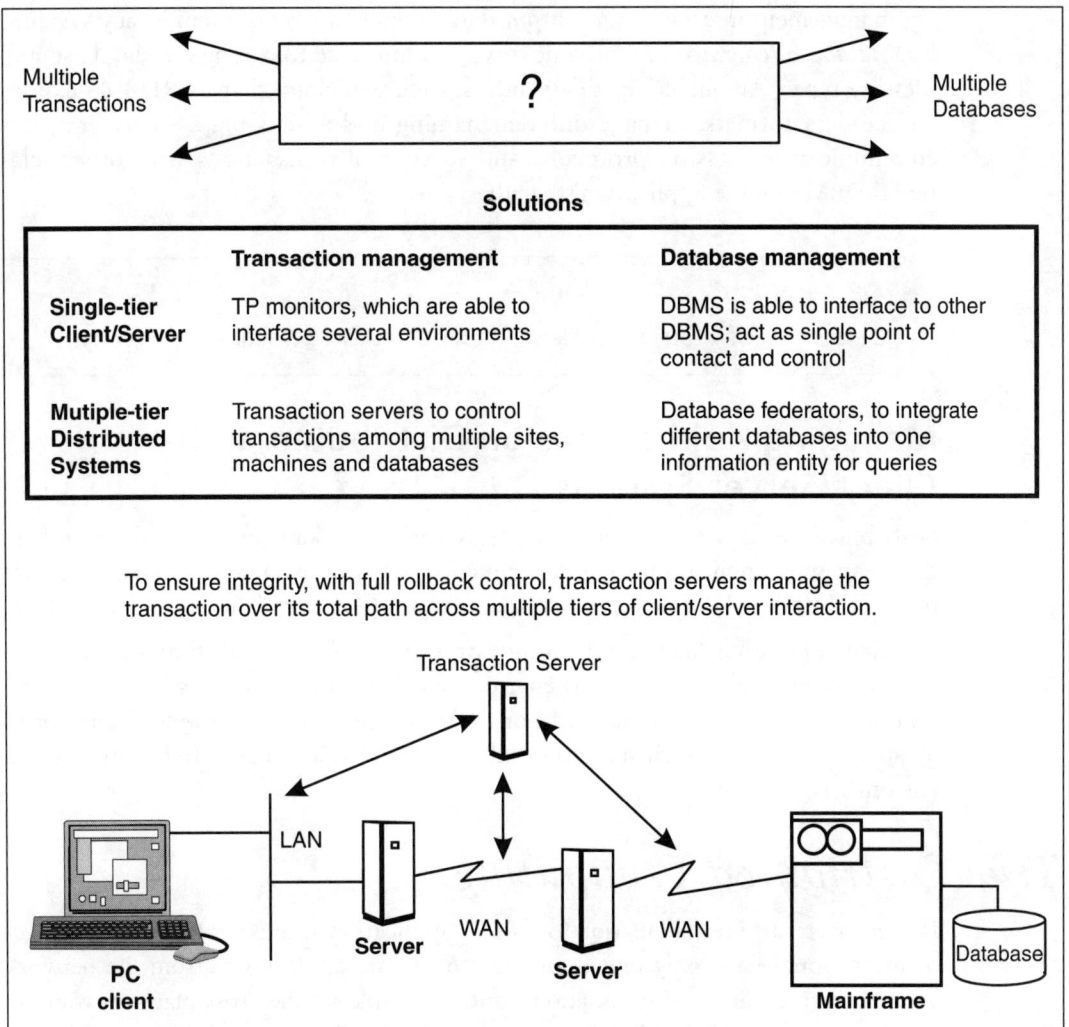

Figure 1.17 *Transaction management solutions handle multiple distributed databases and multiple transactions.*

fic. When a dynamic request has to be set up, and much overhead is incurred in preparation, a transaction server can cut traffic by over 50 percent.

Database Federators

One common cause of headaches is putting different databases and filestores together for the application, perhaps with multiple sessions, when they all have differing management interfaces and output data formats, many of them legacy systems. The *database federator* can provide a way to interface to a range of database and filestore types. Among competing vendors, each will claim that its RDBMS can interface data formats, manage different naming and addressing systems, translate communications session protocols, and so control transactions with other relational DBMS on the application's behalf.

> **TIP**
>
> Database federators can make multiple databases appear as one entity.

Managing Applications on Distributed and Client/Server Systems

Distributed systems management is covered in detail later in the book; note here that managing applications in a distributed systems environment requires action at five levels, and each has specific management problems, as identified in Figure 1.18.

Generally, each layer needs administration tools and fault-fixing tools, integrated into a single management environment for a multivendor system. To date, no universal architectures, methods, or tools to manage all operations cleanly, or to locate and fix faults on client/server and distributed systems exist today; as a result, custom systems reign.

True Distributed Computing

If there were an ideal blueprint for better application interoperation and management, it would have only one component to isolate applications from the network and all the mechanics of transactions, and to handle all the cross-platform transaction management. At this time, however, for true distributed processing, we still need:

- Transparent format conversion.
- Dynamic updating.
- Linking services for objects.
- Scripting languages.
- Groupware support.

These are not available today as a single entity. Previous commercial attempts to achieve this, albeit proprietary, go back to the Xerox Star system (1980), and include an attempt by Apollo with the Domain environment (1983).

LEVEL	KEY PROBLEM
Application	Version control and update procedures; conflicts between applications and utilities
Transaction	Tracking transactions across multiple platforms, for audit and security; multiple rollback to known states on failure; multiple versions of interacting applications
Data Administration	Multiple copy update; central data security and integrity; uncontrolled/unknown end-user versions; errors in access by end-user developers
Systems Software	Version control and update procedures; conflicts between new versions and utilities; multivendor conflicts
Networks	Network managemement down to terminal level, especially over a LAN; multiple vendor network management

Figure 1.18 The most common problems of application management and administration in distributed systems are seen at five levels.

DCE

Further steps are being taken to achieve the goal of a single-entity tool, such as IBM's Open Distributed Computing Systems (ODCS) blueprint, but nothing at the level of a complete single layer will be widely available for the immediate future. The leading attempt today in a shrink-wrapped product is the Distributed Computing Environment (DCE) from the Open Group (a vendor consortium for open systems). DCE's aim is to offer a set of services, principally interapplication communications (with its own RPC and multithreaded control of processes for parallel operations), distributed file sharing, time, security, directories, transaction processing, shared printing, software distribution, GUI interfacing, management of events, and distributed administration. The implementation depends on objects and the object request broker, the ORB (more about this later in the book). DCE provides both a model and the basic source code for vendors to build a standard distributed computing environment, with most of the components hidden from the application programmer. With its architectural blueprint

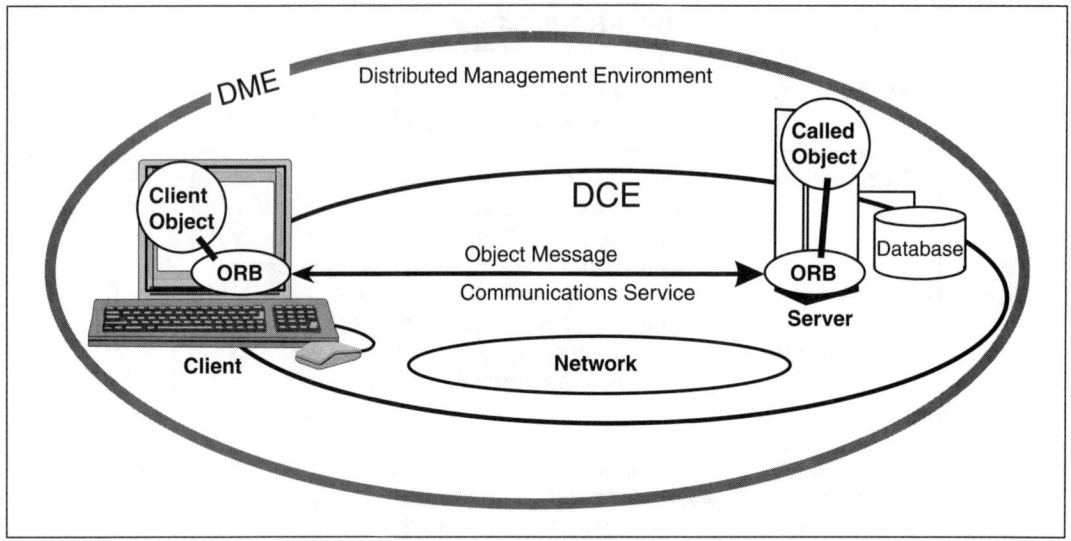

Figure 1.19 *Is the future a shrink-wrapped distributed environment based on DCE, in which remote objects can interwork and DME provides the management?*

for distributed processing, DCE provides a formal framework for distributed and client/server systems.

DCE effectively integrates much of the basic complexity of middleware we have described, with its own RPC and data management elements (Figure 1.19), and adds advanced features for parallelism and performance. DCE intends to embrace current products for its implementation; for instance, to manage transactions under DCE, one possible candidate is Communications Integrator from Covia Technologies. This product was developed for airline reservation systems (Covia was owned by United Airlines and British Airways) to interface applications to existing network protocols. In the eventual implementation, Covia's product may end up as just one component interfaced with multiple other middleware offerings, such as Sun's Open Network Computing. Commercial partial implementations of DCE have appeared from the major systems vendors. DCE support is available for Unix operating systems, as well as for IBM MVS, DEC VMS, IBM OS/2, Microsoft DOS Windows, and Apple MacOS. Some software vendors have considered modifying their applications packages for DCE services and its multithreading capability, as it enables several clients to access the same code in parallel. For instance, systems utilities are being modified to run with DCE for distributed operations, notably the Unix TP monitors such as Transarc Encina, IBM CICS, and Tuxedo. Complete new products based on DCE, such as Atrium's Dazel office server, are also appearing.

STATUS	COMPONENT (OR MECHANISM OR ENVIRONMENT)
In use today	NOS, Network Operating Systems; managers of cross-platform networking
	SQL-based client/server database
	APIs, Application Programming Interfaces, for interfaces to common utilities and services such as communications and operating systems
	RPC, Remote Procedure Call, for remote execution control
	PC package interworking mechanisms such as Microsoft OLE
	PC package interworking mechanisms such as Microsoft DDE
	Librarians and data translators
	Transaction servers
	Distributed databases, using database federators
Leading edge today	Web technology for intranets
Available completely in 1–3 years	Implementations of object models (IBM, Open Group, Microsoft Common Object Model)
	ORB, Object Request Broker: object-based, high-level mechanisms for interapplication communications and control (from OMG)
	Message queue interprocess/interobject communication, specifically:
	Messaging Oriented Middleware, MOM, implemented as MQ by IBM
	DCE, Distributed Computing Environment (from Open Group)
	DME, Distributed Management Environment (from Open Group)
	Web technology with the Internet Interoperability Protocol (IIOP) and the Java Remote Method Invocation

Figure 1.20 Distributed computing approaches and components are at various stages of maturity.

Emerging Components

In summary, we can identify three major stages of maturity in the building block approach for client/server and distributed systems, summarized in Figure 1.20. Web technology offers great productivity through its robust servers and prebuilt components, but much of it is still too primitive for practical use in real distributed systems. For instance, the most touted Web technology language, Java, in its current form is not inherently designed for supporting distributed computing. Java has minimal communications facilities for cooperating processes across a network. Furthermore, it has no notion of built-in state, which is crucial to track the progress of transactions across a network.

The future for building a distributed computing infrastructure lies in three possible directions:

- The older object way, with Open Group's DCE and RPC, or Microsoft's Common Object Model (COM).

- The newer object approach with CORBA (see next chapters) providing an information communications bus (or standard interface of exchange) for data and commands between applications, office systems, and information repositories across the enterprises.

- The WEB way, Java Virtual Machine (JVM) with IIOP, API, applets (see next chapters).

Client/Server Uses

How do you decide what you need to build a distributed system? Ask yourself the following:

1. *What do you need to build?* This is defined by the users' needs: requirements from the number of users online, performance, complexity of applications, and forms of output each class of user needs. This analysis will be the result of several joint application design workshops with the users.

2. *What do you already have?* Assess the current environment.

3. *What is available now?* Which services are commonly available, such as security firewalls and WANs.

4. *What are you using already?* Do you have, for example, 30,000 Windows 3.1 PCs for potential clients machines? If so, forget Java applets on the clients, since Java requires a 32-bit environment.

5. *What legacy systems and databases do you have to draw data from or use as part of your processing in a server mode?*

To help you apply the answers to these questions, we present two examples of building real, large, modern, distributed systems for critical business applications using a number of design choices.

A Data Warehouse Example

In this example, we had little time to build an executive and middle management tool for a leading telecommunications operator. The system had to cope with central management of stock levels across a national system of warehouses, handling everything from a telephone handset for the retail channels to the core backup cards for the trunk switches.

The system had to solve some important problems concerning inventory status, value of stocks, priorities of movements, shrinkage, supplier performance, transporter performance, and accounts for managing several tens of millions of items, from a net present value perspective. After many Joint Applications Development (JAD) sessions, we opted to take data in from multiple legacy sources, scrub it—to make it reliable—and then present it in the various forms as required by the users as an executive dashboard. JAD sessions (described in more detail in Chapter 5) are meetings which take place during an application design and development process between the application developers and the ultimate end users. During these sessions, end users can explain and make more explicit requirements while helping the developers to evaluate design alternatives.

Work began with much effort on the data design. We chose a star data schema. Due to the nature of the problem, the system design evolved around a central repository for integrated data from many systems—so we opted for a data warehouse—and several vendors tendered for the software package. We decided on a client/server implementation due to the dispersed nature of users, data inputs, and processing centers. The chosen package included interconnection to a back-end RDBMS and a server front end with an RPC-based communications server (see Figure 1.21).

We decided to put some processing on a PC client for the screen-generation operations, plus local data calculations and presentation, in order to minimize network traffic and server load. Scripts and screens were designed in Visual Basic for the PC client. A PC stub interacted with a simple communications package via a straightforward RPC, included in the scripting package.

Using JAD workshops leading into a RAD approach for development, the system was available in its initial form just six months from the first joint design meetings.

Example 2: Internet Merchant System with Built-in Workflow

In this case, too, speed was of the essence in solving this major back-office problem. A large utility was necessary to automate all corporate back-office systems to cut

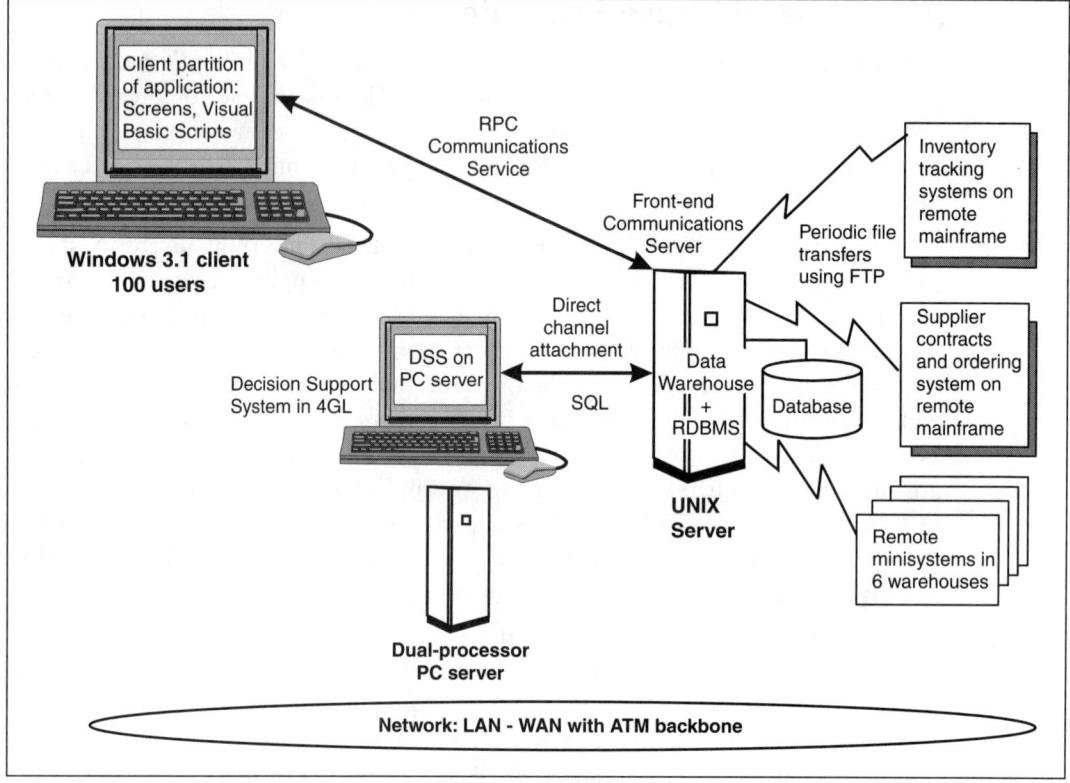

Figure 1.21 *Distributed system design example: A data warehouse for logistics.*

fixed costs rapidly. All procurement functions for operational staff, from ordering vehicles to building repairs and office stationary, were to be automated, with staff doing their own purchasing using built-in authorization/verification—a workflow problem.

For reasons of speed and size (it had to support some 4,000 users interactively), we made the major design decision early: use Web technology for its preformed environment and components in the shape of a Web server as the center of an intranet-based system, topped by a merchant server with a catalogue.

We found, however, that this preformed approach only went so far. Over 50 percent of the complete functionality had to come from programming that was added on top of the Web technology platform, components, and tools. Recognizing this, we chose a workflow package to communicate with the merchant server.

Design decisions revolved around the performance of the software, with a lot of calculations on queuing of transactions. We finally decided to use multiple instances of the Web server to overcome slowness in the workflow package and growth limits in its proprietary database. This action divided the user population among the servers by line of business; thereafter, transactions handled by each server were reduced and gave excellent response times.

The end-user software/hardware/networking package was carefully designed, based on a common browser for a minimal PC client configuration, with access varying from high-speed intranet support down to a modem at 9.6 Kbps. In addition, networks had to be upgraded to cope with the traffic demands of large volumes of HTML screens.

Finally, a lot of design work went into security and design of a powerful set of common services, for robust networking, firewalls, encryption, and authentication; the latter were used by sister projects and so were placed under the long-term support of staff in the operational centers (see Figure 1.22).

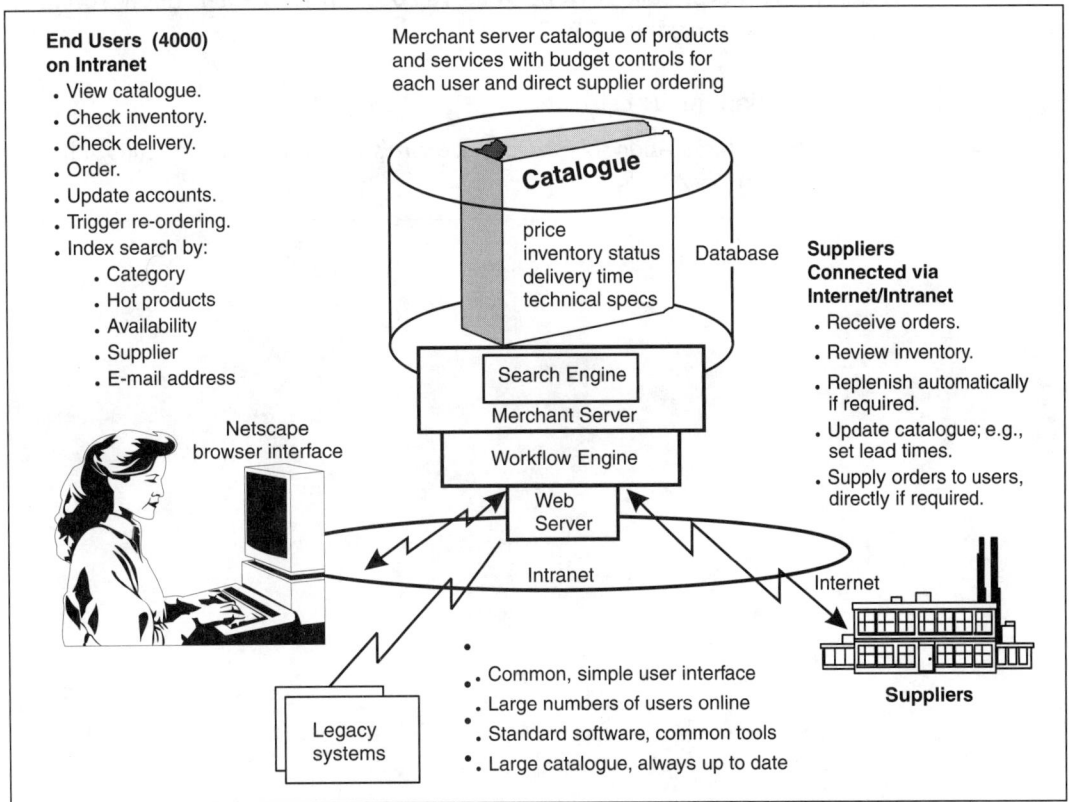

Figure 1.22 *Distributed system design example: A large back-office system for purchasing, based on a merchant server and intranet.*

Conclusions

This chapter addressed some the main ideas behind distributed systems and how they are built, specifically the use of a middleware layer to bind everything together across a network between a client and a server machine. One key concept we only touched on is that of reducing complexity by hiding functionality in black boxes, with a set of services to and from these boxes. We deal with this in greater depth in the next chapter.

FOR FURTHER READING

Guengerich S., D. Graham, M. Miller, and S. McDonald. *Building the Corporate Intranet.* (New York: John Wiley & Sons, Inc.), 1997.

net.Genesis Corp. *Build a World Wide Web Commerce Center.* (New York: John Wiley & Sons, Inc.), 1997.

For transaction queue calculations

J. Martin, *Systems Analysis for Data Transmission.* (Englewood Cliffs, NJ: Prentice-Hall), 1972.

2 USING OBJECTS

The time has come, the Walrus said, to speak of many things: Of shoes, and ships—and sealing wax—Of cabbages and kings—

Through the Looking Glass, and What Alice Found There,
Lewis Carroll, 1871

This chapter:

Gives a brief overview of object-oriented concepts.

Introduces business objects for modeling business processes and problems.

Lists the benefits of using joint requirements capture (JRC) sessions.

Discusses object-oriented software development and competing design approaches.

Explores reuse, including building an object library.

Presents possible object solutions for legacy systems.

Object Basics

No doubt you've heard of objects, but you may be wondering whether objects can have any real impact on business. In this chapter, we show you that objects are more than a new programming toy, and are definitely worth your time. The first benefit objects offer is financial. Objects have generated tens of billions of dollars in sales of software packages, systems, and utilities created using object concepts and languages. PCs, which generate billions in sales, nearly all use objects in graphical user interfaces (GUIs)—they're probably in the PC Windows interface you use everyday. Likewise, the Apple Macintosh is based on object concepts; and the World Wide Web is founded on objects and their interactions.

The future of objects lies in designing and implementing solutions for business systems. In the software industry today, no major vendor can afford not to use object concepts as part of their code production line. When consistently applied, the savings from reuse (another object benefit), can add up to 80 percent of software development time and cost.

Reuse and object concepts impact reliability in software—its integrity. Military software, designed to be ultra-robust and ultra-secure has been object-based for 15-plus years.

Originally, object-oriented concepts and code were used only in the most expensive software for systems operating in life-and-death situations—nuclear power control, military systems, or hazardous industrial plants. Today, object-oriented design is widely used in the mainstream software industry, but its foundation as a security provider has become an essential advantage for distributed systems.

To fully understand the value of objects in distributed business systems, we need a framework from which to view them. Few other technology mechanisms require such a philosophical approach. We'll begin to build that framework at the organic level.

Objects Are Organic

Like people and other organic systems, objects are independent entities, just like cells, and exhibit distinct individual behavior. Moreover, they exist in a class hierarchy that clearly defines that behavior. Objects inherit their behavior patterns from their "parents" and their parents' ancestors. They also may need the support of other objects, in which case, they expect certain services to be provided for them. Objects can cooperate with other objects, according to a predefined behavior in tightly controlled patterns of relationships, where operations follow an expected scheme of events. They can even be "bred" to deal with some level of uncertainty, so that when things go wrong, their behavior is predictable.

Interestingly for us, objects are inherently distributed in their operation, and can be made independently responsible for some task. Most important, they can be designed to act as automatons in a self-organizing, self-regulating community of objects, and if need be, work together while remotely located.

Object philosophy is governed by the following six principles (shown in Figure 2.1). They:

- Are entities capable of interaction.
- Allow us to model our world abstractly.
- Reside in classes and inherit changes made to parents.
- Interpret commands differently in different classes, though the commands remain unchanged.
- Are visible, but hide how they work, making them easy to use.
- Use message request services to limit and control interactions.

The following examples will help clarify the six object principles, which may be grouped under three rules:

- Objects bring us useful description through decomposition.
- Objects exhibit predefined behavior.
- Objects are designed for strong protection.

Behavior

The idea that objects "behave" according to specific patterns may seem odd, but actually, any system can have objects that exhibit specific behavior. For example, you can look at a car as a series of objects—engine, body, transmission, suspension, steering, controls, and electronics—each with a distinct behavior. The engine's behavior is to start, accelerate, decelerate, cruise, or stop. This limited behavior is dictated by its controls and starter motor in order to produce torque to drive the wheels and the dynamo. Similarly, software has interrelated components. The object components invoke other objects to act for them, and they are prompted to respond by other objects. If their structure is persistent and their reactions are consistent, they will exhibit repeated patterns of behavior.

Polymorphism

A command to an object produces a reaction appropriate to the specific object, which is a powerful design concept. It allows us to use a *black box* approach to building business systems. For example, say we want to design a plane that flies by electronic signals ("by the wire") and can be sold in a jet-engine or turboprop version. For either version, the command from the pilot to increase/decrease

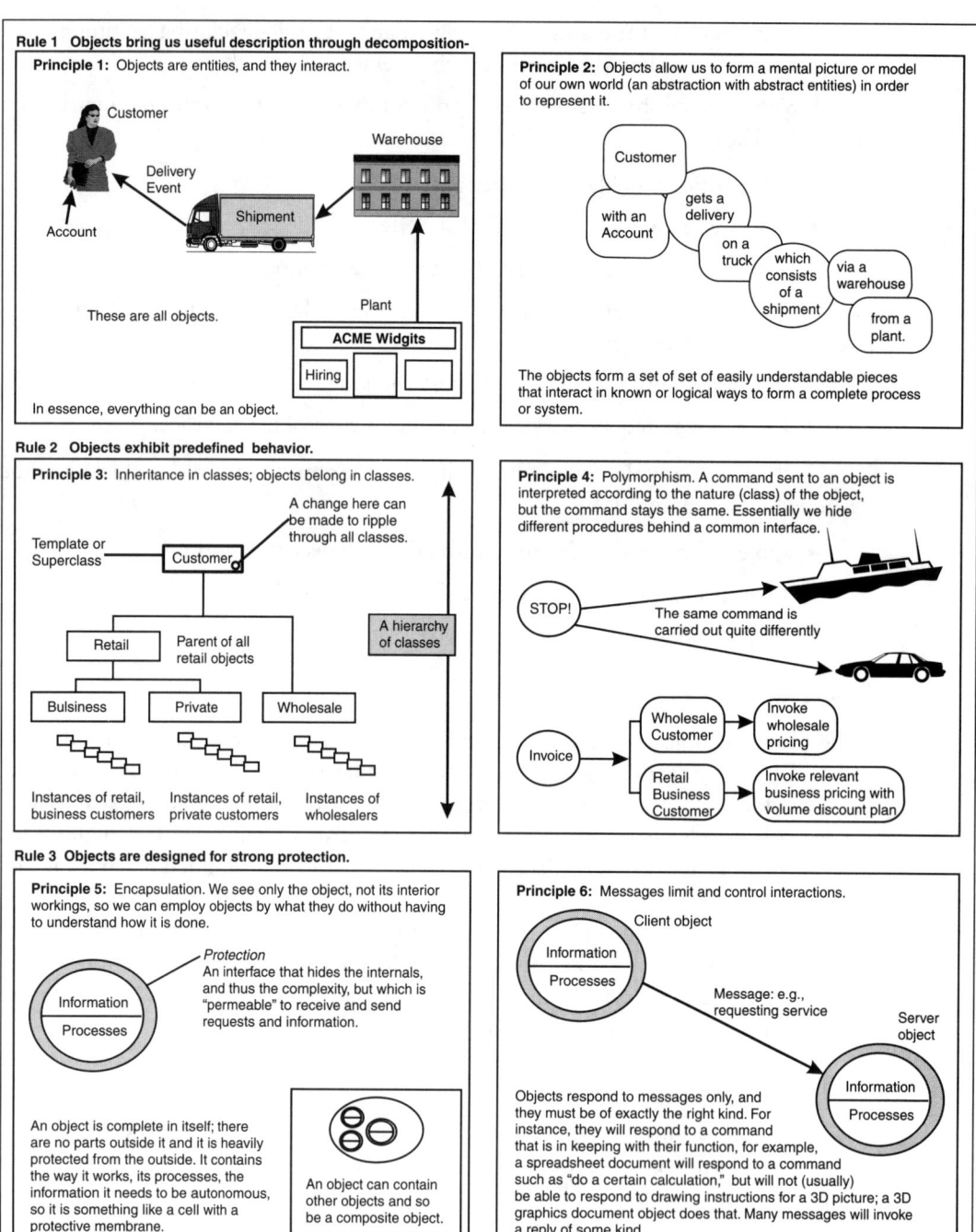

Rule 1 Objects bring us useful description through decomposition-

Principle 1: Objects are entities, and they interact.

Customer

Delivery Event

Account

Shipment

Warehouse

Plant

ACME Widgits

Hiring

These are all objects.

In essence, everything can be an object.

Principle 2: Objects allow us to form a mental picture or model of our own world (an abstraction with abstract entities) in order to represent it.

Customer

with an Account

gets a delivery

on a truck

which consists of a shipment

via a warehouse

from a plant.

The objects form a set of set of easily understandable pieces that interact in known or logical ways to form a complete process or system.

Rule 2 Objects exhibit predefined behavior.

Principle 3: Inheritance in classes; objects belong in classes.

Template or Superclass

Customer

A change here can be made to ripple through all classes.

Retail

Parent of all retail objects

A hierarchy of classes

Bulsiness

Private

Wholesale

Instances of retail, business customers

Instances of retail, private customers

Instances of wholesalers

Principle 4: Polymorphism. A command sent to an object is interpreted according to the nature (class) of the object, but the command stays the same. Essentially we hide different procedures behind a common interface.

STOP!

The same command is carried out quite differently

Invoice

Wholesale Customer

Invoke wholesale pricing

Retail Business Customer

Invoke relevant business pricing with volume discount plan

Rule 3 Objects are designed for strong protection.

Principle 5: Encapsulation. We see only the object, not its interior workings, so we can employ objects by what they do without having to understand how it is done.

Information

Processes

Protection
An interface that hides the internals, and thus the complexity, but which is "permeable" to receive and send requests and information.

An object is complete in itself; there are no parts outside it and it is heavily protected from the outside. It contains the way it works, its processes, the information it needs to be autonomous, so it is something like a cell with a protective membrane.

An object can contain other objects and so be a composite object.

Principle 6: Messages limit and control interactions.

Client object

Information

Processes

Message: e.g., requesting service

Server object

Information

Processes

Objects respond to messages only, and they must be of exactly the right kind. For instance, they will respond to a command that is in keeping with their function, for example, a spreadsheet document will respond to a command such as "do a certain calculation," but will not (usually) be able to respond to drawing instructions for a 3D picture; a 3D graphics document object does that. Many messages will invoke a reply of some kind.

Figure 2.1 *Objects are defined by six principles, expressed as three rules.*

power would be the same, whichever engine type was chosen. The command would not change, but the way it is interpreted within the propulsion object would be quite different. We don't have to understand the engine's internal workings; we only see results. For software, this is a powerful advantage. If a word processing program, for example, sends a print command and some page data to a printer, the WP program need know nothing about that printer's internals; a print driver object will take care of that. That means we can use the same command with any printer type or brand. The software driver object handles differences among printers.

Classes and Inheritance

Objects use the principle of a standard type, or class. A particular object is an instance of its class. Objects in the same class have similar behavior and structure. For example, in banking, you may have different types of accounts, but each is an instance of a generic parent account with specific attributes: a state of credit or debit, a value, an identifier, and a related person or company. The account for person A or company C is a particular instance. With a software class, if we change the parent object, we can make the change ripple through all its descendants. Multiple inheritance can also exist—that is, inheriting characteristics from several types of objects. For instance, a printer driver object for networked laser printers might inherit characteristics from two generic parents, one being a generic laser printer object and the other a network communications driver. So, if the protocol standard used on a LAN is updated to a faster speed, and the laser printer family advanced to a new resolution range, changes in each parent object could be applied to all child objects, with only one change in one known place. To upgrade software without difficulty, inheritance is key.

Protection

Objects take protection seriously. Systems built with objects are much more secure; they are like a series of rooms with walls and clearly defined pathways between them, which are the only ways of communicating. Protection occurs at two levels: consistency, expected behavior, so the whole system is predictable, and internally, protecting the objects' "vitals" (data and code) from the outside world by accepting only specifically formatted messages. What goes on inside an object is protected from the outside. This is part of *encapsulation*.

Encapsulation

Objects are self-contained components of a total system; they are encapsulated, so their complexity is hidden. They may be *composite objects*; that is, they may contain several objects, which themselves can have many parts.

Some of the first (human) users of encapsulation date from the eighteenth century (nature has been at it for billions of years). Swiss watchmakers found that instead of assembling a watch all at once, it was much better and easier to assemble the many parts as a set of stable major components, each of which might have many parts. The effect was to increase their rate of production enormously, for three reasons:

1. The assembly process was much less tricky and therefore faster.

2. When something did not work, it was obvious before assembly, since major components held together and could be tested alone. Nonworking watches became rare because malfunctioning components were detected before assembly. Troubleshooting involved fewer parts, never the whole watch, and so was much faster.

3. The complete product when finished was far more reliable. The watch was built from standard components, tested at each stage, already proven, and continuously improved.

Persistence

In the context of programming, objects have two parts: their own information, as data, and their own processes, which act on, or use, that data. Processing behavior (instructions code) is the object's *method*.

In conventional programming, the processing code and data are completely separate. The code tends to last a long time, and permanent data is stored with constantly changing data. The net result is volatility of all data. In contrast, data in an object is *owned* by that object; it defines that object. If the object data is destroyed, the object no longer exists. It must be *persistent* and last through different sessions, power-downs, overwriting, and even disk crashes if the object-based application is to continue to exist. Moreover, class information must be stored for the life of the application; in fact, it may outlive the application, and be used in and for new developments. With persistence comes *reuse* and storage of objects in a library.

Storing objects in conventional relational databases is inefficient. It can be compared to disassembling a car into its smallest pieces each night, storing the pieces in the garage, and then reassembling it to drive to work the next morning. A new generation of object databases (Poet, Objectivity, Jasmine, Servio Gemstone, Versant, etc.) are aimed at combating such inefficient storage.

The Importance of Objects to Business

Objects are common as software programming tools or approaches. However, objects are also pertinent to business at three levels:

1. As a design tool for solving business problems and defining business systems. We can identify the business processes and then model the main actors as objects.

2. As a software modeling tool to identify the major processes, such as transaction, and model the main actors that participate in the transaction as objects.

3. For the actual programming of the application software; for example, object-oriented programming.

Modeling Business Problems with Objects

Objects let us view a very complex business structure as a series of smaller components, and the object concepts ideas we have just reviewed give us a way to model the total business operation. To begin, we break the business into a separable set of entities, defined by function, where each entity may be composite and each has defined behavior. A variety of corporations have modeled their entire business operations as a set of key objects relating to the major components of the business, for analysis extending even up to board level. Business object modeling has been pursued more in the semiconductor manufacturing industry than in any other. The high-tech nature of that business means most staff have a technical background and can easily follow the object model.

To demonstrate the benefits of using objects at a business systems level, we will examine how information systems (IS) transform the business. First and foremost, objects can help build business systems requirements into information systems; "actors" in software operations can be defined to match the business processes and their components. Later in this chapter we will explore how business object modeling and object-oriented software development converge.

Objects in Software Design

When designing software, the high-level design—the overview without the detail—represents the necessary first step for understanding and modeling. Using separate (and independent) chunks of code, we only have to know their behaviors and relations, not the internal details of how what gets done, gets done. This is a natural way to start implementing a complex system, and the object concept is an ideal approach to seeing distributed systems as sets of interacting, remote component processes.

For example, in a customer ordering system, objects can be used to implement a purchase transaction system. Within the transaction object, we define the minor actors that participate in the transaction as objects at a lower level: a supplier, an order, a delivery, a budget, an authorization, and a payment. Moreover, this high-level instantiation allows us to create an abstraction, and so do something very important to prove our design—this is *simulation*. A prototype system may be far from the final system in implementation (number of users, size of machines, budget required), but it allows us to test the core concept to see if it works. In distributed systems, which are highly complex, simulation can make or break the case for going forward with a project.

Object-Oriented Programming for Application Software

Programming software with objects dates back to the early 1960s, to a language called Simula. In fact, object-oriented (OO) programming may be much older, part of our body cell "programming" with DNA; all organic life may, in fact, be object oriented.

Systems design with objects dates from the 1970s when Xerox PARC (Palo Alto Research Center) produced the first WIMPS (Windows-Icons-Mouse-Pulldown menuS) systems using the notion of a desktop object (of which one class was a document object), a server object, a client object, and a window manager object. Then OO programming was adopted by the military in the late 1970s to create more robust and cheaper software for systems in which failure meant loss of life. It has been used by the military for failproof software and for resilient software, able to withstand attack from a variety of sources.

Object-oriented software development comes at the level of both a development methodology and languages. Object-oriented programming (OOP) refers to programs using separate entities, with classes and entity reuse. Often, but by no means necessarily, this can mean programming in an object-oriented language (OOL)—a language designed for objects. OO languages are designed to create and use classes, with linking, and are often built on top of older non-OO languages (the most obvious here is C++, an extension of C). Two major OOLs dominate the development scene: Smalltalk, originally developed at Xerox PARC, and C++. There are more than 80 others, including Java, OO COBOL, as well as many of the fourth-generation languages (4GLs) now available, which lend themselves to object programming. Today's 4GLs appear much closer in syntax to simple sentences than the older languages such as COBOL or C, which may be a major reason they result in higher programmer productivity (e.g., Natura and Telon). Some 4GLs use distributed objects (e.g., Forté).

OOPs, unfortunately, have the reputation of promising much and delivering little. Differences in development methodologies, along with the guru-speak competing methods inspire, are to blame, as all claim perfection. In practice, object methodologies should be sampled, because each has useful parts, and thus a mix

Table 2.1 OO Development Methods and Authors

METHOD	AUTHORS
Responsibility-driven design	Rebecca Wirfs-Brock
OMT (Object modeling technique)	James Rumbaugh et al.
Objectory method (OO software engineering)	I. Jacobson
Object behavior analysis	Adele Goldberg
OO systems analysis	Sally Schlaer, Stephen Mellor
OO software construction	Bernard Meyers

of several methodologies is often optimal. The major OO methods are shown in Table 2.1.

We will examine responsibility-driven design later in this chapter.

Business Objects

For our purposes here, we define business today as an organization, a culture, processes, and technology. Further, today's organizations are sets of processes combining human resources, business operations with their specific activities, information systems, and fixed assets (buildings, production machines, networks). The processes may stretch across user departments or may be unique to one user department.

But the real picture of everyday business involves a complex interaction among human contacts and organizational structure, responsibilities, motivation, and power centers; jobs and skills; markets and competition; marketing and sales contacts; behavior, at personnel, group, department, and corporate levels; internal culture and values that shape behavior; models in the minds of management about the role of the firm and its goals in the marketplace. How can we capture all of this? In a program? Is it possible?

Modeling the Business and Processes

One way of capturing the life of the firm is to view the business processes as reflecting the real way in which the business works. You must also consider limits imposed by cultural outlook, responsibilities, behavior, human relations, and markets. That's a tall order—especially when talking about building that into software.

To formulate a model, you must identify actors within the business processes using business objects (see Figure 2.2). What do we mean by business objects and

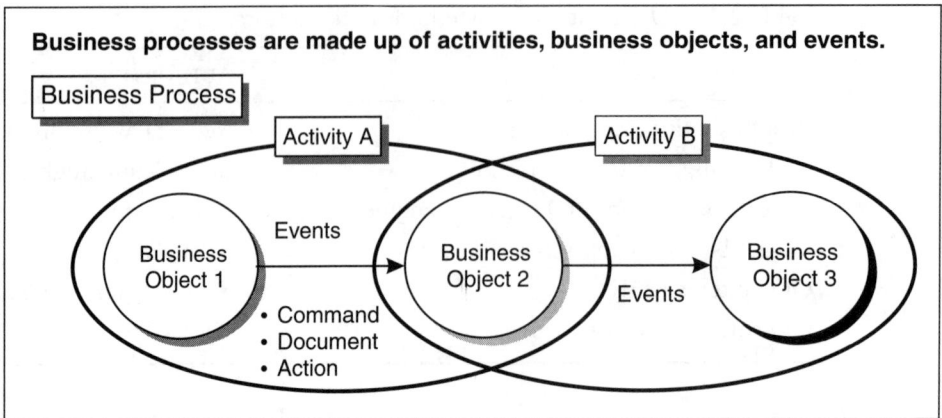

Figure 2.2 *The relation between business processes and business objects.*

business processes? Business objects are the active entities in the business process, and express a certain behavior. Behavior comprises a set of transactions and responses to inputs that follow the business logic or business rules of the organization. Examples of business objects are customers, suppliers, customer bills, accounts.

Business objects can include activities that are difficult to define as specific entities through the behavior of the business object. Normally, we would define a business object to be a "doer," an active noun that carries out actions (verbs). However, a business object could include a whole process in terms of its deliverables and inputs. We might have a billing object that takes in customer sales data and spits out bills, although billing is actually a whole business process, implemented with a set of (sub)business object actors.

The business process description should be implementation neutral in theory. However, it makes sense to show how procedures are really carried out, so that a business object could also represent an information system, if needed. This latter point is important, since introduction of new application systems has an impact on the business, in terms of business processes introduced or altered. A feedback mechanism occurs: once we understand the existing processes, we can introduce an appropriate information system, but the new system streamlines or radically alters the original process.

For example, in a large utility company, employees began entering timesheets, holidays, and overtime hours using a new intranet application. The new system moved responsibility from accounting specialists to individual employees. The new approach reduced administrative costs enormously but restructured administrative processes and job functions.

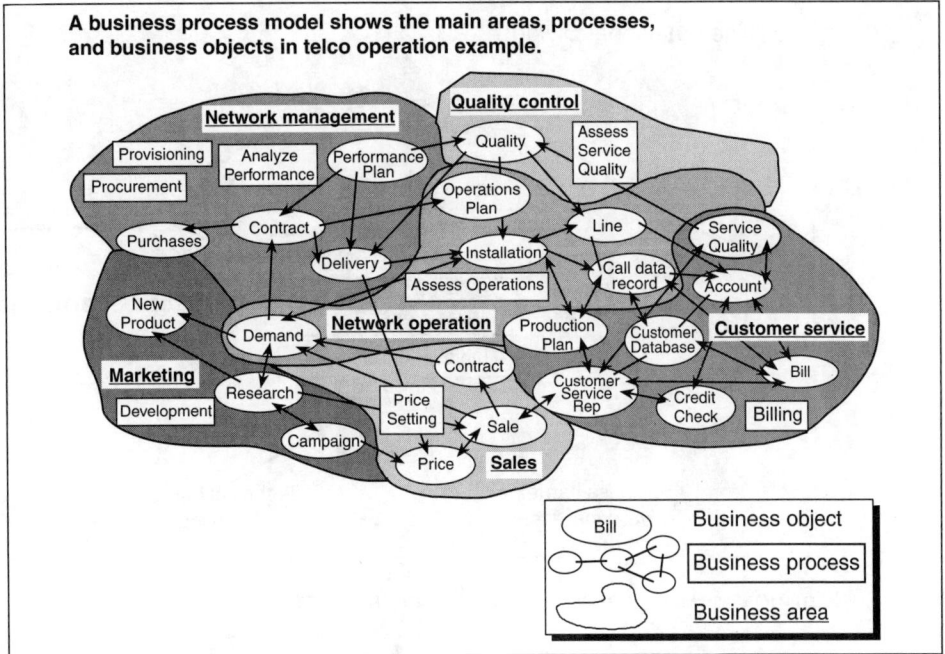

Figure 2.3 *A business process map for a telecommunications company (telco).*

Mapping the Business

We can analyze the entire business as a set of major areas. Business processes run across areas, and business objects are linked in the business processes. See the example in Figure 2.3, which shows a process map for a fictitious telecommunications company. The major business objects include marketing, customers, prices, quality control, and delivery. The objects exist inside each of the main business processes, areas, or domains: customer service, marketing, network operation, and management.

Why is mapping so powerful? Because too often a major rift opens between the business users and the IS department. Users increasingly depend on ever more complex systems, which become increasingly more difficult to explain and define (see Figure 2.4.)

Frameworks for Defining User Requirements

For business to succeed, the aforementioned communications rifts between users and developers must be closed. Business demands applications be delivered on time and exactly aligned with the users' business needs (Figure 2.5). Users and the IS de-

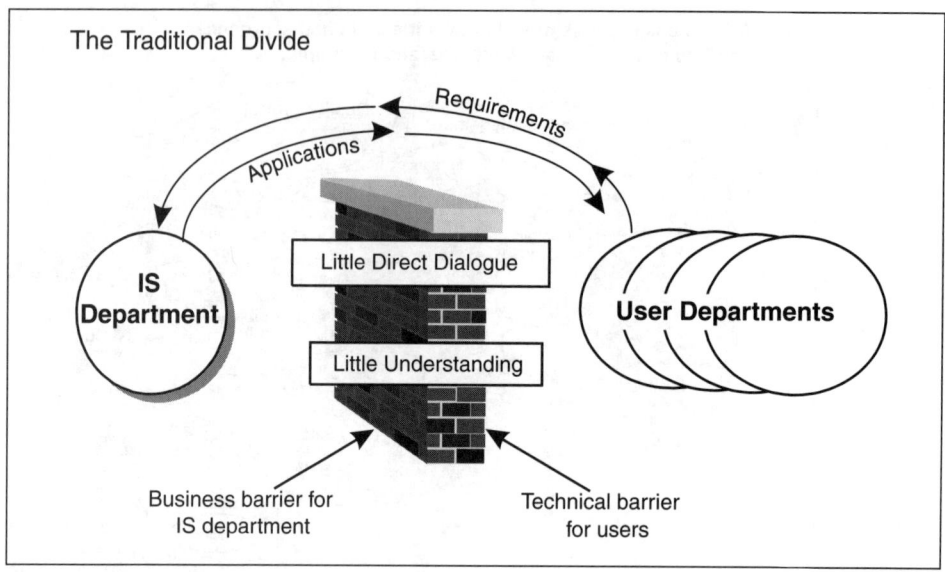

Figure 2.4 The great divide between users and IS.

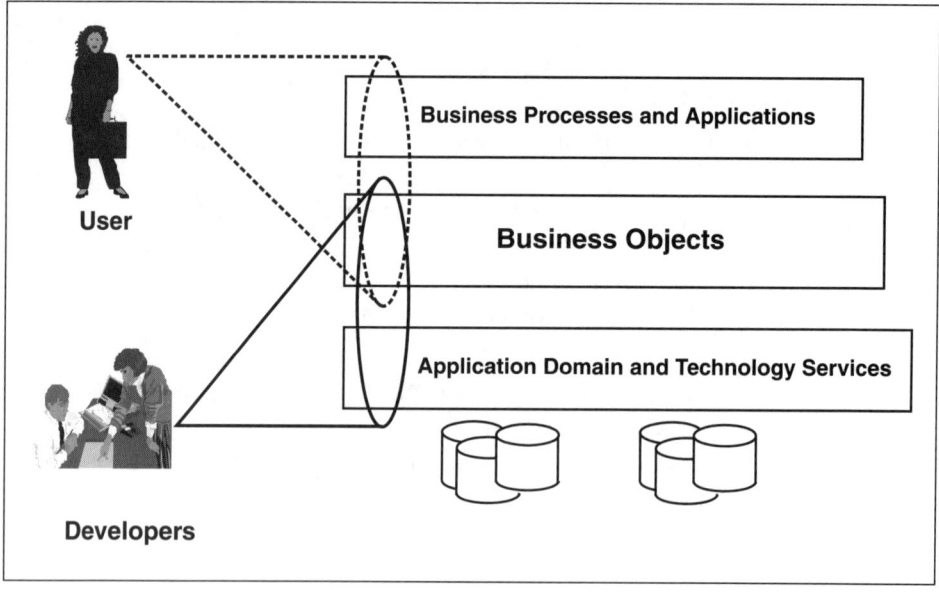

Figure 2.5 Business objects provide a framework for developers and users to communicate effectively.

partment must collaborate for application systems to follow the business more closely. Therefore, it is essential that users and system planners agree on the major actors in the business processes. Business objects provide this new paradigm.

Common terms and concepts must be defined before users and system planners can communicate effectively about application system requirements. The terms should:

- Create a shared business language between the business function and development staffs involved in the software creation (be they project managers, operations personnel, the application implementation team, or the end users).

- Describe the real world in terms of objects, processes, and people.

- Produce a working business model.

A Telco Example

In this telco, business objects are useful for calculating bills and mailing them to customers. Two components, a billing process (highly complex) and a mailing process, are involved. The billing process is diffuse, but could be designed as one (composite) business object. In a telco, billing is highly complex, as it varies with customer type. Separate billing systems could be used for residential and business customers.

We decide to build a fairly generic software application for the billing process. The system is a set of generic components, two of which are the heart of the billing system: a rating engine and its input database. Much of the application is useful for both types of customer, with different rating engines for each class of customer. But with deregulation, a new category of customer suddenly appears—the reseller, who buys local access in bulk in a wholesale mode. The contracts are quite different; calculations are much simpler, but with specific clauses never seen before. Our generic billing business object can be reused for the new business, because it is designed as a set of composite objects in which a new rating engine can be easily added. The mailing object can also be reused.

In the near future, we want to use electronic commerce for the resellers, for online billing. Since the mailing (business) object is also a composite (although the last part of it—bill printing, envelope stuffing—must be discarded), bill data collection, bill layout, and address list management components can be reused in an electronic mail object, with a Web site front end.

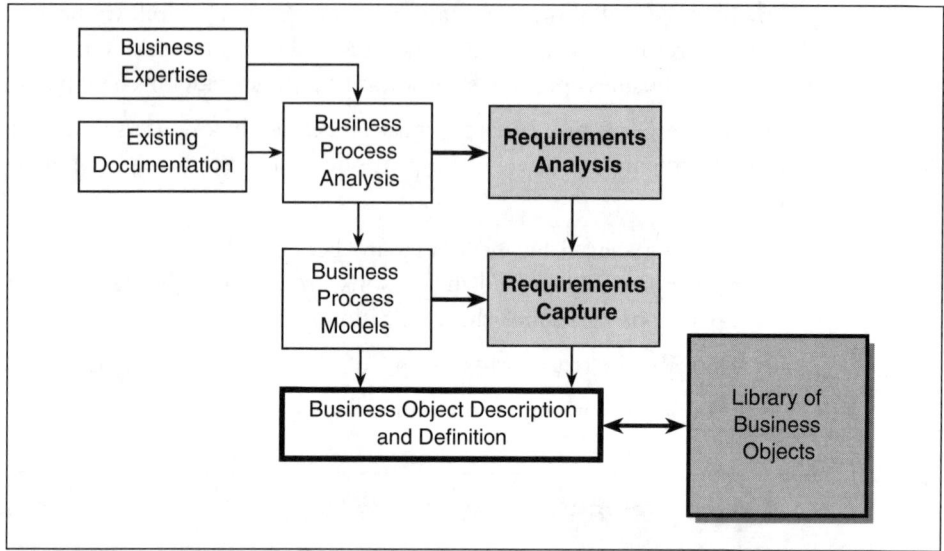

Figure 2.6 *Capturing user requirements with business objects.*

Joint Requirements Capture

We need a specific approach for identifying business objects during user requirements sessions. These objects must reflect requirements capture for new applications. The way forward is a joint requirements capture (JRC) session among the appropriate and knowledgeable users and developers (see Figure 2.6).

In the JRC session we analyze the business processes, build a model of each process, and describe the business objects in clear terms. We examine the existing knowledge about the business, capture the processes of each department, then identify and describe the business objects.

Based on the resulting business object definitions, we can design the software. Software design could mean setting parameters in a software package or selecting appropriate software objects. We can even plan appropriate sizing for optimal performance. The translation process that comes out of a JRC is shown in Figure 2.7.

By using objects and business objects, we have gone far beyond traditional data modeling, in which various user groups get together but often cannot agree on the common definition of a data entity, because it encompasses only static data, not what the purpose of the data is or how it is related. The most famous example of failed data modeling is a railroad company in the United States whose user departments argued for 15 years over the definition of a train (is it the whole train, the locomotive and the railcars, the load, or the financials?).

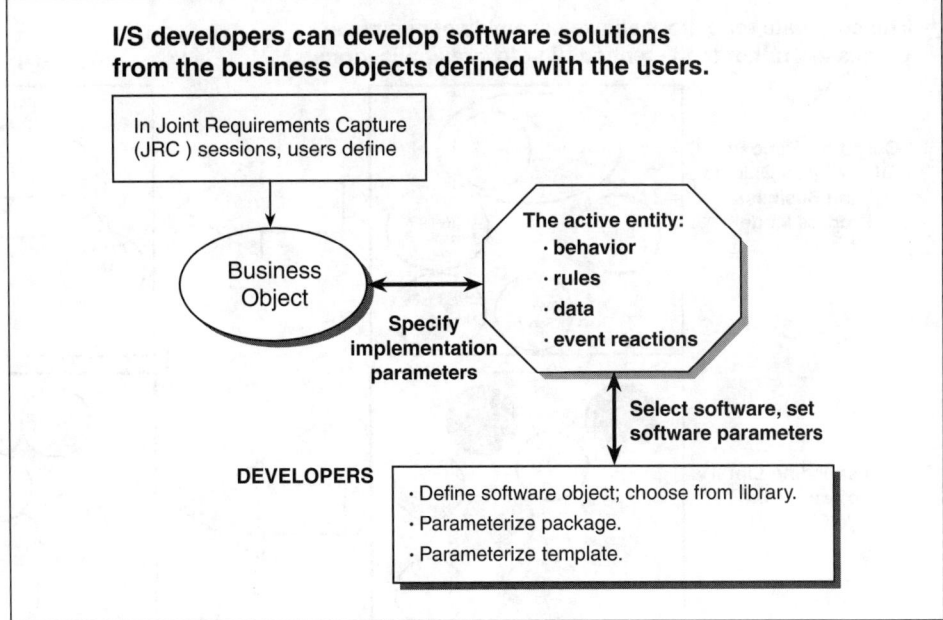

Figure 2.7 *From business objects to object-oriented software design.*

Building an Enterprise Object Library

Eventually we can build a library or repository of business objects, complete with the models of the business processes. Storing the business objects and operational process models paints a complete picture of the operations and the corporate history of the company. If anything changes in the business, we know where to change the business process model and the relevant business objects. Moreover, we can map any change through to the related software. The real payoff of object modeling is power, speed, and control all wrapped up and delivered in one, neat package (see Figure 2.8). Software changes match business changes by using a library of associated software objects.

Distributed Computing Progress

Object-based software is becoming the foundation of distributed processing. A set of standards covers both the definitions of software objects and the specifics of their interoperations. The key component is the object request broker (ORB), which acts as a translator of requests between objects in the same, and different, environments.

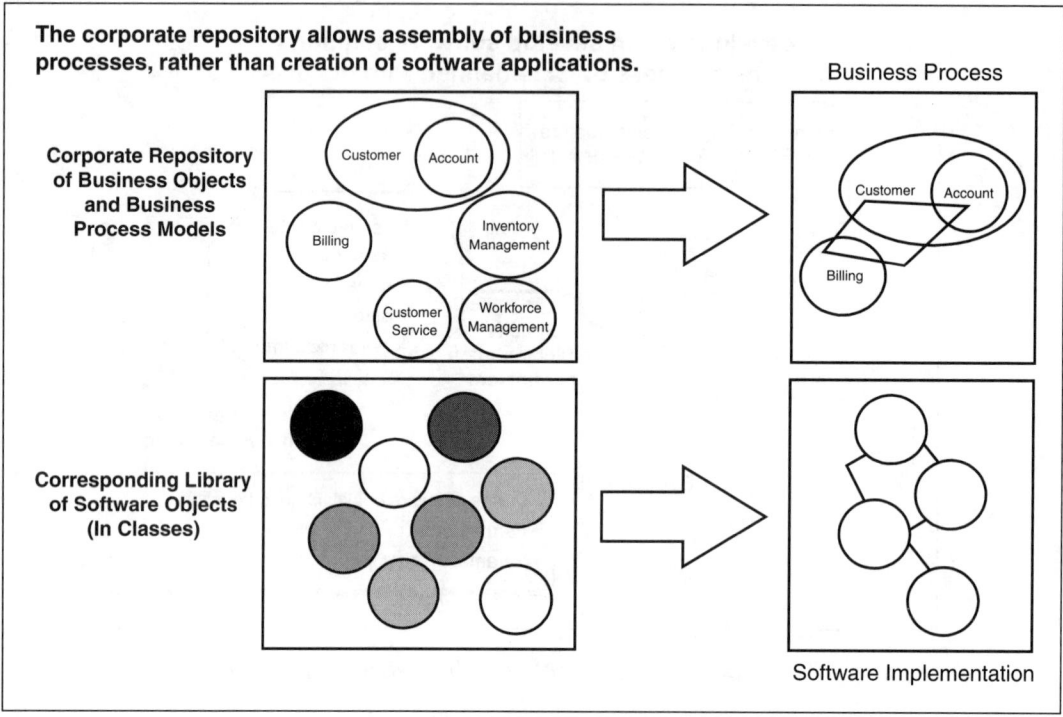

Figure 2.8 Business object libraries capture business knowledge.

OO software in general is developing quickly with:

- Object-oriented databases.

- Application frameworks. These are now available for creating OO programs with no knowledge of the operating system environment (e.g., Borland OWL, Microsoft MFC for PC platforms, or Forté for Unix and other environments; to some extent, Java is in this category).

- Interworking monitors and transaction monitors for object-oriented environments (or object transaction monitors, such as IBM's Component Broker, BEA's Iceberg, and Borland ITS).

Standards Set the Scene

The Object Management Group (OMG), a group of suppliers and users, has been working on a way to enable objects based on different systems to interact over a network. This effort is promising for distributed and client/server systems because interworking will be better defined, more robust, and easier to implement. OMG's architectural model is called Object Management Architecture (OMA).

The key concepts are presented as the Common Object Request Broker Architecture (CORBA), which proposes a number of *object services*, as well as the ORB (object request broker), as illustrated in Figure 2.9. The specification was originally jointly published by OMG and X/Open in April 1992. CORBA implementations run over TCP/IP, the preferred communications protocol. OMG members (such as Compaq/DEC and Hewlett-Packard) have implemented OMG-ORBs on top of the Distributed Computing Environment (DCE), from the Open Software Foundation.

CORBA addresses issues that include:

- The definition of interfaces between objects via a language, the Interface Definition Language (IDL).

- Overcoming differences in hardware and software.

- Distribution of objects (in C++ or Smalltalk) to form interoperating sets of functions.

- Transactions between ORBs.

- The location of distributed objects as a service, the locator service (which is also responsible for the interobject connection setup).

More than 40 vendors have built applications using CORBA or implementations of CORBA. Hewlett-Packard and Sun have incorporated the ORB into their support for interlinked and distributed applications: Sun, originally as Distributed Objects Everywhere (DOE) and Hewlett-Packard, first as Distributed Object Management Facility (DOMF). Microsoft has announced it will make OLE recognize and interface to the ORB, so that it may link existing products, first for the software products of other vendors and their documents, and second, to user-created application objects. For Java programming and Internet software, an Internet version of CORBA exists with the Internet InterOperation Protocol (IIOP).

Given current support, the ORB will play a role in developing future distributed and client/server systems. To date, however, the ORB has been limited in these respects:

- The Object Services Architecture has yet to be fully defined and implemented.

- Different ORB implementations from different suppliers (HP, Hyperdesk, Compaq/DEC, Sun, etc.) did not interwork at first, though the situation improved with the release of CORBA 2.0. Moreover, CORBA initially defined only application-to-ORB interactions, not those of ORB-to-ORB across machines, which proved necessary for multivendor relations.

- Mainframe versions of ORB have only slowly become available. Software AG has announced an ORB delivery that will be compliant with CORBA.

The Object Request Broker is intended to provide interoperability between applications on different machines in multivendor distributed environments. Its major role is to interface different objects, be they applications, utilities, or operating systems, by allowing them to make requests of each other. The ORB specification is the result of a joint proposal from many vendors. The ORB is responsible for all of the mechanisms required to find the object for the requesting application, to prepare the object to receive the request, and to communicate the data making the request. The ORB interface is completely independent of where the object is located or which programming language it is implemented in. Requests are performed according to ORB standards (either the dynamic invocation interface or a stub written in Interface Definition Language (IDL).

Requests for service from a client object are passed via the ORB to a target object:

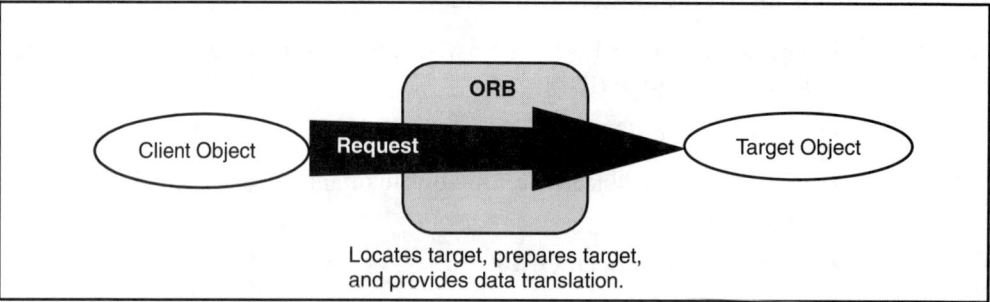

To traverse two different environments, perhaps a client and a server, two ORBs will interface.

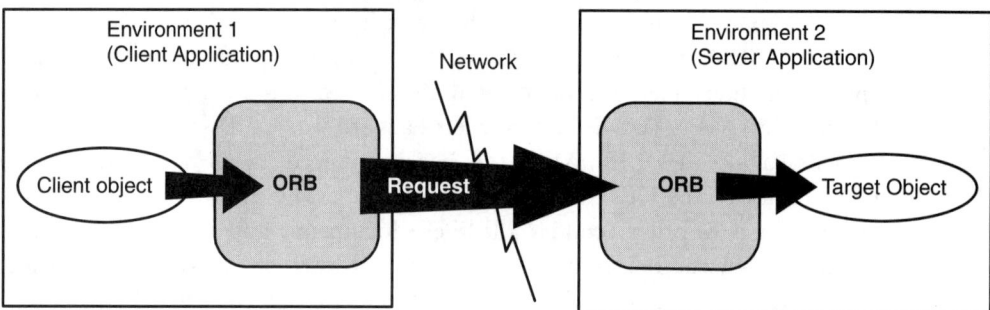

The Object Services Architecture

The Object Services Architecture from OMG defines a number of services that will be of value for development of distributed applications:

- Object Concurrency Control Service: Mediates concurrent access.
- Object Versioning and Configuration Management Services: Supports the identification of alternate versions of existing interfaces and object instances, and the management of mutually consistent collections of these interfaces and instances.
- Object Events Service: Supports the notification of events to communicating objects.

Figure 2.9 *The OMG object request broker (ORB) and the Common ORB Architecture (CORBA).*

New Object Frameworks

Next-generation software design has already begun. Looking even further ahead than DCE and DME is a new range of software that can be included loosely at the level of operating systems or environments; it is aimed specifically at distributed processing and designed for the client/server model. Based on the notions of objects, these environments are being created for workstations interworking with servers over a network. Although the various initiatives differ in major aspects (platforms, compatible software, and basic mechanisms, etc.), all provide a framework in which remote objects in different operating system environments can interact across a network. They tend to compensate for differences in existing operating systems and NOSes by "wrapping around" them in some way. They work by adding an infrastructure to an existing operating system, or by building on a new operating system, through the addition of specific software modules to a basic framework that hosts objects, as illustrated in Figure 2.10.

New-style operating systems are specifically designed for add-ons, with a nucleus or *microkernel* of fundamental functions such as scheduling, and a set of management objects that can be added as required by a systems or software vendor. Such microkernel-based operating systems offer the flexibility to mimic the environments of older operating systems or present to the end user an interface that reflects the older system's idiosyncratic interface "personalities."

The new-style OS offers:

- Extensions of middleware software on top of DCE; for example, from Compaq/DEC and termed Application Frameworks, based on the use of their Object Broker and Microsoft's Component Object Model (COM).

- IBM's system object model (SOM), which solves the problems of inheritance across objects in different languages and from different vendors, with a distributed version (DSOM) for client/server configurations, using an ORB. SOM, first used for OS/2 version 2.0, is at the heart of IBM's Workplace OS, which offers a solution to IBM's abundance of operating systems. Workplace OS provides "personalities" for running applications created for OS/2, Unix (AIX), DOS, and other operating systems.

- Microsoft with its Component Object Model (COM), developed for OLE 2.0 with an object request broker-like structure and a distributed implementation for Windows NT, DCOM. COM offers a model of how objects and their clients interact, covering interface negotiation, error reports and reactions, and memory allocation. Because of Microsoft's relation to a specific hardware architecture (the Intel microprocessor family), interface interaction in COM (unlike CORBA) is specified down to a binary level, as

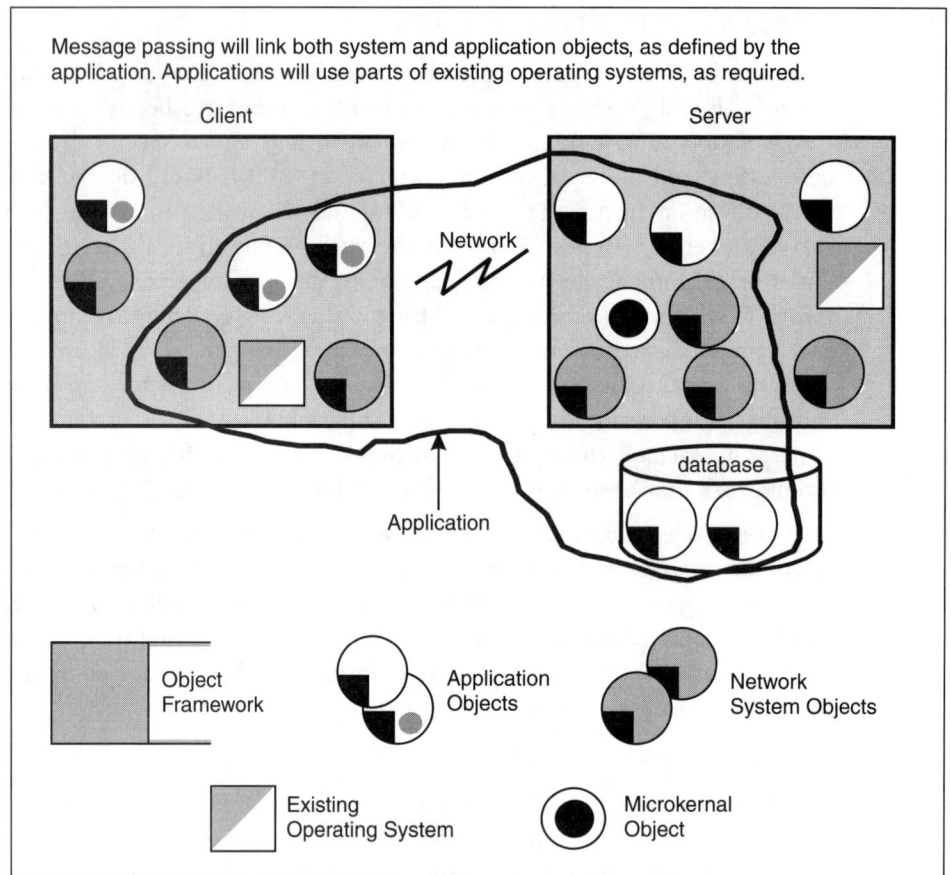

Figure 2.10 *Future distributed systems constructed from object frameworks will link system and application objects across several environments.*

well as at the system level. DCOM's RPC is similar to the DCE RPC. The differences with the OMG's ORB standard are under discussion.

- Apple/NeXT's Distributed Objects (available as NeXTSTEP) has a fully distributed naming service and is available for several platforms. Agreements with Sun for inclusion with Distributed Objects Everywhere will expand the product's impact.

Such advances form the basis for much easier client/server and distributed system development, though true distributed systems may be several years away. Each new object technology is subject to major commercial and technical challenges, and so for the next few years, the distinct components outlined in Chapter 1 are likely to dominate distributed systems building. Common models like CORBA, OMA, DCE, and DME will lead object-based development trends for the near future.

Web Objects

Web technology is being exploited for corporate intranets by progressive companies of all sizes. Private mini-internets, or intranets, are extending from highly effective internal communications to *extranets* for suppliers and customers, and provide a platform for electronic commerce.

The expansion of Web technology correlates to advances in distributed processing, based on simple proven components. Object distribution and communication over a network are ideally suited to Web technology. Intranet communications are triggered by hypertext links, just like Web documents and sites. In addition, in most corporate intranets, the applications require database interaction for general information searches or for business operations. In essence, a set of networked objects receives and sends standardized messages via hidden internal mechanisms.

The Web represents a generic object-oriented client/server model in four levels:

1. *A thin client.* A Web browser such as Netscape Navigator on a PC with Microsoft Windows 3.1 (or more advanced operating system).

2. *A fat server.* A Web server, perhaps with a Merchant server and product catalog on top of it.

3. *An application.* Usually sited on the server, although downloaded applets may be executed on the PC by the browser environment. (This is the basis of the Java mantra "Write Once, Run Anywhere"). The application in C++, Java, JavaScript, a 4GL, or Lotus Notescript executes the business logic of the application.

4. *Network communications in the form of HTML pages sent over the network by the HTTP protocol on top of the lower-level communications in TCP/IP from the HTTP driver (or "daemon") on the server.* A back-end database on the server contains catalog information and all other data.

There are several ways of implementing such a distributed system configuration; the object framework has already arrived in Web technology, as shown in Figure 2.11.

The earliest approaches for a two-way dialogue between client and Web server application were based on a CGI (Common Gateway Interface), which is

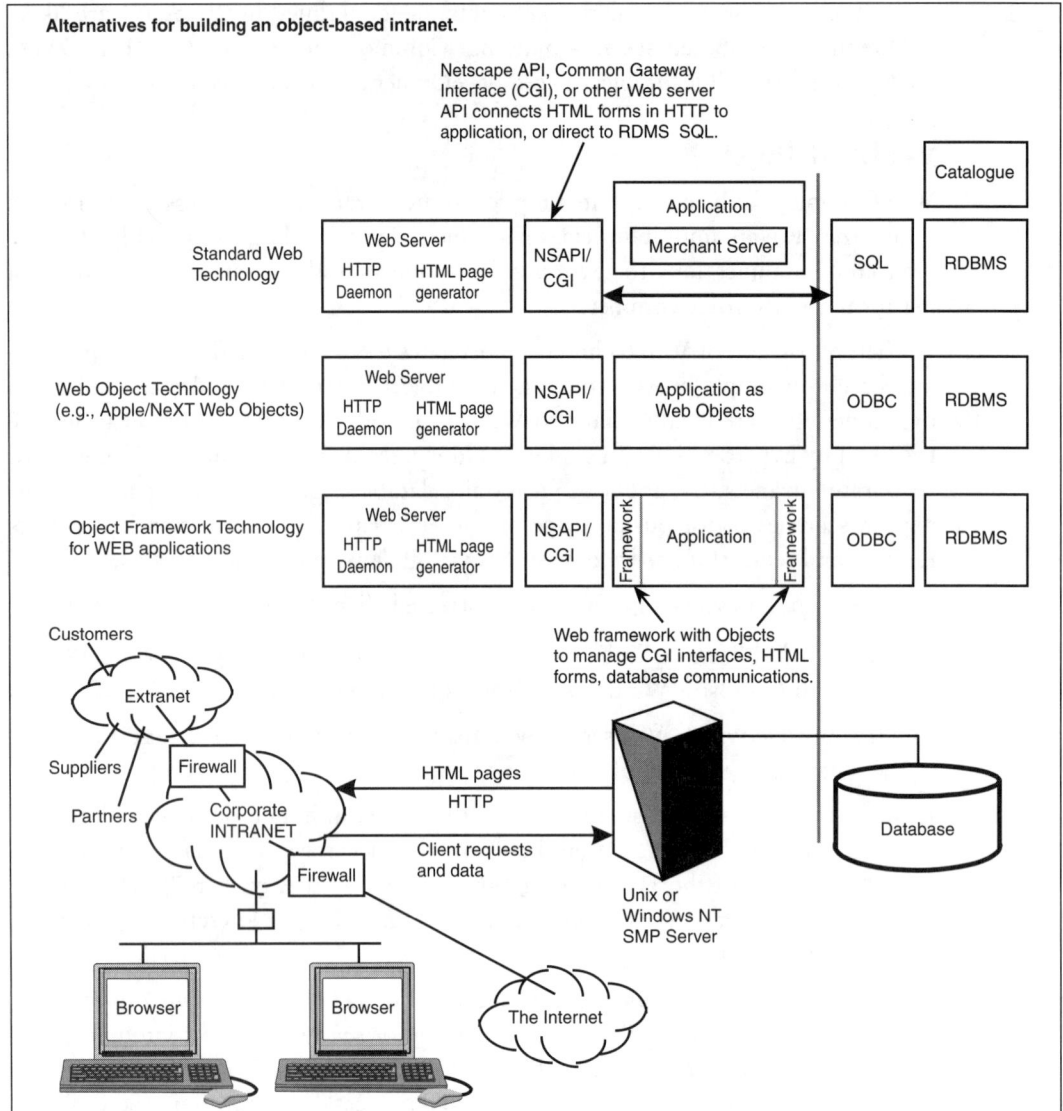

Figure 2.11 *Distributed objects are taking root in Internet/intranet technology for distributed systems.*

form based. HTML was originally static, and pages took some time to be generated. Dynamic HTML now offers a way of processing database queries and generating appropriate HTML pages, or their updates, on the fly, for transmission to browsers. The back-end relational database has been extended to interface with HTML directly (Informix Universal Server or Oracle WebServer). Faster interfaces are essential to increase performance, since Web systems typically have thousands of users, and may be required to handle more than 500 transactions per second at peak.

Interfacing to legacy systems is easier with Web technology. Newer developments in Java provide standard objects (applets) that can be distributed remotely to act as local interfaces, either directly or via CORBA.

A problem with all Web technology today is that most implementations exist as stateless. As discussed in Chapter 1 they have no awareness or memory of their historical condition and its impact on current action requests. Recall that tapping the mouse three times reloads the page from scratch regardless of how much may have been displayed when you hit the mouse button. The display exists exclusively in the moment.

The rapid proliferation of powerful distributed computing technology poses three more obstacles for the well-managed corporation. The first is general security. The use of a powerful firewall server to filter and authenticate IP packets provides only part of the solution. You may need passwords, encryption, a secure sockets layer (SSL) with server authentication (is it really the right server you are logged on to?). An entire *security policy* suddenly becomes paramount. If you are considering electronic payments transactions, then the Secure Electronic Transaction (SET) standards from the card issuers (Visa and MasterCard) and financial authorities are a must.

The second involves hand-over to support and maintenance services beyond the development department. Web systems differ from previous software technology, so software maintenance services may be scarce. Also, Web systems can be rolled out quickly, since any authorized user with a PC and a network connection can download a browser, some applets, and start on the application. You may get no users on day one, then 5,000 on day two, and they will need training and support, including massive help desks.

Certification provides the third obstacle. Although part of security, it in fact becomes a separate problem. Digital certificates for the server and the user provide clearance to use the system. A company officer may register the servers with an external certification authority (trusted third party). This is particularly necessary for creating a virtual private network (VPN) with external partners, suppliers, and customers: an extranet. With an Internet service provider (ISP) for the extranet infrastructure support, digital certification becomes mandatory for safe operation.

Reusing Objects

Once you understand the business models at the levels of processes and objects, and the corresponding software entities have been built, reuse can become a powerful tool. But reuse does not happen overnight; it requires:

- Persuasion, where it counts. Pay your development staff to reuse and assemble, do not pay them to reinvent.

- A change of development culture. Persuasion is the brute-force approach. You also need a complete change in developer and IS department culture.

- Organization of a library with security.

- Care in classification of objects; decisions regarding what is unique and separable; and keywords, indexes, and search engines to find them.

- Time. Reuse only comes into its own after two to three years of building an object library.

- Librarians. Specialized staff to seek out and store objects and models.

A Responsibility Design Approach

As noted, there are many methodologies for OO software design and development, and choosing only one usually results in an ineffective solution; a mix of several methodologies in the OO toolbox will give you the best solutions.

One single approach that deserves particular consideration, however, is responsibility-based design (see Wirfs-Brock, 1990). In this approach, tasks that the software must perform are the responsibilities of some entity (i.e., of some object). These responsibilities exist at three levels:

1. *The total sum of business processes, at the company level.* Responsibility for net output through coordination of all the business processes.

2. *The business process.* Responsibility for delivering a business operation successfully; for example, customer billing.

3. *The business objects at the action or function level.* Perhaps a resource; for example, responsibility for a customer account: keeping the status up to date and performing actions dependent on that state (demanding different bill-chasing treatment if payment is consistently late).

In other words, responsibility makes behaviors and roles evident in the business entities, and clarifies the triggers and responses. Responsibility also defines all the relationships among objects. That means an overall *master* program is not important when designing the software.

Corresponding software can be designed in a similar way to the business, as a set of self-organizing (software) objects that have specific responsibilities. Their built-in interactions and behavior must define the behavior of the collective group in a way that makes it easy to analyze and locate malfunctions. Moreover, as responsibilities are distributed, centralized responsibility is weaker—the overall software solution becomes more robust.

Responsibility-based design starts by defining the software objects from an external view: We know what they must do, but not which internals carry out their function. We then go on to see how autonomous objects can be—how much could each object do without supervision or interference from above? Independence is valuable, so we can minimize the effort expended on other management objects, down to producing only what is essential to provide key checking. We do not have to supervise every step an object takes to achieve its tasks. The net result should be reduced complexity, since we divided up and assigned functions among simpler objects, responsible for specific outputs and results.

Responsibility works for the business objects as well as for their software object implementations. For example, for an airline, we might want to create a business object that is an aircraft. The responsibilities of such an aircraft object could include:

- Traveling from airport to airport according to the preset schedule and along routes set by flight plans.
- Carrying passengers according to a passenger list.
- Providing revenues according to its seat yield and profits according its total operational costs.
- To have a crew, according to the flight crew scheduling.
- Carrying baggage and perhaps freight.
- Paying leasing payments, if leased.

Moreover, it has a responsibility to respond to messages such as:

- Be maintained, according to a maintenance plan dictated by hours of flight.
- Observe notices to flight crew on flight conditions.
- Be insured.
- Be rerouted if required.

The powerful concept of responsibility allows users with very different perspectives to come to agreement about a business object's functions. The next step is to produce software objects corresponding to one function, or responsibility, or to a part of a responsibility or function.

Legacy Systems as Objects

The majority of business software in use in the United States is older than the company buildings in which it is being used. Because changing software is costly in terms of time, money, labor, and difficulty, it may have to last for a long time, which is why most Year 2000 remedies are not about replacing the applications, they're about fixing the code—leaving it in place. Few corporations are taking advantage of the fact that this would be a good time to replace that 10- to 25-year-old code. Why? Because the current software works, and the cost of conversion is more than any business can justify, as illustrated in Figure 2.12.

One reason it costs so much to replace legacy systems is because no one remembers how they work. A legacy system probably was originally designed using a technical model, not a business model, so its level of abstraction is immense, and cannot be bridged today without significant effort and expense. We have lost not only the knowledge, but probably the programmers in whose heads resided the original business and technical logic. The question is: How do we escape from yesterday's systems?

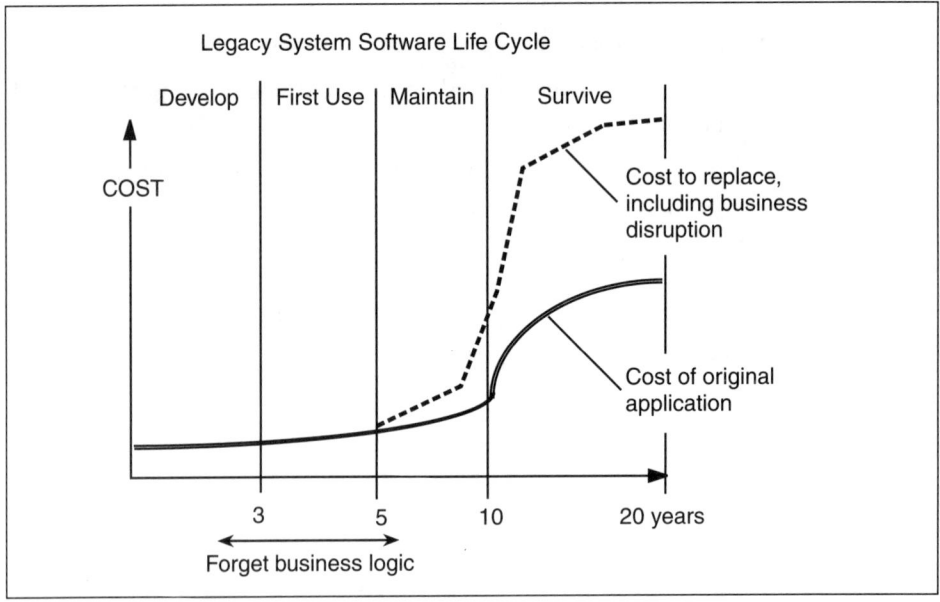

Figure 2.12 *Why legacy systems live on.*

Leveraging Existing Assets

In some ways, existing applications act as a prison; conversion or replacement of the legacy or "cherished" system is just too expensive. So the issue becomes how to bridge the gap between old and new, especially when building a distributed environment. The answer is: object concepts and object technology. We can incorporate today's cherished systems into tomorrow's systems by going further than just screen scraping (defined in the next subsection). Perceived barriers exist, for example these include beliefs that older systems mostly reside on mainframes and that new technology only slowly extends into that realm. The way forward views the mainframes as a just another service provider, as shown in Figure 2.13.

Replace, Revamp, Wrap

Replacement would be the best way forward, if the budget and time allow. Replacement could be a real consideration if a parallel operation and budgets were available, in which case we should use some form of continuing operation of the existing systems while a replacement development is undertaken.

Revamping

Revamping breathes new life into old applications. It has two levels of implementation. The first, *screen scraping* involves adding a GUI front end to a character-based user interface (CHUI). This, however, changes little and certainly does not help interapplication communications much. The second, *interface (re)writing* means adding a data conversion for communication into and out of the database, and perhaps some form of interface to control the processing operations in the main body of code (e.g., "run in batch now with these parameters," etc.), but not adding new functionality.

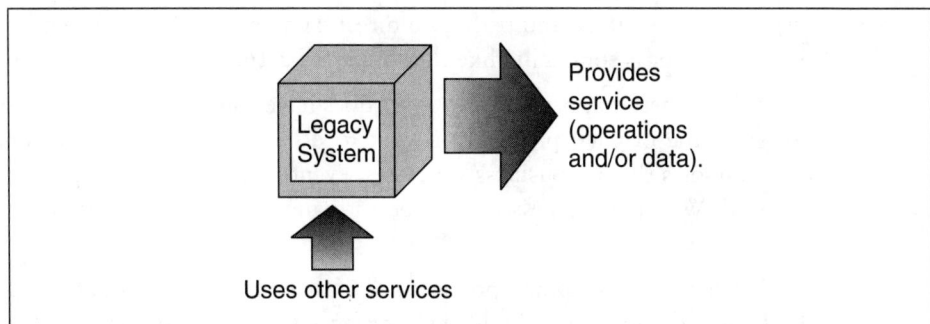

Figure 2.13 We can look at a legacy system as a service to newer applications.

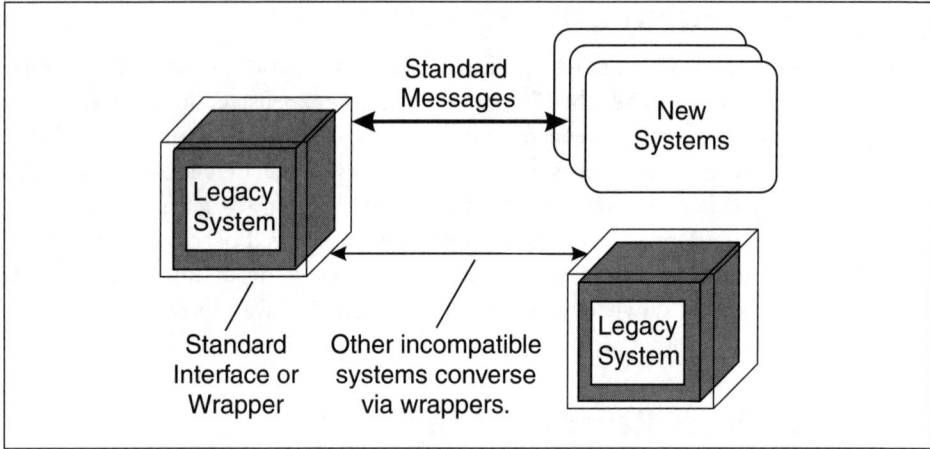

Figure 2.14 *Wrappers act as an interface to turn a legacy system into a service object.*

Wrapping

Wrapping is a better option than revamping. To integrate the older systems, we need a way to bridge to the legacy systems functions and data. Wrappers act as that interface between old and new systems, turning the legacy systems into service objects, as in Figure 2.14.

The wrapper presents the legacy system code as an object that is a complete function (e.g., to handle a shipping order). The logical way to implement wrapping is to exploit the standards for distributed processing already in use and treat the legacy system as a distributed object on the network, which offers a service to other application objects, as in Figure 2.15.

The wrapper actually consists of a way of communicating, a mechanism for interpreting commands, and perhaps a direct data port for fast transfer. The structure of the wrapper is something like that in Figure 2.16.

While a better approach, wrapping does have some drawbacks. For one, it does not solve the original problem of what to do about the aging functionality—if it only supports the old business processes, eventually the legacy application must be replaced. Wrapping can also extort performance penalties—the wrapper takes processing power.

Furthermore, wrapping proves to be viable only where enough is known about the legacy application to build the interfaces for data and controls. If the real semantics of the interface parameters are not understood, the wrapped system will re-

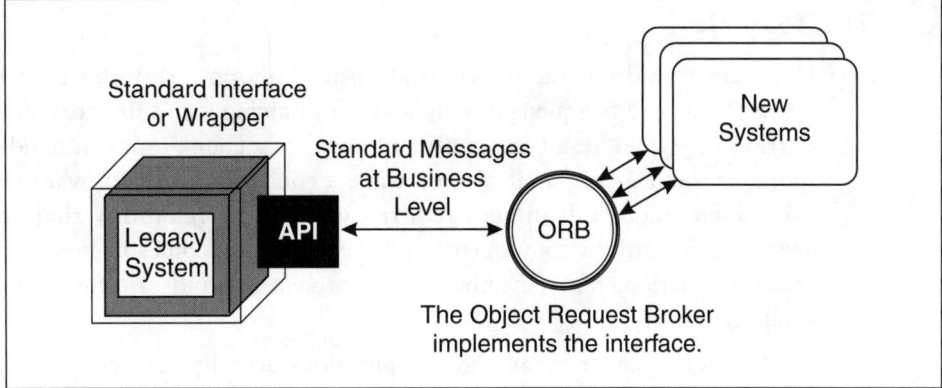

Figure 2.15 *Wrappers allow us to communicate at a service level with old and new systems.*

spond incorrectly; for instance, with the passage of time, fields in a record may have been used for other purposes (e.g., apparently unused fields might actually be used to add a correction factor, so a random value appearing there could cause havoc).

Finally, constructing and using wrappers is straightforward only in certain technical conditions: where legacy code is structured as dynamically linked subroutines and where network communications already support peer-to-peer communications.

We should conclude that wrapping does have a place except as a stopgap measure, and when more functionality is added externally using other applications.

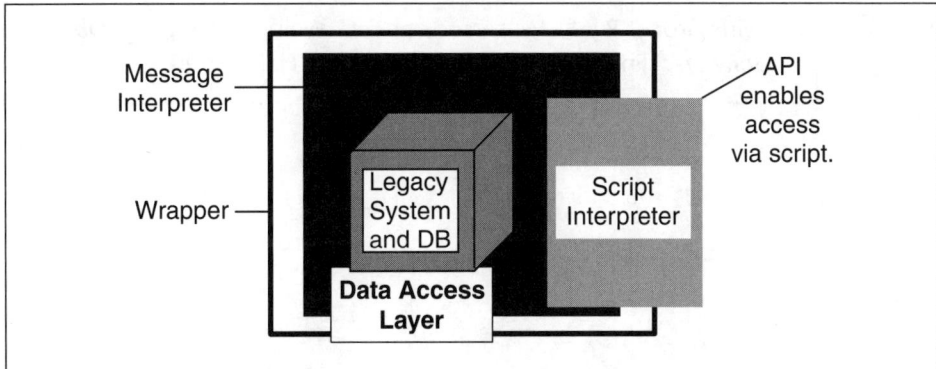

Figure 2.16 *The structure of a wrapped application.*

Conclusions

This chapter laid out the basics of an historically powerful idea used by the Romans: Divide and conquer. Although we are applying it to software complexity, not warring tribes, the result is the same: biting off a chunk you can handle is a wise approach, be it at the level of the business concepts or the software code and its data. Some major advantages realized include the reliability that comes from reusing major proven components and the speed that comes from assembly, as opposed to creation. But remember, this approach demands a different programmer mind-set.

The next chapter details how applications actually get built and operate in a distributed environment.

FOR FURTHER READING

Booch, Grady. "Object-Oriented Development," *IEEE Transactions on Software Engineering*. Vol. SE-12. No. 2., Feb 1986, pgs. 211–231.

Booch, Grady. *Object-Oriented Design with Applications*. (Redwood City, CA: Benjamin/Cummings), 1991.

Goldberg, Adele and D. Robinson. *Smalltalk 80: The Language and Its Implementation*, (Reading, MA: Addison-Wesley), 1983.

Taylor, David. *Object-Oriented Technology: A Manager's Guide*. (Alameda, CA: Servio Corp.), 1990.

Wirfs-Brock, R., B. Wilkerson, and L. Weiner. *Designing Object-Oriented Software*. (Englewood Cliffs, NJ: Prentice-Hall), 1990.

3 BUILDING DISTRIBUTED APPLICATIONS

[He] had the arrogant humility of the man who has learned so much that he is aware of his own ignorance.

Robert A. Heinlein, *Stranger In A Strange Land.*

This chapter:

Describes how applications need to change for distributed computing.

Delineates guidelines for designing a distributed application.

Introduces application partitioning methodologies and their impact.

Warns of pitfalls associated with deployment of distributed applications.

The hottest news on the street these days is Internet/intranet applications, which use the TCP/IP network protocol to pass data between client-based and server-based applications. Even though Internet-based computing has been around since the late 1960s, it wasn't until the creation of the World Wide Web and its associated protocols that distributed computing became mainstream.

To most companies, a distributed application means a database client used to enter, access, and view data stored on a database server. Because this is such a pervasive form of distributed computing, the term client/server has become synonymous with database applications, even though distributed database applications constitute just one use of the technology. This singular association is responsible for one of the greatest misunderstandings of distributed computing in the industry. Since the sending and receiving of data, and its associated error handling, is handled by the database products or by database middleware, developers are lulled into a false sense of comfort and security when building other distributed applications.

Client/server computing covers a much larger domain than simply data access to a centralized database. The terms *client* and *server* represent the *partitioning* of the application; many texts discuss the topic of client/server, but never mention this critical term (see Figure 3.1). The two-tier client/server model, the most common form of partitioning for a distributed application, literally represents where the work is being accomplished. The client itself may or may not do processing, but relative to performing database operations, the database server (service) handles all the client's requests. To remove this partition would result in a single monolithic application that is responsible for reading and writing records from a disk-based file.

> **NOTE**
>
> It is necessary to distinguish between the terms server and service. For many, server is an overloaded term that represents the physical hardware as well as the application. The term service distinctly represents the software that performs a task on behalf of a client's request.

Here are some basic guidelines for defining a distributed application:

Rule 1. Applications have two or more cooperative components, or processes, partitioned by electronic or geographic boundaries.

Rule 2. Applications have, at a minimum, a client process and a server process.

Rule 3. Applications communicate by means of a special process called *marshaling*.

Rule 4. Applications can run either on a single machine or across a network, but each method requires different methods of error handling.

Rule 5. The location of the server is transparent to requesting users and applications.

Let's explore these five rules in more depth.

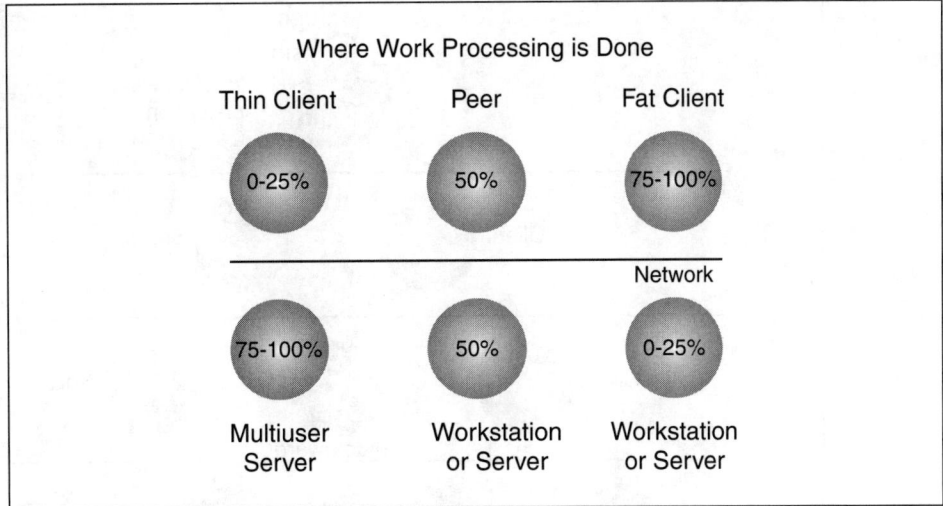

Figure 3.1 *Ways to partition a client/server application.*

In rule 1, we define a distributed application to be two or more cooperative components or processes, such as the database server and database client, partitioned by an electronic or geographic boundary. In this definition, an electronic boundary constitutes process boundaries inside a single computer, such as memory protection; while geographic boundaries are those located on separate computers. The Windows 95/NT clipboard is an example of processes communicating across an electronic boundary; the World Wide Web is an example of processes communicating over a geographic boundary.

Rule 2 states that a distributed applications has, at a minimum, a client and a server. The simplest distributed application is a single client and single server, also commonly known as two-tier. Typically, in a two-tier client/server, the client is tightly bound to the server, which means that the method of communication most likely uses a highly proprietary messaging protocol. To make our distributed application more modular, and hence more reusable, we can add layers between the client and the called server; these layers are the middleware. Middleware solutions are by definition a minimum three-tier solution, but could be unlimited, which leads to an *n*-tier client/server (see Figure 3.2).

Rule 3 concerns the means by which data is passed between the client and the server and its associated middleware layers. All data passed across a partition, whether electronic or geographic, must be marshaled into a format that can be understood by all components involved. For example, if a client wants to send the server the number 1, it must make sure that the structures and byte ordering of the

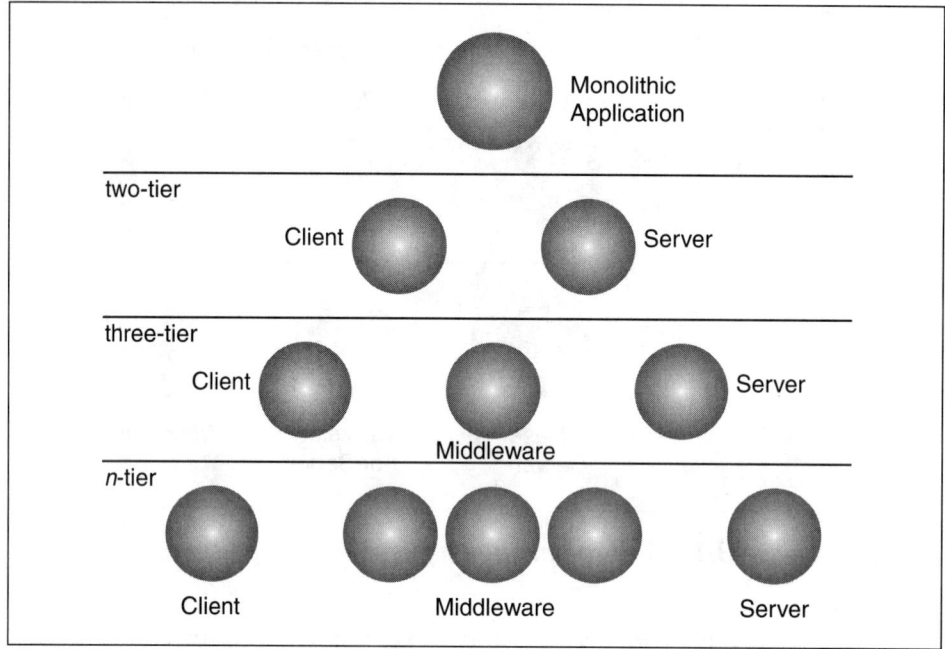

Figure 3.2 *Impact of middleware on client/server tiers.*

server process is the same as the client, or at the very least, that the client understands how to convert the data. For example, the server could choose to deliver a single byte that represents the value 1; or it could deliver it as the ASCII value 1, which is really a byte that has the value of 49. In either case, the client must be aware how to translate the incoming value to 1 for its associated application.

When building a distributed application, rule 3 is particularly important. First, custom marshaling procedures are a leading cause of failure in a distributed system. Attempting to manage and write the code for two or more separate communicating components so that it is identical across all components is risky because both sides must always be using the latest data structures and message formats. Therefore, many developers prefer to use an interface definition language (IDL). An IDL describes the data being sent from the client to the server and how the data will be sent (usually over a remote procedure call). From information furnished by the IDL, code for packaging and sending data is then automatically generated for the programming language of choice. As a result of the totally automated process, the generated code is guaranteed to be clean. IDL is merely text that will be used to generate programming language-specific bindings. It is not an engine.

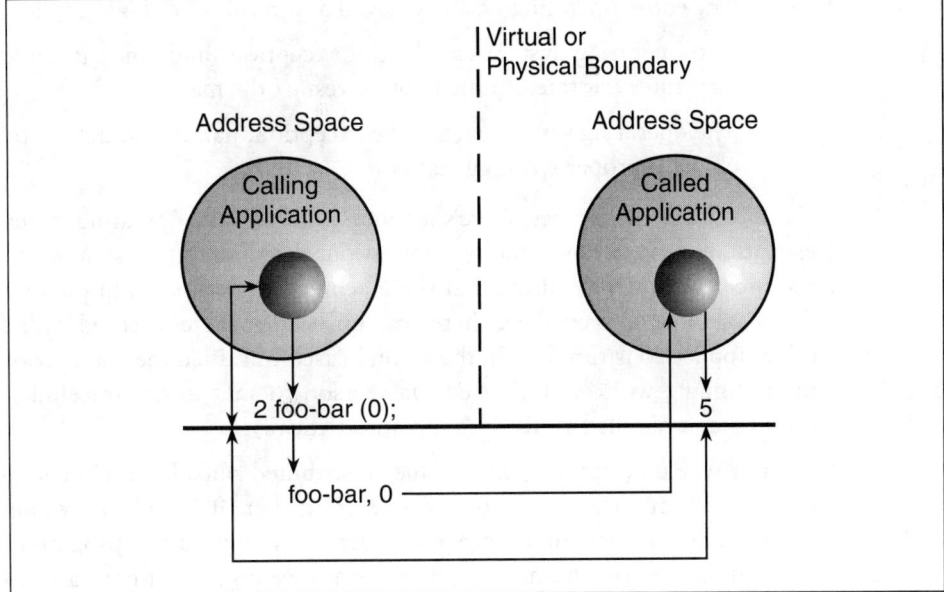

Figure 3.3 *Remote procedure call (RPC) mechanism.*

Marshaling allows clean data to be passed between client, server, and middleware in a consistent manner; but *how* the data is sent is equally important. Early distributed applications used their own messaging scheme, a practice that led to a high rate of failure in distributed applications. This soon gave way to the use of the remote procedure call (RPC). RPC provides a programmatic method of sending data between client, server, and middleware that mimics making a local procedure call. With RPCs, we no longer need the esoteric mnemonics associated with earlier, proprietary messaging schemes. Instead we have a robust programming interface to accomplish the task (see Figure 3.3).

RPCs also help clarify the importance of rules 4 and 5—error handling and location transparency. RPCs give client applications the perception that a function is executing locally, thus providing location transparency. It plays a critical role by ensuring proper error handling in the distributed environment.

To understand the full implications of the distributed model of error handling, think for a moment about your local workstation. As any software vendor will tell you, bug-free software is a myth (a good way of saying it's way too expensive to create). Therefore, at some time, you've probably experienced an application crash. Typically, your workstation responded in one of three ways:

- The entire operating system crashed as a result of a single application failure.

- The operating system caught the exception, and since it could no longer guarantee its state, notified you to restart the machine.

- The operating system caught the exception, handled it, and restored the machine to proper working status.

In each of these cases, there's a common factor: the operating system. When an exception is caused by a faulty application, the operating system acts as a central resource controller, ensuring that the machine runs properly. In the first case, since the whole machine crashed, there was no need to be concerned over the state of other applications running. In the second case, it notified the end user of the danger of continuing work and allowed that person to shut down gracefully. And in the third case, it handled all the cleanup automatically.

But when an application becomes distributed outside of a single machine, we lose the all-important central resource controller. In its place, responsibility for proper handling of remote exceptions generally falls to the programmer. Perhaps this is unfair, and even unnecessary, but since we do not yet have a mainstream distributed operating system, it is the norm.

Passing off error handling to programmers may seem acceptable to organizations just beginning their move to a distributed application environment, such as the Web. But as the Acme Aircraft example in the sidebar illustrates, by doing so, you will be placing a heavy burden on your development staff—a staff which, in all likelihood, has never developed a truly distributed application and therefore cannot anticipate the problems they will encounter.

In the Acme example, a skilled development team anticipated many of the possible faults that could occur, but missed a critical one because they underestimated how variable a distributed application can be. When a client is connected to a server and the server is handling state on behalf of that client, any type of error over that connection will place the system in an indeterminable state. In other words, the client and the server lose their place in the communication, much the way two people chatting on a corner lose the thread of conversation when one gets distracted by a fender bender. Remote exception handling is critical to building a robust distributed application, but so is location *transparency*. Not only is it important to handle remote exceptions; you must handle them seamlessly. The client must not be aware that the process is being distributed (that is, running on a totally different machine).

Location transparency is a critical ingredient to making distributed applications work for nontechnical end users. Imagine if end users had to know the TCP/IP address of every machine involved in a transaction. Take, for example, a

Acme Aircraft

Acme Aircraft is a $70 billion corporation that has just decided to use the Internet to provide its suppliers and customers with access to certain functions of their internal systems, such as order tracking and account status. Accordingly, Acme has decided to write a Java client that will connect with the mainframe systems via the Common Object Request Broker Architecture (CORBA). Members of the development team have completed a Java/CORBA training class, but to date, no one has actually built a distributed object application. The Acme team sensibly deploys their first customer application using a Java client that connects to a Windows NT server that in turn uses SNA to communicate with the mainframe. The system seems to be running smoothly after three weeks of beta testing, so the account manager opens it up to customers. This initial application simply allows customers to track orders as they move through manufacturing; but since tracking accesses corporate databases, the development team naturally follows basic security precautions and requires users to log in.

At this point everything seems straightforward. But then, a very important corporate customer, we'll call him VP Pete, needs to estimate time to delivery of his latest order for a critical sales presentation—but it's 10:00 at night. Initially, this customer perceives the Web site as a lifesaver. Unfortunately, there's a bug in the Windows NT application and the server crashes after VP Pete logs in. Since the Acme team implemented the system with an object request broker, the server process is restarted whenever the end user refreshes the Web page. However, the Acme developers, who had no experience with distributed application error handling, assumed the user was synchronously connected, and therefore, they would not need to track the state of the client's login.

Upshot: When VP Pete refreshed his Web page, he could no longer log in to the system, because the system already deemed him logged in. What had looked like a lifesaver became a boat sinker. Worse, Acme's quality reputation for building reliable custom aircraft was subtly (or not so subtly) damaged by unreliable software.

Consequence: VP Pete will have second thoughts about doing business with ACME in the future because of his bad experience with the company's software.

Web end user who wants to run a Yahoo! search. He or she probably will remember the simple English URL www.yahoo.com, but will he or she remember 195.43.23.1 (the actual TCP/IP address)? Highly doubtful. The Internet Domain Name Service (DNS) is one familiar method used to provide location transparency. It maps those esoteric TCP/IP addresses to descriptive names people can more easily remember.

Believe it or not, most Internet users have no clue that there's a machine at the Yahoo! offices actually running code every time they request a search. They surmise that their own machine is doing the work. This is true of the people who work in your organization's accounting, human resource, and shipping departments. That means you must supply them with the same transparency with a corporate application!

For delivering usable distributed applications to nontechnical end users, the slogan to follow is KISS—for keep it simple, Sam. No matter how many far-flung back-end servers you connect to in order to complete your task, always make the end user believe the processing is happening locally. Usually this just means excluding pop-up error messages such as: "Sorry, cannot connect to LIV01ENG server at this time. Contact your local administrator." Instead, program the erring computer to send a message to an administrator's console describing the problem and the TCP/IP address of the affected machine. The error message to the end user should simply explain that there were difficulties processing his or her request and that the proper staff person has been notified.

A Change in Context

Initially, the term "client/server" described location as well as process. For example, the client was the desktop and the server was the midrange server running in the back office. One of the major changes brought about by the Internet is that desktop machines can collocate both client and server processes simultaneously. That means the original model is broken, making it increasingly important to discuss the requirements for front- and back-office computing independent of the partitioning technologies.

Front-office computing includes all interface with human end users as well as the transfer of information from desktop to desktop. Interfacing with end users embodies the more traditional use of the word client. Transfer of information illustrates the new paradigm: requiring a server component running on each machine to accomplish the task. When designing the front-office portion of a distributed application, important areas to focus on include: security, remote exception handling, and asynchronous accessibility. Let's examine each of these in more detail.

Security

Most organizations store their important data inside a secure machine that resides in a secure room. Distributed applications, however, expose this data electronically to an anonymous endpoint. Therefore, it is important that the logical relationship established between the person sitting at that endpoint and the back office be as accurate a portrayal as possible. That is, the back office should take whatever steps necessary to ensure that the person logging in from a particular endpoint is who he or she claims to be. A number of strong authentication protocols are available to assist with this process, such as DCE Kerberos and Public Key Infrastructures.

Remote Exception Handling

Recall the Acme example to drive home the point that state management is important; but realize that management must be tied into the application exception-handling mechanisms. If the server component of a distributed application goes awry, it is critical that the front office do all that is possible to discern this information when communications start again.

Asynchronous Accessibility

The network cannot be guaranteed; wires get cut, hardware burns out, and software has bugs. Therefore, it is up to the application designer designing the front-office application to handle disconnected states in an efficient manner. For example, if an end user is in the middle of filling out a five-page application, make sure that he or she will not have to repeat all that work if the Web server is unable to process the request at the end.

Back-office computing encompasses all the server operating systems, network services, and management requirements over this and the front-office environment. It is impossible to clearly discern the front office from the back office since they work cooperatively to complete a task. But a good example of the boundary between them can be culled from electronic mail (e-mail). Here end users pass data among other end users and desktops as a front-office function by way of a back-office server and network service—Simple Mail Transfer Protocol, or SMTP.

Back-office components of distributed applications must be robust and sturdy, since these often become the conduits for information across the front office. Imagine, or remember, how frustrating it is to attempt to get your e-mail when the server is unavailable.

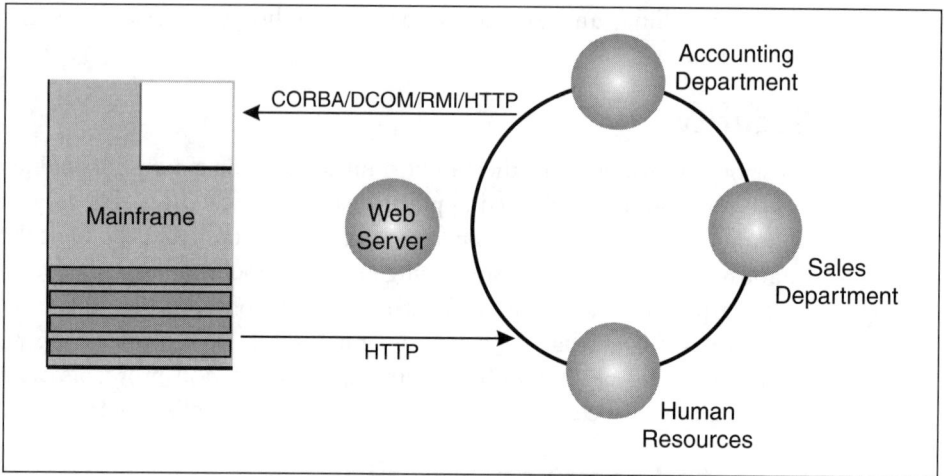

Figure 3.4 *Web application architecture: human resources, accounting, sales linked to Web server linked to mainframe.*

Going Forward

The Web has introduced a new way to deliver distributed applications (as well as a new awareness) that clearly delineates the responsibilities of the front office from those of the back office (see Figure 3.4). In the Web era, the front office is represented by a browser capable of executing logic and displaying a vast amount of data in a variety of formats. This data is retrieved through a Web server that sits at the boundary between the front office and the back office. The same server brokers certain processing tasks between these two. The beauty of this separation lies in its capability to manage IS costs in the enterprise. Developers of expensive software can focus on delivering data engines accessible via the Web server to service a world of business application developers. These developers now have the ability to bring together information in the most productive and efficient way.

Conclusions

This chapter explained the most important aspects to be considered in developing a distributed application. In it we showed that location transparency and error handling functions remain inextricably tied together. We demonstrated that the client/server model of computing does not clearly define the real needs of today's distributed applications. Finally, we showed that application partitioning and machine location now describe different phenomena and therefore are no longer synonymous.

In the next chapter we will look at how the management role of the executive is being reshaped to accommodate the evolving role of IS in the face of emerging technologies and emerging business-focused responsibilities.

FOR FURTHER READING

Chappell, David. *Understanding ActiveX and OLE*. (Redmond, WA: Microsoft Press), 1996.

Koelmel, R. and L. Koelmel. *Implementing Application Solutions in a Client/Server Environment*. (New York: John Wiley & Sons, Inc.), 1994.

Krawczyk, Henryk, Bogdan Wiszniewski, and B. Wiszniewski. *Analysis and Testing of Distributed Software Applications*. (New York: John Wiley & Sons, Inc.), 1997.

Mowbray, Thomas, and R. Zahavi. *The Essential CORBA: Systems Integration Using Distributed Objects*. (New York: John Wiley & Sons, Inc.), 1995.

Watson, Mark. *Creating Java Beans: Components for Distributed Applications*. (New York: John Wiley & Sons, Inc.), 1997.

Part two

MANAGING DISTRIBUTED SYSTEMS

4 EXECUTIVE MANAGEMENT ROLES

> **This chapter defines:**
>
> What executives need to know about systems development.
>
> How a living IS strategic plan can give you a sustainable competitive advantage.
>
> How executive management roles should change to meet the needs of distributed systems.
>
> How adding a chief executive architect to your organization can smooth IS departmental concerns.
>
> Why it is important to remain technologically savvy to retain good employees.

Management Roles for Distributed Systems

The executive branch acts as the brain center of your corporation. The decisions made by chief officers determine whether the corporation maintains and sustains a competitive edge in a growing global economy. Ten years ago, it was not so important for executives to fully understand or be heavily involved in planning the internal IS infrastructure. Today it is imperative.

Not long ago, corporations were building five-year strategic information system plans. In most cases, these plans were really for one or two years with figures run out for five years. Today, a five-year plan is totally unrealistic. Some companies attempt three-year strategic plans, these are more realistic because it normally takes between 18 months and 2 years to develop the described systems. However, even a two-year strategic plan appears to be marginally practical today.

> **TIP**
>
> Ditch the strategic five-year plan in favor of a "living dictate." This dictate should present the overall business goals of the corporation and describe how technology will influence delivery of those goals.

The Internet—the distribution of both process and data over a network—has caused the business environment to change and adapt rapidly. Strategic plans developed earlier than two years ago could not have anticipated the widespread use of this emerging technology and, therefore, could not have incorporated all the required infrastructure changes brought about by this revolution. These changes sometimes require massive expenditures on wiring, equipment, software, programming, and training.

Changes in Your Neighborhood

By neighborhood we mean the base of competitors for your business. With the expansion of electronic communications in emerging markets in India, China, and the Philippines, your neighborhood has expanded tremendously. It is important to recognize that because emerging markets often have poor telecommunications infrastructure, they have moved straight-away to wireless configurations. This gives them an advantage over the United States and Canada which have strong legacy wire-line services.

Currently, millions of people already count on wireless communications to run their lives and businesses. They function from palmtop devices that send and retrieve messages from all over the world. Perhaps you are one of these people who has your essential information delivered to you the minute it becomes available. Or are you one of those glad *not* to have instant data access, for fear of information overload? If so, consider this: With the proper filtering and configuration, it is possible to establish a system that delivers only critical information.

We all know that knowledge is power, but it is important not to confuse raw data with knowledge. If your business is to manufacture and sell staplers, you will want to know instantly that your fiercest competitor just merged with a large conglomerate, whereas you probably don't need to know the weather for that day unless your travel plans may be impacted by a storm. The point is, controlling the flow of information is even more important as the global economy begins to swing into high gear. The global economy is a 24-hour environment. What did you miss while you were sleeping?

To be a successful executive in this new global economy will require a much closer association with technology. Many executives have already made the transition from technophobe to technophile—though some remain unable to download and read e-mail unassisted. Without question, those executives who learn to use technology resources will be far more capable of making intelligent decisions in the increasingly time-pressured workplace.

Systems Development for Executives

It is important that all corporate executives understand the importance of their information systems to the overall well-being of their companies. That said, it is not necessary for an executive to understand, say, the difference between gigabit routers and Asynchronous Transfer Mode (ATM) routers.

For executives, knowing the types and capabilities of the company's systems will give them an intellectual edge, much the way an army general understands his or her advantage because of knowledge of the capabilities of a particular weapon in a particular situation. In many cases, the army general may not have hands-on experience with that weapon, and may not understand how it works, but he or she certainly understands its implications. President Truman never personally saw the awesome power of the atomic bomb, but he knew the advantage it would give the Allied Forces in World War II.

> **TIP**
>
> Think of your information systems as a weapon against your competition.

U.S.-based financial firms have always been leaders in technology implementation for competitive advantage. For years computer technology conference attendees have been clamoring for real-world information regarding implementation of leading-edge technology, but have been unable to obtain it. Understandably, companies employing new technologies are tight-lipped about them, as they wisely view their systems as an advantage over the competition. Consequently, they also tend to spend the most money on hiring and keeping the talent able to learn and employ these new technologies quickly.

Knowing What's Really Important

We've established that information systems are important, but exactly what about them is essential for executives to know? Is that COBOL or C++ program written last week all that valuable to the overall viability or worth of the company? The answer is that, to some degree, all code written has some intrinsic value to the company if as nothing more than a record of services received for funds rendered. But, truly, the most important part of information systems is the data they take in and store. For the most part, the programs are nothing more than vehicles for entering and retrieving said data.

Almost as important are the rules embedded in these programs. Every company has embedded in their software the rules by which they process a particular piece of data. These rules transform the input dataset to create that which is stored permanently inside the company's electronic vaults. It is these business rules that form the foundation of the corporation's competitive advantage. However, when these rules are locked away in irretrievable source code, maintenance and reengineering becomes a much more difficult task. Irretrievable business rules mean your competitive advantage is reduced.

Fundamentals of Living Systems

If (and this is a big if) your organization is capable of converting its existing legacy code to newer source code, what should the role of the executive branch be? Traditionally, this has fallen into the mystical domain of the directors and vice presidents of information system departments. We are recommending, instead, that predominately nontechnical executives take a hand in this process, because when executives understand the fundamentals of so-called living systems, they can help guide efforts to revamp legacy applications.

The concept of living systems is borrowed from the biological research community. It describes a system that is continually evolving. More important, living systems behave differently when interacting with other systems than when viewed in isolation.

To date, most information systems have been built in relative isolation; that is, the premises and requirements were to solve a single problem with little forethought as to what the solution's impact might be on other information system requirements. Consider the formidable number of proprietary data formats and database schemes in any one organization. It would take a Herculean effort to integrate these older systems into the new enterprise system.

As information systems become an integral part of the enterprise's existence, leaders charged with running the company must have a role in defining information

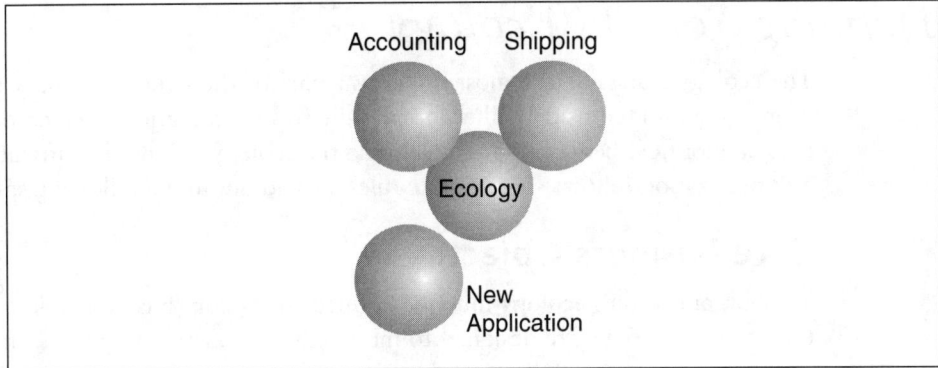

Figure 4.1 *A living system.*

systems. Clearly, it is not proper for a chief executive officer to decide whether the company should be developing in C++ or Java, but he or she should have a foundation of knowledge that enables him or her to make decisions related to IS. A good foundation can be synthesized by understanding living systems. Moreover, the principles of living systems can be appreciated by both the layperson and technician alike.

For the purpose of this chapter, we define living systems by three simple properties (see Figure 4.1):

- An ecology defines the environment where individual nodes will live. A node can be a process, a program or a business division or department.

- A new node can express itself uniquely, but must also provide a definition of that expression to the ecology.

- It must be possible to create a flow from any one node to another within the ecology.

As long as these properties are maintained, the living system can continue to grow and evolve.

NOTE

This definition of a living system is very generic. It could be applied to many aspects of running an organization, but we will examine it within the construct of building information systems. After all, theory without practical execution and examples is not very useful.

Defining Your IS Ecology

The ecology stands as the most important part of the living system. If not defined properly, all nodes inside will eventually die from "starvation," which occurs when data cannot flow between nodes. Defining the ecology will not be difficult as long as an organization follows some simple rules, as laid out in the following subsections.

Core Business Objectives

Your organization's ecology must be defined by its core business objectives. Often, information systems are designed to meet only the existing requirements of current computing processes. For example, a manufacturing organization might build its systems around the need to move and store large computer-aided design (CAD) models. Certainly this is an important requirement of the physical infrastructure, but the actual goal of such an organization is to build, say, a car or a stapler. More important is getting as many cars or staplers as profitably possible into the hands of consumers. Depending on the business model, this can mean that the car or stapler must be the highest quality available on the market, while costing the least to manufacture in the shortest possible time. Therefore the distribution channels should be constantly supplied with product in an effective, but cost-effective manner. In short, the manufacturer's ecology must support a complement of systems designed to accomplish this mission.

Nourishment

Once the ecology is defined, it is natural to want to fill it with living nodes. If the ecology has been well designed, a naturally defined template will make it possible to create nodes that will thrive in this ecology. An ecology must nourish its nodes. This may sound strange, but this is an excellent design paradigm for next-generation systems.

Nourishment of a node takes the form of a consistent flow of data that meets the requirements of the business goals. For example, say that one of the features of the ecology is to keep the distribution channel well-supplied in a cost-effective manner. This will take an evaluation of records from shipping, accounting, and sales. Assume that your existing information systems define your ecology: Is it capable of nourishing the node responsible for calculating this output? Granted, with computers, anything is possible since it's really all zeros and ones, but could you build this node and drop it into your ecology tomorrow without interacting with any other system designer or group? If not, then your ecology does not nourish your nodes, and eventually, this will inhibit growth. In the real world, you will require more resources than you have available to generate nourishing pathways.

Leading the New Paradigm

Executive management must demand and drive the process of designing new information systems. Why and how? For two key reasons: First, the process rewards participants who complete the task assigned, not those providing the most qualitative solution; second, only the group that understands the "big picture" can ensure that a component will continue as a premise of the living system and not block growth.

For too long now, IS has been a bottom-up environment; that is, the requirements come in through a top- or medium-level person, but are delegated to the engineering/development staff. This staff is then responsible for turning requirements into reality, and often are given the freedom to use the tools they are most comfortable with to create the system. The results of such a loose creative development process are a mix of hardware platforms, operating systems, and middleware. Because it is important that the engineering staff not be stripped of their creative edge, the problem for management is trying to maintain quality control over the resulting mishmash of system elements.

Because of the growing dependence on information systems to keep the company running, the IS department must become a top-down environment. Executive-level managers do not need to get involved with daily decision making, but they should be responsible for providing a corporate framework, or reference specification, with which all applications must comply. For example, the executive branch could issue a document stating that all new applications must comply with certain parameters, such as object-model compliance, reusability requirements, network services requirements, and so on. Defining the IS ecology expedites this process. And like the ecology itself, this document must grow and evolve with the IS industry.

In theory, this is sound advice, but how can you guarantee that emerging technological directions will be compatible with systems based upon the existing document? We address this question throughout this book. In each section, try to identify the properties that make your organization's infrastructure modular. Maintaining a high-degree of modularity is critical to developing living systems.

What about Legacy Systems?

Today, the word legacy is used by vendors to describe any application or system currently in place. This is nothing more than a superb marketing ploy to encourage you to buy and use the vendors' new product to make your old systems work like new. The catch phrase is "like new."

Most of the extant applications in organizations today were not inherited (in the sense of left to them by "ancestors") but were created by those organizations. Thus they are not legacy, but merely *older* applications. True legacy systems are those from which the source code is missing and/or the author(s) is unknown or nowhere to be found.

Consider this: Millions of lines of code are executing everywhere every day, processing mission-critical data that runs companies, and nobody knows how it works! Does this represent a sound business philosophy? Do you believe that you can compete globally with this foundation? An old Yiddish proverb says, "With a strong foundation, a home can withstand anything; but with a weak foundation, kerplat!" Complicating legacy issues is that the processes that were analyzed to create your legacy applications probably do not accurately represent the way the company does business today. Therefore additional postprocessing is added on top of the original processing to make it useful for the way business operates today.

To Reengineer or Extend, That Is the Question

The best answer is to reengineer. It may sound like an overused solution, but with the newer technologies born of the Internet era, and with today's advanced rapid application development tools, organizations have an opportunity to reevaluate the automated process and reimplement the code in as little as three weeks. More important, reengineered solutions can feed into the living system, allowing them to evolve and thrive with the changing needs of the company.

Ask yourself: Why is your company in business? If the answer is that your company exists to generate a profit so that all the employees and the shareholders can improve their lives, then let's look at what it really takes to win your game. (If you are a not-for-profit, this section may not apply to you.) Let's assume you've reengineered your entire organization using as your guide some of the hundreds of books available today and/or according to the advice of consultants. Why do they avoid

---

NOTE

If you are a young startup, or an established company in an emerging market, your systems are directly related to the future success and viability of your company. Build them with care, ensure their proper maintenance, and most important, never allow yourself to believe a system is complete. Tomorrow it will need new functionality to face a new challenge.

> **NOTE**
>
> If you haven't decided to throw away legacy applications today, it is likely you will keep it until the day you turn off the host machine.

telling you that the best long-term solution is to get rid of legacy systems? Well, we're telling you here: Rid yourself of legacy systems now! Why? Your competition is a young startup or an established company in an emerging market. These companies are not plagued by legacy, and they are ambitious, which means they will try to take over your market share; and they just might succeed.

Are we saying that you have to replace every last single piece of code? No, because as soon as you finished one round, you would have to start over again. Rather, we aim to take you through the development leading to a healthy flow of electronic information. Any applications running today older than three years (and some younger) are most likely the result of an automated process. As the goals of the business and its competing environment change, these processes must change as well.

At one time, computers were designed to simplify and speed redundant tasks. Unfortunately, when information systems were designed and built, the tasks they modeled were not evaluated for their productivity, but merely as electronic mimics of redundant human processes, which is a minimal use of the capabilities of the powerful machines that pervade our desktops and back offices.

The first step is to evaluate the process to which each piece of legacy code contributes. Examine the foundation upon which the code was designed and ask the following questions:

- Is this truly a productive method of accomplishing the task?
- Is the outcome of this process providing the company with all the information it needs to make effective decisions?
- Can this process be combined with another to be accomplished in less time or through outsourcing? (Remember the adage: Do what you do best, and let someone else do the rest.)

Chances are that over 75 percent of the applications now running on computers in most large corporations do not accurately represent their intended task. In fact, there are probably a host of peripheral processes that postprocess the data to extract additional morsels of data from the original outcome. These postprocesses have been added continuously through the years so that is almost impossible to dissect the system without it falling apart.

If after evaluating a running process, you conclude that the process would be designed no differently today, by all means *don't* replace it. We're not advocating change for the sake of change. There are more than enough methods to connect this older code to newer systems if necessary. Your goal should be to perform what amounts to heart transplant surgery on your company's information systems. Moreover, you want to replace the old poorly functioning heart with a young, strong one.

> **NOTE:**
>
> Your information systems are the heart of the company. To ensure survival, they must be strong and healthy.

When You Needed It Yesterday

Imagine how effective your information systems could be if they were rebuilt using the latest knowledge and techniques. The main obstacle to achieving that state is the amount of time and money it would take. Take heart, this section will help you clear that hurdle.

Today's rapid application development environments are at the point now that you can produce a solid application in a matter of days instead of months. Thanks in particular to the World Wide Web and the pervasiveness of the Internet, building and deploying applications is easier than ever.

Essential Design Components

Six design components are required for applications: data, input, output, processing (rules), platform, and audience. Of the six, the last two, platform and audience, typically cause the most problems; processing is usually the second most troublesome, and input the third. Data is usually available or can be synthesized from a number of sources; and output is typically a no-brainer if the other requirements can be satisfied. Let's examine these design components in more depth.

Platform is the physical hardware and operating system required to deploy the application. Choosing a platform for new applications today is one of the greatest challenges facing an IS department. For starters, you have to determine whether the application should be written for Microsoft Windows or Macintosh or Unix. To answer this question, you must understand the hardware currently deployed throughout your organization; but more important, you must understand the audience that will use the application. It may be, for example, that an application such as electronic expense reporting needs to be developed for both Unix and Windows.

You must also consider the long-term impact of the decision to develop an application for a particular platform. For example, graphics- and multimedia-intensive companies are often Macintosh-based. But you must consider what will happen if the Mac platform becomes obsolete. Of course, no one can predict such sweeping changes in the market, and you should not allow fear to deter you from making the best decision at the moment; however, never lose sight of the fact that platform and audience make up the most critical components when developing and purchasing applications for the company.

> **TIP**
>
> Platform and audience increase the cost and time for application delivery.

We explored the effect of the Web on information systems in Chapter 3, Building Distributed Applications, and therefore will not dwell on the technical aspects here. Just keep in mind as you read this chapter that the Internet and the Web change the implications that platform and audience have on deploying applications. For one, Web applications can help overcome obstacles of platform and audience, and thus should motivate companies to rethink earlier strategies, in particular those that preclude the overhaul of information systems.

Processing is partly affected by platform, but also by partitioning. Partitioning defines where in a distributed process an actual unit of work will be accomplished. If all the processing is done on the server, building and deploying that particular type of application is simple. If, however, the processing needs to be done where the end user is operating, the equation is much more complex. Again, we come face to face with the problems associated with platform and audience. Here, too, the Web has heightened awareness. And the Web offers a solution. Scripting languages for Web applications define logic for presentation among diverse platforms and audiences. Every scripting language requires an interpreter to evaluate code and perform a process. This means that although scripting may not be the correct solution for highly complex logic, it can handle simple routine chores and use available local processing power.

The Chief Executive Architect

As information systems have come to impact more on the business process, the number of technical roles in the executive branch has grown. The most common additions are the chief information officer (CIO) and the chief technical officer (CTO). The CIO is primarily concerned with connecting the information systems to the core business. But to adequately meet that challenge today, a CIO must have a specialized background. When the CIO does not have that background, many organizations respond by instituting the CTO role. Both the CIO and CTO are important to the technological well-being of the company.

But those two positions create the need for a third: the chief executive architect (CEA), to link the choices the CTO makes with the vision of the CIO. The CEA is trained in the science of information system's architecture; he or she views the organization as a very large-scale system that needs a set of well-defined interfaces to provide interoperability. These well-defined interfaces can then be used in defining

---

Ace Order Fulfillment

Order fulfillment usually requires cooperation of multiple departments such as sales, shipping, and the warehouse. In the Ace Book Company, each department has its own information systems designed to automate and simplify processing. But at Ace (and many other companies), information systems were not designed to communicate from the start.

Along comes the Ace CIO, who decides that the company could improve customer satisfaction by fulfilling orders faster than its competition (Acme). To fill orders faster, all systems across all departments will have to start working cooperatively.

In a common scenario, the CIO hands the task of making systems interoperate to the CTO, who finds a technology to make the disparate systems communicate, or decides to implement a whole new enterprise system for order fulfillment. Unfortunately, in this case, the entire corporate information system needs overhaul, and the CTO only fixes the surface of the order fulfillment problem.

A complete review of the process for handling order fulfillment shows that a book order is generated in the sales system, which creates two hard-copy reports: a warehouse packaging list and a shipping manifest. When these reports arrive at their destinations, they are compared to the current systems in those departments and either fulfilled or placed on

the CIO's vision, and the CTO can select the right technology to implement these interfaces. The Ace Book Company sidebar illustrates this three-way implementation.

It is important to understand the role of each of the executive branch members described in the Ace example. The CIO is responsible for reiterating that order fulfillment is important to customer satisfaction. The CIO must then decide how IS will correct the problems from an information systems perspective. Any concomitant personnel and cultural changes will be handled by human resources executive branch members.

The Ace example also highlights the importance of having a high-level group that crosses departmental boundaries to keep an eye on cross-departmental processes. It is equally important that the organization recognize that every pro-

back order. Complicating the process is that the shipping department must match its shipping requests with drop-offs from the warehouse.

Although fixing the data systems would help sales and customer service provide more accurate delivery dates, it would do little to speed the time it takes to fulfill an order. With the assistance of a CEA, the entire interdepartment process is redesigned to show where data must flow and when. For example, all sales go into a repository to be filled on a first come, first served basis (with priority override). The warehouse system uses this repository to generate packaging lists based upon available inventory. After a book order is boxed, it is marked in the system; a shipping docket is generated and placed with the outgoing box to be used by shipping to ensure prompt delivery. The CEA is responsible for designing the structure of the order in the repository to ensure its usefulness to all departments. For example, the CEA defines the requirement for the warehouse to expose its books-on-order to generate more accurate ship dates.

Once this interdepartmental process has been designed, the CTO fulfills his or her role of selecting the necessary technologies for implementation (if necessary), and generates an internal project to program and deploy the systems where appropriate. The project manager and system architect then implement the logic necessary for the individual departments. For example, for sales and customer service, they provide the approximate ship date based upon current inventory and books on order.

grammer does not necessarily have the qualifications necessary to analyze corporate processes. The qualifications for a CEA or in the CEA's group should include:

- The ability to think abstractly.
- Experience that includes the successful design of a large-scale or enterprise-scale system.
- A thorough understanding of the core business objectives.
- An entrepreneurial spirit.
- The ability to communicate complex technical information simply.
- An understanding of object-oriented design techniques.

The CEA should also be capable of designing the IS ecology and maintaining its vision. The CEA should work with the CTO to examine how emerging technologies will impact their business and how they should be incorporated into the IS ecology. Finally, the CEA should also work with the CIO to more clearly identify where there are bottlenecks in the information infrastructure and to transition these into the living system.

> **NOTE**
> The CEA's role is to deliver, maintain, and orient the organization's information infrastructure into a living system.

Managing Employees and Technology

As an executive officer, employee satisfaction is one of your key concerns. A primary goal should be a low turnover rate, because, obviously, high turnover can result in organizational inefficiency. Before the widespread use of the personal computer and the Internet, employee satisfaction was defined by the establishment of work hours, workplace conditions, benefits, and other related factors. In today's global economy, all that has changed.

To support this new environment, management must recognize the need to implement supportive technologies. Telecommuting, high-speed Internet access, and around-the-clock access to e-mail and data are mandatory features required to support the new breed of employee. Today's employees judge their management's ability to guide the company by how well it adapts to and how fast it adopts cutting-edge technology. Jane and Joe Employee will regard insufficient or unreliable Internet access as an indicator that management is not technology savvy and thus will probably be left behind as the global economy emerges. Such an employee will not want to join or stay with a company with that profile.

> **TIP**
>
> Recognize the technology expectations of your employees. Keep in mind: Nobody wants to play for the losing team.

Joining the Internet Age

For the Fortune 1000, Internet access costs probably are not a significant issue, but for small and midsized companies, merging on the so-called information superhighway can be a complex and expensive proposition. Specialized knowledge is required in the areas of communications, computer hardware and software, and high-tech security. In addition, the cost of high-speed digital lines is huge compared to regular business services lines. It's easy to understand how a small company could be overwhelmed by plans to move to Internet technologies.

This section, therefore, offers a brief overview of the steps to take to bring your company into the age of the Internet. It is not necessary for every executive to understand these technologies in depth; following paragraphs itemize where you can go for various services and what they should cost.

Obtain a Domain Name

The InterNIC is an organization that maintains the domain registry, the list of all domain names on the Internet. There is a $100 fee for a two-year registration, and most Internet service providers (ISP) will obtain this name and link it with their network on your behalf. A domain name is an ASCII representation of your numeric Internet address; for example, you and your employees and customers will only have to remember the domain *joe.com* because the service translates it to the numerical address 199.0.0.1, which is necessary for routing information. The ISP will charge you a nominal fee, usually around $75 to set up an account and domain.

Decide on an Access Method

Base this decision solely on your cost and speed requirements. Decide how you will connect to the ISP to send and retrieve e-mail and access the Web. Table 4.1 itemizes the different connect options and typical benefits and pitfalls for using each. (It does not account for establishing a Web presence.)

Table 4.1 Internet Connection Options

METHOD	SPEED	AVERAGE COSTS	BENEFITS/PITFALLS
Local Area Network Modem Pool	14.4 Kbps– 33.6Kb	Setup: $250/Modem $50/User Account Monthly: $20/User Account $50–$70/phone charges	Benefits: Low-cost Disadvantages: Access not guaranteed (busy, down lines, etc.) Slow
Leased-line	56 Kbps	Setup: $500–$2000/hardware $250–$750/account Monthly: $300–$750/account	Benefits: Moderate cost Constant access for entire network Disadvantages: Moderate to slow speed
Integrated Services Digital Network (ISDN)	128 Kbps	Setup: $250–$1500 hardware $250–$750/account Monthly: $250–$750/account $300/phone charges	Benefits: Moderate cost High-speed Disadvantages: Access is not guaranteed; expensive with heavy usage
Digital Subscriber Line (DSL)/T1 and Fractional T1	128 Kbps– 1.5 Mbps	Setup: $2800–$4000/hardware $750–$2000/account Monthly: $800–$2400/usage $750–$2000/account	Benefits: Guaranteed high-speed access for entire network Disadvantages: Expensive; usually used to establish a Web presence

Hire Help to Configure an Internet Access Server

If the ISP already supports TCP/IP networking, an Internet access server may be implemented without additional resources. Otherwise, you will have to install a TCP/IP network.

Consider the Implications

Before granting access to your employees to the Internet, you may want to consult with legal counsel regarding the implications of your employees' actions in the public domain. You should also implement Internet usage policies before letting your employees go online through the company's setup. This policy should cover the following issues:

- *Security.* This includes internal security, network security, and data security, among others. Security policies must define which actions will warrant reprimand or termination. The aim is to ensure that confidential company information does not leak into the public domain. Consult a network security expert.

- *Downloading.* Downloading software inappropriately from the network can breach software licenses or introduce the threat of destructive (virus-infected) software. Therefore, downloading policy must address both these issues. Furthermore, a new threat is e-mailed executable content, which when opened, wreaks havoc. So policy should also define downloaded content as any data received via any network service, such as e-mail, newsgroups, file transfer protocol, Web, or gopher.

- *Posting.* Besides being a source of information, the Web can also serve as a collaborative environment. Chat rooms and newsgroups provide forums for people to express their opinions openly. For corporations, unfortunately, this can become a nightmare. Most regulatory agencies have been unable to determine responsibility for posted content when addressed from a corporate domain. This means that if one of your employees posts offensive or confidential data to a public forum, your company could become embroiled in a lawsuit. Again, consult legal counsel regarding protecting the company from legal action.

- *Storage.* Content downloaded from the Internet can quickly fill data storage space. For example, employees may share their findings with other employees by placing content in a common area on the network. Assuming this content does not breach the downloading section of the policy, establish guidelines for how long these "nuggets" will exist on the network and how much space to allot them. At the same time, be careful not to deter information-sharing activities, which can save hours of work for another employee at a later point in time. On the other hand, you don't want to spend dollars and network space supporting a game warehouse for your employees.

- *Usage.* Monitoring employee usage is a tricky area of concern, because it borders on infringement of privacy issues. Nevertheless, do not let this deter you from implementing a policy and accompanying software to monitor employees' online use. The safest way is to measure the time an employee spends on Internet transmissions outside the company, rather than on the addresses being accessed.

Virtual Private Networks

Besides providing Internet access to your employees in the corporate workplace, your employees may also need to telecommute. Remote access can be an expensive proposition to manage internally, especially for small or midsized businesses. As a solution, many companies are teaming with local ISPs to create *virtual private networks* (VPNs) over the Internet.

VPNs work via a secure channel between the corporation and the employee. The ISP assumes all responsibility for providing points of presence (POP), that is, access points into which remote users can dial and which provide a secure route to the corporate servers. Partnering with an ISP for this service is advisable because the ISP can provide a secure connection behind its firewall (a network service that blocks unwarranted access), thus limiting security breaches.

Conclusions

In the age of diminishing quality human resources, no company can afford to lose valuable employees to a competitor; in short, these people could mean the difference between success and failure. By implementing technology wisely and properly, you can help them get their jobs done more efficiently and effectively. And if you establish clear policies to guard against abuse of these privileges, you will have a complete package.

In this chapter we emphasized the impact of information technology on the executive branch of the corporation. As we approach competing in a global economy, computer and information systems become increasingly important to the daily operations and decision-making processes of a company. Executives that continue to delegate complete responsibility for these systems' creation and maintenance may eventually find themselves behind their competition and unprepared to leverage emerging technologies for financial gain.

We proposed a framework for use to evaluate technological directions without requiring executives to become mired in the complexities of implementation. The living system model can be used to evaluate a single application or an entire technology's utility in the enterprise.

The Chief Executive Architect is a new position proposed not only to augment the Chief Information Office and the Chief Technology Office, but to also complete the information management requirements. The CEA's responsibility is to manage the interfaces between departments and ensure that data can flow freely between their information systems without requiring enterprise-wide data definitions.

It is also important for management to exploit technology to retain the best resources. Today, management is being evaluated by employees and potential employees by their level of use of new technologies. A good employee is more likely to take a position with a company that has full Internet access, electronic mail, and high-end workstations before they take one with a company that's still using Windows 3.1 on Intel-486-based PCs.

As an extension to this chapter, Chapter 5 addresses some critical decisions IS managers will have to make regarding the future of their information systems.

FOR FURTHER READING

Brooks, Frederick P. *The Mythical Man-Month: Essays on Software Engineering.* (Reading, MA: Addison-Wesley), 1995.

Gates, Bill, N. Myhrvold, and P. Rinearson. *The Road Ahead.* (New York: Penguin USA), 1996.

Moore, Geoffrey A. *Inside the Tornado: Marketing Strategies from Silicon Valley's Cutting Edge.* (New York: HarperBusiness), 1995.

Peters, Thomas J. *The Circle of Innovation: You Can't Shrink Your Way to Greatness.* (New York: Knopf), 1997.

5 CHOOSING THE ARCHITECTURE

Multitudes in the valley of decision.

Book of Joel

This chapter details:
Why CIOs must plan effectively for the future of the corporate information system.
How new application systems are defining the "hollow" company.
The role of the information systems department.
Essentials for choosing the right systems architecture.
Why distributed systems are right for your business.
Why joint application development (JAD) is invaluable.
How to deal with legacy systems.
Systems delivery options: build, buy, outsource, or a combination.

Information Systems in Business

CIOs too often fail to address pressing business concerns raised by their boards and operating units, and thus don't last long in the position. In the U.S. telecommunications industry, the average time in the post of CIO is less than two years.

This chapter outlines the critical IS decision-making process from a business viewpoint, specifically addressing those decisions that relate to the use of and development of distributed environments. Here are some of the questions corporate managers should be asking:

- What are my information system needs as dictated by the business strategy, tactics, and type of operations?

- How do I assess the health of the IS relationship with users so that I can manage it effectively? How can I understand the real needs of users?

- What is the appropriate technical architecture for my operating needs, and under what circumstances should I choose a distributed environment?

- Should I buy or build systems, or outsource all services; which option makes financial sense? (Note: This is also a CFO-type question, which resides at the core of the gap between IS and the operating units.)

- What are the approaches to development that will better address user needs?

- How do I effectively withdraw from yesterday's systems and break the lock-in dependency to older systems and processes?

In subsequent chapters we respond to the questions of technical concern, such as distributed system environments and employing objects to achieve realistic goals; we also address human resources and organizational concerns, such as how to reskill for tomorrow.

The Hollow Company

We are seeing the appearance of the *hollow company,* a series of operations based on and integrated by computing that requires fewer and fewer employees. In any business, whether consumer goods production, public utilities, telecommunications, finance, or medicine, the computer department can mean the difference between success and failure. Systems allow us to increase geographic competitive scope by enabling cheaper and faster coordination across boundaries for both markets and supply chain, while at the same time cutting the cost and time of coordination and control with outside partners. As IS moves toward center stage to become the key department in many companies, alignment of IS with business is critical. IS did not play such a crucial role as recently as 15 or even 10 years ago. But slowly our view of what constitutes the substance of the company is changing from one of physical productive capacity, sales channels, and supply chains, with large numbers of operatives, to a series of processes running across vertical departments such as procurement, production, and marketing. Driven by information services, this shift in focus has occurred in stages.

Initially, application systems automated discrete functions in a piecemeal, independent, and somewhat opportunistic manner. Slowly, systems were integrated, and information such as customer data in billing could be shared with customer support, and then with marketing. Eventually, a cross-functional processlike workflow was entirely remodeled around information systems; as a result, IS was able to form the basis for the processes and their management.

Now the next generation of systems integration is occurring. The migration to interlocking services is often led by the user departments, with intranets and Web technology as the building blocks. But it goes further than just the streamlining and reshaping of the processes. The systems are the core of the business. In telemarketing, retail, insurance, or telebanking with automatic tellers, we "hollow" out the company and refill it with application systems. It is notable that such application systems are based equally on advanced telecommunications technology and computing, with the computing primarily distributed, and only very rarely standalone.

Technologies such as voice response and computer-integrated telephony (CIT) for call centers are becoming as important as the databases themselves. Centralized architectures are used for certain functions on a pragmatic basis; this means that IBM's thesis that the mainframe is not dead, that it has instead become a server based on cheaper standard technology with multiprocessors, will still hold true in the twenty-first century. However, suppliers often lag behind commercial needs in the area of electronic commerce. For example, the standard merchant server Web platforms that handle electronic commerce over the Web are really no more than credit card front ends and a catalogue for products. Real users need budget controls, sophisticated procurement processes, and business-to-business checks for everyday operations. The IS department has a core role to play in the electronic commerce area, adding functionality for distributed processing on top of the basic server platforms, be they from Netscape, IBM, Microsoft, or Oracle, or others.

At the same time, a more general corporate movement is concentrating entirely on the core competencies—the real added value. Peripheral activities are becoming progressively externalized, though closely linked and controlled through information systems. For example, many car assemblers still manufacture a lot of their own components, although their real added value is not in their manufacture but in their assembly (thus car assemblers create over 50 percent of the car value in Europe, against under 30 percent in Japan). In contrast, ICL, a computer company in the United Kingdom, has spun off a seemingly core part of its operation, circuit-board production, as a separate company, which supplies ICL as one customer among many. ICL's core operations no longer include board manufacture, only systems sales and systems integration.

Because businesses are increasingly dependent on computing for functions like marketing forecasts, account tracking, and customer service, the form of computing a business chooses is changing. Normally, the new form of computing concentrates on optimizing the core business processes. The nature of the new model, the development approach, and even ownership reflect both the business as a whole and the competitive position of that company in its industry. A newly recruited Canadian CIO in air travel remarked during a massive turnaround that there was no way the old company could compete effectively because the systems were a reflection of the industry in 1970.

Moreover, information systems are providing the middle layer of control, and at the same time reducing the costs of that control. In addition, because the company's core business knowledge and modus operandi is usually coded into the main applications, the concept of the firm is being redefined by its use of computer systems. As a result, companies are becoming increasingly sclerotic while their computer dependence increases. It is now more difficult to change code on old machines and databases than to change the physical business processes themselves. Case in point: A major airline reservation system still has parts specially manufactured for UNIVAC machines, which disappeared from computing more than 20 years ago.

Too many corporations have coded their everyday operations into unchangeable code. The Year 2000 crisis is symptomatic of this dependence and of the difficulty of untangling from yesterday's spaghetti code. Coincidentally, today's business processes can change each year with the market; thus, corporations must become far more flexible—that is, put computer power where it is needed, changing what it does without stopping the whole commercial operation.

At the lower level of daily operations, systems distributed all over the corporation form the glue that holds the workings of the organization together, including e-mail, shared files and documents, and intranet services such as time-keeping or vacation posting. This is a suitable working definition of what we mean by distributed systems in business—putting computer power where it's useful—on the desktop or down the hall, not isolated in a remote centralized data center.

The integration of IS with all levels of business operations continues to increase in importance. Distributed systems are often implemented to give a business a competitive edge, as illustrated in Figure 5.1.

Here are some examples of how companies use distributed information systems to build a competitive advantage:

- Retail operations with a supply chain linked to stock control and per-store, per-item sales use distributed systems for super-efficient inventory control,

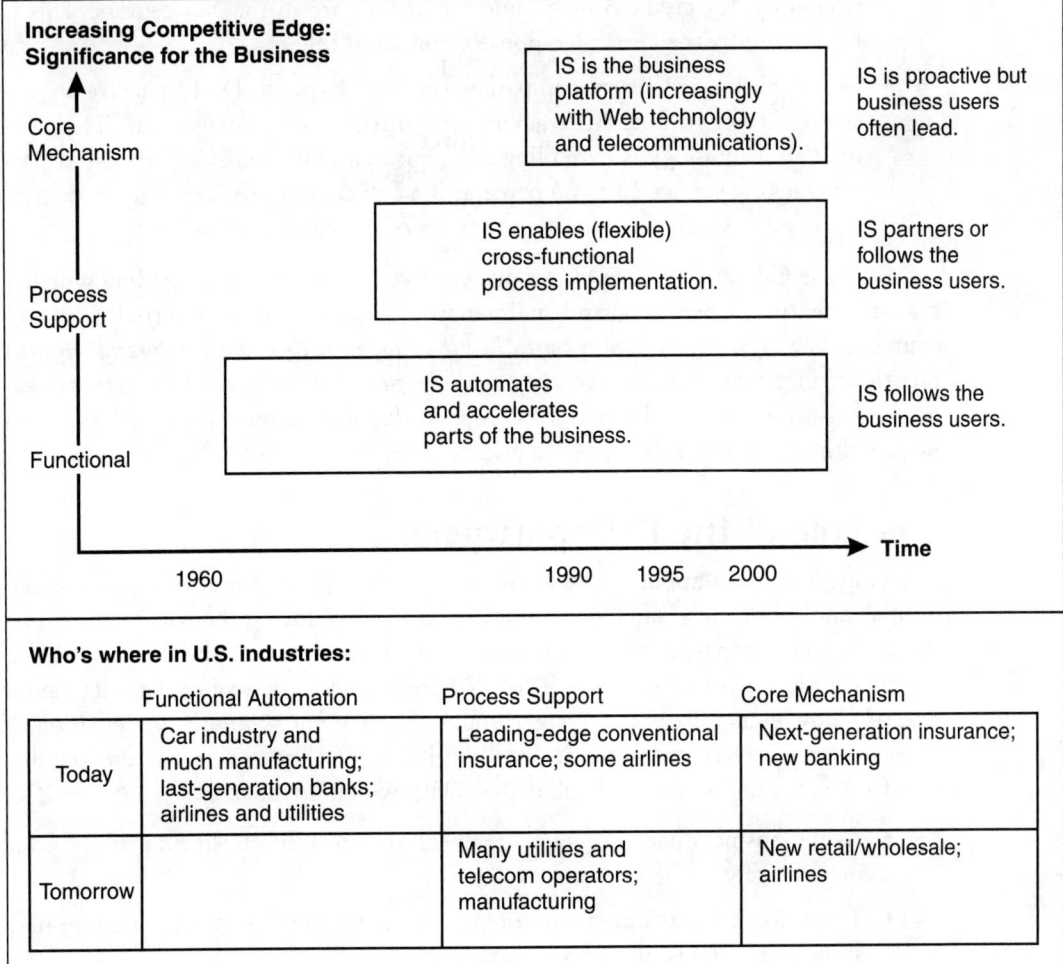

Increasing Competitive Edge: Significance for the Business

Core Mechanism — IS is the business platform (increasingly with Web technology and telecommunications). / IS is proactive but business users often lead.

Process Support — IS enables (flexible) cross-functional process implementation. / IS partners or follows the business users.

Functional — IS automates and accelerates parts of the business. / IS follows the business users.

Time: 1960 — 1990 — 1995 — 2000

Who's where in U.S. industries:

	Functional Automation	Process Support	Core Mechanism
Today	Car industry and much manufacturing; last-generation banks; airlines and utilities	Leading-edge conventional insurance; some airlines	Next-generation insurance; new banking
Tomorrow		Many utilities and telecom operators; manufacturing	New retail/wholesale; airlines

Figure 5.1 The development of IS, which leads to a competitive edge.

replenishment, and pricing. Wal-Mart has built a $100 billion operation using distributed systems.

- Boston Market uses distributed systems to drive its growth in fast foods by lowering the cost of operations through automation of much of the back-office operation, as well as supply chain management and production quality controls.

- In the insurance industry, a new business model has appeared based on telephone selling and backed by distributed systems for computer-integrated telephony, for credit control, and customer care in the call centers. This is being used by the Direct Response Group and others.

- Major package delivery companies (Federal Express, DHL) survive by excelling in networking for tracking and distribution management. Their use of Web technology is extending this. For example, FedEx's Web-based parcel-tracking service costs 20 percent of a call center; this is extending distributed systems into the homes and offices of the customer base.

Both the CIO and the CFO must answer two questions when deciding whether systems creation, operation, and maintenance should be done internally or outsourced: *Is the system's function central to the business, or is it a peripheral support function?*; in either case, *should they run the function, or give it to external experts?* This leads to a third question: *Where do distributed systems fit with the business?* (Although it might be better to ask: *Where don't distributed systems fit?*)

The Role of the IS Department

Ironically, just when applications software is becoming the center of many companies, a number of those same companies seem to be reducing the role of the information systems department, even outsourcing its functions. Is this because the IS department has lost its (traditional) role, or not found its new one? A fundamental question now facing many IS management teams is: *What should be the position of IS in the business?* To answer that question, it is necessary to consider the key drivers for change in the role of the IS department, which include:

- As the business pace heats up, it is necessary to track business evolution far more closely in the systems developed.

- Transition to distributed environments: More complex systems require new skills and systems in user departments.

- Users function at a higher skill level by using technology to accomplish what once required skills that were the exclusive domain of gurus and experts. The pervasive PC offers one graphic example. Relative novices perform sophisticated data manipulation and are able to easily create reports and presentations with professional polish. Applying the power of technology at a level of expertise which was once the exclusive domain of gurus and experts with simplified, sophisticated interfaces is now well within the abilities of the novice.

- Improving interworking [crossing and involving interaction and cooperation in all the possible permutations and combinations (among, between, at all levels as well as up, down, and across) the organizational and tool hierarchy] relationships with the users is essential.

- It may be necessary to move away from custom development to packages.

- The changing nature of software technology means that more complete solutions can interwork more easily (for example, Web technology, which is often user-driven, and object technology for wider reach into customer homes with e-commerce). This also yields greater reliability while handling greater complexity at lower cost.

Traditionally, the IS department has played two roles. The first was a service role. From its pool of resources, IS provided basic computing and office automation services, rather like mail distribution or cleaning services. Usually, it was not regarded as a profit center, but operated from a central budget on time and materials. Similarly, it was rarely the focus of systems excellence or a source of user satisfaction.

The second traditional IS role was that of follower, that is, as a supplier of user departments requirements. It reacted to user demands, it did not anticipate, and was often so separated from the business that it could have been the responsibility of an external vendor of software services. In the follower role, IS occasionally had contracts with the user departments and therefore was occasionally considered a profit center. While playing this role, IS was often despised by the users and usually at war with one operational unit or another.

Deciding the future role of IS is the job of the IS director, but there exists no one right answer. Moreover, two additional roles are becoming apparent, shaped by the new drivers. The first, creative partner, enables the expression of new business ideas by the business divisions as they occur in a more real-time approach to development; and second, as lead, to take a proactive look around at the market, the competition, and the technology, and then to suggest user solutions.

In the lead role, one of the biggest challenges facing IS management is keeping pace with changes in technology. This nowhere more evident than with distributed systems. As business users begin to take greater initiatives with technology and exercise budget powers to stay ahead, today's CIO and management team must constantly be aware of:

- *User perception.* The IS department must be a trusted partner; otherwise, a serious communications gap may develop.

- *The position of the IS department in the value chain of the corporation.* Are IS personnel maintaining a favorable position by doing what the business wants, or are they allowing the systems to stray from goals?

By making key decisions concerning the IS department, the CIO and team members will be able to align the applications portfolio with the needs of various business users, which will ensure maximum worker efficiency. In order to meet user needs, the IS organization must build a structure from which to deliver the most appropriate systems. The management plan you implement can be the determining factor in whether IS will become a profit center or a cost center in your organization.

Choosing an Architecture

As businesses evolve, they need computer architectures that match the patterns of business operations and internal structures. In other words, as human operations change and application systems develop, the computer architecture must evolve accordingly. More often now, organizations are managed as a set of collaborating units linked into a business process, as shown in Figure 5.2. The centralized command and control structure is more rare these days.

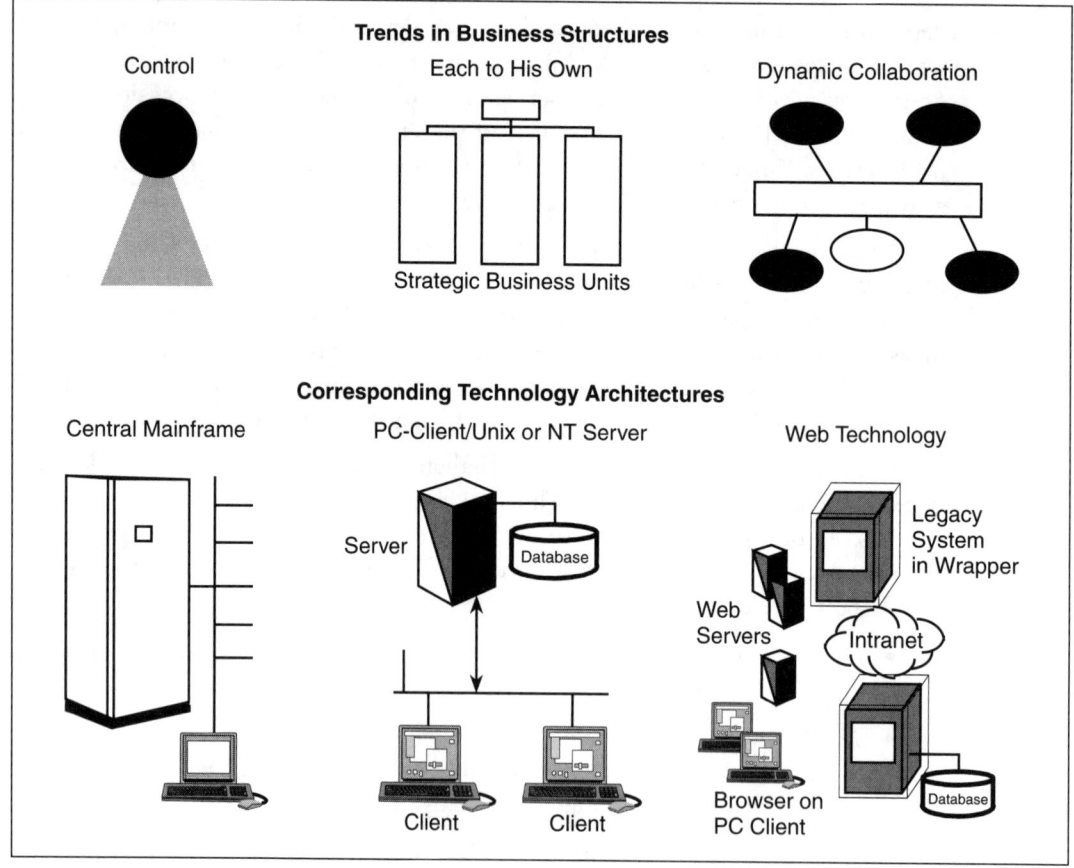

Figure 5.2 Trends in business and technology architectures.

In this context, we can look at what distributed environments offer business. Today, a distributed processing structure is the right one for most business needs because computing power fills all parts of the so-called hollow company. Distributed environments put the computing power where it is needed—where the business makes money. Not surprisingly, the majority of business processes have come to rely on some form of distributed computer power during the last 10 years, as illustrated in Table 5.1.

Table 5.1 Distributed Systems in the Business Sector

INDUSTRY	CORE PROCESSES REQUIRING DISTRIBUTED SYSTEMS
Retailing	Point of sales Supply chain with warehouse and delivery control Marketing and pricing
Manufacturing	Process control Supply chain control Distribution chain control Customer ordering
Banking and Financial Services	Retail banking (ATM networks) Trading for shares, foreign exchange rate management, etc. Settlements and consolidations EFT and bank clearing
Telecommunications and Utilities	Customer care Distribution network control and maintenance Billing
Delivery and Logistics	Customer ordering Distribution network control Vehicle location, security, and delivery tracking
Air Travel	Reservations Flight and crew scheduling

Why Distributed Systems?

In business terms—that is, as the links between the IS architecture and the corporation—this section gives a brief overview of the advantages of and reasons for using distributed systems. We start by listing five business reasons for migrating to distributed computing:

1. *To put computing power where the money is made.* When users are given flexible systems to work with, they have the autonomy they need to be productive. For example, at a car dealership, the dealer should be able to search from the desktop, on the Web or via direct links, other dealers' inventories for a customer's request for, say, a convertible model in yellow. Applications must be shaped to a business pattern of interlocking organic modules, within the corporation and externally, to seed growth markets like electronic commerce.

2. *To establish resilience and redundancy.* It is essential to provide backup computing power and backup copies of data and documents. Consider if a centralized airline reservation system goes down: Even when the hot standby (a system operating in tandem with the online system in order to take over the operational role of that system in the event of its failure) comes up, it may have only half-updated files, or transactions may have been lost.

3. *To gain a competitive advantage.* Where speed means having the competitive edge, distributed systems can help. For example, bond dealers in Tokyo, London, and New York can share price information, trade locally, and perform reconciliation processes in remote sites as disparate as Florida, the Caribbean, and India.

4. *To meet the demands of complexity.* A central scheduling system can seem like the best concept but prove to be the worst solution. For instance, in package distribution, local applications intelligence (able to process data) is needed to enter changes, accidents, and anomalies, and even to rearrange deliveries (routes, schedules, priority of service) even if coordination decisions and schedules are normally set up to be performed at a centralized, remote location. This is not quite redundancy; it's more like sharing the load. As a cautionary example, consider the major European airline that lost 20,000 pieces of baggage in a single incident when the central tracking system at its major hub failed. With a local system, branches could have continued tracking luggage in their flight areas.

5. *To create an organic model of computing.* Your model should include the ability to do the following:

> *Offer local ownership of resources.* Match specialist needs, organizational pressures, and budget control, especially where information is power. An example is warehouses, whose managers like to have their own systems, because when they have to rely on a distant central system, every time the network goes down, they are lost. With local ownership, they can control the data and its integrity.

> *Gather and share information.* Make vital information available to users throughout the organization An example is procurement. If an order has been passed by a user department, many people may be involved in the process, from authorization to ordering to tracking the delivery. A secure intranet Web-based system is ideal for sharing data on a procurement transaction.

> *Link old systems and new.* Link legacy systems and databases with the new business processes and give access across the organization. An example is customer service in telcos. Many telcos have very old back-office and accounts systems that may have to be linked into the latest customer service systems to deal with queries, as well as to external credit control checks. All of this data may be linked to a convergent billing system, for long-distance, local, mobile, CATV, and CLASS services (a must to compete in today's markets). This system uses the credit control information for specialized bill treatment depending on credit record (prepayment demands).

Why Not Distributed Systems?

Now that we've considered when and why it's beneficial to use distributed systems, it's important to consider when *not* to use the distributed computing model, when the alternatives—centralized computing power supporting only dumb terminals, or standalone systems—are wiser choices. Table 5.2 helps to make the determination.

Generally, nondistributed systems are best for situations with security problems, or for noncore functions where the feeling is: "It works well today, and it would cost more to replace it, so leave it alone." Centralizing all processing does offer greater control and is often much easier and cheaper to set up and support.

Table 5.2 Nondistributed Systems: Centralized and Standalone Functions

POSSIBLE CANDIDATE FUNCTION	SYSTEM TYPE	BENEFIT
Treasury and Corporate Finance (selected functions)	Centralized, standalone	Security
Personnel Systems (selected functions)	Standalone, standalone	Security
Utility Billing Systems	Centralized	Protect investments
Back-Office Functions, e.g., payroll	Centralized (standalone?)	Minimize training and new system overheads
Centralized Functions Sold to Outside Organizations, e.g., older airline reservation systems	Centralized	Reduce external interference, security

What Constitutes a Software Architecture?

Distributed systems tend to emphasize one of the most important concepts of a "future-proof" systems strategy: building a complete *software infrastructure*. This constitutes much more than support, it comprises a set of components from which the applications are constructed. But when we look at a total software strategy for the organization, we have to consider all areas, not just applications and their components. So when choosing an architecture, keep in mind that it must incorporate at least six components of software architecture configuration. The arrangement of these six architectural components from the standpoint of a distributed environment is shown in Figure 5.3. Both lower layers can be viewed as a set of technical services for the application components, and serve as development tools, as well as data resource support.

Objects: Why Use Them?

Although some corporations have achieved success with object technology, it has proved elusive for many others. Despite all the uproar over objects, some estimates indicate a lower success rate than predicted five years ago. Early successes were due, in part, to the fact that object technology projects were staffed only by experts, who were knowledgeable in and comfortable with key object technology concepts.

One Swedish corporation that builds electronic intelligence systems for naval vessels reduced its software costs progressively by 80 percent over a period of five years through reuse of common classes. In contrast, a major telco tried to intro-

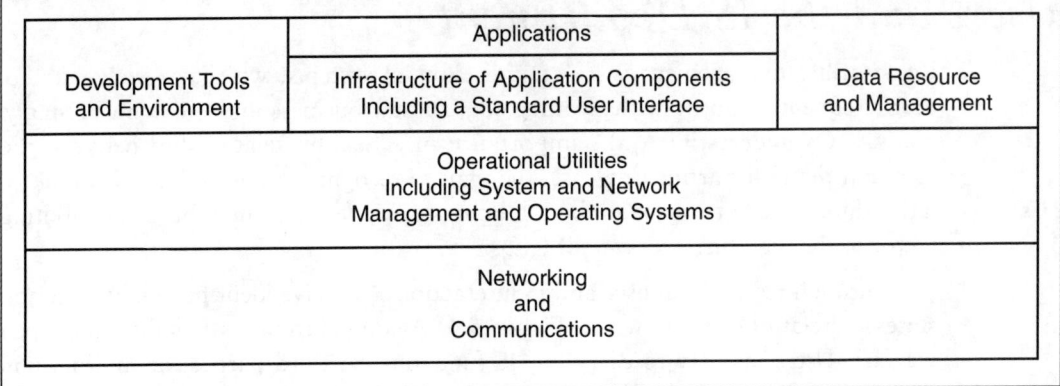

Figure 5.3 *The components of a software architecture.*

duce object-oriented programming through a series of development tools, but failed to achieve any measurable success because its programmers were not trained to think in new terms, especially of reuse, and no library of software objects was set up.

The bottom line is, object technology concepts can be used successfully for distributed systems, but they must be used with care. The sections that follow discuss how to use object technology effectively with distributed systems. Traditionally, object technology has been used in programming, but the central concepts are of most value to the business at the following three levels.

1. *The lowest level of programming.* In building applications, objects allow you to form stable "nuggets" of software. In a haphazard environment like a network, distributed systems must have parts that work consistently and provide the business with reliable systems, not a chaos of technologies. Moreover, *proven nuggets* allow reuse to flourish. The business benefits from reuse are undeniable: time-to-market for new applications can be cut by up to 80 percent.

2. *The software design level.* The concepts of divide and conquer and complexity and reuse make networking much simpler.

3. *The business process level.* Objects are invaluable for business process modeling because they can form the bridge between the users' and developers' concepts.

(Refer back to Chapter 2 for a more in-depth discussion of distributed objects in business applications.)

Users and the IS Department

Relationship management is key for distributed systems, which, as we've stated, more frequently appear at the leading edge of new business initiatives. Surprisingly, many CIOs underestimate the importance of a healthy relationship between the user and the IS department; worse, they fail to recognize a bad or deteriorating relationship. Failure to manage these relationships effectively may be a contributing factor to the high turnover rate of CIOs.

Through research on user and IS interactions, we have identified eight common states of relations, as shown in Figure 5.4. At one extreme is hostility and open warfare. Users may try to carry out IS functions via third parties, or internally in their business units, if they have budget control. At the same time, users may influence the CFO to outsource IS or to eliminate the IS department altogether. At the other extreme, the IS department is a proactive business leader, pinpointing the most beneficial advances in technology and acting to introduce them to the company.

Most IS departments, however, find themselves somewhere in the middle: The users are customers, and perhaps there is a slightly closer relationship, in which the users are treasured clients. But in both cases, the users largely determine which sys-

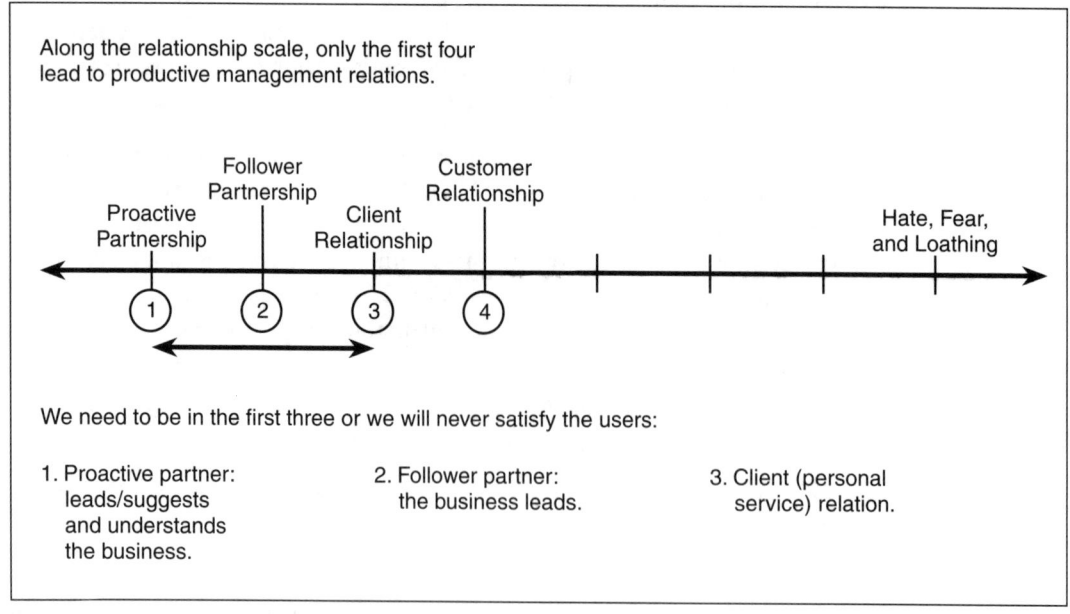

Figure 5.4 Eight models of relations between users and the IS department.

tems are required, although there is usually a gap between user and IS department decision making, instead of a collaborative process.

Understanding the End User

When the business users define needs and the IS department follows to meet their demands, it is unsatisfactory to both. This traditional situation is shown in Figure 5.5.

When business users and the IS department don't work together to build applications they come in direct conflict with business requirements, which is the effective strategic alignment between the business and the systems needs. The IS function should be to deliver and support optimal systems.

To get the tight coupling required between the IS function and the users requires understanding at three levels. Ask yourself these three questions: First, *what is the core business?* Consider your answer for now and in five years. This analysis will require board-level access to understand the corporate strategy and its systems implications. It may mean placing IS in the limelight for increased board discussion and analysis.

Second, *which needs affect systems development?* Does the company want applications developed from scratch to meet business needs, or is an off-the-shelf

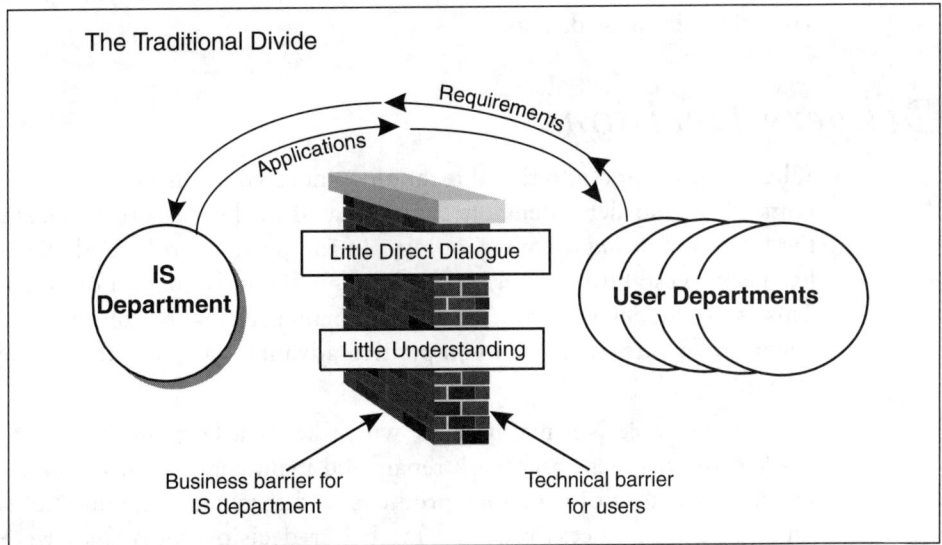

Figure 5.5 The gap between end users and the IS department.

product the expected "quick-fix" to be updated when new technology becomes available? The answer to this question is crystal clear in some industries. For instance, in telecommunications, most start-up companies want the billing system working in a matter of weeks—any CIO who suggests development from scratch will not be around to collect the annual bonus.

Third, *which needs define the systems?* Ask this question when the action is in the business units, because capturing their requirements is essential. Unfortunately, such information gathering demands teamwork and business skills not available in many IS departments (financial services industries usually representing the exception that proves the rule). Moreover, cross-functional systems will extend across several business units and may require particular diplomacy to unearth real requirements and elicit cooperation. In the next section, we look at approaches to deal with cross-departmental system requirements.

At the root of the three-question approach is understanding the corporate culture and "mental phase of development" of the use of information technology. In addition, you must be able to identify the key functions of each separate business unit. For instance, in any telco, the business customer service division has to be able to individually tailor offerings for the 100 top accounts. In contrast, the residential customer service division must serve the mass market and still offer individualized customer services (call interrupt, voice mail, etc.) at a low cost. The systems needs differ considerably, but too few CIO and senior IS staff recognize the business demands behind their differences. The lesson is simple: protect your job by listening carefully to business demands.

Delivery Decisions

What software and additional technology does your business need? The business units—being so dependent on computing of all kinds—are increasingly taking the lead in choosing new technology. In the past, the role of the IS department has been to establish strategy, especially for the introduction of new technology. This is no longer the case. Enterprise managers are far more technologically adept and aware—and gain competitive advantage in their field by agile use of technology.

One example is a major telco, which keeps a large inventory of every part stocked for emergency network repair and maintenance. This is in addition to a massive inventory of telephone products sold through its tie-in retail shop chain. Operating this process required far better decision tools than were currently available to middle management, especially as the business expanded. The business managers selected the solution which involved a decision on whether to try out new technology. The IS department neither found a solution, or made the hard decisions on implementation, as detailed in the example below.

Capturing User Requirements

To make good delivery decisions, you must have a thorough understanding of user requirements and the business environment. The question is how to close the gap between user requirements and system shortcomings? Traditionally, development has followed the linear, or waterfall, approach, by which a user request (usually not fully understood) is presented, a conceptual design is fashioned, a detailed design follows, and then coding begins. Overlooked requirements are added piecemeal for later integration and testing. Inevitably, these fail.

You cannot afford to risk that functions, the operating system, or the business role of application systems will fail, or will no longer fit the bill after a short period of time. Moreover, testing at the end of a development project always spells trouble. For example, a postdevelopment test proved a company's new network was a hundred times too slow, the server was not sized correctly, and that the number of pages requested per user in the new intranet application was far greater than expected. As a result, the system failed at 40 users, instead of supporting 4,000, as planned.

A Data Warehouse Example

A company needed the capability to track deliveries and manage inventory in its two national warehouses, as well as to track tied-up capital, deliveries in hand, and supplier performance, including the freight transports. The business unit had a large number of legacy systems, some dating back ten years on accounts, inventory, and orders; it also had a set of warehouse systems in each warehouse, none of which could tell management its current position, stock-outs, shrinkage, and so on. To bring together old and new data in a decision support system (DSS), with a dashboard for executive information systems, statistics, and reporting, the company had to find a new approach. The business unit (not IS) decided on a data warehouse solution. The IS department was then asked to respond. The data warehouse solution was constructed very quickly using rapid development techniques, with a new technology on top: a customizable DSS package for a PC server. The whole system was available in nine months.

Approach

For distributed systems you need a faster approach, more directly linked to the business. Many successful fast-to-market applications are being developed using *joint application development* (JAD). JAD captures user requirements in a far more detailed and business-aware manner. It forms one part of a development method we discuss shortly, a faster development path known as *rapid application development* (RAD). JAD is a subtle and fairly difficult process, and usually requires the support of outside experts to initiate and run. But it is the only way to get a complex system's working requirements identified quickly and accurately. As a part of RAD, JAD helps to contribute to up to 80 percent reductions in time and development costs. JAD has, for example, cut a four-year project to four months.

Using JAD, you create groups of key users who know the application area and how the business will use the application; they are in the same workshop or working area as the developers from IS. These users should have the ability to see changes in processes, not just in today's practices. More important, users (and developers) in the JAD process must be empowered to decide where the application will change current (or even create new) processes.

The basics of successful JAD is an entirely new psychological relationship at both the individual and managerial levels, between business users and IS. The elements of this relationship depend on constructing a cultural bridge between the two sides—which may be a major shock to both. This bridge is built during a series on intense work sessions.

Special people are required for JAD to work; one key player is the JAD session facilitator, who is facilitated by technical scribes who note everything and prepare the decision documents. JAD works only when a level playing field for capturing requirements has been laid; that is, all those knowledgeable about the business processes, whether a VP or a mail-room junior, must have equal say. A good session facilitator assures equal and effective communication. Groupware tools, enabling everyone in the session to make suggestions (anonymously) on an electronic whiteboard can also be beneficial by eliminating "intimidation by rank."

But the process of understanding and implementing JAD is as much about learning what *not* to do. Following are some JAD "don'ts":

- *Don't fail to get top management's strong commitment.* JAD requires effort, time, and money, and takes staff (over which IS has no control) away from their core tasks. The process must take precedence over other business preoccupations, which often is an issue with top management support.

- *Don't have a weak facilitator.* The facilitator must be very knowledgeable and diplomatic, yet forceful to ensure that no one person dominates a session. The facilitator must also be well-trained in order to guide the JAD sessions to their ultimate goals. (Having a backup facilitator is a good idea, to prevent burnout.)

- *Don't fail to get the best people available into JAD sessions.* Out of your JAD sessions come the requirements. What goes into the session are people and their ideas; if they are deficient, your application will be, too. That said, don't insist that these people attend all sessions as a full-time commitment, or you will risk having half-hearted interest.

- *Don't fail to prepare a detailed agenda for each session.* This should include requirements to be captured and definitions to be made; and make sure the language of this agenda is at a business (not a technical) level. The aforementioned technical scribe should be an ace at capturing, writing, and quickly structuring, because she or he will be the main author of your deliverables, the requirements documents, with its screens, business logic flows, and calculations, which should appear later the same day for distribution.

- *Don't listen to the wrong people.* Listen to the people who work the business processes every day, not those in the corporate structure too far removed from daily practices to really know the ins and outs of these.

To Buy or to Build

For CIOs and CFOs everywhere, determining whether to buy or build is the biggest decision they will make regarding IS. And this is a decision that must be made repeatedly because the shape of the business is constantly changing. Furthermore, the decision has expanded from software considerations, and now includes:

- Application packages versus internal software development.
- Human resources; contract personnel versus full-time employees.
- Whether to outsource the whole corporate IS function.
- Whether to outsource some services for the IS department operations (e.g., data center operations), or for the core business (e.g., computerized bill printing in a utility).

All these decisions are related; how much you buy dictates whether you even need an IS department! If you decide you do, the build or buy decisions also dictate what shape the department will take, whether or not it will contain application development capability, for example.

We consider packages and outsourcing decisions in greater detail a little later. For software and human resources, the build or buy decision is dictated not only by the firm's business position now and in the future, but by the realities of the market: Can you find (and keep) the software skills you need to build your specialized applications. Once found, is the better strategy to buy the one (skills) or the other (applications) into the organization?

Determining whether to contract software staff (rather than go with some form of outsourcing) is often a question of culture. In telecommunications, one large operator (with 30 million customers) has an IS department of 6,000. Another of similar revenue size has an IS department of only 1,700, but contracts another 4,000. Which model is best? For some companies, as a matter of tradition and culture, most staff are employed internally. When financial realities bite, you may be forced to build an IS department that is highly dependent on contract staff—but that falls just short of total outsourcing. Just be aware that when you use contract software staff, you must manage not only staff but suppliers as well.

Generally, IS departments with high ratios of contract staff have the following characteristics.

- A far higher rate of loss of knowledge about the applications and databases, because the staff are transient.
- Poor continuity between dependent projects.
- Difficulties in project management because staff have disparate loyalties and lack a sense of corporate spirit.
- Increased payroll costs per person (although this can be the reverse in certain highly paid corporations).
- Difficulties in assigning responsibilities to external staff.

However, the CFO sees the following results: lower fixed costs in payroll, greater labor flexibility, highly paid and exceptional skills are available on an as-needed basis, more "assignability" and better tracking of costs by project.

Making the Outsourcing Decision

Contracting out to meet all, or some, IS requirements is increasingly viewed as an advantageous strategy. (Note: The actual process is considered in detail in Chapter 7.) Often seen as a euphemism for cutting costs, the decision is in fact far more complex. In the realm of distributed systems, outsourcing takes on a new meaning. It is a way for large and small organizations to control geographically dispersed resources; manage the onslaught of new technology that the business needs but that the capital budget may not be able to support; and obtain deep technical expertise on the latest distributed processing technologies, skills that are becoming increasingly scarce (such people are attracted to the specialist outsourcing companies since the career path is wider than that in a corporation, whose main concern is, say, banking or tire production).

Outsourcing in particular has strong appeal in those corporate circumstances whose needs extend beyond technical considerations to include a change in competitive scope. Such companies are:

- Those globalizing rapidly, and therefore requiring sophisticated support overseas, where today they have nothing. A working global infrastructure is third on the list of management prerogatives when expanding overseas, after a suitable economy and political situation and availability of a skilled workforce.

- Those that want to absorb new companies and integrate them technically, but need to concentrate resources on the acquisitions and subsequent mergers, leaving technology to others.

- Those forming numerous industry partnerships; for example, with the supply chain in the manufacturing industries.

- Those whose current IS setup is weak or very limited and must immediately expand it to become competitive in terms of technology, costs, reliability, capacity, or new skills.

Dealing with the Past

As noted in earlier chapters, most organizations have extensive legacy systems, which cannot be replaced overnight for one or more of the following reasons: too often they are core systems and thus cannot be shut down; they work, at least in the way the organization used to work, and sometimes still does today; they are monolithic, complex, and mysterious, whose original logic is lost in time; the operating environment is a large expensive data center, for centralized hosts, with a large attendant staff who themselves pose a change problem.

Typically the legacy system is specific in function, devoted to a single segment of a business process; often it runs on a large mainframe, using a software technology that is 10 to 25 years old. The majority of large U.S. corporations still depend on IBM CICS transaction processors and have IMS data files, the latter often attached to systems running in batch mode. Combined, these factors limit legacy systems in evolutionary potential. The result: Most large organizations today are slowly spending many millions or billions of dollars over 5 to 10 years to escape from yesterday's systems.

Solutions for Legacy Systems

Is there a way forward out of this quandary? Many corporations can find a solution from the following list:

1. Give the application a midlife boost by adding a new front end to gain a simpler, friendlier end-user interface, which may be on a PC client.

2. Rewrite all or some of the logic for a new platform, without the limitations (reliability, unfriendliness, batch use, centralized operations).

3. If the functions are no longer part of the core business, wall off the legacy systems from the mission-critical systems, and leave them to whither and die. Outsourcing support may be an option here.

4. Replace the legacy system with a package covering 75 percent of the old functionality but on a new platform, with logic that better meets current needs.

5. Repackage and integrate the system as a data or information server for the single dedicated function of the current application whose architecture then serves as an input to the next generation of systems. This is especially useful for databases.

6. Integrate as part of a larger function set in a new application, as one component.

7. Extend base functionality by adding a new application system.

8. Replicate the system on new platforms (again, as a server) to offer distributed and perhaps transactional operations from a previous batch centralized system.

Legacy People and Legacy Thinking

Instead of "legacy," you'll hear major corporation call their Jurassic systems "cherished." In so doing, they extend value not only to the systems, but to the staff who maintain them and who may often be crucial to the organization.

We've said that such systems usually indicate a need for change. But does this apply to the people who maintain the systems, too? The answer is, yes and no. Yes, when the mind-set as well as the skills have to be updated. If, for example, the normal mode of thinking is to switch all transactions via the central mainframe, a better architecture with a new remote Web server and PCs with browsers (that may also access some mainframe facilities) will not even be considered. So the design has to be by people who will have this wider vision of solutions.

However, the answer is "no" if the selected solution requires maintaining cherished systems of some form—the people should not change. And furthermore a line of succession, to hand on knowledge, must be planned.

For instance, in cases where the mainframe is retained as a large server, or wrappers are added around existing mainframe applications, the value of cherished developers is unquestioned, and they should be rewarded accordingly. In other architectures, where the mainframe applications have to be walled off, alternative scenarios must be considered, such as:

- Outsource the staff in some form of facilities management deal to an environment where their skills have more of a future.

- Retrain for new roles and new technologies. This can have a much higher success rate than many expect, resulting in up to 70 percent reuse of staff.

- Prepare for outplacement. If the cherished staff have to be downsized, the most successful operations offer reskilling packages prior to the outplacement phase. Such programs limit separation costs and can make the whole process humane and manageable, with lower legal risks.

One final note. Legacy systems, software standards, and people are not one-time issues. They are elements in an ongoing corporate process in market evolution. Systems and staff must be implemented with this in mind; plan for change, because in one way or another, we are always escaping from yesterday's systems.

Choosing and Tailoring Packages

Packages can offer a quick solution to many crucial IS problems. In a distributed environment, a server with a package can give the whole organization new functionality in weeks, perhaps even overnight. For some businesses, using them is the only way forward. In telecommunications, for example, customer care and billing packages are almost the only way to get to market fast, especially for the new mobile operators, resellers, and late entrants to the market. And the major incumbent telecom operators, with their large specially developed billing applications or highly customized packages, often suffer from legacy system problems and cannot afford the expense either in terms of money or time to create from scratch.

Package catalogues defined by industry and by function present a numbing array of choices, and evaluating them all requires close study and field testing for performance and functionality, perhaps in conjunction with reviews of existing installations. Generally, there are two strategies to take when considering using packages:

- Choose a number of different packages from different vendors for point solutions. These must be integrated into other applications, whether built in-house or using additional off-the-shelf packages. The PC environment is a case in point: Spreadsheets are often used to front-end much bigger applications built in-house.

- Use a large integrated generic package, such as those from the SAP company with their R3 family of packaged business process applications and others to cover a whole range of functions and provide an applications infrastructure.

Here are some rules of thumb to follow when considering packages in a distributed environment:

- Point applications are often successful functions for packages, where the function is well defined and package choice is wide. These include human resources, accounts, payroll, and sales support.

- Look for solution examples to those industries that have a tradition of integrating complete package solutions, such as billing and customer care in telecommunications, or MRP II in manufacturing.

Generic Packages

The boundary dividing those companies that use or don't use packages is blurring thanks to the success of the major customizable generic packages that cover a wide range of core functions, including production, inventory, accounts, suppliers, and customer deliveries—such as SAP R3. Most such packages have either mainframe or client server versions for Unix servers and Microsoft Windows NT servers with PC clients.

But when considering generic packages, be aware of four major factors impacting implementation:

1. Generic packages are highly complex and so may require two to three years to install. This is not just a software installation; establishing the package becomes a major IS project over this period and usually involves the users and their knowledge of the business processes.

2. Generic packages may change the core processes' operations, as they often contain an inherent business model, which forces commonality in all affected areas. In the chemicals and pharmaceuticals industries, where strong common IS controls over many research and manufacturing processes and production sites are a key to success, generic packages have become popular.

3. Database definitions and structures all may have to be changed to align with the package's data requirements. But the biggest problems

can be political—dealing with the "data druids" who protect and feed the corporate data repositories.

4. Decisions made on installation can be binding for many years, so systems' agility for the business may have to be sacrificed. However, generic package vendors are moving to balance customization with standardization by the selection of components. For example, Baan's (from the Netherlands) Triton product uses the object technology approach to customize through component selection. Other vendors such as Marcam (Waltham, Massachusetts) sell an enterprise resource-planning package, Protean, that offers customization by selection of objects (more than 2,000 classes), as well as an inherent business model.

To sum up, IS managers can use packages to quickly acquire functionality, acquire industry-best practices within one package, and reduce development and maintenance costs and risks.

These advantages must be balanced against these potential disadvantages:

- The solution offered by the package may be okay for today, but not for tomorrow; it may not be upgradeable, meaning you could be stuck with yesterday's decision for several years.

- Packages, at best, are only an approximate fit, usually containing 50 to 80 percent of required functions.

- You may become strategically dependent upon the quality and financial health of the supplier; if the package is critical and the supplier fails to deliver, your enterprise could be at risk.

- Packages tend to impose a data architecture, and thus may be difficult (or impossible) to interface to existing systems and networks, and therefore will require significant tailoring and integration effort. These efforts may have to extend to getting inputs and outputs right.

- User staff may require retraining, as a package may impose a different user-interface technology.

- Because packages are available to all competitors, they may offer little competitive advantage.

Getting the Best from Generic Packages

When using a point solution package, the following suggestions will help you achieve greater success and flexibility in a distributed environment.

- Use the corporate business model to select your package. This means understanding time-to-market for the function to be supported; fit to users' needs, now and in three years' time; possibility of reuse of the package's functions and data. The actual methodology may dictate that some of the functions in a package will not be at all useful; however, that is not necessarily a reason for rejecting it, as it may contain certain critical functions which you can use and forget the rest.

- In a distributed environment, turn the package function into a service that can be shared across the organization and other applications. The service then forms one application component within the application architecture.

To be effective with these suggestions, you have to choose a package that is both open and flexible. Today "open" implies not just industry standards for programming (an applications programming interface, API), network, and database access, but for Web capabilities as well. This means perhaps more than TCP/IP/HTTP connections for browser interface/HTML page generation; it means using the standards developed by consortia of package vendors—the Open Applications Group (OAG) in particular. The OAG is concentrating on APIs and a standard electronic document for interchanges between packages—the business object document (BOD) and its model (BODM)—which incorporates commands for actions, plus synchronization, as well as data based on the RPC and the CORBA concepts. A BOD may be issued for a particular industry or function; for example, there is one enabling general ledger packages to take transactions from inventory packages.

More common today is a new theme on the package concept, templates, highly parameterizable packages that offer flexibility, although they do require more work to get operational. Templates are similar to generic customizable packages, but tend to focus on one process or a process set in a single industry—for example, on the customer support, billing, and network operations in gas utilities. Templates offer a smart compromise for business systems agility, as the user can hit near 90 percent functionality in weeks to months of customizing. (An extension of this idea, which we discuss more later, is object sets for a particular industry process.)

Development Methods

Traditionally, teams have developed applications in a linear process—from a functional specification given by the user department to conceptual design through detailed design, coding, integrating, and testing. At the end of a period from six months to many years, many teams had to abandon such projects, because they were not getting anywhere, or were way over budget, and/or failed to meet users' current needs. Despite a mass of "structured methodologies" (all with tongue-twisting acronyms/names such as SSADM, SADT, Merise) and techniques described as "egoless programming," statistics suggest that 50 percent of projects are around 180 percent or more over budget (for an accumulated cost of more than $60 billion) while 30 percent of new software projects are canceled before completion (at a total cost of around $80 billion).

Rapid Application Development

There is an alternative approach to development. This new technique, while aimed at faster development, actually saves time and money as well, while reducing risks, and therefore preventing project cancellations. It's the aforementioned rapid application development (RAD). Is it right for your company? Probably, if it falls into one of the following categories:

- Projects where user satisfaction is critical, and fit to user specifications must be accurate.
- Mission-critical systems where risk of failure must be minimized.
- Small and large projects where time is of the essence.

RAD, however, generates major pressure and requires support from top management in the user community. RAD is seen as inappropriate for highly technical, precision-driven projects such as real-time industrial controls or telecommunications network management, since RAD advances in approximate steps. (But note, this view is being challenged now since multiple trials have shown precise fit and viability in highly complex technical solutions.)

The overall aim of RAD is to produce maximum functionality within a strictly limited development time frame. RAD uses "timeboxes" to enforce deadlines. The 80 percent success rate is shown in Figure 5.6.

RAD is a radical departure from tradition. Users communicate with developers in a specially designed environment guided by carefully chosen new players in development, each taking a specific role. Users are involved throughout the joint applications development (JAD) cycles, including:

- Planning, in joint requirements planning sessions (JRP).
- User requirements capture (JRC) sessions.
- Testing and critiquing of the results of development; that is, a set of prototypes.

RAD has been conceptualized as a step-by-step process which "spirals" in ever decreasing circles onto the completed solution. Figure 5.7 illustrates the spiral.

RAD is successful because it manages risk so well. How? With its iterative cycles, RAD is equivalent to taking a short step, seeing where you are, then advancing

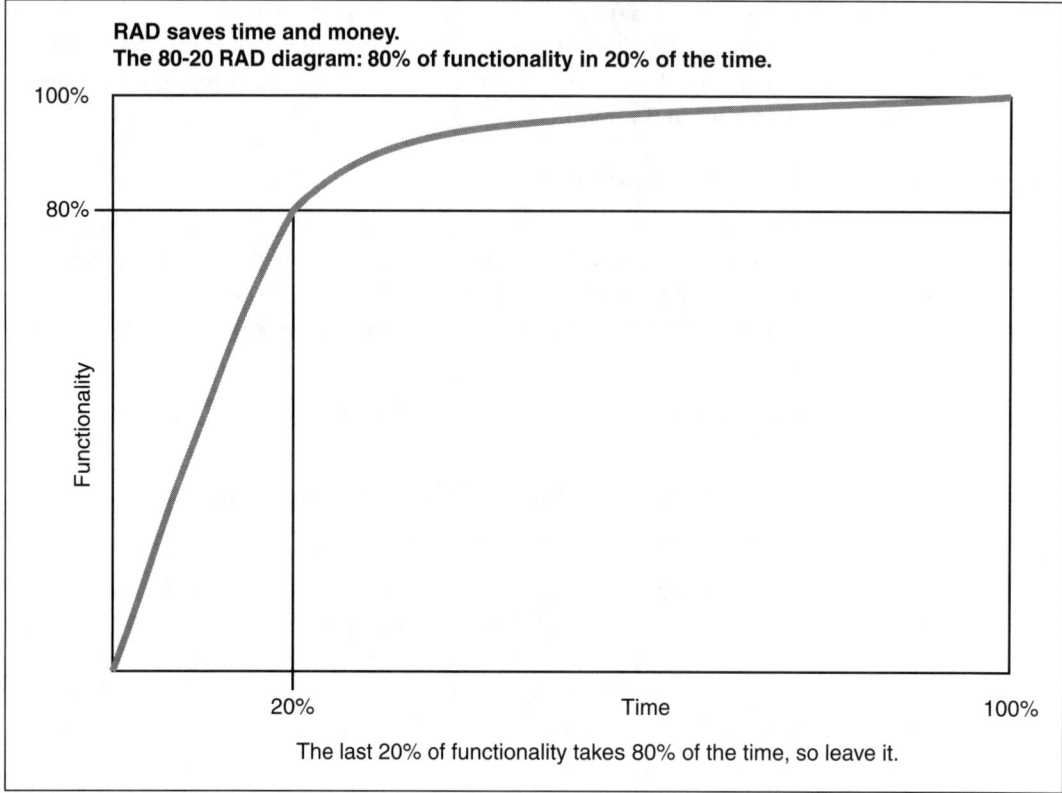

RAD saves time and money.
The 80-20 RAD diagram: 80% of functionality in 20% of the time.

Figure 5.6 RAD usage accelerates delivery time typically by 80 percent.

over another small piece of the task, always taking stock with a prototype that indicates your final working version. Then you start again. Figure 5.8 illustrates iterative development.

When RAD fails, often it is for reasons different from those occurring with many traditional approaches (e.g., failure of technical design, failure to really listen to the users, or lack of project direction). RAD may fail for reasons that are subliminal in traditional projects, but become explicit in RAD development, that is, the psychology of teams. Using RAD creates a real pressure cooker, especially for developers. Poor team dynamics and structuring become evident in the first month, and it is psychology—aimed at motivation and team structuring—that leads to repair and recovery. Psychological factors have always been the keys to successful software development; but it is only since timely software has gained importance that the power of team development has come to the forefront, and

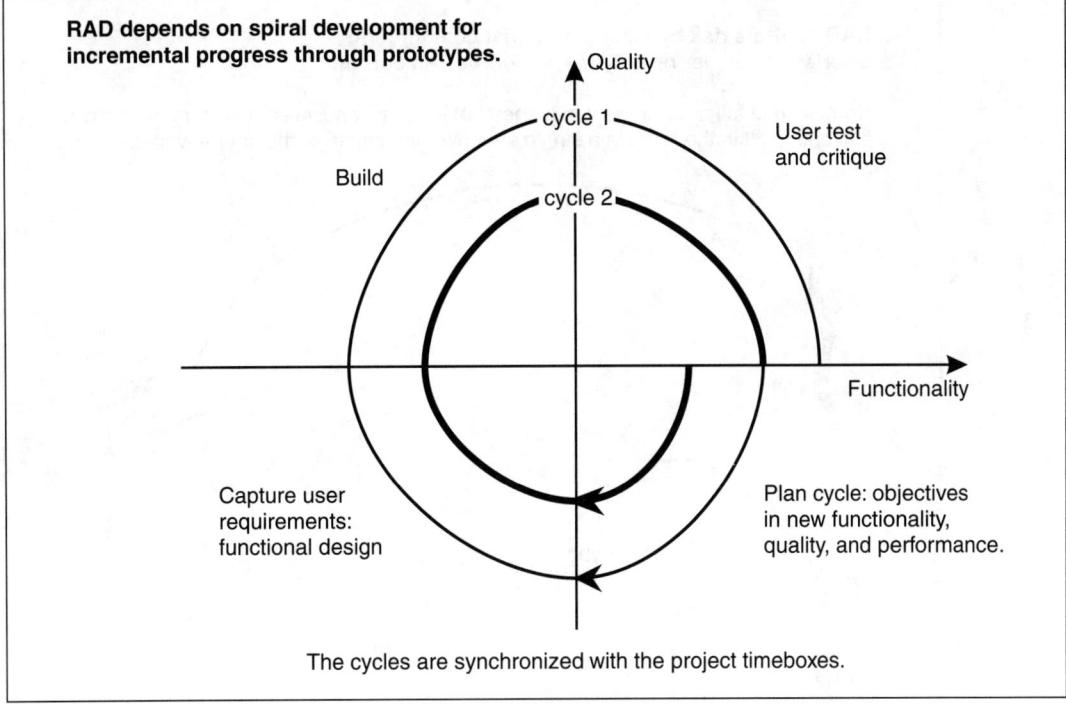

RAD depends on spiral development for incremental progress through prototypes.

Quality

cycle 1

cycle 2

Build

User test and critique

Functionality

Capture user requirements: functional design

Plan cycle: objectives in new functionality, quality, and performance.

The cycles are synchronized with the project timeboxes.

Figure 5.7 The RAD spiral development cycle.

more expressive team development techniques have replaced earlier repressive methodologies.

Organization of the IS Function

We have left organization of the IS function until the end of the chapter because the structure of the organization must follow its functions and weaknesses, not the other way around. Otherwise, organizational functionality and strength will be constrained by structure.

In distributed environments, the IS department must be organized to cope with dispersed decisions regarding the implementation of new systems in the business units, a far wider range of skills, and perhaps new user relationships, because the systems are placed more in these units and less in the data centers. Understanding the culture of the organization must be part of the IS department's structuring. Specialized skills must be accumulated in response to external pressures of markets, industry, legislation, and so on. Nowadays, absorbing computing technologies from

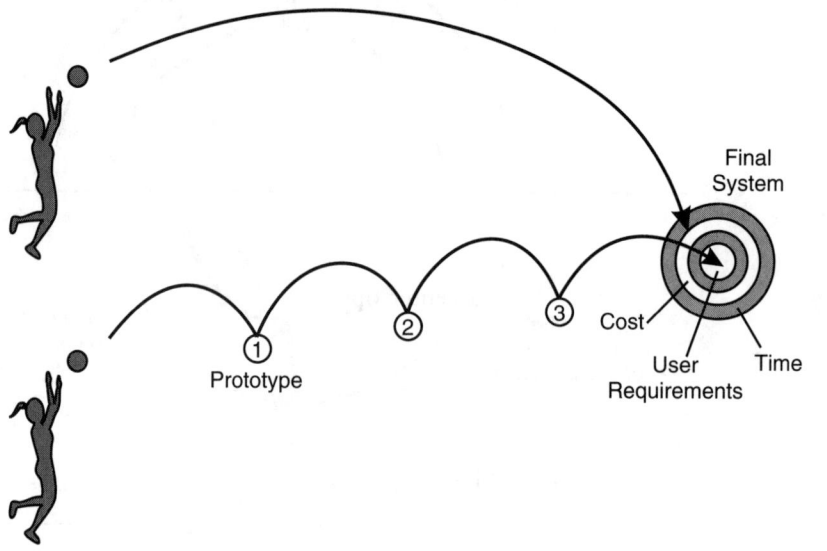

**RAD controls risk by aiming at a final goal through
a series of smaller prototypes, which we can correct.**

Normal waterfall development is a one-shot process, equivalent to having to throw a
ball and get it in the hoop in a single shot over the length of the court—very high risk

Final
System

③ Cost

② Time

① User

Prototype Requirements

RAD manages risk via a series of shorter steps with an evaluation of performance,
functionality, and quality in terms of user requirements at each step; thus errors can
be corrected as the occur, while strict control of time in timeboxes ensures on-time
delivery of the key functions.

Figure 5.8 RAD *helps to control risk through iterative development.*

the users, whether they come from ATM networks in banking or Web technology in
marketing, must also form part of the natural behavior of IS.

Goals for the future (dictating the new IS organization) should include the following:

- Understanding of the core business and its technologies.

- Support of the core business, in a partnering role.

- Flexibility, to accommodate new business, technology, architectures, and integration of more external resources, including outside experts and outsourced partners for specialist roles such as data center operations.

- Creativity.

- Proactive attitudes.

- People development (to broaden skills and increase flexibility).

To plan for the future, many IS departments are instituting a process-based IS structure. The new organization model requires: an innovation process, planning, development, user support maintenance and service provisions, and infrastructure management/technical support/standards.

New types of operatives will replace the old pools of programmers/analysts/ project managers, up to 10 to 20 percent of development staff, and as much as 80 to 90 percent on maintenance of existing applications. New basic building blocks of the IS department will include teams (especially for RAD); centers of expertise for RAD, networking, database, client server, Web technology, application services and infrastructure, data center operations, and applications by business unit; and consultants to the users.

Core activities will move away from pure development and maintenance to building an application infrastructure, with reusable components and services. The IS department, as a knowledge-based organization with project work, would bene-fit greatly from adopting a team-based organization, coordinated by human re-source managers, with several types of teams, organized according to the following criteria:

- Expertise with tools, networking, database, maintenance, and so on.

- Cross-functional process, such as billing and customer service.

- Function, including accounts, marketing, sales.

- Strategic business unit (SBU); for example, by "customer" department.

- Goal task forces with specific missions.

- Team type mixing, with short and long lifetimes.

The result of the new team structure is shown in Figure 5.9. This structure is organized around the three work entities: processes, work teams, and centers of ex-cellence and expertise.

Conclusions

In summary, this chapter has captured some quite complex managerial concepts which include such things as an examination of the place information systems have in company operations both today and tomorrow. A review of the role of the IS de-

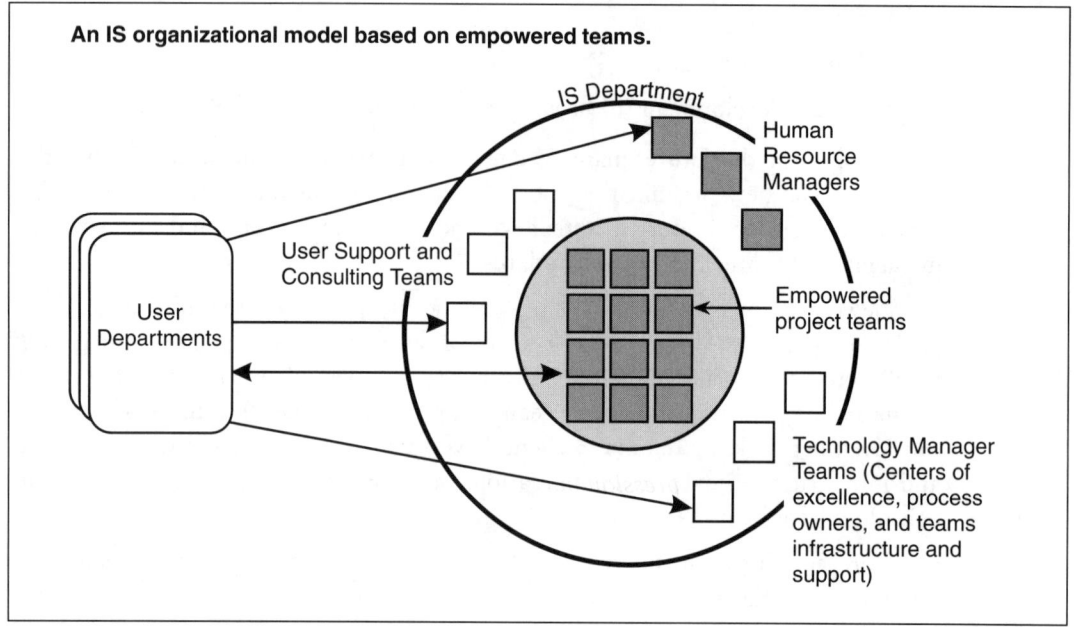

Figure 5.9 *Structure of the IS department of the future.*

partment in relation to the business, the possibility of a new IS department structure, as well as reasons for choosing distributed systems. We examined at the macro-level the IS relationship with user departments, its quality, and the role that implies for IS. Finally, we provided a discussion of some new approaches for managing user relationships at a micro-level, as well as techniques for capturing user requirements. These form the background for Chapter 6, in which we examine how management roles will be redefined for distributed systems.

FOR FURTHER READING

McConnell, Steve. *Rapid Development.* (Redmond, WA: Microsoft Press), 1996.

Wood, Jane and Denise Silver. *Joint Application Development.* (New York: John Wiley & Sons, Inc.), 1995.

6 THE MANAGEMENT LANDSCAPE

His expression may often be called bald ... but it is bald as the bare mountain tops are bald, with a baldness full of grandeur.

Matthew Arnold, *Essays in Criticism* Second Series (1888)

This chapter:

Explains distributed management modeling, including management tasks, functions, and services.

Defines management elements: the hardware and software that interact in a management system for a distributed network.

Identifies methods for identifying and categorizing system elements.

Describes the tasks that management tools perform.

Presents an overview of events: recording, reporting, handling.

The move to distributed environments in conjunction with increasing business and competitive pressures mandate a maximum return on every invested effort and resource. Understanding how, why, and what happens in distributed management and the underlying distributed environment is essential for business managers and technical staff who must work together to find the right network solutions. Vendors now explain their product technologies so that the business consumer and the technical implementation staff can work cooperatively to apply them. The explosive emergence of service-level management, service-level agreements, business process views, and applications management attest to the genuine efforts by vendors to address current problems.

Distributed technology development staff and business managers understand that the vendor products they choose must solve business problems. The widespread use of Internet technologies have familiarized some business managers with distributed environments, but to many, network operations and management are still mysterious. Understanding the network and management functions will help you, as an IS decision maker, to position vendors, evaluate alternative solutions, and discuss the underlying solution technologies with your staff.

The Distributed Management Model

Designing and managing distributed systems is a complex task requiring the creative application of the experience, knowledge, and abilities of system planners and developers. However, creative freedom may also cause confusion, chaos, and redundancy. Standards and models help to focus efforts without unduly limiting creativity.

Models separate well-defined tasks into broad categories of functions and services. They give tool and platform providers an architectural standard to guide development efforts for complementary and integrateable solutions. Standards guide layout, data format, data inclusion, interfaces, and so on, and allow different, independently developed tools to interact.

Many models have been proposed to formally define the architectures, functions, and approaches to building and maintaining a network for distributed managers. The OSI seven-layer model described in Chapter 1 characterizes the structure of the network, defining how information is communicated and connections are made when linking systems and devices in a network. This seven-layer model provides a valuable framework for discussing and understanding communications between systems, as well as the allocation of tasks to implement interconnection within a network. This holds true even though the details of the implementation by individual vendors vary significantly.

NOTE

If a vendor product differs in detail from the OSI model, the differences are usually well documented and explained.

OSI models have proven particularly useful in demonstrating the need for standards and standardized implementation interfaces for network communication. The influence of these models is reflected in everything done in distributed computing, ranging from the design of applications to the measurement of network device and system element performance.

Models help break down complex tasks into easily understood parts. By explicitly identifying the series of tasks, functions, or activities that taken collectively achieve a result, models enable us to concentrate on these incremental steps to success. Models allow us to understand and, hopefully, improve the understanding, efficiency, and effectiveness of complex tasks. This improved understanding allows for better decision making in the selection among competing products, the implementation of solutions, and so forth.

The task of managing distributed networks and systems provides an opportunity to acquire understanding through modeling. Dividing the complex process of management into smaller agreed-upon steps and activities benefits developers, vendors, and users. By differentiating between standards, shared tasks, and specific management functions, developers can focus their ingenuity on areas that will provide clear competitive advantage. By clearly defining tasks and functions, vendors can articulate their unique advantage. Finally, placing a "stake in the ground" definition of management and the constituent tasks allows the users (purchasers as well as operators) to evaluate and compare various solutions. In the next section we discuss an OSI model for distributed management.

Building the Management Model

The OSI management model gives us three standards for management service:

- *Management functional areas.* Generic management *objectives* applied to any managed entity.

- *Management functions.* Generic *tasks* or actions performed in management functional areas.

- *Management services.* Low-level *commands* executed to carry out management functions.

These three standards build on one another. For example, performance management is an *objective* that *tasks* such as alarm reporting and event handling perform to monitor and report on how resources are being used. These functions use low-level *command* services such as GET (information about a resource) and CREATE (an event report). See Figure 6.1.

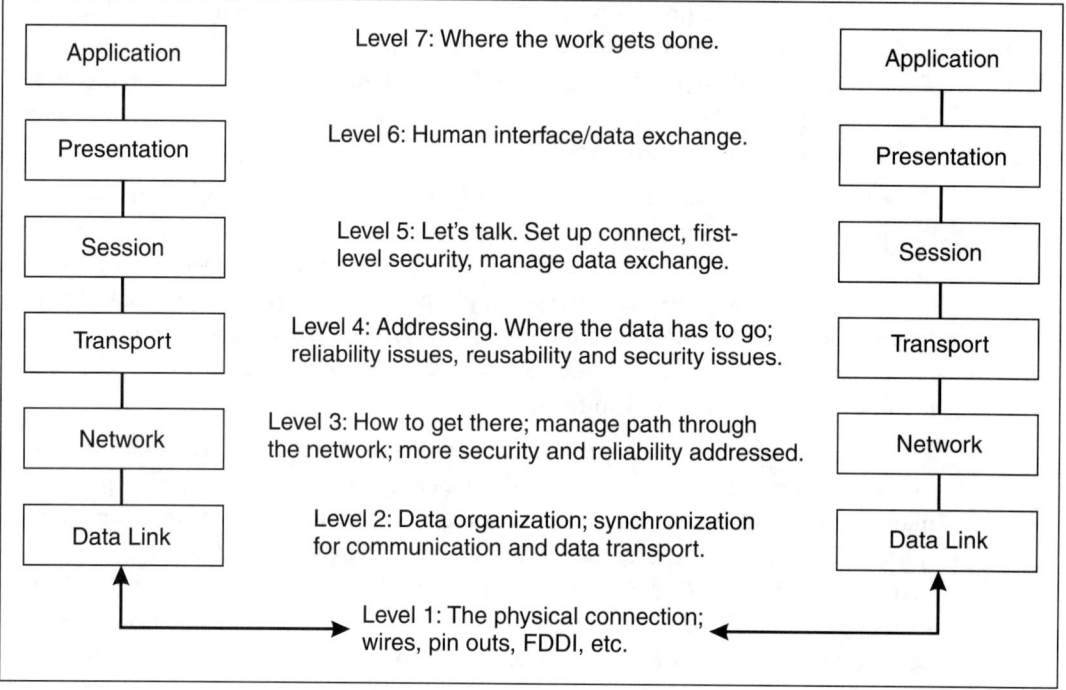

Figure 6.1 The OSI model and management.

Management Tasks

Management functional areas specify the primary management tasks. These are generic tasks that can be applied to any managed system, device, or service. The ISO has defined specific areas of management functionality and services as part of its OSI model. Included in the OSI model are the following functional areas.

Fault Management This area accounts for tools that report problems, record problem occurrence, and initiate and track corrective action. The level of functionality varies with purchaser, product, and vendor; in one, it may be sufficient to simply record and report an event or fault, whereas in other instances, fault management must include a whole sequence of actions. The system must notify users and schedule and track corrective processes by monitoring the creation and use of a shared database of problems, causes, resolution procedures, and time taken to resolve the problem.

Complete fault management requires greater investment, but will pay off by reducing repair time or by preventing problems altogether. A comprehensive fault management system also reduces costs by educating users about common problem resolution so that expensive support staff can be put to better use.

Asset Management Asset management includes tools that collect data needed for tracking, accounting, and managing hardware, software, and system resources. The data collected may be as simple as an itemized list of asset serial numbers, purchase dates, and prices, or as complicated as an automated monitoring and recording system that periodically checks for and records changes to the managed devices, providing the resulting data to accounting as well as other applications.

Configuration Management In this area are the tools that collect and record data about settings, capacities, and states of managed devices. Configuration management tools also provide device-descriptive data like serial numbers, and collect network configuration data (how and where a device fits into the network). These tools can track and record data-detailing support arrangements, including contact information; some will even accumulate inventory and accounting information and feed it to asset management and accounting applications.

Performance Management Performance management tools collect information that reveals how efficiently and completely devices, systems, networks, and even applications are being utilized. The most common tools available collect and report performance information on the monitored systems and devices in isolation. Reporting occurs on processor or disk capacity utilization, response times for transactions, traffic rates, and densities for networks or switch times. However, integrated performance information (performance of recognizable business transactions) is far more interesting to systems and business administrators. The ability to record, report, and tune the performance of the monthly billing process, for example, is far more useful than producing records of disk utilization or transactions per second. The standards, processes, and products necessary to support such tracking have begun to appear.

Security Management Security management tools provide access control, authentication, integrity, and confidentiality. Security tools check user permission to access systems and functions, verify user identification, protect data and files from corruption, and put mechanisms in place to prevent unauthorized capture and reading of data during transmission.

Traditionally, management functional areas have not been fully integrated in most systems for three main reasons:

1. Systems and network management are treated as separate disciplines.

2. Management ability has been restricted to monitoring and controlling individual hardware and systems elements.

3. Management interest has focused on the performance of individual devices.

Individual solution vendors have started to include each of the functional areas as an integral, portable element of their total product. Since IS departments have become increasingly responsible for linking their activities to specific business objectives, interest and focus has shifted. Successful management of a cooperating complex of individuals, systems, and devices depends on a more informative, fully integrated management view. Systems and network management have started to converge and focus on total service management and application management.

Service-Level Agreements

The new business-oriented focus of IS managers has led to the creation of service-level agreements (SLAs). SLAs represent contracts between service providers (e.g., telecommunications service providers) and their customers (e.g., a corporation) specifying a level of service delivery as the basis for payment and performance evaluation. SLAs will be treated more extensively later in this book, but for this discussion, understand that early versions used metrics or measured values (e.g., annual device uptime) that were easy to collect but not always realistically meaningful to the user of IS services. Such metrics reflected device reliability but did not translate to any meaningful business service.

SLAs started to emerge as part of the common vision in the IS world in early 1995. They appeared as agreements between IS administrators and business functions (e.g., accounting or sales). The ability to establish a visible, direct link between IS and business operations satisfied the unmet needs of many high-pressure interests. The pressure to provide meaningful metrics led to innovative responses from both existing solution providers and emerging competitors. The ability to define *business process views*, *end-to-end performance tracking*, and *applications performance monitoring* became a required element of every solution provider's selling points.

The separation of systems, network, hardware, and software may make sense from an operational view, and in many cases will continue even with the growing crop of robust, flexible management tools; however, service-level agreements require us to paint a complete picture of interactions needed for successful delivery of a complete service for elements distributed throughout the networked environment. IS must implement the management functional areas across heterogeneous managed elements.

Management Functions

OSI created and maintains a set of standard management functions that consistently specify the separate tasks needed for a complete systems management solution. This list includes:

Object management. Tasks that identify the format and content of the object entities, which define the elements, systems, and applications to be managed.

State management. Tasks that identify and record the state, condition, and readings for a managed device.

Relationship reporting. Tasks that record and report on the managed device as it relates to its location in the network; connections to other resources; dependencies with other systems; and so forth.

Alarm reporting. Tasks that establish the seriousness of an alarm, and create events when predefined criteria have been met or thresholds exceeded.

Event report management. Tasks that analyze, process, and present reports about events and alarms.

Log control. Tasks that record events, alarms, and so on.

Security alarm reporting. Because of the critical nature of this area, tasks required to initiate and report events related to security are defined as a separate function.

Security audit trail. Tasks that track and maintain a history of the activities related to security events.

Access control. Tasks that implement and track activities related to gaining access to devices, systems, applications, and services.

Account metering. Tasks that track usage, both frequency and number.

Workload monitoring. Tasks that manage the workload placed on devices, systems, processors, and so on.

Scheduling. Tasks that set, monitor, and implement the scheduling of activities and jobs.

Summarization. Tasks dedicated to collecting and rolling up data, events, and so on.

Management Services

Common Management Information Service Elements (CMISE) define the basic commands used by the systems management functions to perform their tasks. These service elements combine with the Common Management Information Protocol (CMIP) to communicate with agents on the managed devices. The services consist of elemental functions such as:

GET. The service used to take a numeric or logical reading on a managed device, element, system, or application.

SET. The management service used to fix a numeric or logical value or reading.

DELETE. The management service used to delete a setting or value on a managed device, element, system, or application.

The remaining service commands include CREATE, which generates an event; CANCEL-GET, which stops an action; ACTION, which describes a response to an event; and EVENT REPORT, which reports an event. These represent the most primitive command level used to implement the management application.

Summary

We now have a background in the underpinnings of the distributed management model. We also have a context within which to fit the various tasks that must be accomplished to implement a distributed solution, whether for management or the delivery of any service. Distributed application implementation is not magic, but it does require attention to detail and careful steps. At the very lowest level, the *primitives* show the limited set of services upon which the whole model is built. The *functions* show how each action taken must be broken into a series of separate activities, then collated and coordinated to deliver the highest level of managerial activity.

We have seen how the virtually unlimited number of ways to implement a management solution has been given some degree of control by agreeing upon a defined set of functions with complete freedom to be innovative in their implementation. These models give the manufacturers of solutions some guidance for implementing their tools. They divide the challenge into addressable segments so that every new tool and managed element does not require a custom interface or solution. The model also demonstrates the overlap of basic functions in systems and network management.

Developers require standards for interfaces, communications protocols, collected management data, and formats before they can create a complete solution. The model provides the underlying rationalization of constituent parts and opens discussions that yield these standards.

Management Elements

To implement and apply the tasks of distributed management, a number of separate hardware and software elements need to cooperate and interact. Figure 6.2 shows the elements involved, which include:

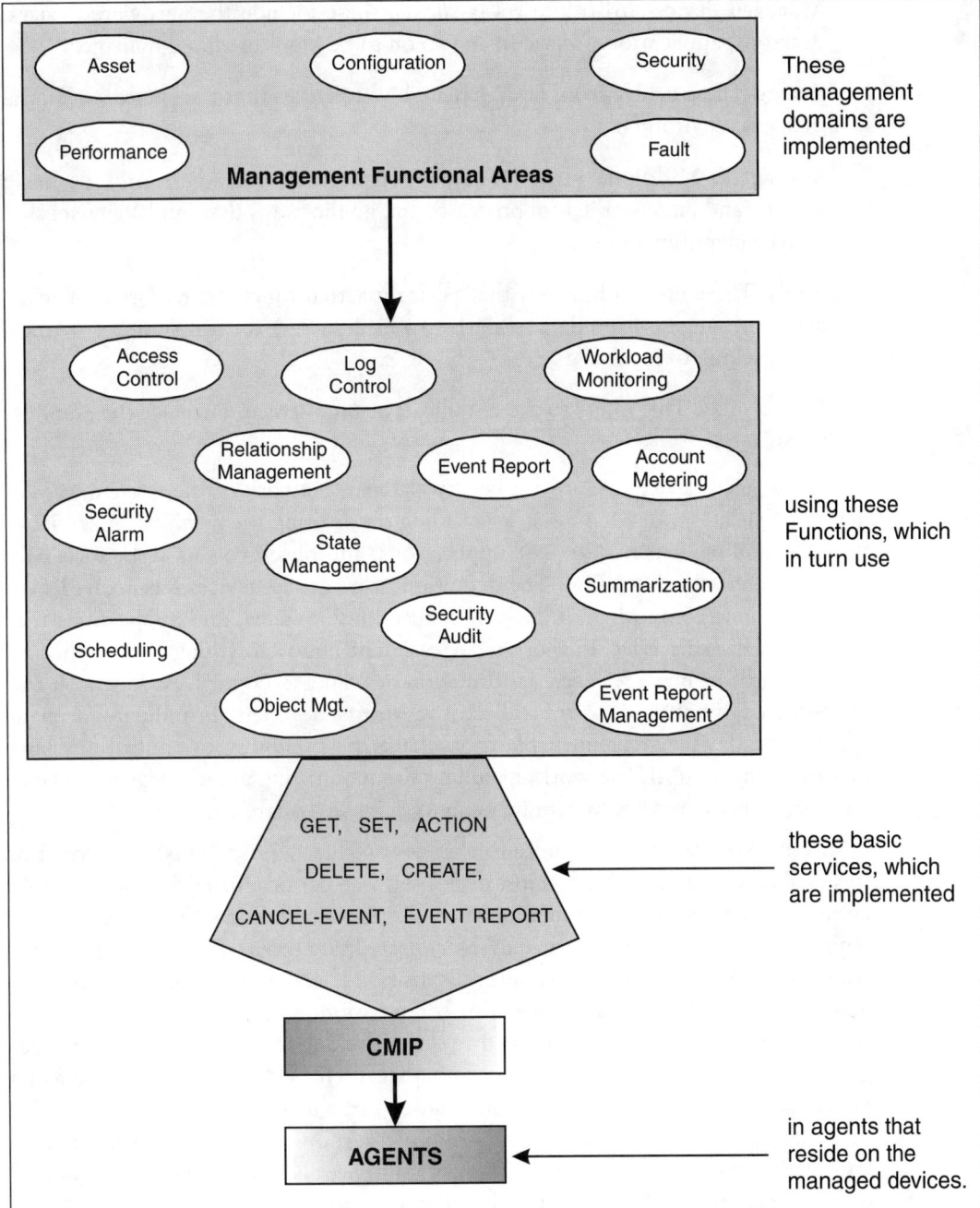

Figure 6.2 Elements in a management system.

Managed devices. Also known as *clients*, these include the hardware devices, desktops, applications, services, and so on to be monitored and managed.

Events. These evolve from or are created by activities that take place within the managed environment.

Managers. Middle-level or management platform managers provide basic servers, and manage the tool processes and applications that implement specific management functions.

Tools. These are applications that perform actual functions required for management, ranging from data analysis to autodiscovery to trouble ticket creation and tracking to reporting.

User display. This refers to the graphical, or *blue screen*, interface the administrator sees.

A managed device (client) can be any element: network traffic, system, system device, application, or even a service residing on or using the network. A service is the collection of elements, devices, applications, and files involved in the successful delivery of a desired function. The definition of managed devices has evolved over time to include composites of devices, connections, systems, and applications that deliver or define a service. In short, a device can be almost anything about which an administrator or manager needs information or wants to control. As long as it can be measured, monitored, or controlled, it represents a potential candidate for management. Today's management platforms have the capability to control anything that can connect to the network, including fire monitoring and control equipment, lighting, security, and heating and cooling systems in "smart" buildings.

Events are created in response to changes in state (a board fails), as a result of specified preconditions (packets lost over a set time period), or in response to other events (fixed thresholds exceeded or too slow response time to a user). Each event requires a decision or action; it may be collected, analyzed, discarded, correlated, stored, or forwarded. The decision for disposition is made on the basis of explicitly defined and specified rules. An event or combination of events may initiate a complex string of activities or be deemed irrelevant and ignored. The *intelligence* that generates events typically resides on the managed client. It can be as simple as an SNMP (Simple Network Management Protocol) trap generated when a device fails, or as sophisticated as a complex automatic response event. An event can be launched as the result of the correlation of multiple, disparate events or the output of a programmed analysis performed on the managed system.

An event initiates a string of related activities, which may include:

- Turning a device indicator red on the management GUI.
- Automatically initiating a call to a manager.
- Creating a trouble ticket record of the event.
- Reallocating processing to minimize performance impact.
- Notifying a list of end users affected by the failure.
- Scheduling follow-up activities to track resolution of the problem.

Events may also be the result of an inquiry to the managed device (e.g., reading a counter), which occurs when the management software *polls* devices at set intervals. Alerts must be handled, accumulated, passed on, and displayed, whether the result of a single event or created as the result of a sophisticated analysis.

Management solution products come in two forms: The *manager-of-managers* (M-o-Ms) act as central management control points, while *integration managers* provide frameworks and platforms with a basic set of services for use by specialized tools.

Manager-of-managers collect the data and coordinate the functioning of tools, management suites, and management platforms. Services include consolidation and reformatting of data stored in multiple, incompatible formats, and multiplatform and cross-tool event correlation, as well as report creation and generation services. M-o-Ms, sold as standalone products, serve as mechanisms to hide the idiosyncrasies and incompatibilities that result from attempting data collection and control using collections-of-point products. As management platform and framework products became more robust, reliable, and easier to use, they seemed to threaten the M-o-M market niche. However, the demand for enterprisewide service-level management created a demand for even more sophisticated high-level information management, which these products are evolving to address.

Integration managers provide a basic set of services in a framework or platform environment with well-defined application interfaces to allow tool integration. Typical services include event management, user interfaces, autodiscovery, scheduling, virus scanning, reporting, object repository, and object libraries. Specialized management tools and applications access these common services, thus avoiding redundant activities, databases, and so forth.

Tools developed as specific applications implement each of the various management tasks, such as performance analysis, storage management, security checking, and so forth. These have traditionally been developed as independently functioning applications. Tool independence has resulted in problems with redundant functionality, duplicated activities, and multiple redundant databases, as well as the problem of consolidating redundant and incompatible data. Redundant data occurs when either a single event triggers multiple failure alarms (say a network connection that fails equals one failure alarm, and all systems downstream are now isolated; each triggers a separate "failed system" event, n events), or multiple tools report the same event; for example, a filling disk slows response time on a monitored application (a capacity monitor triggers an event as the disk usage exceeds the threshold value; the application monitor triggers an event as response time slows). A variety of techniques and architectures, described shortly, have been developed to address these problems and reduce excessive load on resources.

The user display gives the operations manager a view into the status of the managed devices, systems, applications, or network. The format of the interface ranges from a three-dimensional, "real life" view to a simple two-dimensional network graphic to a text-only listing of error messages and condition statements. Some tools provide the ability to embed graphic representation and architectural layouts. Device and equipment detail can be displayed to the level of rack layouts, meter readings, adjustable settings of thresholds, state indicators, and operational levels. Visual aids can greatly facilitate troubleshooting, problem analysis, and correction. Tool vendors show the layout and interface as they see fit. Some follow a Windows-style format. The best platform products allow for the integration of all tools, and provide a consistent presentation format with an overview of total system status. In addition, the products allow the manager, whatever his or her responsibility—network, systems, operations or business—(with a few mouse clicks) to drill down for additional detail about events, alarms, and conditions. Consistent icons, formats, patterns of data presentation, and access on all screen interfaces help administrators learn to use the tool, reduce training time, and improve efficiency.

Summary

Management models evolved from the need to develop a vocabulary and syntax to discuss, design, and implement management tools for complex systems. Identifying and categorizing system elements allows us to construct independent, interactive, and cooperating management systems. Now that we understand the basic functioning of each element, we need to examine how to put management models to work. Management tools options are vast, and while this choice allows free rein of the imagination and competitive creativity to develop better approaches, the downside becomes apparent when attempting to evaluate, integrate, and apply tools from multiple vendors. Fortunately the problem was recognized, and standard management models emerged. The management models provide a context and architecture around which solutions have been developed. The next section deals with the implementation of management models and management tool responsibilities.

Management Tool Roles

As mentioned earlier, management tool applications have been created to perform the various management functions. However, as always, the devil is in the details. Tools tend to be fragmented—focused on solving a particular segment of the problem and not as neatly compartmentalized as suggested by the OSI list. Tools reflect the creativity and focus of their developers. Tools ostensibly intended to perform different functions may have overlapping features, but with enough underlying variation to make them valid additions to a complete toolchest. The following sections look at the functions and roles of the various management tools.

Product Management

Product management tools provide the functions needed to administer day-to-day operations of the managed systems and elements. Typical tasks provide for:

Workflow management. Job scheduling, output distribution.

System and application availability. Monitoring the state of the managed element.

Console operations. Status display and remote control.

Workflow management provides the capability to automatically schedule jobs, track dependencies, restart failed jobs, and assure the backout of changes when a job or series of jobs fail to complete. This tool may also contain functionality to initiate phone calls, send mail, and launch predefined and scripted procedures. Some tools include facilities to create and route status reports and summaries, either as an integrated function or through an interface to a separate application.

Another function typical of production management tools is the capability to monitor the status and availability of systems and applications, that is, checking and reporting on whether the device operates and is being used within guidelines. If not, as part its functionality, the tool can provide for automatic load balancing (starting a backup system or rerouting jobs among available resources).

Finally, all console operations—display of data, remotely setting or resetting switches, thresholds, or levels—are included. The console opens a window to the state of the enterprise, network, or LAN. The coordination of management functions, such as user management, adds, moves, and changes that must be initiated or performed manually round out the responsibilities and functions covered.

Fault Management

Fault management tools record, analyze, track, and fix faults and problems when they occur. Specific applications exist to address the following functions: help desk;

problem identification, trouble ticket tracking, resolution; and postresolution analysis, correction, prevention.

The help desk exists to respond to end-user questions and concerns. Virtually all help desks are responsible for reactive response. When a network outage or system or application failure occurs, the help desk will dispatch workers, respond to user concerns and questions, suggest corrective action, and so forth. Typically they provide answers to requests for service; answer questions about a set of supported applications; and arrange for changes in service, access levels, and resource availability. Many organizations have expanded the help desk responsibility to include *proactive* functions—tracking frequently asked questions, applications, resources, or services with the most problem calls and so forth. Based on an analysis, corrective measures can be planned and implemented, including public bulletin boards with responses to frequently asked questions (FAQs), special and periodic training, focused and enhanced support teams, and even recommendations for purchase of additional or new resources to meet increased demand.

Some problem resolution requires corrective action that is not automatic, and requires overt recording, tracking, and monitoring to assure a satisfactory resolution. This process of initiating, tracking, monitoring, and administering trouble tickets falls within the realm of the help desk staff. In many organizations, they have the additional responsibility of building and administering an active database of problem resolution information. A problems database can help identify and reduce repeat problems, facilitate and speed resolution of repeat problems, and enhance team problem resolution ability by sharing experiences. In some leading-edge companies, problem database information is accessible to end users who may find the key to resolving their problem without involving the support staff.

Network Management

Network management tools collect data and report on the state of network elements, connections, and devices. This includes collections of information about the devices that can be used by other applications. Specific functions common to all network management solution products include network topology, traffic analysis, alerts, correlation, and problem identification.

Network management tools will automatically discover all the devices, systems, and elements connected to a network. In the best implementations, collected information can be shared with license management, inventory, and asset management functions. Good tools offer options to display a specified subset of devices (or all devices) discovered via a graphical interface. A variety of views can be displayed, including progressively more detailed views of network elements, specific classes of devices, a single vendor's devices, or only those managed elements involved in the delivery of a specific service. Service-level agreements, sparked by the need for system management, have increased flexibility and functionality in building displays. Included in the discovery function is the capability to limit the discovery function. Typically, after the initial discovery process, periodic checks send only changes in the environment to the network or operations manager.

After tying management and display to specific hardware platforms, all major vendors are beginning to provide *browser-based monitoring*. It is important to note that these monitors do not include the capability to set or change settings on managed elements. Remote control of any managed device is a highly desirable capability for system administrators and managers, as it holds forth the promise of truly mobile management. Obstacles to the delivery of remote control management have arisen around issues of how best to:

- Maintain network security.

- Protect the network from unauthorized, potentially fatal tampering.

- Permit remote control.

The threat of unauthorized or unplanned changes to network integrity (let alone performance) represents the stuff of nightmares for network managers. This remains true whether changes are initiated with or without malicious intent. Potential for disruption of service and consequent financial loss from unwanted system changes is limitless. Preventing and protecting against such threats has been and remains a challenge for browser-based distributed management interfaces. Network managers will take extreme measures to restrict authorization to modify settings, addresses, and so forth. Remote access invariably means a security compromise. Until recently, when the first solutions began to appear, the trade-off cost of convenience for security had been deemed too high.

In late 1997, the major solution vendors in network management committed to various levels of remote management and control:

- Hewlett-Packard delivers the capability to manage Internet servers from a browser, with the technology in-house to implement more comprehensive widespread control.

- Sun and IBM-Tivoli announced display monitoring capability, with plans in place for control capability.

- Computer Associates International announced beta testing of full browser-based management and control of all managed devices, including a full range of Java-based applications, hardware, and devices.

Network managers frequently offer software-based probes to monitor network traffic at varying levels of detail. Most tools can report on traffic volumes and behavior for each of the different protocol types used on a network segment. More sophisticated tools offer the ability to track the source and destination of traffic, not just at the device (system or LAN segment) but also to the application level. This more detailed information provides greatly improved specificity for management control. The availability of improved *quality of data* allows for more accurate accounting and reporting for delivery of service.

Once information and events have been generated, they require further analysis to determine significance, accumulate statistics, generate requests for or initiate action, and so forth. The ability to *correlate* data from disparate sources eases problem analysis and speeds the remedy. All vendors provide some built-in correlation capabilities. All have negotiated agreements with external software partners to provide additional capability. Systems administrators are demanding even more powerful correlation engines be built into the platform or as part of a manager-of-managers. Vendors already have begun to respond, initially by offering correlation engines as options and, gradually, by bundling the functionality into their core products.

Tools used in network management range from applications geared to the management of a single family of devices from a single vendor (such as a BAY Networks or 3Com) to complex, integrated *management platforms*. Platforms provide basic services to a variety of management tools. In addition to the enterprise-oriented solutions that define the space, LAN-focused solutions exist with a more limited range of functionality.

Implementation architectures range from sophisticated object-based, intelligent network models (Cabletron's Spectrum), which infer the state of devices and linkages from collected data, to those that reflect the *real state* of the network, based on event data (Hewlett-Packard's OpenView, Sunsoft's Enterprise Manager, IBM-Tivoli's NetView).

Network management and systems management represent two distinct activities, each composed of a number of discrete functions. When we speak of function, we refer to the totality of the task to be done; for example, the function of performance management refers to the totality of activity involved in tracking and reporting how a device, system, person, or other element performs. Management functions include: performance management, storage management, problem management, and so forth. The delivery of a function requires specific functionality, discrete actions or activities such as event collection, event filtering, analysis, and so on. The actual discrete and detailed list of functionality delivered in accomplishing a management function varies with the vendor's implementation. The decision of which functionality to deliver depends upon a variety of interacting issues and capabilities that range from the design concept behind the solution architect to the experience and ability of the implementation team to the state of technology to the level of competition. Until relatively recently in the vast majority of corporations, the actual management functions involved in network and systems management have traditionally been viewed and addressed discretely because they were seen as the responsibilities of separate, nonoverlapping groups.

After many years of existence separate from systems management, the convergence of function and functionality in the two umbrella management (systems and network) tasks has been explicitly recognized. The increased visibility and importance of distributed, mission-critical applications involving the transient interaction of elements, devices, systems, files, and applications spread across and throughout the enterprise have helped fuel this convergence. System administrators need a management and reporting system that will give them a view of the total environment.

Performance Management

Performance management means reporting how efficiently a resource is being used or is functioning. Data collection is one part of performance management used to track how much or how little bandwidth, memory resources, processing capacity, or other volume measure of a resource is in use or has been consumed. Functions performed by performance management tools include:

- *Identify performance bottlenecks.* Monitor system and network resource utilization, including memory, traffic volume, user response time, and more.

- *Capacity planning.* Collect and analyze data to warn of saturation, and identify where more resources are needed.

- *Load balancing.* Spread processing, storage, print, connection, and message routing over available resources for optimal system efficiency.

Off-the-shelf products in the past reported only part of the information the system administrator needed, and were concentrated on individual resource states. System administrators need to be able to track problems to a specific source. Being able to collect traffic data and see the specific origins and destinations allows the administrator to report how efficiently the overall system is functioning. The ability to monitor the interaction of all system devices helps ensure efficient utilization of resources. Whereas once solutions required expensive, custom software, the widespread demand for end-to-end views is resulting in products that offer processes and tools for data collection designed to provide a more comprehensive view.

Complex mission-critical networks require speedy identification and resolution of situations that interrupt the smooth, consistent, predictable delivery of services. Malfunctioning programs or devices, excessive traffic volume, or filled disks can cause serious, even fatal failure. Performance tools monitor states including the amount of memory in use, the amount of memory still available, or the amount of bandwidth consumed on a network at any particular time. Exceeding predefined thresholds results in an *event*, which can be immediately forwarded to an administrator or held for further processing or even correlation. Events may be reported only when a specific number of events are created over a time interval or when specific types of events occur in conjunction. Data from event-monitoring tools can be accumulated and stored for later analysis. Storage time can vary from a few minutes to weeks or months, based on the requirements of the system, device, or service. Data for some system or network elements may be irrelevant for problem identification and troubletracing minutes after collection; or in the case of computer-controlled radiation therapy, require storage for years.

Performance monitoring tools gather data that can be used to authenticate the need to purchase additional equipment or resources. Most organizations operate under budgetary and resource constraints. Analysis of network traffic data, printer queues, memory utilization, inquiry response time, and so forth can provide valuable information to guide solutions design and resource acquisition decisions. Some tools include applications that enable simulation and what-if modeling of various loads, traffic patterns, response times, and so forth, to determine the impact on system operations.

Finally, some tools also provide "look-ahead" and "look-around" capabilities that enable the administrator to actively or automatically reallocate processing loads, reroute network traffic, or even prevent or delay application execution in order to avoid service degradation. (Note: These tools frequently require significant configuration and process knowledge on the part of the administrator.)

Asset Management

Asset management provides data and information to the end user, as well as data for successful tracking, accounting, and management of hardware, software, and system assets. Asset management tools:

- Identify, track, and manage IS assets including hardware, software, data, and users, and record information about managed resources ranging from HR files to resource lists.

- Maintain hardware and software inventory: system, software, and network configuration management.

- Conduct program management, including license tracking, distribution, and change control.
- Perform storage and data management, backup, and restore functions.
- Implement security measures, including authorization and authentication.
- Perform resource accounting and chargeback.

Most major enterprises face a major problem in tracking IS assets: Few can reliably identify the configuration, let alone the location of all PCs, servers, laptops, and other devices in their network. Most platform vendors and IS managers can tell stories of finding previously unknown devices and systems in an existing network by running an *autodiscovery* program.

Data and information you need to record includes:

- *Device descriptive data.* Serial number, version number, release IDs, and so on.
- *Network configuration.* How and where the device fits in the network, port numbers, and so on.
- *Support arrangements.* Internal support contact, external contracts, terms and conditions, call lists.
- *Inventory and accounting information.* Purchase date, price, ownership, inventory value.

Configuration management tools provide the capability to store and manage configuration and descriptive information for all resources by recording data collected in a database. The tool should be able to automatically collect and record information and to initiate periodic checks to ensure accuracy and detect changes. Some tools have built-in agents that automatically monitor state information, which can then proactively send data about changes to a central manager to update and synchronize records. Ideally, all data would be stored in "open," accessible formats, which could be shared by all management applications and tools. Data could then be used for accounting functions, software distributors, change management, discovery, and more, as appropriate. Unfortunately, no universal standard exists for data format and storage today (although candidates do exist). This has led to the development of tools that collect data previously gathered by the various independent tools and platforms and reformat it for common access and analysis.

Once configuration data has been collected, changes must be recorded and appropriate action taken if required, such as when a change is unauthorized or in violation of policy. This represents an exhausting, detailed, and error-prone task in any but the smallest businesses. The task of monitoring system changes is called *change management.* Novadigm, Inc. introduced the concept of *desired state* management several years ago with the introduction of its EDM change management software. For example, the systems administrator defines the desired state of the managed system; the EDM solution then monitors the device and initiates whichever tasks are necessary to return to the desired state when a discrepancy occurs. All this happens automatically, with the administrator required only to provide the initial desired state, identify managed elements, and prepare the basic procedures for corrective installs and policy administration rules. The initial EDM application was restricted to software and data management; that is, the administrator decides Office 97 should be used for all word processing and office activities. EDM can check for and remove earlier versions or even nonstandard (in this case, Corel Office) applications. Or, the sales manager changes the pricing file for this month's quotes. All sales reps must use this most recent pricing file to create quotes, change management checks, and replace files to assure that all have the correct version.

Other vendors have picked up on this model, which identifies a desired running state, monitors the device or system for deviations, then automatically initiates corrective action to return to the desired state when necessary. They have been applying it to other management areas where changes need to be controlled. As an example, the administrator's state definition just referred to can just as easily be an enterprise policy that defines the desktop configuration, including programs and permissions applicable for a type of user, say a design engineer. The design engineer policy defines the computing environment in terms of application access, file access, desktop configuration, and so forth, available to all design engineers in the company. The applications automatically monitor all computing environments defined as belonging to design engineers for conformance to the established policies, and initiate corrective action as needed.

Program management tools make it possible to track and manage the use of licensed application software. This includes managing and administering the distribution of software and files. Distribution management products may provide the capability to create and distribute changes and updates to data files and applications or enable full automation of the process. The more sophisticated distribution applications require more initial setup and training, but can ultimately represent a significant savings for IS staff. These programs can precheck to ensure that free space and application and version dependencies have been satisfied prior to attempting installation. They can automatically *roll out* and *roll back* to ensure successful, enterprisewide synchronized updates to data files and applications.

Included in this class of management applications are those that perform storage and data management, as well as backup and restore functions. These functions cover processes for storage of media and frequency of backup, along with data and files that will be backed up at specified intervals. For enterprise-scale operations, the process definition and administration can represent as much as 60 percent of the effort, with the tool providing the remaining 40 percent.

Program management tools define and implement security procedures as well as processes that monitor and report on user account and access activity. Security represents one of the most critical and neglected areas in distributed environments. The very nature of distributed computing aggravates the problem of implementing secure processes and procedures.

Security functions include the following tasks:

- *Access control.* Verifies that the user or application has permission to access files, data, applications, or services.

- *User authentication.* Validates the identify of the user or program.

- *Integrity.* Ensures files, data, and applications remain uncorrupted and secure from attack.

- *Confidentiality.* Protects data and files from being read except by those with the proper key.

In addition to these basic functions, other specialized tools implement and manage firewall protection and help define and implement policies for secure remote access control. Again, in this area, success will be the result of carefully defined and administered processes that complement the selected tools. No tool alone can provide anything beyond a minimal assurance of security.

Security has been defined at multiple levels, from the casual implementation of a personal PC to a highly secured, physically isolated system required for government projects. Security levels have been defined by the government (in a document commonly known as the Orange book) as follows:

A1—Verified design; the highest level of protection

B3—Security domains

B2—Structured protection

B1—Labeled security protection

C2—Controlled access protection

C1—Discretionary security protection

D—Minimal protection

The U.S. government maintains a program to test and certify the level of security implemented in a product. As an example, Windows NT has been certified at the C2 security level.

A fundamental trade-off at each level occurs between ease of use and access for the user and level of security. Each escalation in security places an increasing demand upon the end user (in terms of procedures to follow) that cannot be safely automated. Most enterprises function with what to many seems like an amazingly low level of security. A clear understanding of security needs and the associated costs can best be reached in consultation with an expert in the area.

Finally, accounting and chargeback systems collect and report statistics on who uses which application, data, hardware, and communication resources. Chargeback in the best of situations provides a clear recording of how resources have been consumed, providing IS with a focus for planned growth in resources (network expansion; printer, storage, workstation, and PC purchases). Because chargeback systems record information about who uses resources, they make it easier to identify the appropriate end users (heavy users of system or network resources) for recommendations on improved and new services. They also help to allocate IS costs to the heaviest users of the resources.

Unfortunately, in some implementations, accounting and chargeback become battlegrounds of special interests, causing departments to expend effort and creativity to subvert controls, disguise use, and avoid use of services. Departments avoid chargeback by enlisting unofficial local support staff, stealing time from their regular duties, or working with off-budget resources to conceal true expenditures. Chargeback avoidance hides true IS costs from the organization and wastes resources. This has led some organizations to support IS by a tithe against all operating departments, thus making management of IS costs difficult and arbitrary.

A solution used by some leading companies combines allocated and unallocated costs. The business managers work with IS to define a threshold level of services and resources, which if exceeded, initiates a chargeback to the department. Detailed accounting and use records, even when not used for actual cost allocation, provide invaluable management control data.

Summary

We have separated management tool functions into a number of independent categories. It is possible to institute a structure to network management solutions, through collaborative efforts of your business managers and IS team, and without restricting ingenuity that could give you a competitive advantage. The result, while not perfect, allows freedom of expression in network management solutions. The descriptions of the tools preserve sufficient commonality in expected functions and services to enable you to make informed comparisons regarding the functionality of the various products being promoted today. The taxonomy of management tasks outlined are common to all systems, communications devices, networks, or services. The formal definition of common management tasks has set the stage for comprehensive, integrated solutions that can provide a universally applicable management tool set on a single platform. Furthermore, it has raised the competitive performance bar for vendors by heightening expectations among users in ease of use, level of available management control, and so forth; but the penultimate solution remains in the future.

Events in the Management System

This section provides a generic description of the actions and functions involved in event creation and handling, data storage, the various management functions, information display, and reporting.

The Anatomy of an Event

Let's examine what happens when a management event occurs. An event is created as the result of the direct action of a device, say the failure of a connection, or indirectly by a software-generated response to the active monitoring for a change in the value, state, or condition of a monitored entity. The failure of a system to respond to an inquiry, or a response time exceeding a preestablished threshold, would result in an event.

Events may be actual descriptions of individual conditional instances or values, or may represent a value or accumulation of values. The event may be stored locally, analyzed locally, or sent to a remote management server for storage or analysis. After event information is analyzed, an alert may be generated. Alerts designate events that were created specifically as the result of a defined error or problem condition.

> **NOTE**
> All alerts are events, but not all events result in alerts.

Even in normally functioning systems and networks, many events occur that are inconsequential. Significance can be determined by volume, value, accumulation, or uniqueness. It is not at all unusual for thousands of events to be ignored or discarded without generating an alert. Just as the physicist must identify the single significant event from the tens of thousands of collision events that occur in a particle experiment, the monitoring manager wants only alarms for those events with the potential to significantly impact reliable service delivery. Significant alerts must be further processed to either initiate some corrective action or to notify the administrator of an actual or looming problem.

Event data will almost never be discarded immediately without an attempt at recording or summarizing. In the event of a catastrophic network or system failure, such raw data can yield information that is invaluable for identifying the circumstances or conditions that led to failure, or to establish trending data that point to imminent failure. If not preserved completely intact, the data will be accumulated as a count, frequency rate, or in some low-impact format, and preserved. In some instances, such historical data will be preserved for a limited time interval (say minutes or hours); in other instances, the data will be stored for weeks or months. The storage and accumulation time frame will usually be determined by the operations manager.

Strategies for preservation differ. Some implementations accumulate the data locally, passing the data to a central data storage repository either periodically (e.g., hourly) or during periods of low network utilization (e.g., during lunch breaks, after work hours). For example, data can be accumulated locally on the sampling system or a middle-level data collecting system. These local storage processors can perform a level of analysis, filtering the data and keeping only significant events or retaining only a sample of summary information to be used should additional analysis prove necessary in the event of a major system or network failure. It is also possible to determine the data collection and preservation option dynamically. Events, device and system states, and interactions can be evaluated, with data analysis and storage taking place as specified according to a centrally defined policy or set of conditions.

Events and Tool Behavior

An event can be the output of a management tool. As an example, a configuration management tool examines the current state of a managed device, comparing its current state to the expected or desired state. Upon recognizing a difference, it initiates an event. The event is processed by an event management tool that generates an action to eliminate or reconcile and record the difference. The actual action taken will typically be coordinated by a *management platform*.

A single event can be processed by multiple management tools, or it may trigger a chain of independent actions. The actual functionality and tasks performed by

Short History of Tools

Initially, vendors designed tools to service only their devices and families of devices; thus tool capabilities varied from vendor to vendor. They might be full-function, performing a range of tasks that included:

Monitor. Merely recording states and values.

Control. The ability to change state and set values.

Manage. Define access, allocate resources, create reports, store and correlate data, and so on.

When tool vendors designed their tools to be standalone, each optimized the functions, interfaces, and capabilities for their specific devices. This approach performed best in homogeneous environments. It was heavily favored by vendors but was less attractive to IS departments, which while favoring homogeneous solutions (to minimize the range of devices to be learned and the fingerpointing that occurred when problem solving) were more often than not forced to deal with and support heterogeneous environments. Purchasing essentially incompatible management tools wasted resources in terms of learning curves, redundancy in functionality, and an inability to easily (or even with great effort) gain a comprehensive view of the managed environment.

Gradually, tool providers responded to pressure to expand their tool functionality to support generic device functions. This alleviated some of the redundancy problem; but support of foreign devices was always at the expense of flexibility and functionality. Problems were extreme especially in the areas of event capture, management, storage, display, analysis, and reporting. The solution seemed obvious: Create a management platform with common services that all tools could share. And that is why management platforms and frameworks were conceived.

each tool varies with the intent and implementation plan of the vendor and that of the enterprise.

Events and Automated Manager Behavior

Early on, many devices merely stored events and data, and remote automated manager devices would periodically poll devices to check for meaningful events or data.

A Banking Event

A bank has an automated change management system, which includes configuration, and asset management element that is monitored by an automated policy administration tool. Additional memory is installed to a monitored system. A configuration management tool, detecting that the amount of memory on the monitored system has increased, creates an event. The event is sent to the monitoring management station, where a check is made against the policy to see if such a change is authorized. If this is an authorized or permitted change, a variety of actions begin.

- There is an update to the device information file in the configuration management application.

- An event is generated to update the asset-monitoring application.

- In some environments, the update of all involved tools will be automatically handled by events generated by the management platform.

The level of tool integration and automation determines the number and transparency of the actions taken as a result of any significant event.

This approach allowed minimal local footprints, in terms of physical size as well as resources (e.g., memory) consumed, and intelligence, in terms of the range of tasks performed, values checked, or decisions made without reference to a remote server. However, it caused management data traffic on the network, which meant that meaningful, business-related traffic had to compete for existing communication bandwidth. In the case of very active, medium-sized networks, this caused a real problem; it significantly reduced the amount of meaningful work accomplished because management commands and data exchange consumed scarce resources.

Local analysis requires local intelligence and resources. This increases the cost of the device, but is preferable (in most cases) to the potential overload caused by unregulated forwarding of all events to a central location. Local analysis can be as simple as setting and resetting a counter to trigger an alert event only at a specific numeric threshold; or it may be as sophisticated as the correlation of multiple events generated by different devices or elements in the system.

Finally, the event may be forwarded to a remote management server for storage, collection, correlation, and analysis. Today, many systems include a combination of these designs, in which local analysis will analyze, filter, correlate, and consolidate events to reduce their number and ensure that only truly significant and serious ones will be passed along to a remote manager.

Let's look at how an alert can be handled. (Note: Here, "managers" refer to the management programs that process collected data.) Once an event has taken place and its significance established, an alert, possibly along with some local detail data, will be sent to a remote manager. What takes place then will depend upon the manager, the management function, the design of the system, as well as the state of the system. The manager can be an intermediate stop for the accumulation of information from a collection of devices or interrelated systems, or it may be the centralized, high-level manager accumulating, acting, and reporting on the end-to-end state of a business process.

Any automated management tool can handle a limited amount of input from the devices, systems, desktops, or applications under its control. Intermediate management servers (processors) play a critical role in enabling management solutions to scale to handle very large, complex networks. When an alert arrives at the mid-level manager, several things take place: The data may be stored in a local database to await processing with subsequent alerts. In some applications, the data may be converted to a common data format prior to storage. The conversion may be an integrated function embedded in the manager. It may also be performed by a specialized application tool that operates in conjunction with the manager. Depending on the level of previous analysis, the alert can be passed to a specialized application for immediate correlation with other alerts. If it is sufficiently severe, it may be displayed to an actual local, human network manager (or merely appear on a monitor) to warn of eminent disaster or the need for corrective action. The alert will be passed on to the central manager immediately if sufficiently serious or on a periodic basis.

The central manager can also handle alerts in a number of different ways depending on the design of the system. If there is no intermediate manager, alert processing will include the activities described there. Similar processing may be performed by the central manager even if there is intermediate processing, which may be the case if there is an escalation process for extremely serious or ignored alerts.

In some automatic management systems, the central manager merely reports on the status of the enterprise environment. Alerts will generate corrective action either locally or at an intermediate manager. In other configurations, all alert processing, recording, and action take place at the central manager. An alert arriving at one of these central managers may initiate an automatic message to the help desk function informing them that a database is not accessible and an application will not run. The level of information and response again depends on the implementation. Assuming a fully automated management function, the help desk could proactively send messages to all affected end users. The notification could include an estimated time when service will be restored.

With the notification to the help desk, the manager may initiate corrective action with a diagnostic program, the output of which may be a trouble ticket, assigning and scheduling the corrective action which includes suggestions for the repair, replacement, and so on. The manager may also generate automated corrective action in terms of rerouting traffic, rescheduling applications, or load balancing.

Conclusions

Events initiate activity within a distributed management system. Events can be ignored, accumulated, analyzed, and passed among managers and management tools. An event or collection of events deemed significant will generate an action. An action can be a record in a log, a change in the state or color of a display icon, a message on a screen, or a series of actions. The series of actions initiated by an alarm can include recording the alarm, generating a trouble ticket, generating an e-mail or telephone message, scheduling a follow-up action or an active adjustment to systems or network activities.

Automatic event manager tools and management tools and functions have been the subject of intense scrutiny and study. Their tasks and responsibilities have been defined, divided, and implemented in a multitude of ways. Standard models, interfaces, protocols, and formats have been and continue to be defined to provide some structure to the development and delivery of distributed management tools.

With in excess of 20 years of effort, standards and processes in support of management solutions continue to challenge and generate controversy. Vendors, developers, and network managers who buy solutions will continue to work together and in contention to move toward more automated, integrated, and effective distributed management solutions.

Tool design and implementation should include not just the immediate task at hand but, as much as possible, should consider how a tool is used. Considering the processes of tool application and problem solving will yield a network management solution that operates effectively, intuitively, and efficiently. In the next chapter we look at the evolution of the distributed network management toolbox.

FOR FURTHER READING

Czegel, Barbara. *Running an Effective Help Desk, Second Edition*. (New York: John Wiley & Sons, Inc.), 1998.

Elbert, B. and B. Martyna. *Client/Server Computing*. (Boston: Artech House), 1994.

Hegering, H. and S. Abeck. *Integrated Network and Systems Management*. (Reading, MA: Addison-Wesley), 1994.

McConnell, John. *Managing Client/Server Environments*. (Englewood Cliffs, NJ: Prentice-Hall), 1996.

Orfali, R., D. Harkey, and J. Edwards. *The Essential Client/Server Survival Guide, Second Edition*. (New York: John Wiley & Sons, Inc.), 1996.

7 UNDERSTANDING THE MANAGEMENT TOOLBOX

Give us the tools and we will finish the job.

Winston Churchill, Radio broadcast, February 9, 1941

This chapter:

Examines the evolution of distributed management from discrete views of managed elements to business process views.

Explains the origins of the distributed management toolbox.

Classifies the different types of tools.

Matches the solutions architecture to the problem architecture unique to your enterprise environment.

In the past, distributed systems management has been divided into discrete functions which were handled by isolated subgroups of the IS department. This discrete, or "stove pipe," approach worked for the IS personnel who managed part of the system—a LAN or group of LANs—but was not conducive to painting a comprehensive picture of the end-to-end operations that global businesses now require. The inherent weaknesses in existing management solutions became undeniable as sophisticated business managers and end users more often demanded that IS service delivery make a measurable positive business contribution (see Figure 7.1).

Figure 7.1 *Why discrete management approaches don't work for distributed systems today.*

Tool Classifications

Vendor tools have become increasingly sophisticated to meet the demands of the distributed computing community. The economics of smarter devices and the tools to support them made them attractive to IS departments with the inherent promise of greater service reliability and less downtime due to failure. For vendors, they meant better margins and closer, more interactive, and numerous service links to their customers.

Early tools were classified by the general task(s) the tool performed (see Figure 7.2).

- *Development tools.* Task oriented; used to create and develop applications, provide version control, testing functions, and so forth.

- *Classical management tools.* Information delivery and analysis-oriented tools.

- *Standalone test systems.* Intended to be used independently, typically to perform a single, specific task. These systems include *test sets,* instruments to

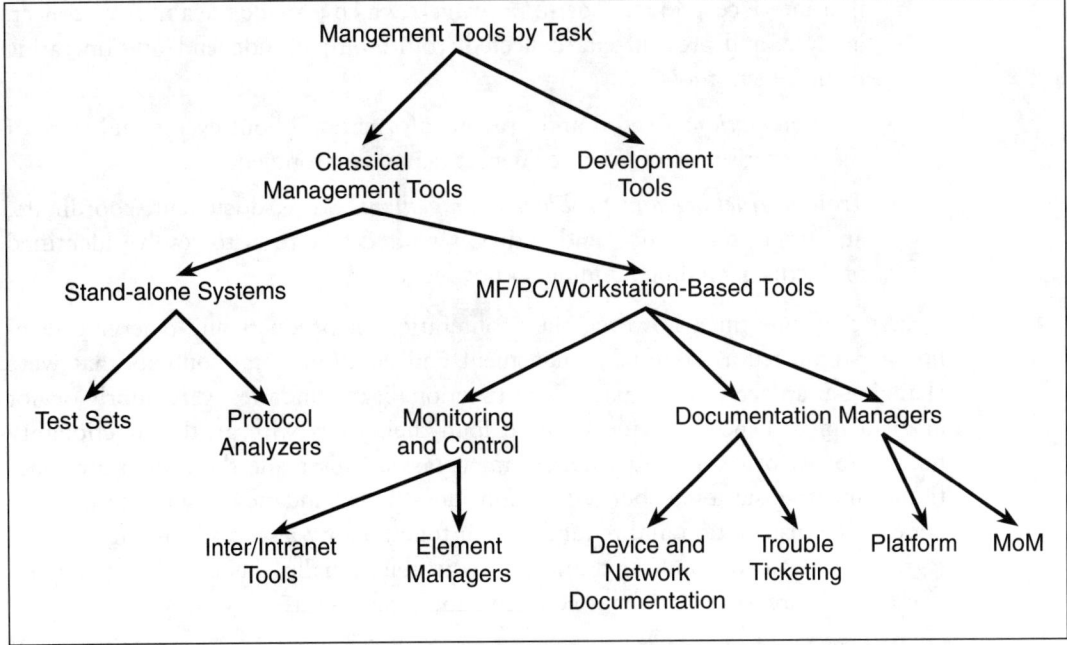

Figure 7.2 Classification of tools by task.

examine and test electrical or transmission characteristics such as oscillo-scopes, ammeters, or frequency test generators; and *protocol analyzers*, so-phisticated systems that examine the *bit stream* moving across the connecting network wire, record traffic volumes, and perform varying levels of analysis.

- *Mainframe/PC/workstation/server-based.* More complex, comprehensive tools that may or may not be coordinated and integrated, intended to func-tion with other tools. These divide into tools that provide *monitoring and control,* used to collect information, and set or change instruments and con-trols; and *Internet and intranet tools* and used to monitor and manage Inter-net and intranet activities.

- *Element and device managers.* Work with a single brand or class of devices, such as Cisco routers or Wintel desktop systems.

- *Managers.* Provide the coordination and integration of functions, applica-tions, and/or data to allow easier collection, analysis, and presentation of data. These include *platforms,* which provide a group of basic services for event storage, analysis, and presentation of results, typically via a graphical user interface; and *manager-of-managers* which provide the ability to collect, analyze, and present data collected from multiple, independently operating management tools.

- *Documentation.* Record and present information about events and state of the enterprise, workgroup, or departmental environment.

- *Trouble tracking and problem management.* Store, document, coordinate, and track information and activities related to efforts to resolve identified problems, including building a knowledge database.

At the same time, however, the proliferation of products and emerging technologies required a scope of management and environmental contexts that were changing at an accelerating pace. Tool functionality boundaries were poorly or not at all defined; hence, providers would load their tools with all the functionality needed to perform all related management tasks. This made the tools fully functional and free-standing, but led to considerable redundancy as new tools were added. The distribution and redundancy in functionality also made attempts to integrate these tools complicated and unpredictable. Finally, the situation generated market pressure to design a more cohesive tool architecture.

Business and market forces exerted pressure for a more integrated functional architecture. Focused, independent management views of basic system elements and network devices could not meet the demand for a clear view of the performance of multiple, dynamic, transiently interacting parts. The initial, early requirement for device state tracking became a much more complex task necessitating the management of multiple, interacting objects. The convergence of isolated, distributed component views into a unified, comprehensive representation of interconnected interactions moved the emphasis from technology to the presentation of a comprehensible business process.

Unfortunately, early tools, with their incompatible and independent data collection and storage capabilities, provided little to help IS staff who were expected to manage distributed systems based on a broader vision of the business and its enabling services. This broader vision, called a *business process view,* requires a much more coordinated and integrated view of enterprise operations, one that pulls together all the interoperating and interconnected elements involved in the delivery of critical services.

This view differs from but complements the business approach that IS must take to present its capabilities. The view speaks to the presentation and representation of the status of the devices and systems used in the delivery of a productive service and the results or monitoring the involved elements. The approach refers to a mind-set and methodology for articulating the application of IS expertise to resolve business issues. A business process view has become essential in enterprise environments; while much more complex to assemble, its goal is simplicity in presentation. We simplify distributed system management by highlighting only critical data and situations and by flagging situations in terms of threats to service delivery rather than the state of the individual devices. While state and performance data on individual devices or systems is still needed for analysis and corrective action, the information needed for successful management identifies only service interrupts and delays.

NOTE

Tools for successful management of distributed systems flag only data related to service interrupts and delays.

Because of rigorous business pressures, and today's tight budgets, the results and output from system management tools must be immediately comprehensible in terms of business impact. This eventually led to a more rigorously defined structure for management tools, as described in Chapter 6.

Today's tools are grouped according to the management function and services they provide (see Figure 7.3). This grouping complements the generally accepted distributed management model.

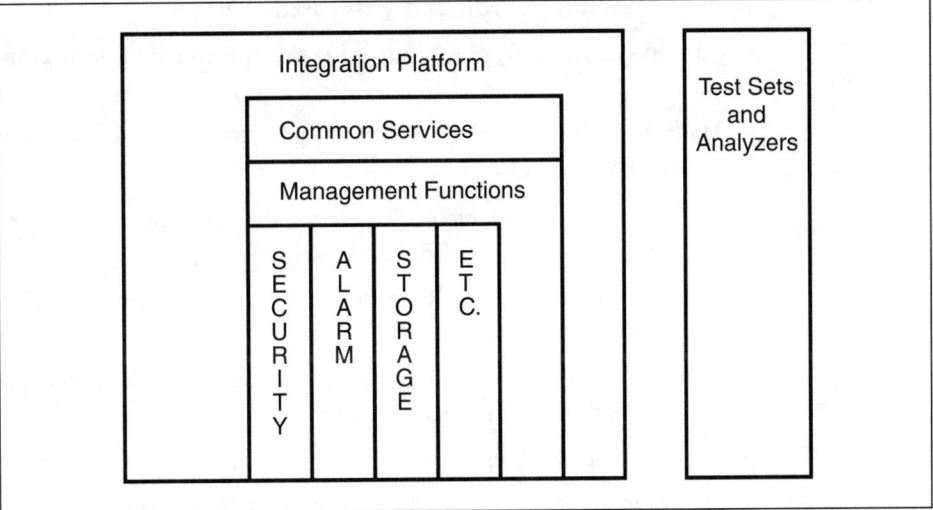

Figure 7.3 Management tools by function.

Current tool groups include:

- *Test sets and analyzers.* Perform the same function as their predecessors.

- *Management integration platforms/frameworks/suites.* Provide a context (identified as either a platform, framework, or manager) to facilitate access to a standard set of services for use by multiple, specialized, independent application tools, including *manager-of-managers,* consolidators of data and information from multiple management tools and applications (some include basic data integration services); and *platforms/frameworks,* architectures of application programming interfaces and integration capabilities that provide common services, including event management, data handling, and presentation services to a flexible collection of focused management applications. *Management suites* consist of groups of already or easily integrated tools that work with and complement frameworks and platforms. Such suites have been most prevalent in the desktop space.

- *Management common services.* Services used by both network and systems management tools, provided by integration platforms or frameworks:

    Data storage. Manages the storage and access of data and databases.

    Event handling. Capture and direct events.

    Analysis. Perform correlation, data reduction, averaging, etc. on collected data.

    Presentation. GUIs and Web-based interfaces.

- *Communication.* Applications to establish and maintain communication links.

- *Application functions.* Specialized applications to perform specific management functions such as:

    Account management. Provide services and processing for tracking and reporting resource usage.

    Fault management. Recording, tracking, monitoring, and reporting efforts at problem resolution.

    Help desk. Provide services to end users in education, problem resolution, and service initiation.

    Trouble ticketing. Assign and monitor efforts to resolve problems.

    Performance management. Monitor and report on the utilization of resources.

Configuration management. Collect, maintain, and report configuration data of managed resources.

Production management. Manage workflow and process management.

Change management. Track and initiate action in response to specified changes on monitored resources.

Software distribution. Provide automatic monitoring, creation, and distribution of changes to software application and data files.

Security management. Track and report activities related to security of the managed devices.

Management Implications

The separation and grouping of management tasks within individual product implementations remains, of necessity, somewhat arbitrary. Vendor tool providers will make the ultimate decision of how to group and bundle functionality based on their perception of the problem to be solved, their expertise, and the target market. The enterprise systems manager, when considering the distributed systems and network solutions, must understand his or her own enterprise architecture and environment. A process for evaluation of solutions is provided in Chapter 8, but for now, keep in mind the following list of general issues when reviewing solutions.

Before purchasing a new vendor solution, ensure that you and your staff have considered and understand the following:

- Current installed tools and the functions they perform.
- Problems to be resolved and in what priority.
- The architecture of the potential solutions.
- How the solution distributes functional responsibility.
- How the solution's architecture and procedures match your internal organizational methodology.
- Provision for integration with existing tools.
- Provision for integration with a platform or framework.

Next we address the forces driving the initial forays into distributed management by reviewing the business drivers behind the early solutions and the solutions architecture, which brought early success and still influences today's solutions, to both their benefit and disadvantage.

Origins of Distributed Management

Originally, tools monitored rather than managed applications. They provided state information, typically only indicating whether the device was operating or had failed, giving very little in the way of value-added data. As customers began to demand more reliability and functionality in operation, vendors were driven to develop tools to manage their devices.

However, when the device or tool failed, more often than not, it required an on-site visit to reset or replace the device, change trip levels, or redefine failure limits. These simple indicators allowed some improvement in service by quickly alerting administrators of failed devices. But competition-strapped business customers were interested in more significant information and productivity improvements. They wanted devices and tools that provided more information—data on the state of operating conditions prior to failure or alarms, interactions with other devices. Given this information, the operations staff could start to analyze causes and, with the knowledge gained, prevent future failures. Such data could also be used to predict and minimize negative effects downstream.

By adding intelligence to a simple monitoring device, vendors increased its utility to the customer *and* made a bigger profit. For example, a simple hub sells for around $99. With sufficient intelligence and controls to reset remotely; change settings, collect, analyze, and report status information, and so on, the price rises to $599 while the production costs increase far less. The intelligent device with significantly enhanced utility to the customer helped increase both revenue and profit margins for the vendor.

By using an intelligent tool, a single network or systems operations manager can monitor and manage many more devices. This makes it possible to detect, correct, and even avoid problem conditions, leading directly to a decrease in the number and length of service interruptions and outages. Facilitating the delivery of more reliable network services can easily outweigh the additional costs incurred.

Not surprisingly, customers began clamoring for the enhanced tools, called *smart devices*. Vendors responded by building even more sophisticated management tools for their line of products, building information collection and control capability into their hubs, routers, systems, and so on, each in a unique manner. These tools proved to be a very real competitive advantage, with the additional benefit of more closely linking the customer to a single brand or vendor.

Various strategies were employed by vendors to increase functionality. Independent and startup tool providers, with little or no installed base of solutions, used the latest technology and techniques to initiate highly functional but not necessarily compatible solutions. They hoped to penetrate markets and build market share by offering leading-edge functionality. In the rush to market, however, they did not always put their products through the rigorous performance and scalability testing necessary to deliver quality products. These vendors were not always careful to provide features or use standard interfaces that made them easy to integrate with existing tools. Though products operated as promised in small installations, they often would fail dramatically when networks grew beyond a few thousand nodes or under heavy user demand. The situation has improved significantly in today's market but *caveat emptor* still applies.

Vendors with a significant installed base found it necessary to balance serving the needs of their base by carefully evolving the introduction of functionality of potentially disruptive new technology. Especially for breakthrough or new technologies, most solution providers felt they had to anticipate, plan, and design for backward compatibility. This atmosphere permeates the mainframe and Unix technology environments. For PCs, the major solution provider, Microsoft (for example, with its Word for Windows product), repeatedly introduces new versions with apparently minimal attention paid to backward compatibility.

The good news is that many vendors do develop, test, and refine enhanced functionality, while introducing it over time. First, they make the new technology available on a project basis to very large enterprises and then gradually introduce it as a product enhancement. This strategy works for tool suppliers with an existing, robust customization services capability.

The pace of introduction and integration of new functionality has always been a balancing act. On the one hand is the potential revenue to be gained by leapfrogging competition with unique, innovative products and technologies. On the other hand, the development cost of built-in backward integration cannot be ignored, nor can the potential revenue from lucrative custom services, nor the risk of lost sales if implementation proves too complex. Some business customers accuse vendors of moving to productize enhancements only when competitive pressures and consumer demand force their hand.

One response to these tensions were system and network device management vendors offering complete solutions in-house, integrated around a management framework or platform intended to provide stable management environments with standard interfaces, into which new products and technologies could be easily introduced. They would provide basic services that the operations staff could expand over time as new products with new desirable features were made available. These vendors seemed to be the perfect hedge to the "technology analysts's" promise of newer, faster, better products appearing every six to nine months, long before the cost of expensive current products would be amortized.

Vendors initially provided primitive management platforms optimized to collect, analyze, report, and control devices. They operated according to rules that catered to and optimized performance based upon the idiosyncrasies of their own devices. Unfortunately, this led to a proliferation of techniques, formats, and controls while each vendor concentrated on optimizing for its specific tools. Also, customers who purchased multiple tools, each operating independently, ended up with repeated and redundant services. It was not unusual for a customer with multiple management tools to have a separate discovery process, separate databases, and a different user interface for each tool. And each tool imposed its own demands on scarce systems resources and added to network overhead traffic. The situation was tolerable only as long as a customer stayed with a single vendor's line of equipment; but inevitably, this replication of function led to problems in the more typical heterogeneous environment.

As the complexity of network and system environments increased, so did their heterogeneity. It became increasingly difficult and unattractive to remain in a single-vendor environment. Heterogeneous networks necessitate purchasing, installing, and training on multiple incompatible management products (see Figure 7.4). This results in a less productive and efficient utilization of resources, since

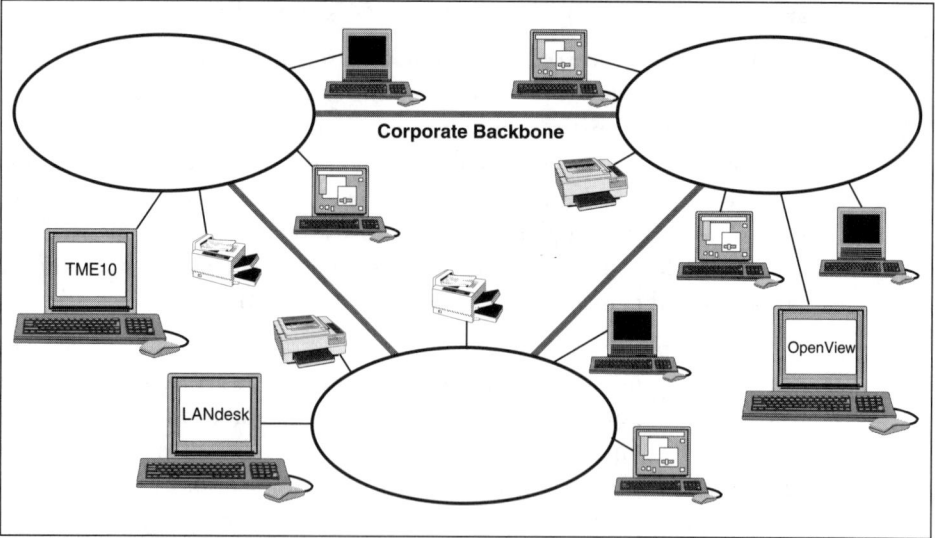

Figure 7.4 *Vendor integration.*

the various tools individually discover network devices, monitor changes, capture and store events in unique formats, and so forth. Hence, there was increasing pressure to design and deliver standard tools for data collection, data storage, and manipulation.

Vendors realized the advantages of expanding their management and monitoring capability to include competitive devices. Each had to balance customer satisfaction with the loss of performance advantage. Tools originally optimized for specific products were modified to support generic devices, frequently with diminished efficiency. With all the lip service paid to the demand for and attractiveness of *open solutions*, effective proprietary solutions can yield tremendous returns even when somewhat lacking in overall quality of performance and reliability in operation. There exist a profusion of desktop products providing dramatic evidence of this phenomenon.

Business customers became more sophisticated and demanding as the benefits of standardized interfaces and control mechanisms became obvious. Contributing to the interest in a suite of standardized services were the inflated resource demands and costs incurred because of redundant data collection and storage. This added to the cost of (near constant) training required to become expert and maintain expertise in the use of new management solutions from multiple vendors. This led to the appearance of management frameworks for heterogeneous devices and systems.

With standardized frameworks, the best tool providers could concentrate on developing the richest functional management capabilities, while the framework concentrated on bringing all the information and common control functions into one common management environment.

Of course, in real-life implementations, the division of functionality would not be all that simple, precise, and clear. Hence, the emergence of standards and standards bodies, the publication of APIs, and of competing, standards-based platforms. All of these efforts have been directed at facilitating the creation and integration of tools with platforms, and ultimately to simplify the life of the manager of distributed environments.

Finally, device providers themselves were not immune to these benefits. While remaining reluctant to sacrifice either the competitive advantage of *lock-in* provided by their tools or the inherent performance advantage of a tool optimized for a particular family of products, they recognized the potential benefits of a single point of integration with common, consistent user interface. The result was a rush to create what culminated in the multiple types of framework and platform solutions discussed in the next section.

General Product Architectures

Because every vendor uses unique definitions to categorize solutions, the following subsections attempt to reduce the confusion in terms and function.

Point Products

Point products are designed to solve a single very specific problem. They focus on doing a limited number of management-related tasks very well, such as storage management, automated software distribution, router management, or, more generally, event management.

Point products may be restricted to the configuration management of a single vendor's devices or family of devices. They may also perform a single management function across multiple devices and systems. They range in functionality from those that operate like small, custom-written utility applications to sophisticated solutions that can monitor, detect, and adjust to changes in the managed devices. Many point products (see Figure 7.5) emerged as tool providers recognized that they could earn additional revenue if failed or failing equipment could proactively inform the IS staff to take corrective action or even initiate corrective actions themselves. Performance was optimized for the specific device or family of devices with little concern for integration or management of other devices.

Even when acknowledged and provided for in the tool design, integration for a multifunction heterogeneous solution causes aggravation and adds cost, regardless

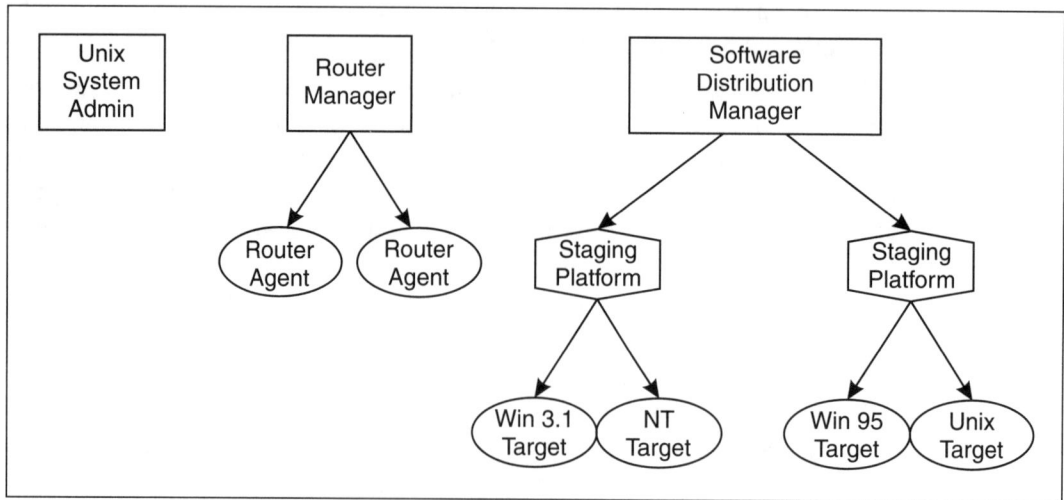

Figure 7.5 *Point products.*

of whether it's performed locally by the IS team or through the use of outside contractors. If not carefully defined, the integration effort often is incomplete, adding development costs to the redundant effort cost.

Some say that given the pace of change and introduction of products, the best solutions will be built around point products locally integrated. The success of such an approach is discussed more fully in Chapter 8. In general, the locally integrated point approach makes the most sense for businesses that provide technology integration services.

Management Suites

Management suites integrate the management tools and functions often from several vendors or solution providers into a single package, offering a set of (often casually) integrated functions. These are particularly prevalent in the desktop environment but also exist for mainframe and client/server environments. For these latter two, it is usually a single vendor providing a suite of tools. The management suites provide one-stop shopping (see Figure 7.6) for solutions that streamline specific administrative tasks such as asset management, virus checking, server management, charting, database management, and configuration checking for a single LAN, collection of LANs or even a distributed data center environment.

Typically these tools will be accessible from a single management console. They may share data implemented with a similar look-and-feel for all of the functional modules in the suite. Some of these solutions scale to perform their limited tasks very well for large organizations consisting of thousands of nodes. Others do not

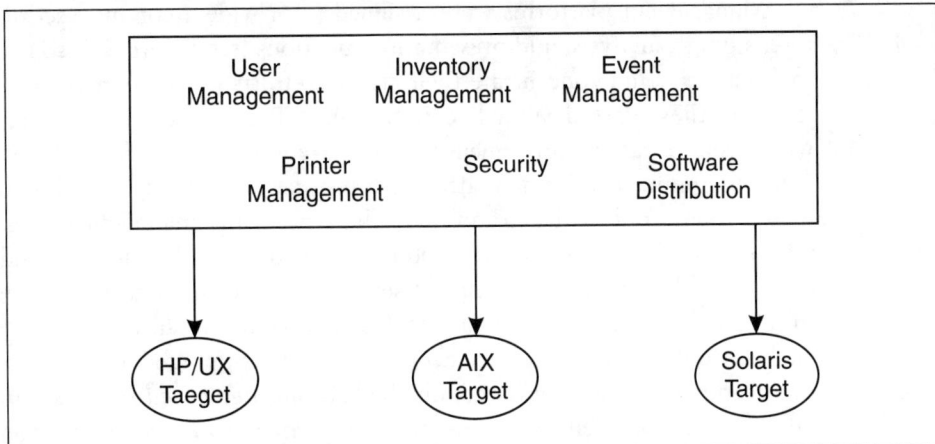

Figure 7.6 System administration suites.

scale well, compelling IS teams to demand integration with more robust enterprise platform solutions.

Conflicts arise when local administrators have implemented a management solution and the enterprise administrator chooses a central control platform. Local administrators become reluctant to hand control to remote managers or balk at learning a new system. Standard APIs for exchange of data and commands between enterprise platforms and LAN solutions exist to address this problem. Some enterprise solutions provide full integration of the popular LAN management solutions. Both approaches permit local administrators to function with little or no change, while enterprise managers receive the information they need for a comprehensive view of the entire system with the potential to exercise local management commands remotely.

Some vendors have started to offer focused solutions based on system administration suites fully integrated with their enterprise offerings. Other major platform providers have responded by forming closer partnerships with existing suite providers, even financing integration efforts.

Systems and Network Management Platforms

Systems and network management platforms provide a set of common services used by independent management applications as they perform their specialized functions. These solutions target management of the total enterprise, covering the gamut of heterogeneous systems, networks, and devices. Architecture must scale to embrace tens of thousands of managed resources, integrate with diverse management tools, and distribute control across multiple management domains.

Management platforms were designed to provide a common set of event capture, storage, analysis, and presentation functions (see Figure 7.7) so that tools and tool makers could concentrate their creative efforts on the particular management function they were designed to implement. Thus, a security management tool would concentrate on implementing robust, reliable security for the network or systems environment. A breach, attempted breach, or warning according to predetermined rules would cause an event to be sent to the management platform. The platform would receive the event, store it in a common data format, and report the event according to a predetermined set of rules. Storing data from multiple monitoring applications in a common format allows for sophisticated correlation and analysis to determine necessary action, including tripping alarms, resetting devices, notification of the appropriate individual, *knowledge-based response*, and so forth. Tool providers concentrate on developing the richest functional management capabilities, while platform providers offered basic communications, analysis, reporting, and storage services in a standardized format.

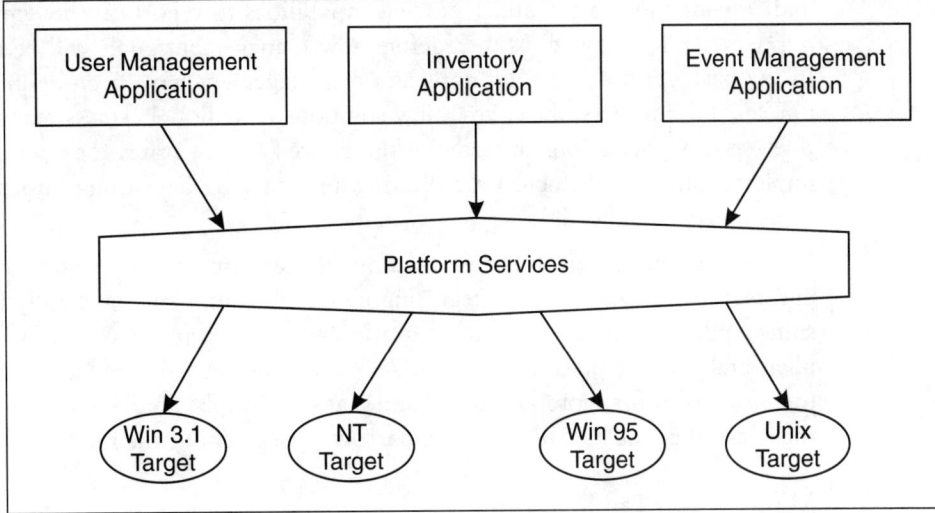

***Figure** 7.7 Systems and network management platforms.*

Typically, platform and framework providers make significant use of standards, both proprietary and generic, in implementation. This facilitates the integration of new and emerging products and technologies. All vendors take great pains to provide well-documented APIs along with integration services and development toolkits to facilitate interoperation with numerous specialized applications. All major platform providers conduct ongoing aggressive partnership recruiting and support programs to grow a large body of better integrated complementary management applications.

Manager-of-Managers Platforms

Manager-of-managers (M-o-M) platforms are intended to work with and depend upon the functioning of other tools and application suites. They pull together data collected by other, specialized tools including other management platforms, and manage data stored in multiple databases or reformatted and stored by the M-o-M in a common format. They also provide mechanisms for further data processing and coordinated presentation. They address the issues of scalability, multiple data formats, event analysis, information presentation, and heterogeneous environments. They have typically been handicapped by the limited number of data formats or event schemes they can manage, as well as a requirement for customized data collection modules.

The development and enhancement of platform and framework solutions has threatened the M-o-M market niche. In response, existing products are enhanced and provide monitoring and reporting capabilities to report on the *end-to-end delivery of services* as well as to redefine how management goals will be articulated. In the past, service level and application management have been defined in terms unrelated to business objectives. New solutions will allow business managers to define service expectations in terms of the desired service states for operation. These implementations will focus on collecting and tracking data using information that is only recently collectible.

Integration responsibility is a major differentiator among suites, frameworks, and platforms. The task of integrating new tools into a suite generally falls on the suite vendor, whereas platform integration generally depends on a third-party supplier, and not the platform vendor. As major platform providers respond to customer demand for more and better integration of tools, analysis, and presentation, this class of products will address a narrowing segment of the market.

Management Implications

With all of these tools, platforms, and suites to choose from, what is the enterprise manager to do? Use caution: Understand the problem and state the goal explicitly before choosing the appropriate path. Technical issues to keep in mind are discussed in the next section. Here are some methodological and administrative issues to consider when looking at potential solutions:

- The current enterprise (administrative, managerial, or technical) environment. Avoid attempting to introduce a radically different architecture in one step.
- The architecture of the solution. Determine how it complements or clashes with the current enterprise culture. A conflict in architectures or environment may, in fact, be the appropriate approach; however, it should be selected and known in advance so that appropriate plans for the introduction, education, and orientation are put into place.

These solutions are not mutually exclusive in content, place, or time; any or all of these approaches may provide the exact solution fit with various pieces of the management problem at different places in the enterprise and at different times.

Technical Issues with End-to-End Solutions

With such a comprehensive set of capabilities, does anything stand in the way of offering full end-to-end service-level management? Ironically, the greatest obstacle is the overwhelming variety of tools available, compounded by rapidly changing technology and lack of a standard data format. Major vendors often only reluctantly cooperate on the adoption and reconciliation of even slightly overlapping standards. The coordinated efforts of vendors to delay delivery of truly useful standards is nothing new (witness the history of Unix). The potential benefits for tool writers, vendors, and customers from standards for a management data format and instrumentation makes the lack of cooperation especially frustrating.

In response, some businesses create their own custom solution from best-of-breed tools. These businesses determine and implement the degree of integration and functionality needed. But to succeed, the custom approach requires an in-house tool expertise and integration techniques—and satisfactory completion is still not guaranteed.

The custom solution approach assumes that the IS team is best employed sharpening generic integration skills rather than on IS services customized to the business and its competitive challenges. Information technology and information systems staff should not be used as generic staff organizations rather than as unique corporate assets. Consider the senior IS manager whose biggest concern was consistent e-mail access from remote locations. In his mind, the most immediate concern and contribution to the business by IS was e-mail accessibility. He did not ask IS staff to work on enhanced processing capability or more robust automated systems management.

The point is not whether or not smoothly functioning and easily accessible e-mail contributes to the operation of the business entity but that in this executive's mind (as confirmed during further conversations) there existed no link between IS activity and a responsibility for business profitability or positioning for competitive advantage. The IS staff had not demonstrated their potential for contributing to any such advantage or improvement to profitability. The real risk here is the loss of control of a significant business asset in unique IS knowledge and capabilities through outsourcing. Outsourcing often becomes the cost reduction solution of choice when the IS team lacks direct visible links to or is not considered to be measurably contributing to business goals.

Common standalone tools are optimized to address a specific or limited set of management functions, with little concern for sharing data or integration. In a custom integrated management system, each tool may act independently to perform its own discovery; some even detect, collect, and store event data in proprietary databases—a redundant effort and resource load. The tools may also trigger their own corrective actions or requests based on information that may or may not correlate with other event data. Even correlation of data becomes problematic when each tool uses its own unique format. Tool incompatibility has led to tools that sweep event data into a common format for correlation and evaluation.

The redundant and inefficient use of resources is a well-known network management problem. Unfortunately, equipment vendors handicap themselves by unilaterally adhering to industry standards—look at Microsoft's success pushing proprietary solutions for any number of computing and networking demands.

Similarly, the world of network management lacks standards for data configuration, storage, and access among platforms, vendors, and tools. Vendors continue to provide locally optimized performance and control, but at the expense of true interoperability and open solutions. Vendors would rather not risk the downside of unilateral standards adherence, in terms of performance degradation, complexity, or overhead; it would merely provide a sales advantage to the proprietary, nonstandard, but more efficient solution available from a competitor.

Suite, framework, and platform products attempt to address the problem in two ways: first, through delivery of a comprehensive set of tools that share common base services for discovery, data collection, and storing; and second, through the provision of comprehensive, well-documented APIs that allow bidirectional access to and sharing of information.

The first approach—a comprehensive tool set—can fail because virtually all meaningful implementations of distributed management solutions require inclusion of existing and therefore, almost certainly incompatible legacy products; this translates into substantial additional developmental effort to integrate tools.

The second method—the use of APIs—fails because it can require too much development effort. A rule of thumb is that management tools must achieve payoff at no more than 18 and 24 months, with increasing pressures to reduce these further. Development and integration needs may discourage purchase or forestall full use of the tool.

The manager-of-managers mentioned earlier in this chapter seemed to offer one solution to inefficient resource use by adding another level of service: They accept event information and coordinate the processing and presentation of information. And though providing a workable solution, they tended to grow basic services to better secure their niche, thus adding overhead and complexity to the management process. So while they were able to work with the most popular existing platforms and tools, they required additional integration and customization services for emerging tools.

An alternative approach looks to industry-wide cooperation by vendors, developers, and business consumers for the creation of standard data formats. One promising initiative is the Common Information Model (CIM) proposed by the Desktop Management Task Force (DMTF), in Portland, Oregon, an independent industry-wide organization formed in 1992. This effort focuses on defining a standard set of formats for data collection and storage for object-oriented, Web-based data management. It requires the cooperative effort of some 200 (and growing) contributors, some keenly competitive, some (perhaps altruistically) contributing to reach a workable, but lowest-common-denominator solution.

> **NOTE**
>
> A number of significant and worthwhile efforts are under way in this area of defining APIs, standards, and interface standardization. Some have gone on so long that they exist as mere academic exercises for "standards roadshow" groupies. Others are mere platforms for showcasing vendor (not so subtle) efforts at establishing a competitive advantage. Use your IS staff to identify and evaluate the efforts most necessary and useful to your success. Then actively support and influence the effort, because some will succeed regardless of your involvement. It is better to have influenced the standard to your benefit than to have to react to its potentially hampering impact.

Custom Solutions Using Best-of-Breed Options

Solution providers must select high-volume platforms to optimize their appeal. Business customers want platforms that support all currently installed management tools, as well as any they may want to install in the future (see Figure 7.8). They need a platform that allows them to integrate, correlate, and report all events occurring in the managed environment, from the desktop to the enterprise. Unfortunately, such a solution does not exist; all have their advantages and disadvantages. Every solution reflects the assumptions and views of its architect and design team, which can be very specific. Purchasers, on the other hand, must clearly define and understand the problem or set of problems they want to solve if they are to select an appropriate platform. It requires significant discipline for a team to clearly define and bound the problem definition.

Every platform solution represents an attempt to address the same general class of management problem; they intend to provide a common set of services to be used by multiple specialized management tools. The base services include such activities as discovery, event capture, data management, storage, and the display of information derived from the data. Fundamental, supplemental management services plug in to the base platform. Integration of third-party solutions should be easy to implement because of the standards-based application

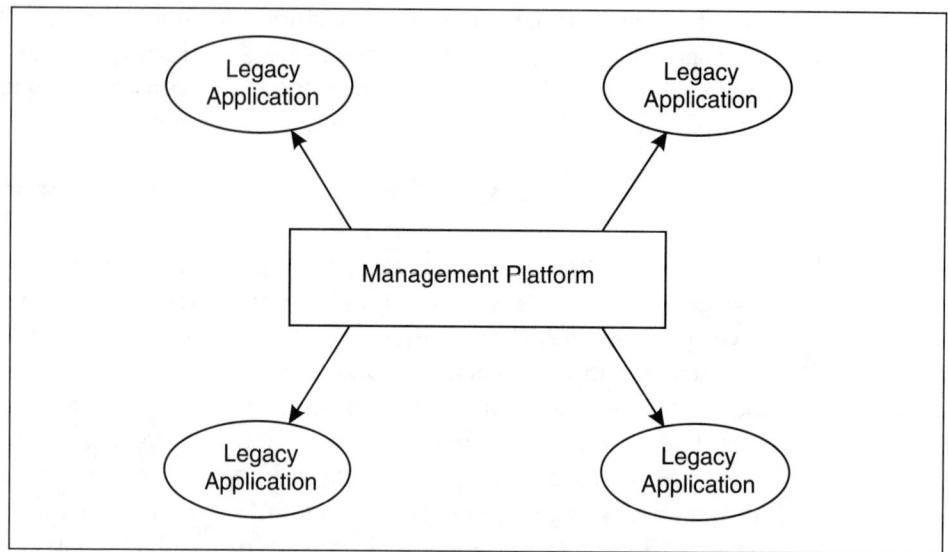

Figure 7.8 User integration.

program interfaces (APIs) provided. These APIs define the format, syntax, and content that are expected when applications attempt to interface to the platform or framework.

Early on, ease of tool integration with platforms tended to be overstated by the provider; or rather the complexity was not fully articulated. This caused problems for early adopters and developers of tools that had to be integrated with multiple platforms, ranging from poorly documented specifications to interface specs thinly disguised as proprietary lock-ins.

Lack of discipline and structure in distributed management evaluation projects doomed many solutions. The projects were too ambitious and overextended, marked by poorly defined objectives or failure to match a solution architecture to enterprise needs. The result: failed projects.

Dissatisfied end users blamed poorly functioning IS teams, who blamed vendors for misrepresenting tools. In truth, the fault lay in all areas. Enterprise managers may have failed to exercise good judgment or tight processes in screening potential solutions, for reasons ranging from oversized review staff to lack of process to a simple response to enterprise politics.

Mismatch between solutions and problems coupled with overly optimistic descriptions of integrated functionality caused widespread skepticism over the utility of platforms. Business customers were afraid of risking the success of the manage-

> **Poor Management Product Selection**
>
> A major manufacturing firm selected for the final evaluation:
>
> - One product that provided only minimal desired functionality.
>
> - One product built around and targeted for a platform explicitly excluded from the standard corporate operating environment.
>
> - One product that provided a full-function and totally automated solution.
>
> Clearly, the fundamental problem, the requirements listing, and priority for resolution were not explicitly defined in this case.

ment project by using a potentially inappropriate platform or building a solution from best-of-breed products.

For a while, popular opinion said to ignore platforms totally, that an enterprise should go with best-of-breed solutions in isolation or customize the integration process with internal resources or third-party integration facilities. This view held that platforms would soon be irrelevant; that they were high risk, low function, and created by vendors only to serve as competitive lock-ins. Some consultants went so far as to state that product improvements were occurring at such a pace that one day's solution could be discarded and replaced by the next best-of-breed candidate in 12 months or less with no significant loss, and that IS operations managers should embrace this as their core management tool strategy. This recommendation ignored the costs associated with learning a tool and the costs of installation and implementation, as well as resistance to changing a tool, process, or procedure once it has become familiar.

While the best-of-breed approach still has its adherents, most enterprises would be better off following an alternative path. Options range from an integration platform, incrementally adding functionality, to use of independent suites for incremental implementation of local control.

Next we discuss emerging ways to address weaknesses of current solutions. Then we talk about matching solution implementation and architecture to the problem.

Other Emerging Answers

Platform and framework vendors offer a wide variety of integration aids and services. They want to encourage adoption of their product by as many tool providers and business customers as possible. Efforts include:

- Attempts to proactively define, implement, and deliver cross-industry standards.

- Distribution of standards-based (both generic and proprietary) integration toolkits.

- Aggressive partnership alliance programs.

- Creating industry-focused integration service organizations.

Another approach proposes data, format, and access standards for *metering* applications. A common standard for metering applications means that management tools and platforms would no longer be burdened by incompatible data formats and content, thus making their task less complicated. The intent is to define syntactical and content standards usable by both platform providers and solution creators. Application developers would have an idea of the kinds of information that the users and systems and network administrators of management platforms and tools find useful. The standard would specify the data to be collected, the formats for storage, and how to make it available to embedded management services. Working with IS staff who use management applications would help identify the relevant data. The developers would build into the application the ability to collect, store, and enable access to the data. Collection of the specific data and information standards would be incorporated by application developers.

A metering approach makes a great deal of sense. Unfortunately, to date, it has found limited acceptance with platform providers, although some with solution providers. The major problem, as with the adoption of most standards, is the vendors' fear of surrendering competitive advantage. Vendor A may propose and provide all of the infrastructure for adoption of the standard, but vendors B and C will not adopt the mechanism as it exists because they fear yielding a competitive advantage, or because they have their own proposal ready to announce. We have succeeded in raising the issue and dialogue to a higher level of visibility, but to date remain far from a complete solution. Management application users have to pressure their vendors and solution providers to coalesce around a solution.

As an alternative to application metrics, vendors have proposed customized management for a comprehensive view of a specific business application, groups of applications, or services. These customized views of managed elements allow the administrator to create a view of devices, systems, applications, and elements linked according to specific criteria; that is, delivery of service. For any specific business service, all of the elements involved can be monitored from the status of a single icon. In this approach, the applications and monitored elements require no customization or designed-in functionality; the management platform or tool works with available data. This offers a definite improvement over the current situation, but must still deal with incompatible data structures if the view involves independent tools, with the consequent limitations on data correlation and analysis. Information available for review and analysis remains uncoordinated and nonstandard. The manager has available only what the device or application designer decided to include, with no consistent format or data structure.

Another approach is to hire a consulting firm to work with businesses to design and implement service-level management. An experienced team will custom-build the end-to-end solution based on existing tools and platforms. This solution has the advantage of making an experienced and expert team instantly available. With proper structuring, expertise can be transferred into the client organization to avoid problems of outside dependency.

Overall, the value of each solution must be judged case by case, based on factors such as cost, compatibility with the existing business environment, and concerns about vendor dependency. Cost may not be a deciding factor: The price gap between the use of external versus internal consultants narrows when allowing for hidden costs associated with learning, experience, and extended implementation times for internally led projects. In the same way, a business slow to accept external direction will weigh against the use of external services. Finally, an enterprise prepared for a successful transfer of knowledge will be able to avoid undesired vendor dependencies and lean in favor of an external solution.

World Wide Web standards offer the potential for a significant level of presentation and data integration, plus administrator mobility. Essentially, all vendors of distributed management solutions provide browser-based interfaces. Due to security concerns, Web-based tools initially were read-only, but this is rapidly changing; technologies like Java-based applets can provide fully customizable management functionality. Current efforts may resolve today's very real security and authorization issues, which inhibit much extranet and Internet activity.

Newly emerging service-level management tools such as Micromuse's Netcool suite include specific capabilities that more powerfully address the task of storing and making data available in a common format and structure for easy correlation and analysis. These products differ from existing data collection products in that they perform no real direct event collection functions, relying instead upon existing tools and platforms (e.g., HP OpenView, non-SNMP systems, etc.) to collect and pass raw event data to them. Passively receiving event data in multiple formats, these tools convert the data to a common format and store it in a single database for analysis and consolidation. They deliver great flexibility in indexing and keying to permit multiple sort criteria. Accompanying tools allow the system or network administrator to automatically analyze, filter, correlate, and present the data for a comprehensive management view. The more robust tools permit initiation of corrective actions based on sophisticated decision-making criteria. The built-in ease of use and implementation sets metric tools apart from many of the existing M-o-M and platform solutions. One evaluation metric for these tools is the absolute number of different protocols and data formats they can handle out of the box.

> **NOTE**
>
> These tools perform such a fundamental data integration service, we believe that the functionality they offer will be absorbed by and implemented within all of the major platforms in the near future.

Management Implications

There is little doubt of the full-scale assault being launched by emerging software firms and platforms to find solutions to all of the distributed computing management problems. Nevertheless, challenges will remain because IS personnel who use the tools will continue to demand enhanced, automated functionality. An IS or business manager should keep the following in mind when reviewing potential solutions:

- Know and fully document the data requirements and status of the existing installed management tool base.

- Query the actual level and status of integration among existing or potential tools and the platform or framework being evaluated. Integration is done at multiple levels; full sharing of data and results is *not* the typical level, although it may be the most desirable.

- Understand the required level of integration. Full integration may be desired, but the additional cost or effort to implement it may not be necessary.

- A full and exact fit off the shelf is unattainable today. Any vendor who commits to this should be avoided. Recognize that an 80 percent or better fit to current requirements, with convergence to a better fit over time, may prove to be a better solution than a custom 100 percent fit.

- Monitor emerging products, tools, and technologies. The rapid evolution and introduction of new functionality is the rule, not the exception. Use experts to validate the utility of an emerging product or technology; the true test of value is whether an approach resolves more problems than it creates.

Next we review the task of ensuring that the solution addresses the problem it is intended to resolve. All too often, misguided efforts have led to the adoption of an inappropriate solution. Any process can be subverted by the misapplication of creativity and intelligence in support of the wrong solution. The next section will help you reduce the risk of choosing the wrong solution by raising your level of awareness of the need to keep operational facts in mind during the selection process.

Matching Solutions to Problems

Architecture underlies the functions and tasks performed by a product, and determines the effectiveness and efficiency of any solution when it comes to resolving distributed management problems. It also, and almost more critically, reflects the solution architect's vision of the problem, the enterprise, how the product functions, and how to attack the problem. As an example, Tivoli's TME 10, along with Bull's ISM, Computer Associates TNG, and Hewlett-Packards OpenView, represent the most widely used systems and network management and integration platforms available on the market. These products compete head to head. Any comprehensive feature-function analysis would be hard-pressed to find any of them suffering from a glaring lack in capability. To make up for whatever may be lacking in an individual product, each vendor will have formed alliances with other suppliers, and sometimes the same ones, for third-party solutions. Virtually any one platform can be made to fit any enterprise structure and need. But at what cost—and why?

The significant differentiation between these platforms resides deeper, in their architecture, and needs to be understood to achieve the best match. The specifics of how the solution has been implemented carries implications for the enterprise selecting the solution. All too often, the assumptions of the solution architect are not recognized as affecting the choice of solution. For example, one platform positions itself as a standards-based, cross-vendor integration platform to facilitate policy-based management in an enterprise built around a distributed client/server model. The assumptions underlying this model are reflected in its strengths and weaknesses as a solution. An organization with centrally set and controlled policies, with a flat structure of distributed, heterogeneous LANs will find this an attractive solution. A strongly hierarchical organization, with many layers of networks and systems will find this solution more problematic, for if control and policies are set and administered locally, the organization will find the solution overfeatured.

Business consumers have several decisions to make. Should they select one of the platforms, gambling that it will survive and evolve to fit their business requirements? Should they choose a best-of-breed tool, counting on a fast return on investment and an accelerated pace of new product introduction that will allow them to switch to a better-suited solution certain to be available in 12 to 24 months?

Continuous and unrelenting competitive pressures combined with the increasingly sophisticated demands and expectations of consumers combine to motivate platform solution providers to decrease the complexity of utilization while increasing functionality. They also drive vendors to identify and address their respective actual and perceived weaknesses. Pressures from one another as well as from emerging companies drives all vendors to increase the utility and uniqueness of their products. Focus is rapidly moving away from straightforward comparisons based on function lists to evaluations based on the facility and intuitiveness of the tool. To evaluate tool intuitiveness, you need an in-depth knowledge of how the tool is used in problem resolution, combined with an intimate familiarity with the tool's architecture. Intuitive tool functionality will be a major area of competition, and the business consumer will reap the major benefit.

Incompatible Problem Definition and Solutions Architecture

In the ongoing battle between vendors and customers over delivered versus promised functionality, too little attention has been paid to ensuring that the architecture of the product/solution complements the identified problem. Every product architect has a vision of the problem to be solved as well as the environment in which the product must function. A product forced to fit either the environment or the problem will always be less successful than one that fits both. In the complex environments where system and network tools are used, the right choices become even more critical.

On one hand, vendors have the responsibility to provide a fair description of the features, functions, and environmental expectations of their solutions. On the other hand, enterprise purchasers should be honest and detailed in identifying and prioritizing requirements as well as constraints surrounding the problem to be attacked. Often, sufficient ambiguity exists in both product specification and product description to cause misunderstandings and dissatisfaction. The solution requires discipline on both sides, as well as the services of dispassionate analysts who have a thorough understanding of product architectures and implementation.

For example, one management platform product may be designed for use in a distributed, heterogeneous environment with an emphasis on locally tracked and implemented policy-driven management. Another may be focused on providing event-driven response to distributed servers, with an emphasis on centralized, hierarchical control. The former will not easily fit into an environment where centralized control is considered a high priority, or where data on policy violations is ignored. The latter will be less successful in an environment where local groups have considerable autonomy in behavior and configuration, setting their own policies and standards.

Virtually any distributed management platform or tool can be *made* to fit an environment or resolve a problem. Vendors, implementors, and value-added resellers (VARs) are happy to provide customization services to provide the best fit—and using one of them may make the most sense to achieve the identified goals and needs of the enterprise. Customization efforts are not objectionable. But the purchaser must extend the effort to achieve a clear definition of goals, a bounded description of the problem to be solved, and a clear prioritization of identified requirements to minimize required effort and ensure the best fit of product to need.

The IS manager must also judge the suitability of attempting to introduce radically innovative products and technologies based on the capabilities of their resources and organizational environmental norms and level of tolerance. An enterprise in which IS costs represent a small portion of overall expenses can be far more tolerant of experimental, cutting-edge applications. When combined with visionary management, some organizations can reasonably undertake the risks inherent in exploring the limits of the creative application of IS services to develop a competitive business advantage. Enterprises that are able to experiment help push the leading edge of distributed management, but unfortunately are very limited in number. For most IS organizations, the competition-driven facts of life leave little latitude for experimentation. They must pace their introduction and adoption of new technologies and products with thorough testing and special attention to ensure sufficient improvement in efficiencies, facilitated processes, reduction in product time to market, or improved information quality to ensure payback.

Emergence of Service-Level Management

More and more IS organizations today find themselves being evaluated on their direct contribution to the competitive and business advantage of the enterprise. Those that cannot clearly link their activities to an identifiable benefit, improved product positioning, customer advantage, or reduction in costs find themselves having to do more with less resources, or even face the threat of outsourcing. IS has little time, energy, or inclination to allocate on gratuitous customization or products with extended learning curves.

Total cost of ownership (TCO) of client/server and computing technology and operations has been the fad phrase applied to efforts to identify and manage the cost of what has been viewed as an overhead operation. This is a misplaced priority. IS represents an asset and resource that should be measured on its contribution to business success. IS has the potential to increase competitiveness and improve business profitability, an issue explored in more depth in Chapter 5.

The search has been for a solution that integrates cleanly with existing, installed products; comes with a well-defined interface to expand functionality; and is usable out of the box. Attempts to provide this capability aren't new. Solutions available from a range of vendors all attempt to provide an integrated framework or platform complete with multiple, integrated management functions. These products offer the capability to discover, monitor, and report on multiple vendor devices. In much the same way, systems managers appeared, offering centralized, policy-based functions such as user management, software distribution, and services accessible to third-party management applications. These solutions raised the level of competition and fed expectations for more sophisticated, easy-to-use, and integrated solutions. Controversy over the financial payback of integrated approaches provides considerable and continuous fodder for consultant and analyst discussions and journalistic bombast.

There is no doubt, however, that we need to view network management from the perspective of the business as a whole. For service provider and enterprise manager alike, escalating competitive pressures combine with the reliance on sophisticated, distributed services to push business issues to the forefront. It is no longer acceptable to promote element, device, or link availability as a measure of performance while relinquishing business to extended design cycle times or lost access to a data or pricing file. For example, showing 99.998 percent switch reliability is meaningless if the pricing file in Los Angeles is inaccessible due to a server crash. It is generally acknowledged that metrics and performance tracking must expand in focus to take into account the reliable delivery of a total service.

Enhanced perspective requires a dynamic view and management of all resources (switches, network paths, applications, etc.), no matter how transiently involved in the implementation of the service. While this idea is not new to managers of telephony or LAN/WAN networks, only recently have major vendors and emerging solution providers begun aggressively promoting end-to-end service capabilities as part of their solution sets and product plans.

End-to-end service delivery and reporting has become the model for distributed management. This function goes by several names, including *service management*, *jurisdictional management*, and *service-level agreement* (SLA) management. The question network managers face is whether current tools and products—let alone the IS organization itself—are up to the challenge.

Management Implications

Finding the best and most appropriate solutions requires a disciplined process of evaluation, one of quality not quantity of input. An evaluation project plan should include:

- *Statement of goal.* Resolve all problems or a critical three?

- *Well-defined problem statement.* Simple file transfer or dynamic software change management?

- *Performance metrics.* Determine what will change as an indicator of success.

- *Document boundaries.* What is possible given the corporate culture, priorities, financial, and administrative restrictions?

- *Understand the solution choices.* Not just what they do but how they do it and the underlying problems they are designed to address.

- *Research the solution provider.* Interview satisfied *and* dissatisfied customers.

- *Pilot the solution.* Plan and execute a test in a controlled environment to shake down the implementation.

Let's go into each of these in more depth.

Goal Statement Goal statements may reflect either an overly ambitious statement of objectives or too narrow a focus on a tactical problem. Overambition can mean a never-ending project that fails to deliver the expected problem relief—an eventual cash sink and an excuse for delayed action. Too narrow a focus can mean underwhelming achievement with no significant, visible contribution to business goals.

The goal must realistically reflect enterprise commitment, bound the project scope to recognizable achievement, and be backed up by corporate commitment with an appropriate assignment of resources.

Define and Understand the Problem In practice, a clear problem definition proves difficult. The rich array of features and functions available can confuse a selection process that focuses on "horse-race" comparisons of functionality. A vague problem definition leads to a requirement set whose functionality is irrelevant or incompatible with the managing environment. As an example, a tool built upon policy-based management and control will end up as expensive shelfware in an enterprise environment without both the will and authority to enforce them. A sophisticated automatic change management system is an expensive and overly complex solution when compared to a simple automatic file and application distribution capability for automatic software distribution. An enterprise may find considerable savings in the more sophisticated solution, which can automatically detect the need, create the minimal package needed, verify satisfaction of installation parameters, and install necessary software changes in a heterogeneous environment.

Identify a Metric to Verify Success All too often, projects begin and end with too little thought given to fixing the measure of success. It is necessary to determine and document *at the outset* how success will be measured and defined. Record the metric prior to the implementation, at periodic test points during the implementation process, and at the completion of the project. The relationship between project activities and efforts and the influence on the metric should be clear, explicit, and understandable by all team members and management monitors.

Document Implicit and Explicit Solution Boundaries Corporate culture, environmental restrictions, organizational constraints, personnel restrictions, resource limitations, as well as technical limits can all impact the search for a solution. Identifying these restrictions at the start of the solution search process can reduce search time, improve the quality of the final solution, and minimize wasted efforts.

Fully Understand the Solution and the Architectural and Design Intent Underlying a product is a large collection of assumptions about the problem and the environment in which it exists and in which the solution will be introduced. Understanding this prior to selection and implementation can prevent a gross mismatch and significantly enhance ultimate satisfaction. It isn't that any of the today's management platform solutions can't be made to fit any environment; it is just that there is often a better match between the assumptions and design intent for some solutions and some organizations and their problems. A flat, distributed organization with much local control with only casual reporting relationships to a central organization will be more easily and completely satisfied by a solution whose architecture reflects this structure than with one that assumes a strong, hierarchical focus with power and control residing in a single, central department. This will frequently require more up-front analysis and investigation, and few firms are willing to explicitly reduce the size of their potential market. Services available from any of the technical, analytical consulting firms, *not* systems integrators, can provide the neutral expertise and information required. Such firms offer solutions help either through custom consulting services, which analyze your unique business requirements, or less expensively through research subscription services which provide periodic reports comparing the capabilities of tools and platforms.

Review and Research the Solution Provider This means interviewing satisfied as well as dissatisfied customers. Preferably these will be enterprises whose problems, size, and interests represent as close a match to yours as reasonable. Any reputable vendor will furnish references. Also, be sure to determine the level of postsales support you will require, and determine whether the vendor can meet it. As documented in the trade press, even the largest and most established firms can run into staffing shortage problems when faced with an explosion in success and product demand that has not been foreseen.

Implement a Pilot Program A pilot program, whether full blown or in the form of a phased implementation, will help uncover and resolve the inevitable unexpected and unforeseen incompatibilities and problems inherent in any project. When affordable, a full-blown pilot, implemented and run totally separate from the production environment, provides the highest level of security and rigorous shakedown. But even doing a phased implementation in a controlled environment will help reduce the problems encountered in the rollout.

Follow Implementation with Discipline The success of any process is limited by the diligence and discipline of its application. Frequently, even existing processes tend to be ignored, excused because of the critical nature of the current problem or limited time available to the evaluation team. If you face problems, delay the project, assign new staff, or define a more realistic schedule. Otherwise, you may end up hiring a consulting firm to fix problems caused by of a lack of discipline in following an existing process, or because accountability for adherence is ignored. Adherence to a well-defined, disciplined process rests well within the control of the evaluation team. If the process doesn't exist, their first responsibility should be to define and document it.

Conclusions

Discontent with today's distributed management functionality results from a combination of inflated expectations, a lack of understanding products and problem focus, and the pressure to tie technology performance directly to business success. Too many of today's systems report what's measurable, not what's meaningful to the business manager. Fundamental to the presentation of a business-focused view is the correlation and analysis of collected data into a relevant and comprehensible presentation.

Today's tools and management solutions are rapidly evolving from an environment geared to quickly identifying and responding to element failure to one focused on providing a comprehensive view of business services with proactive problem solving or avoidance. Recognizing and responding to existing integration and functionality gaps, tool providers, IS operations, executives, and vendors must work together to develop creative responses at multiple levels. These range from new embedded tools that provide automatic data consolidation to enhanced analysis tools to agreement and implementation on standardized information collection and presentation formats.

Intelligent business practices go a long way toward creating the best management toolbox for an IS organization. Technology-rich IS customers must expand their view of IS from that of a mere infrastructure provider to one of an active partner whose powerful tools provide the capability to address business problems and enable significant competitive advantage. Information systems and technology organizations represent corporate assets that can and must be encouraged to contribute to resolving business problems and increasing competitiveness. IS must learn to identify their potential for contribution as well as their resource needs in terms not only of the cost of utilizing them but of their contribution to business success as well. Service management, service-level agreements, and application management provide the building blocks to this communication.

Having completed a review of the various alternative approaches to distributed management solutions and the various vendor offerings, the next chapter provides a methodology for selecting the appropriate solution.

FOR FURTHER READING

Boar, Bernard H. *Practical Steps for Aligning Information Technology with Business Strategies*. (New York: John Wiley & Sons, Inc.), 1994.

Jay, Anthony. *Management & Machiavelli*. (San Diego: Pfeiffer & Company), 1994.

8 EVALUATING MANAGEMENT SOLUTIONS

> No one can encompass the unencompassable.
>
> Alexei Konstantinovich Tolstoi,
> *Collected Works of Kosma Prutkov*, 1884

This chapter addresses:

Media, vendor, and customer roles.

Why you need a management solution selection process.

Assumptions about management operational models and how they affect vendor solution design.

Questions to guide the management solution selection process.

Why IS must provide quality service and then document and publicize the value of the IS team to the organization.

Media, Vendor, and Customer Roles

It is estimated that 70 percent of distributed management platform-based solution attempts fail. Article after article in the trade press detail the failures of what are, paradoxically, the most popular distributed management solutions. Descriptions abound of overstated, underperforming applications foisted on unsuspecting and innocent searchers for IS solutions at all levels.

What's going on? Are management solution vendors the twentieth-century equivalent of the nineteenth-century "instant and universal" curative medicine peddler? Are the major solutions providers the functional equivalent of the proverbial sleazy used-car salesmen? Or does the problem lie with customers who fail to follow a disciplined process of problem identification, requirements collection, prioritization, coupled with careful implementation planning? The answer is not black and white.

In any case, assigning blame will not help build a working solution. But by analyzing why the hype exists, we can learn how to devise action plans to help us avoid the pitfalls. This chapter examines potential problems and pitfalls with vendor solutions and establishes guidelines to help you get what you need as well as what you pay for.

Reading the Headlines

Bad news always outsells good news, even in the professional press. Technically literate readers are no less engaged by headlines, story leads, and consultant anecdotes that hint or tell of controversy, conflict, and failure. But such reports won't necessarily provide the detail needed to help you avoid your own failures; and frequently they misrepresent the advanced state of technology as well as ignoring the successful implementations. Remember, stories of failure also help drive the demand for consultant and analyst services.

To get the full picture of the situation, you must use good judgment, keeping in mind that there are two sides to any story; vendors, implementers, and customers all share the responsibility for project successes and failures. Newsworthy stories, relating both the good and the bad can help maintain a balance between overenthusiastic vendor claims and gloom-and-doom scenarios that increase demand for expert hand-holding.

TIP

Read the articles in the trade press for significant information. But question why the technology failed. Try to see beyond the journalist's view for the reasons the project went awry. Ask how important the technology or functions discussed are to *your* situation. Be on the lookout for lessons, then—examine, evaluate, and relate them to your own situation, experiences, and requirements.

Understanding Vendors

Advertising and enthusiastic sales reps give vendors the impetus to inflate functionality, ease of use, and integration of their products. While sometimes justified by past experiences, confrontational and adversarial relationships between vendors and clients do not contribute to successful projects.

Vendors expend great effort to align their product to customer identified needs—as well as to detail and document the mechanisms used by customers to make product selection decisions. Unfortunately, at times, their responses to market cues are too slow. Thus they may miss a shift in solution priorities or even fail to respond to satisfaction surveys and feedback that provide advance warning of changes in requirements and expectations. Numerous other stories tell of customers left in the lurch as vendors shift product plans. Even dominant, apparently unassailable market leaders can fall when (even technically superior) products fail to address newly identified requirements. Vendors will eventually see their markets collapse if they fail to remain current with such expectations.

Fortunately for customers and unfortunately for slow-to-respond vendors, the market for solutions remains dynamic, innovative, and highly competitive. Alert competitors can spot a potentially lucrative market niche or functionality gap quickly, assess their ability to profitably (and credibly, but not necessarily effectively) address it, then act on a positive assessment. However, there always exists a risk that the proffered solution will fall far short of what the customer expects.

For example, when systems managers suddenly began to focus on business and service-linked views of the distributed system, service-level agreements and business-related views were delivered in vendor products in mere months, as a way to replace stovepipe, device-focused management reporting. Unfortunately, a rigorous examination of many of the initial solutions revealed far less than the integrated, correlated, and filtered information required for business and service management. In addition, the effort required to implement a truly useful presentation frequently required custom consulting and development services. Vendors who presented a straightforward explanation of the complexity and effort required initially suffered

TIP

Ask the right questions. Sophisticated consumers must frame very specific questions and investigate products in detail to ensure a close match between *required, promised,* and *delivered* functionality. Vendor enthusiasm aside, it falls on the consumer to check that what is promised matches what is delivered.

because less scrupulous solution providers promised out-of-the-box integrated management and reporting capabilities.

Being a Good Customer

IS organizations often have not just one, but several different solution applications already on-site for consideration. Whether purchased, loaned for evaluation, or bundled with a hardware purchase, they are rarely used to basic, let alone full potential. Reasons for not using the application include: "They're old copies that no one knows how to use," or "I would be held accountable if a problem occurred using the tool," or "No one has enough time to learn to use the tool properly." At other companies, problems occur even when the selection of a solution was the result of an extensive, internal evaluation process. Problems with fit, application, functionality, or suitability appear and raise serious doubts about the solution's usefulness, or work against their full, effective application. Underutilization is at the heart of many of the reported solutions horror stories.

Customers, whether defined in the narrow sense of the user of the solution (operations staff) or in the broader sense of those making the buying decisions bear, part of the blame for confusion about the criteria for solution selection. It requires the cooperative effort of both to define solution requirements and to conduct an accurate assessment of alternative solutions. Vendors need a clear message from the customer that defines the basis for comparison among competing products; they need to understand how the product will be used. Successful solution selection results from an often complex, multifaceted process integrating and balancing a wide variety of priorities and influences. Customers often fail to understand the limitations and advantages of the solution offered to them. They may be just as much in the dark about the priorities and product requirements of the problems they are attempting to resolve. How do customers know if the solution works with their operating environment, their implementation processes, and even the very real problem to be solved?

> **TIP**
>
> Be disciplined when determining needs. Apparently "cool" features may prove useless when applied to your specific environment or mode of operation. Don't let vendors get away with mere checklists of important features. Insist on demonstrations of critical features; verify that features are easy to access and do not require extensive customization to be used productively.

Summary

If the reports on the failure of IS management solution projects are to be believed, the corporate landscape should be littered with the bodies of shell-shocked, damaged, and destroyed IS managers paying the ultimate price for their foolish choices. The fact that so many remain ambulatory, however, doesn't invalidate the anecdotal and reported horror stories. Rather it suggests that:

- Life goes on pretty much as usual; successful implementations will follow from well thought out and executed evaluation/implementation processes.

- IS staff spend way too much time recovering from the results of poor selection/evaluation processes and incorrect product choices.

- The IS trade, press, analysts, and consumers enjoy reading about how someone else has failed. Why? Either to gape in horror or to learn something from the postmortem to help them avoid it in their own lives.

All this leads to the question: Is extraordinary effort or special process required to bring IS projects to a successful conclusion? Whatever the answer, can we describe and quantify the selection process? The next major section addresses these questions, but first we will look at the vendor/customer decision-making environment.

How Vendors and Customers Can Work Together

Vendors need to know their markets, products, and the problems they wish to resolve. They need to understand that customers make decisions not just from a checklist of features but based on the perceived value of the solution as one part of a multipart equation. Service, quality, price, functionality, and value all play a part, not as isolated elements but in combination and in relation to all the potential competitive solutions. Vendors should never forget that the solution set for the customer includes doing nothing, that is, making a decision to continue in the current mode of operation until either a better solution emerges, the current situation becomes completely intolerable, or priorities change sufficiently to force resolution.

Customers (again, in both senses) have to understand and clearly communicate their requirements and decision criteria to vendors. They need to exercise due diligence in researching products. It is necessary to understand not only the overt capabilities and limitations of the management solution package, but also those buried and inherent as part of the architecture, design, and assumptions made about the problems to be solved and the operational environment.

Creating a Selection Process

Sifting through today's solutions in search of the most appropriate product requires a disciplined evaluation process. The process must focus on the quality of knowledge obtained from the research, not merely the quantity of input. The telephony case study illustrates the importance of a quality evaluation.

In addition to carefully controlling both the size and makeup of the team, you need a disciplined process of evaluation, again, one of quality not quantity of input, following the criteria discussed throughout this chapter. The important sections of a successful plan include these points:

1. Follow a well-defined project process and stick with it.

2. Clearly define both the goal and the problem to be solved.

3. Establish performance metrics.

4. Understand the vendor and the solution choices.

5. Run a pilot of the solution.

It is critical to differentiate, understand, and maintain the difference between short- and long-term goals. Avoid attempting to pursue conflicting goals. Sequence and prioritize goals, don't unconsciously compromise one set of goals for another. To achieve your goals, you must be able to *complete* the process. In any high-visibility project there is a temptation to expand the goal set to include just one more critical function. Yielding to that temptation is a virtual guarantee of failure; it dilutes resources, impacts well-laid plans, and results in a loss of focus.

> **TIP**
>
> Set priorities and goals early, make them public, keep them visible, and focus, focus, focus.

Understanding Your Needs

So far we have addressed the various roles, responsibilities, and structures of management solutions, and have examined the goals driving both the providers and users of solutions. Now we discuss the importance of developing an in-depth understanding of needs. Beyond a listing of requirements, you must recognize that a correctly selected and effective IS management solution will impact the operational environment of the enterprise. Doing so can help to avoid attempting to introduce

> **Telephony Case Study**
>
> A major telephony service provider undertook a search for a distributed systems management solution. Project plans called for a well-documented, well-defined, and well-disciplined process to be followed. Particular attention was to be paid to ensure careful identification and prioritization of requirements in each of the five targeted management domains: problem management, help desk, performance management, security management, and configuration management.
>
> Unfortunately, the teams organized to collect and prioritize requirements were composed of groups of 3 to 15 people representing a range of constituencies from desktop users to IS teams. Because all participants had an equal opportunity to squelch a compromise, endless bickering ensued until there was virtually no chance of a successful resolution. After three months of operation, the project was brought to a merciful but painful end by an external acquisition. The acquiring partner sliced through the out-of-control process by mandating and imposing an existing management solution. While not the best approach, the initial pieces of the phased implementation were completed successfully, a solution that could have been implemented within months of the project initiation if done properly.

unacceptable change and facilitate the adoption of the solution. Spending most of one's waking hours within an organization does not assure the necessary appreciation and understanding of the embedded enterprise management *operational model* (see the next subsection); the political ramifications of choosing a management solution; or how specific management tasks get done. Nor does it help with the identification of the necessary information, who uses it and how, as well who shares what information. Remember, not all information is worth collecting.

Distributed Management Operational Models

Enterprises and businesses organize and operate around specific operational models. By operational model, we mean the model that drives and organizes all corporate processes from information gathering, storing, and processing to administrative and management control. An almost entropic event, this organization happens by default even if an overt decision has not been made to embrace a specific model. Although, here, we are looking specifically at the model for distributed systems and network management, it applies to the entire organization (the scope of this book precludes exploring the enterprise impact).

We have identified three operational model design centers competing for mind-share today:

Event oriented. Based on and reactive to events as they occur; product examples include management platforms such as Hewlett Packard's OpenView and Computer Associates' TNG.

Workflow/process oriented. Promoted and realized using applications such as SAP R/3 or PeopleSoft.

Policy driven. Typically hierarchical and centralized in nature, the focus is on automated implementation of centrally defined policies; Tivoli's TME 10 represents a good solution example.

Remember, these are representative types; in actual implementation, a specific enterprise may very well function with, and include, a blend of these types.

Event-Driven Organizations

For *event-driven* management, the emphasis is on monitoring and reacting to alarms and triggers in the managed system. Priority is given to tracking events: collecting, analyzing, and identifying the useful bits of data from the thousands or tens of thousands of irrelevant or insignificant samples.

The search for Nobel prize–winning data in experimental physics provides a good analogy. Scientists spend months designing and setting up experiments to arrange collisions and collect data during the few seconds after particle generation, acceleration, and collision take place. From the tens of millions of *events* that result, fewer than ten have the potential to yield information that can materially advance the state of knowledge. The work of the theoretical technician focuses on sifting through mountains of data for those significant few events.

The processes and procedures developed in event-driven organizations will reflect the distributed focus. The emphasis will be on pushing problem identification and correction close to the occurrence of the event to prevent collateral damage from proliferating throughout the system. Control and administrative authority will be distributed—pushed out to where the action takes place.

Process-Driven Organizations

For our purposes, *process-driven* organizations operate according to predefined data, information, and workflows, and procedures enforced through application suites. Application metaphors lie at the heart of such solutions as SAP R/3, Baan

Co., and PeopleSoft. These applications reflect the belief that businesses succeed when tasks and functions are carried out in a manner organized for maximize value to the customer. This translates to an efficient operation as a combination of parallel and sequential workflow processes.

Process-driven organizations use the concept of a supply chain, starting with the most basic operations of sales, engineering, purchasing, manufacturing, and distribution, positing that the concept of a sequential flow of data, tasks, and materials is too limiting and time wasting. The new organizational focus of IS sees the customer as a pervasive influence and interface for all organizations. The customer first and foremost is the ultimate consumer of the enterprise deliverables. The internal desktop user, accounting department, manufacturing, sales, and engineering functions in the organization are all seen as part of the comprehensive set of service delivery mechanisms of the services or products that form the core function of the business. All activities, tasks, responsibilities, and data have to be focused upon and organized to support the concerns of this ultimate customer.

Hierarchical and application-oriented focus is replaced by an emphasis on transaction processing and monitoring that operates in real time. This operational mode calls for multiple, interactive, and evolving interfaces between the functional groups both within and outside of the enterprise.

Policy-Driven Organizations

Policy-driven organizations follow a more traditional, centralized administrative and managerial model. At their most rigorous, central management groups define policies for desktop configuration, application access, information sharing, and so on. These policies are then enforced at a local level. Enforcement can take the form of automatic reconfiguration to the desired state, lock-out of the offending system, or simple notification to an administrator for further evaluation and action. Reporting may also be a simple entry in a data file, filed for future reference or left to grow until the file becomes unmanageable. This automatic monitoring process for configurations and settings can consume significant resources; problems arise when the organizational and management structure don't support the administrative structure. The insurance company sidebar illustrates problems with policy-driven management models.

Of course, few organizations today rigorously adhere to a single administrative model. Some functions naturally operate more effectively in one or the other models, and different parts of an organization can operate under a totally different model. The intent here is to increase sensitivity to the existence of the multiple styles and show the potential positive and negative impact of the management solutions in the enterprise.

> **Policy-Driven Insurance Company**
>
> An insurance company endured a drawn-out, expensive requirements definition and product evaluation process. After the final phase of the evaluation and implementation had begun, management changed; IS staffing was "rationalized," and outside consulting services were terminated. The product selected as the backbone enterprise management solution assumed a strong centralized IS organization.
>
> The reorganization left a decimated, token central IS administrative staff, with most power, managerial decision making, and administration policy residing in independent divisions. After a year of operation, the management system, while it provided all of the promised functionality, had become an overpriced extravagance to the central IS staff. Some of the most powerful automation and tracking functions of the solution served no useful function, as managerial responsibility was no longer their responsibility. They would have been far better served to choose a solution that focused on providing distributed, autonomous event-driven monitoring and management. With such a solution, policies and procedures could have been defined that ensured only globally interesting anomalies would be brought to the attention of the central management staff.

Politics

In every organization, politics plays a role. The impact can be subversive and damaging, or it can be overt and fundamentally supportive. Business politics has frequently been denigrated and dismissed. However, political activity and sensitivity, born of necessity, exists and survives because it serves an organizational and human relationship purpose. Management solutions impact far beyond the immediate individuals involved in network or system management.

Introducing a management solution can radically shift the centers of control and power within an organization. How these shifts are recognized and accepted will depend on how the changes have been presented. Working to ensure that changes in process and responsibility have been fully documented and agreed upon in advance will go a long way toward smoothing the implementation and acceptance of a new solution.

Political activity is positive when it facilitates and accelerates accomplishment in support of corporate and enterprise principles and goals. It is perverse when it subverts appropriate controls, promotes individual goals at the expense of the long-term benefit of the enterprise, or violates moral principles.

Politics cannot be ignored or denied without risk. The impact of doing so can manifest itself in the mandatory inclusion or exclusion of vendors in an evaluation process based on positive or negative experiences in the past. Politics can mandate a higher than apparently justified priority for a particular requirement or group of requirements. It may also take the form of implementation of a particular management domain in order to gain approval. While a politically motivated decision may not require explicit documentation, you can avoid potential landmines by recognizing they exist, determining how to integrate or adapt them to the needs of the project, and making them work in support of the project. They represent a need that must be addressed. Recognize and plan in advance how to address the concerns and needs of the various constituencies affected by the management system.

Process

It is important to critically examine and understand the management discovery, analysis, and resolution process if the desired solution is to deliver more than a checklist of features. The goal is to provide a tool to enhance the efficient tracking of problems, to root out causes, and aid in prompt resolution of problems. It is critical to document and understand how the management work gets done. To accomplish this, tap your existing enterprise experts in analytic and problem resolution processes; they can provide valuable help in requirement generation, as well help balance the evaluation process.

More often than it should, requirement definitions end up driven by vendor-generated, marketing-driven functionality lists. Attention shifts to a vendor's strong points, which may provide functionality not relevant to the enterprise and the way it operates. Technical analysts can also be seen as complicit in these "horse-race" evaluations. Feature and function lists can be relatively easily generated and scored. They can provide a false sense of security for decision making with their so-called scores. If you are able to point out weaknesses, vendors can learn to address them quickly.

The requirements definition demands more than a mere surface understanding of process. It includes understanding and appreciating the analytic procedures your IS management team will follow; only then can the selection team determine whether the tool will be useful. For example, an unsorted list of IP addresses is not a useful way of presenting information if you are looking for a few bad addresses; the product would be more useful if the list were sorted with errors appearing first. The procedures of interest include those that utilize available event data, as well as those that drive the directed search for additional data as part of the analytic process. The goal is to determine if the product "thinks" like your management staff and anticipates the next step in the problem resolution process.

Vendors, customers, and analysts recognize that as competition heats up and products mature, new areas of evaluation and competition have to found. Tool efficiency and effectiveness can be increased as an outcome of a thorough understanding of how the tool is used, and of the analytic and management processes. Evaluation teams that understand the processes can ask more intelligent and informative questions of vendors and analysts to ensure a better fit between their needs and selected products.

The evolution from feature/function lists to utilization-engineered solutions takes time. It requires concerted effort from vendors for implementation, customers for functionality definition, and analysts to increase the visibility of the issue. Some vendors, recognizing this new level of competition, have begun to focus engineering efforts on delivering such enhancements. In the end, vendors will respond only to pressure from their customers. Therefore, the more fully, clearly, and forcibly the consumer articulates the need, the more quickly, effectively, and comprehensively vendors will respond.

Data Value

Finally, it is important to identify what is truly useful data. There is a tendency to assume that any available data that can be collected is useful. Therefore, specific efforts should identify exactly what data, in which specific formats, is relevant to the management process.

There has been significant confusion about multiple data repositories versus replicated databases versus shared databases. The problem arises from the perceived wasted effort of collecting redundant data and maintaining the same data in multiple locations. It seems obvious that data and information collected from an automated discovery process for the network management system should feed into asset and configuration management applications. On the other hand, event data from a network device failure does not have to be accessible to a systems manager unless it affects his or her system or service delivery.

To identify the important and useful information, you must understand who uses what data and for how long. To that end, look for and document who shares what information. Use this new-found knowledge to understand and bound the collection and analysis of management information. More than enough has been written about the risks and difficulties surrounding the selection and implementation of management solutions. The resolution of complex problems is the result of hard work backed by clear thinking and analysis.

What to Look for in a Management Solution

This section reviews strategies and key operational concepts frequently overlooked by IS organizations. Long-term strategic plans have a way of failing to keep pace with events. All too frequently the process of detailing directions and strategies becomes an end in itself, each version barely published before the process of revision begins again. On the other hand, if one has not defined a destination, any movement can be (mis)represented as progress. The destinations and guidelines discussed in the following sections are worthwhile for any organization. Therefore, we talk about the necessity of IS taking an active role in understanding and driving enterprise success. IS must become a recognized partner in driving the success of the business by creatively anticipating and meeting customer needs.

This section also addresses the need for IS to understand the architectural implications of the solutions it analyzes and proposes for implementation. A conscious analysis represents less of an issue for internally developed and implemented solutions than it is for the selection and purchase of off-the-shelf and semicustom solutions. No one with the ability to read or who is within hearing distance of an organization attempting to implement one of today's integrated reengineering application suites can be unaware of their impact on the enterprise.

Finally, in this section we discuss some behavior metrics and design standards that indicate customer-friendly, industry-leading solution providers. Honeyed words from silver-tongued promoters provide no real assurance of robust, effective solutions less likely to tie you to a single vendor. In the words of Ronald Reagan, "trust with verification." We provide some advice on just what to look for from vendors to protect your long-term solution viability.

Facilitating Business Success

Too often in the past, IS teams have adopted a reactive attitude that challenges business executives to understand how to use IS services most effectively. An "if they want it they will ask us" approach worked early on, when automated data processing on a gigantic scale provided obvious cost advantages. However, in today's world of global competition, shrinking budgets, and thin margins, every segment of the business must prove its contribution—particularly since the promised reductions in the cost of computing through distributed processing have been overwhelmed by the cost of management and administration. If IS is only good for computer maintenance, then outsourcing becomes a viable option. Here we recommend that IS recognize and actively promote its role as a critical resource in the enterprise, one with the ability to contribute directly to improved competitiveness and success.

IS management should be active in the problem definition and resolution process. IS management and staff need to understand what drives the business success and competitive advantage in their enterprise. Only then can they devise solutions and services based on the creative application of their total resources.

If there is no history of creative IS engagement in the business problem resolution process, leaping unprepared into the process will almost guarantee failure. Take the time to identify a strong player in the business team and enlist him or her as a partner. This person need not be a technology expert, but should understand how technology is applied and be able to quantify the business benefits. Pick a partner who can help prepare and present the business case for the involvement of the IS organization.

IS's potential contribution to business success is rooted in its virtually unlimited ability to provide automated and accelerated services customized to satisfy end-user needs. IS contributes by identifying, analyzing, tracking, and crafting a response to the unique requirements of large numbers of departments and individual end users. The ability to automate, coordinate, and collect data on the thousands of interacting pieces involved in the delivery of a service to an end user requires skills, capabilities, and functions inherent in this organization. To lose the department's capabilities or have them pass into the control of an organization external to the enterprise may mean you are unnecessarily surrendering your competitive advantage.

IS must overtly undertake to document and publicize its ability to drive competitive business advantage. This requires that IS staff and management understand the business they serve and how new technologies will impact the business, the end users, and competitors. It is only with this comprehensive view of the environment in which they function that they can effectively and efficiently define and deliver exceptional services. While cost control is important, revenue enhancement ultimately must come from increased revenues. The IS solution contribution will be based on their contribution to business success through an increase in these revenues, the realization of competitive advantage, and the resolution of business problems.

Cost Control or Solution Investment?

It goes without saying that the IS department exists to provide services to profit-making enterprises. Even for those such as service-focused organizations where profit does not represent a primary goal, few organizations outside of the government define success based solely on the growth in the size of their budget. Even organizations devoted to nonprofit research will typically have some level of contribution or cost-benefit performance requirement.

Business success can be defined in many ways. Take time to identify and understand the definition of success as well as the business goals of the organization.

Remember, what actually exists as the major business objective may not be the obvious, traditional goal. Few managers would argue against a focus on quantifying and reducing the cost of operations. However, a focus on controlling costs that improves margins but sacrifices postsales support in a market crying for reliable support services may actually lead to a loss of business.

Much has been made of total cost of ownership (TCO) as a driving strategy for acquisition and utilization of IS resources. Notoriously difficult to pin down, it is next to impossible to prove that cost is decreasing over time. The real risk is that the emphasis on cost and cost-focused control in IS has been overemphasized to the point where IS is not recognized as a valuable part of the business. No one argues for an unrestrained growth in expenses or to ignore cost management—these are and will remain important; the real goal is to find ways to apply resources in support of increasing and facilitating revenues. Identify activities that contribute to business success, competitive advantage, and creative resolution of business problems. Using IS resources to attract customers and satisfy their needs more quickly, efficiently, and effectively will shift the business view of IS as a cost center to IS as a revenue driver; thus IS will be seen as a valuable resource.

How Business Views IS

What does senior management expect from the IS department? Too often, corporate executives do not understand the current potential of IS as a valuable corporate resource. In a major aerospace company, for example, senior management was asked what they saw as the greatest possible contribution their IS team could make. What did they say? Effective maintenance of electronic mail! These managers appeared unaware of potential contributions to competitive advantage and savings in engineering, operations, manufacturing, and sales through further innovative application of IS capabilities. Aerospace is an industry where consolidation and budget cuts have significantly raised the level of price- and cost-focused competition. A focus by IS on any one of these specific areas had the potential for dramatic payoff.

The executives' attitude reflected poorly on both IS and corporate management, but also represented a major threat to the IS manager. The IS department either contributes to and is directly involved in the success of the enterprise or it has no rational business reason to exist. If the contribution or potential for contribution remains unrecognized or unheeded, outsourcing of resources makes undeniable business sense. (See the discussion on outsourcing in Chapter 11.)

Designing Valued Services

The end users (customers) of any business, service, or product make decisions about how to allocate and use limited resources. The decision process involves multiple steps, including:

1. *Identify the need for a product or service.* A problem, business advantage, or capability that hinders success and must be addressed.

2. *Prioritize the need.* How critical or threatening to the life of the enterprise is this particular problem; does it represent a level of threat that mandates utilization of resources to address it?

3. *Identify alternative solutions.* What are the alternative ways to resolve the problem or issue?

4. *Define and prioritize selection criteria.* What are the requirements or features of an acceptable solution?

5. *Evaluate and choose.*

Any consumer or purchaser of goods or services goes through these five steps. The depth of analysis and effort applied to each step, however, varies considerably. While all steps would make for an interesting discussion, at this point, we will look only at the fourth step. Does a taxonomy of decision criteria exist, or can one be developed? Can you create criteria that act across the range of product decisions made every day in all industries in a wide variety of situations? More specifically, can IS identify a process that allows it to design services to meet the selection criteria of its users? The answer has to be yes. You must look at IS as a business that must compete with alternative sources of services. The IS department today must consider itself in competition for business resources. The decision for allocation of resources—where to add staff, whether to outsource or maintain services in-house, which applications to buy or develop—will be made on the basis of business benefit. The following discussion defines the context within which IS can design its offerings and a strategy to promote them.

Two types of situations exist. In one, IS enjoys a privileged position in a captured market. Its contribution is well recognized with no talk of outsourcing. This is akin to the position of a vendor with a product so unique and targeted that no competition exists. The other, more frequently encountered situation requires a selection from among multiple products, all of which meet the basic requirements. Here the question is one of perceived relative value or judgment of potential contribution.

In the first case, deciding on services means little more than checking the validity and criticality of requirements, and setting priorities for delivery of services. IS can select and choose among products and technologies according to its own agenda and schedule, with some concessions to customer demands. This wonderful situation rarely exists. No manager, let alone one in IS, should feel complacent about his or her role in an enterprise without a direct, well-known, visible, and documented link to business contribution.

In the other case, much more realistic and common, IS must compete both within and outside the enterprise for resources. Managers must understand that decisions impacting their efforts will be made on the basis of perceived value or contribution, both absolutely and in relation to alternative sources of business services, including those not related to IS.

IS must develop a detailed understanding of how end users and corporate executives understand and value its services. Traditional customer satisfaction surveys have proven woefully inadequate in presenting an accurate picture of service ability. Unfortunately it is still common for such surveys to present results in dramatic conflict with actual user experiences.

Surveys of satisfaction can fail for three reasons: the questions don't reflect the actual indicators or measures of customer satisfaction; the methodology for collection is flawed; or the data is accurate but the interpretation is flawed or conclusions ignored. Fortunately, examples of the first case have become increasingly rare as users have become more aggressive in demanding service metrics they understand. For example, a network operations group once reported its service levels based on server and network uptime but now rates performance on the basis of the availability of the sales-pricing application.

As an example of the second case, a systems operations department in a networking firm rated its IS operations service organization based on direct feedback obtained from in-house customer surveys. The feedback yielded consistently high ratings so it surprised the department when it was presented with an outsourcing proposal for desktop services as a cost reduction. They neglected to benchmark themselves and demonstrate their total service value against all alternatives.

Finally, a major minicomputer manufacturer conducted biannual surveys of customer perceptions of product functionality, buying decision criteria, and purchase plans. Despite widespread recognition of feature and function superiority of its product, the survey consistently pointed to customer plans to move to a competitive platform. The manufacturer failed to acknowledge that none of its highly rated features appeared on the list of top ten decision criteria as documented by the surveyed customers.

Service-level agreements (SLAs) hold forth the promise of providing more accurate and realistic measurements of service. These attempt to relate IS performance to more comprehensive, business-focused results by measuring and reporting on end-to-end service delivery. SLAs collect and present information on devices, applications, and services required to accomplish a business task. Initial indications are encouraging, but use caution: SLAs may measure and report performance metrics unrelated to actual quality of service.

IS managers must understand how their services can be used by their consumers. Measures of the right information will provide an accurate picture of the path to greater effectiveness and contribution. The IS manager's goal must be to drive IS investment, development, and implementation to provide services that help the business end user do his or her job efficiently.

The delivery of services that satisfies the end user begins at the most basic level: delivering "defect-free" services. You must provide customers with a system that is free of errors and failures in service, and meet a predefined level of quality-controlled performance. Providing reliable network access, consistently installing new user accounts with appropriate permission levels, and ensuring reliable access to servers and printers are examples of good quality of service.

While critical, this level of service represents only a first step; next comes what we describe as a focus on identifying and meeting the customer's unique needs, a step marked by the use of customer satisfaction surveys and analyses. As discussed earlier, valid information and feedback that provide valuable guidance for continued improvement comes only when these evaluations accurately measure and reflect performance valued by and of value to the customer. The hallmark is that of a *customer-driven* IS department—necessary but not sufficient for "best-in-class" performance.

The next process directs attention to quality of service and *perceived* value of service. You must identify and understand how your corporate executives and end users view value IS, especially with respect to the competition and alternative service providers.

Value versus Cost

It's important not to focus on costs at the expense of value and quality. For example, paper plates and plastic forks don't compete with fine china and silver dinnerware; each targets a specific market niche, with clearly differentiated utility versus value evaluations. Even within the low-priced disposal dinnerware market, differentiation exists. Plates that fold or fall apart before the end of a picnic will not be a good value however low the price. If you buy the cheap plates, you have to use three or four to equal the quality of one good plate. The same concept applies to IS services. Low budgets or associated costs don't translate to good value for the money. An IS budget that exceeds industry norms while providing significant competitive advantage may, in fact, represent a bargain. Unfortunately, research and effort directed at documenting IS contribution and best practices are not readily available.

IS management must expend effort to understand what it takes to establish and maintain recognized superior performance relative to competitors. This drives the need to understand not just articulated requirements and evaluation metrics but to understand the decision context. Just what defines a superior service or product? Is it response time? Is it ease of use? In the context of evaluation and comparison, what determines and influences it must be understood. A sales organization may be satisfied with online, dial-in access to pricing and configuration services operated with a remote connection until they discover that the competition can produce a visual model with customer requested modifications, parts list, purchase orders, and committed delivery date before they walk out the door.

IS must understand and manage the information that establishes and sets end-user expectations. This doesn't mean concealing or misrepresenting data; it does mean identifying and communicating appropriate measures and indicators of quality, then clearly demonstrating how they and their services meet these criteria.

Finally, the ultimate level of customer-focused service valuation involves the total enterprise in anticipating and developing strategies for service based entirely around the customer. Bradley T. Gale, in his book *Managing Customer Value*, provides a detailed quantitative methodology for driving toward a customer value-based enterprise.

Matching Solutions with Operations

Every organization operates with its own set of assumptions, hierarchy, and institutional focus. Every solution is developed within a context and set of expectations about the problem it will address and the environment within which it will operate. The implementation of a solution will proceed more easily and be more readily accepted when expectations (on the part of the users) match the assumptions (on the part of the solution selectors).

Finding a proper solutions match is an area frequently overlooked, but so fundamental that it bears repeating. As an example, distributed systems management solutions have been developed with at least four different underlying visions. These are:

1. *Network focused.* Operating from the assumption that distributed systems depend most upon the underlying network, events that occur on the backbone network impact and drive management response; for ex-

ample, Hewlett-Packard's OpenView provides comprehensive network management with integrated extensions to provide server management, user administration, operations, and desktop management.

2. *Centralized, policy-driven.* Operating from the assumption that the organization is driven by policies emanating from a centralized organization but administered locally; for example, Tivoli's TME 10 offers a framework of services in support of the automated definition and distributed implementation of centrally defined management policies and configuration profiles, extensions provide event management, help desk, and so on.

3. *Management domain-focused.* Operating from the assumption that the organization will be driven by prioritized focus on the major management domains implemented in phases; for example, Bull's AccessMaster with its modular, toolkit approach that builds from a focus on enterprise security.

4. *Automated, event-driven distributed management.* Operating from the assumption that the organization focuses on identifying and resolving problems that trigger alarms in the monitored systems, network, applications, and services; for example, Computer Associates TNG, which offers comprehensive, integrated event-driven management across all domains for monitoring networks, applications, systems, and services.

Each of these solutions can form the basis for much the same range of distributed management functions, either directly or from third-party software partners. However, the key differentiation is in the specifics of implementation, level of integration of specific functions, and the focus of their original design.

The process of implementation and introduction into an enterprise will be affected by the compatibility between the original design intent and enterprise operation. Once feature/function compatibility has been established, the next level of questions can be addressed. The specific questions to test for compatibility will depend on the priorities and processes of management administration of the individual organization. Although the complete list of questions and topical areas to cover exceeds the scope of this book, and will depend upon the priorities and problems to be addressed, some of the relevant areas of inquiry and sample lists of questions to ask in each area follow:

Design Concept

What is the underlying design concept of the solution? Event-driven? Policy-driven? Domain-focused?

How closely does the solution design match *your* management operations?

What does the solution assume as the management control infrastructure? Centralized management and control? Centralized policy definition? Distributed policy implementation?

What does the solution assume for information and data flow?

What does the solution assume for control flow and responsibility?

What flexibility is built into the solution to adapt to organizational realities?

Enterprise Administrative Issues

Where does the authority for definition of desktop configurations lie?

Who takes action when a management policy is violated?

Who is responsible for defining and implementing management policy?

What level of configuration control applies in the enterprise? In individual departments? At what locations?

Who can make changes to settings on network devices when services are interrupted? In what domains? Locally? Nationally? In other geographic regions?

Service-level Views

Who is responsible for resources shared among multiple processes and services?

Which services require end-to-end management?

Which policies exist for implementing service-level views?

Do administrators with service-level views of IS resources require management control over all resources related to that service? Or do they only need monitoring capabilities?

Who can make changes to the service views?

How are service views maintained and updated so they accurately reflect the resources involved?

Event Correlation Concerns

Who is responsible for assigning and tracking corrective action on remote systems? On network problems? For enterprise-wide customer-focused services? For global services?

What is the best way to capture your administrators' experience in solving problems? Event correlation rules? Searchable case-based database? Combination of both?

What resources are available for creating, testing, and updating event correlation rules?

Performance Management Responsibilities

Who is responsible for tracking application and service performance from an end-user perspective?

Should performance management be automated?

What level of performance management is needed?

Where should performance management be automated?

How much internal application development occurs?

Who controls and monitors internal development activity?

Does the corporation have a policy for application management?

Does the corporation have a policy for service delivery management?

Who defines and has responsibility for policies regarding performance management?

What policies and guidelines exist for building performance management data collection into the application?

What types of information needs to be collected for real-time management? Capacity planning?

Automated Administration Concerns

Who is responsible for ongoing automation and tuning of management tasks and processes?

What type of actions can be taken automatically?

What is the policy for controlling devices located in remote domains?

What is the policy for initiating corrective actions in remote domains?

What corrective actions can be automated?

What is the correct combination of automated action and process activity?

Which escalation policies should be implemented?

Which automated "override" capabilities should be implemented?

This represents just a small sample of potential questions to be asked. Vendors with comprehensive lists of functionality and customer benefits are extremely adept at directing priorities that favor their products. This comes as no surprise, since they would not grow very fast or be very successful if they could not provide a compelling argument in favor of purchasing their products. However, this definitely does not translate to an ability to help you identify specifically what your selection criteria should be. Vendors usually are willing to cooperate and provide support to your own resources as you collect data to understand what they do well and what the don't do well. IS managers can consult a variety of online resources to help them gather information on relevant evaluation issues and strategies, including vendor Web sites and independent technical analyst Web sites, such as www.dhbrown.com, www.summitonline.com, and www.ncfocus.com.

Finally, vendors can respond quickly to trends, once recognized, by rephrasing product marketing material. If you have the available resources, it helps to understand the application and utilization of technology. Beware of vendors unwilling to provide information about how solutions are implemented.

Vendor Attitudes

Vendor behavior and attitudes can yield significant clues to their acceptability as long-term, even short-term business partners. The following are good indicators of vendors that are genuinely concerned with the long-term success of their clients. Each, by itself, cannot guarantee a suitable partner for long-term relationship, the point being, do not overlook standard due diligence. Each does, however, suggest a seriousness of purpose and attention to detail supportive of successful relationships.

To identify a vendor with a forward focus in solutions development, ask, does the vendor solution:

1. Support innovation in implementation?

2. Emphasize use of existing, standardized infrastructure to implement services when possible?

3. Demonstrate understanding of how the tool will be used in real-life terms?

Solutions designed to allow for innovation in problem solution implementation suggest the provider is interested in relationships based on providing long-term service and support. It isn't always possible to build modular solutions or those that provide for adaptation as newer technologies and solutions emerge; however, it is nearly always appropriate to look for and allow for future introduction of better solutions.

Clients, customers, and vendors must establish their own value structures for open versus proprietary infrastructure and solutions. The standards embraced, as well as the overall strategy with respect to standards and emerging technologies, very much depends upon the enterprise, it's infrastructure strategy, and the internal profile of expertise. Most enterprise IS organizational resources should be focused on addressing the business issues and challenges—*not* on extending the boundaries of technology.

The level of importance of standards and longevity expectations vary with solution type and area of specific application. The determination of the impact of a solution must be overtly and carefully considered. No experienced IS manager can be unaware of the number of applications and "quickie" solutions that have found unexpected, widespread acceptance, and thus become key components of success. When designed, implemented, and delivered without careful thought to long-term consequences, weaknesses in adaptability and evolution become major headaches downstream. What is important is the process of understanding, evaluating, and weighing the implications of standards, architecture, and enterprise impact.

While arguments rage, in the area of *open* standards-based solutions versus *closed* proprietary solutions, the decision is far from certain. Consider the task of identifying and evaluating the trade-off of current functionality and availability at the expense of a proprietary implementation while balancing the risk of vendor lock-in versus a measure (how much is real?) of vendor independence with somewhat lower levels of functionality.

Consider, too, the issue of the apparently always just-over-the-horizon application portability of open Unix versus the ubiquitous presence and acceptance of very proprietary Windows NT. Arguments rage over reliability, security, functionality, and so on to eternity. The fact remains, each satisfies the needs of large numbers of users.

Another important indicator, especially as solutions mature, is the ability to demonstrate expertise and understanding in the use of the tool. Early in the product life cycle, feature/function lists can provide valuable data for choosing between products. Unfortunately, in today's highly competitive arena, with shrinking intervals between new versions, feature/function lists quickly become obsolete or irrelevant. Few detailed feature/function comparisons are valid for more than 12 months, and many for even shorter periods of time.

More important is a tool that reflects a knowledge of how it will be used and focuses on increasing the effectiveness and efficiency in application. Feature/function lists only scratch the surface in problem resolution. Anticipating the next information to be requested, facilitating the next data search, or automatically presenting data in the most useable format to the user are all good indicators of a committed vendor.

A developer who has an in-depth understanding of how a tool is used should be able to create a tool that is more efficient in its application as well as easier to use. A developer with extensive experience in network device management and problem troubleshooting should be able to design a more efficient tool than a developer who concentrates only on meeting a feature/function list. Documentation, user interfaces, and the automated processes embedded in the tool will provide evidence of the ability of the developer.

Conclusions

Discontent with today's distributed management functionality results from overinflated expectations combined with the missing link that ties IS activities to business success. Many of today's systems report what's easily measurable, not what's meaningful to the business manager. Fundamental to the presentation of a useable view is the correlation, analysis, and reduction of collected data into a relevant and comprehensible informative presentation of the business benefit.

Today's tools and management solutions are evolving from an environment focused on quickly identifying and responding to element failure to one focused on monitoring the delivery of comprehensive business services. Recognizing and responding to the functionality gap, tool providers, IS operations executives, and vendors have been developing responses at multiple levels. These range from newly developed tools for data consolidation and analysis to custom consulting services to customized views to defining standards for management data content, availability, and format.

Intelligent business practices go a long way in creating the best management toolbox for an IS organization. Technology-rich IS end users and corporate executives must expand their view of IS from that of a mere infrastructure provider to that of an active partner with powerful tools and capability to creatively address business problems. Only then can IS focus on delivering real solutions in terms of the business service management required to directly contribute to improving both competitiveness and profitability.

In the next chapter we discuss the challenges IS must face as the skills necessary for success undergo radical change in a period marked by a shortage of capable staff. The chapter includes a discussion of alternative solutions, as well as a description of the newly emerging IS development environment.

FOR FURTHER READING

Fergeson, Paul and Geoff Huston. *Quality of Service.* (New York: John Wiley & Sons, Inc.), 1998.

Gale, Bradley T. *Managing Customer Value.* (New York: Free Press), 1994.

Part three

THE NEW SHAPE OF DISTRIBUTED SYSTEMS

9 RESKILLING FOR TOMORROW

Tomorrow to fresh woods, and pastures new...

from *Lycidas*, John Milton, 1606–1674

> ## This chapter outlines:
>
> **An action plan for dealing with skills shortages.**
>
> **How to build effective development teams.**
>
> **Developer culture and how to introduce reuse.**
>
> **Where end users fit in the new distributed environment and development process.**

We cannot enter new distributed worlds without the skills to use in them. The complexity of distributed systems differs from and exceeds the previous generation of mainframe systems. Development organizations that migrate to distributed systems using Web technologies, even those with experience in older client/server systems, have more difficulties due to a lack of skills than for any other single reason. We can attribute these problems to a shortage of the new skill set necessary to deal with the more complex technical nature of distributed systems not found in any other environment.

The new skills set must meet three current business demands:

- *New technology.* Web technology, client/server, object technology, new tools.

- *A new business process for software development.* This process must respond far faster to demands of end users, while delivering results closely targeted to business requirements.

- *A new approach to development.* Systems integration, with an understanding of interfaces between components and reuse wherever possible.

Staffing requirements do not stop at types of skills; the highest-quality people must be available to learn and apply the range of skills required. Distributed systems are not the place for the inexperienced members of a development team to acquire and hone skills. To address the people side of building distributed systems, we will discuss the following issues: the skills required, solutions to the skills shortage, how to manage the development process, and how to use teams.

For starters, you need a team with a highly diversified set of technical skills balanced between application development and interfacing, with networking skills at the forefront in a systems integration approach (see Table 9.1).

Although the following sections concentrate on the newer technical skills for distributed systems and their long-term support, note that we included legacy skills in the table. These remain important and should not be overlooked or dismissed. Linking legacy systems to the new generation can represent 50 percent of the effort in many projects. Lack of knowledge of legacy systems can constitute 90 percent of the design problem when replacing the historic with newer technology. Thus, organizations must retain legacy skills. Referring to legacy systems as "cherished" represents just one way of avoiding pejorative labels for systems as well as the people who know them. As noted earlier, care should be taken when identifying "cherished" systems to avoid using this as an excuse to avoid a justifiable effort to let go of the application and move forward with a new version. When facing Year 2000 problems, such apparently small distinctions could be crucial in retaining and recognizing key skills.

NOTE

Staffing inadequacies can be the biggest barrier to building distributed systems.

But more than just enhanced technical skills are necessary to build distributed systems. Building a more complex system calls for a different, enhanced set of people skills, too. Software development is, at its most basic, a human, not a technical process.

Table 9.1 Necessary Distributed Systems Team Skills

Technology or Area	Skills
Web Technology	Web server setup and HTTP operations.
	HTML Web page editing and setup.
	Java and JavaScript programming, with client applets.
	Programming for browsers.
	Web server platform performance testing and tuning.
Security	Certification and password management.
	Firewall setup and operations.
	Interfacing from Web server to workflow and other applications.
	Network traffic sizing and optimization.
Transaction Design	Splitting/partitioning experience.
	Transaction analysis and traffic-generation knowledge.
	Transaction server knowledge/programming.
	Browser or client software processing.
	Transaction support.
Data Design	Across multiple platforms with extracts from legacy databases, all based on inputs from the business end users.
Database with SQL Access	Implementation for PC, server, and database/filing systems on a mainframe.
	SQL tools use for application development and interworking.
	Stored procedures programming.
	Database TP performance and growth in operation.
Screen Design	GUI screen painting and MS Windows usage, and/or other GUI if used.
Network Design	Traffic estimation, with HTML pages, LAN/WAN design.
	Network element choice and configuration, TP traffic loads.
PC	PC package interfacing; DDE, OLE use; MS Windows Software developer's kit for GUI-based applications; MS Visual Basic; key PC packages for networked operation (spreadsheets, word processors).

(continues)

Table 9.1 Necessary Distributed Systems Team Skills (*Continued*)

TECHNOLOGY OR AREA	SKILLS
Middleware Software/NOS	Setup and debugging for LAN/WAN: Netware, etc., including use of the requestor, NOS protocols like IPX, NLM, TCP/IP and others; ORB and RPC technology.
LAN/WAN Setup	LAN and interface card setup and debugging.
Servers	Unix, Windows NT, plus other proprietary OS if used (MS Windows 95, DEC VMS, IBM OS/2, DOS, or OS/400, etc.).
RAD	RAD approach trainers. RAD team project managers. JRP/JAD session facilitators. End-user trainers. Prototyping and iterative development process skills.
Reuse Development	Reuse habits and ethos. Library skills. Librarians.
Object-Oriented Languages	Object-oriented principles, techniques, and programming.
Specific Tools Skills	4GLs, GUI painters, RPC generators, SQL generators.
Programming	C or C++, VB Script, VisualAge/Java, etc.
Legacy Systems	Knowledge of business logic and the technical interfacing for data and processing; traditional mainframe skills (DB/2, CICS, SNA, COBOL), plus APPC and OO Cobol, C.
Rollout	Business manager skills in rolling out new applications to many end users. Help desk setup. First-level help desk personnel; end-user business-level skills. Second- and third-level help desk (technical and part of IS).

Solutions to the Skills Shortage

There are three major solutions to the skills shortage: retraining, new recruitment, and some form of outsourcing.

Intensive Training

Often, existing staff can be retrained; but be aware that some of your technical staff, who are familiar only with older, single-machine environments, may be too mainframe oriented. A move to a distributed, multivendor environment with iterative development and prototyping represents a fundamental and significant change of development culture. Select only the most suitable (in this case, meaning "adaptable") staff because your team must be open to new ideas, as well as ready and able to apply them at work. A positive work attitude will help ensure success. In addition, motivation and the concept of teamwork are important.

> **NOTE**
>
> Not all technical staff will be candidates for the distributed system development team.

Attitude differences throughout the IS department go largely unrecognized and unacknowledged. Programmers, along with other traditional members of a development team—such as systems analysts—all respond to widely different motivations; that is, different from both other personnel in the corporation as well as IS department management. Although salary remains a common concern, people on development teams tend to be more interested in personal satisfaction or in job gratification than those in management or sales positions for instance. Software professionals in general maintain a more intense interest in and assign greater value to their ideas than in external relationships, positions, and titles. Moreover, while some surveys report that IS professionals function by thinking rather than feeling, this is not necessarily the case. Most IS professionals are as driven by emotion as any employee, and as such are just as susceptible to motivation, and demotivation, generated by management actions and enterprise events.

Generally, IS managers function under a different value system regarding work and what motivates them from the IS development teams reporting to them. Developers tend to value a few close personal relationships, as well as their individuality, lifestyles, and peer recognition. Managers, in contrast, tend to value corporate awards, the size of the staff they "command," salary, and perceived corporate status. This clash of attitudes can lead to a mutual incomprehension, and represents a major cause of failure for many projects. To avoid or minimize differences in cultural values, it is essential to find a highly skilled manager who is aware of cultural expectations and has both the knowledge and ability to form teams successfully.

New Recruitment

Although a few organizations have chosen to take the new recruitment route, more commonly, once development has begun, the IS manager begins to look for an injection of new skills. This occurs frequently in the areas of Web technology, networking, and database usage, or for a specific technique such as RAD (mature RAD experience is probably the most elusive skill) or a specific language such as Java. Wide-ranging Web and PC skills remain difficult to develop and thus require time to hone to desired levels. The same is true for substantive C, NOS, and server experience. As a consequence, staff with specialized skills are and will continue to be difficult to find and expensive to recruit.

Outsourcing

Some organizations have been successful in using third parties to develop particular areas of the system without relinquishing project control. These third parties are often the original software or hardware suppliers of a particular link in the distributed and client/server system chain. Because they offer the most complete knowledge of the problems inherent in their own kit and the associated software interfacing problems, they can often provide the best solutions.

> **TIP**
>
> Use your suppliers for development work where possible.

When major new developments are beyond the skills, tools, and number of staff available in the IT department, total outsourcing may be the only reasonable way forward. Just be aware that choosing this option means strategic dependence, which is not a favorable position for your business. Still, it can be used successfully, as these outsourcing examples point out:

> **TIP**
>
> Outsource only if the IT department is unable to support development internally.

- A major U.S. airline used a systems integration specialist for a new generation of reservation system, which was an extension of the old reservation system.

- A New York brokerage used a local systems integrator for a $100 million development in back-office extensions and new front-office client/server systems.

NOTE

Total outsourcing can mean strategic dependence.

Systems integration specialists have their own proprietary tools, such as application integrators, which can be essential for pulling together new distributed systems and existing systems. But when you use an outside team, you have to address the questions of how to monitor their performance, how to organize internally for control, and how to negotiate a contract. The answers to those questions are presented in Chapter 10.

New Project Management Style

A new kind of total project management becomes necessary for client/server and distributed systems. It's a style that comprises use of outsourcing; requires particular skills for the multiple platforms with sets of teams; and includes a move toward

---

How to Use Suppliers

A major European building society used its mainframe supplier for some of its development work. The supplier of its branch system communications acted as the main contractor for creating a communications network into the mainframe. The relationship with the mainframe supplier proved very useful for porting a particular software module between Unix platforms (even though the target Unix machine came from another supplier).

An alternative is the "boutique" approach, pulling in small, highly expert suppliers for a short period to focus on specific subjects (Java, Web technology, RAD, etc.). They can give the necessary support as well as train or coach your employees in the new techniques. This has the advantage of enhancing your staff skills while completing a project and avoiding continuing dependency on outside contractors or consultants.

more object-oriented design and development by instilling an effective reuse culture. Furthermore, when required for far faster delivery, a RAD development environment may have to be introduced.

To implement this style successfully requires a revolutionary change in mind-set and end-user relations. Because the skills set required is extremely diverse, the most common approach calls for the enterprise to invest in the short-term use of specialists. These people may be found in the suppliers of the software platforms or even hardware platform vendors.

> **TIP**
>
> You need a project management style to suit the new skills, players, and methodologies appropriate for systems integration.

Managing Partial Outsourcing

As noted earlier, many distributed systems development projects effectively outsource only certain functions to suppliers (total outsourcing is detailed in Chapter 10). Suffice it to say, developing a mission-critical system in part by using outside contractors demands a mastery of the special management skills required to handle a team consisting of organizations, skills that are in strong contrast to as well as distinct from those of internal IS staff management. Managing a group of suppliers presents a formidable challenge, since each supplier may prefer, or take refuge in, finger-pointing instead of actively helping to resolve the myriad potential problems that can occur, even with the most careful handling.

> **NOTE**
>
> Outsourcing some skills requires a "team of organizations" approach and close supervision of the outsources.

Therefore, human relations management of external suppliers and outside contractors is as critical (perhaps more so) for project success than internal team management. Interfaces, agendas, and individual schedules with time lines all need to be defined and mutually agreed upon for each partner. Likewise, it is essential to share aims and targets with all partners at both the business and the technical level.

Take note of the use of the word "partnership" in this discussion: Successful projects require just that, partnerships, not subcontractor and contractor cold wars. Specifically, choose suppliers based on their ability to interface to other suppliers and willingness to offer support, as much as on their technical performance. This is especially true where the IS department lacks strength in a particular area. Successful project management with supplier partners is also dependent upon:

- End-user participation in the functional requirements specification.
- Personal networking and information links into suppliers.
- A set of performance-related payments for each external development partner, linked to the total plan with schedules and timelines.

Personal networking and information links into suppliers become far more important than with normal development projects. Targeted efforts in this regard will yield inside product information, extra effort for software creation and hardware configuring, and especially, additional help for commissioning and debugging. Close long-term relations with outsourcing partners will also enable you to apply pressure at critical moments to get the job done.

> **NOTE**
>
> When using major supplier outsourcing, it is essential to clearly define schedules and deliverables.

After rollout to end users, you will need to establish a permanent management committee (which includes the partners) for a monthly review of system performance, maintenance, and upgrade needs. This committee will rule over the lifetime of the system, from commissioning on. Thus the committee should be composed of representatives from the end-user organizations, the IS department, and the systems integration team.

In total outsourcing situations, end-user organizations become closely tied to the systems integrator. Therefore, the decision to outsource must be carefully considered, followed by a close evaluation of each contender. Organizations may exploit particular leverage for satisfactory performance, for example, by being or becoming a partial owner of the systems integrator. Such ownership of the systems integrator reflects the strategic importance of distributed and client/server systems to the business. This strategy is common in parts of Europe; for instance, in France, where major banks tend to hold a significant share in their chosen systems integrator. Similarly, in the United States, such relationships are common in the airline industry.

Managing Teams with Different Skills

On large projects, you may find it necessary to organize teams by platform, while including staff who can work in multiple platforms. Platform-related team planning helps to achieve the level of communication necessary for the more complex distributed processing development. Teams that are too large and monolithic tend to be hard to motivate and have trouble communicating effectively. You may also be able to strengthen the systems integration team by mixing internal and external staff, if you have decided to outsource certain skills.

> **TIP**
>
> View your systems integration staff as a set of teams with different skills, and apportion people to teams appropriately.

> **NOTE**
>
> To organize teams by platform, you need cross-platform workers.

There is, however, a risk associated with dividing into mini-teams by platform. Mini-teams can suffer from a lack of communication if you don't make a conscious effort to add "glue people" and to use continual test reviews to integrate everyone's activities. You will also need personnel who can work across areas, along with those targeted to spread information. A formal cross-analysis and coordination procedure between mini-teams is also important. In summary, a well-planned organizational structure is part of the systems integration method: Teams work on specific problems or components, and the results must be continuously integrated and tested together.

> **NOTE**
>
> Interfacing skills at the application level (and below) are essential.

In general, there is a need for team skills, so look for staff who can work together, who can put aside individual agendas for the good of the project. Generally, the important distributed system team skills can be divided into vertical and horizontal aspects, as illustrated in Figure 9.1.

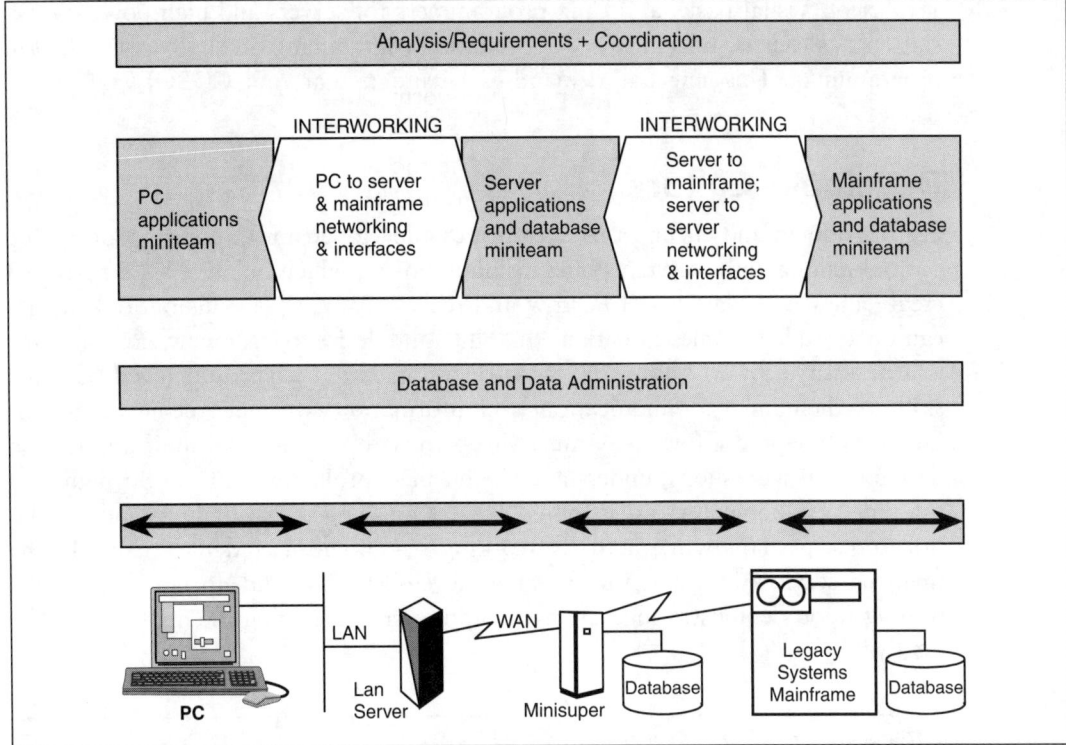

Figure 9.1 Vertical and horizontal skill delineations.

Horizontal skill sets provide cross-platform competence, which means developers do more than create the applications, they develop application services as well. Developers in the PC and server arena may have knowledge about interfacing to servers and mainframes, although sometimes only at a high level (SQL calls, for example). The database administrator, too, is a key team member of the distributed and client/server systems team; they are essential for monitoring data location, copies, updates, and structures, as well as controlling the schemas and views of each platform for shared information.

Vertical skills are defined as single-platform, single-machine for application and/or database development. Many traditional mainframe developers fit in this category.

One vendor of major methods and tools describes mini-team divisions in terms of client, mainframe, and database programmers. Though COBOL developers can be used on the mainframe platforms, more frequently, developers need C, Java,

JavaScript, Visual Basic, and Unix programmers for servers and high-power work-stations, as well as skills in stored procedures programming on databases with SQL programming. This new skill demand can mandate that your COBOL staff be re-trained.

Developer Culture

For distributed and client/server systems, the developer must adopt a prototyping outlook, along with a systems integration mind-set, which involves a shift from "I create anew each day" to "I borrow and reuse." A multiple skills outlook with a can-do attitude becomes essential. An ability and desire to learn new environments is a necessity, not an option or bonus. Developers must have enhanced personal skills, as the human communications and information exchange role now demands far more time and effort; they must sit down with end users in joint application design (JAD) workshops, understand the business problems, and run through pro-totyping development as a distributed process by using screen builders and simula-tion tools, perhaps while actually working in the end-user departments. In the financial services industry, for example, developers may end up working on the trading floor, demonstrating, testing, adapting, and changing the application "on the fly."

> **NOTE**
> Developers need to take a can-do approach to end users and their work-station requirements.

Multiskilled Team Members

Ask yourself: "Can all the skills I need be found in one person? And if so, do I want them in one person?" Experience with LAN server development has shown that one person with several skills is better than several people each having only one of those skills, especially when the job calls for debugging and integration. Develop-ment organizations should insist that at least some of the team members in the PC and server areas (like PC applications and PC networking) have a minimum of two skills each.

Developer Education

If internal staff are to be retrained, outside knowledge sources become essential, as they can provide outside trainers as well as offer first-hand input based on their experiences in similar projects. Two major resources for many IS development staffs have been tool vendors and key suppliers.

Another strategy calls for IS development staff to use higher-level tools to minimize skills and training needed. Examples of these tools include:

- High-level screen painters.
- Use of components from object libraries, generalized or specialized (for financial or telecommunications industries).
- Client/server development tools/benches or environments with 4GLs; the 4GL gearing can be two to five times that of a 3GL such as C or COBOL. Tools like Forté and Seer HPS come as complete development environments with a 4GL inside them.
- SQL interfaces and RDBMS programming with stored procedures.
- Use of components from Web technology applications for intranets (Web merchant servers, Web servers, browsers, etc.). Complete environments for Web technology development also exist (IBM's Visual Age for Java).
- RPC libraries, to reduce communications protocol knowledge and RPC writing (especially to reduce APPC/LU6.2 skills).

NOTE

To teach a large number of developers RAD techniques, "training the trainer" is often the best approach.

Reuse

For reuse to work in practice, you will need a new style of developer organization. Even for smaller projects, where each platform may have only one development person, business models with their business entities, application objects, and services must be used uniformly. To ensure parallel development, you need an object library and access procedures. In addition, you must have formal procedures for including and advertising new objects, for version control, and for updating developers about what is available overall. Electronic mail systems with shared files and a cross-referenced index can provide a basis for your library system.

Unfortunately, the concept of reuse continues to be difficult to instill as a discipline in programmers, who naturally prefer to be creative. Efforts that can help to motivate a change in developer culture can be as simple and straightforward as instituting a reward system for identifying reusable modules in the repository. However, usually far greater effort is required. One leading object-oriented software supplier pays a bonus each month for each line that is borrowed, *not* written. A model for reuse is outlined in Figure 9.2.

NOTE

Object-oriented reuse requires new management systems, cultures, and compensation packages for development staff.

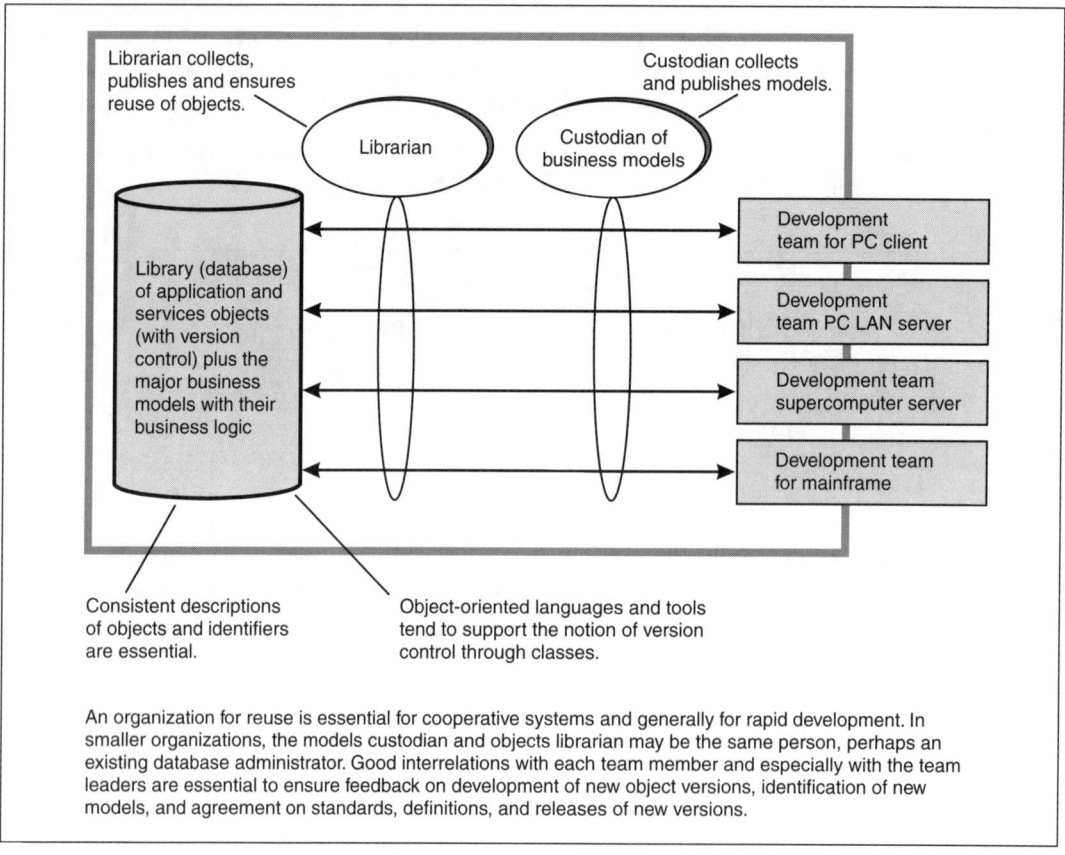

Figure 9.2 An organizational model for reuse.

The Role of End Users

In today's new distributed computing environments, end users, and the business managers who represent them, are more likely to be involved in the development and ongoing maintenance of the network and business applications. Distributed systems and the staff who develop and support them are part of a total business process view that must involve end users.

End Users Help Guide RAD

One of the most challenging and radical changes coming to an IS department near you is the joint application development (JAD) trend. In this approach, instead of great walls dividing users and developers, the two sides form a single team. The next step is to use this much closer cooperation to accelerate development from two to five times with "RAD." In rapid application development (RAD), your corporation's business groups must participate, then buy into, and eventually "own" the applications. This represents a reversal of the traditional IS department setup. End-user guided development is inevitable in some organizations, and the IS department must choose between initiating and controlling it to some extent, waiting to be forced into it, or facing outsourcing and the loss of their jobs.

There are several stages to RAD introduction, and each requires a unique set of skills for both the IT development team and the business managers from each department, who represent their employees as end users in the JAD process. The RAD introduction process requires the following skills:

Education and communication. Sales skills to top business managers.

Initial pilot projects. Training skills for JRP/JAD sessions, in which the business managers are trained by IS to participate, then to control, and finally to take responsibility for, and even manage IS development of their business applications, from an end-user standpoint.

Application rollout. The business managers must become skilled in rolling out new applications to hundreds or thousands of end users, which requires a level of training resources often far beyond what the current IS development/maintenance staff can offer. It therefore requires an end-user-centered task force. Rollout may include the setup and operation of a first-level help desk, although second- and third-level help may be more technical and thus remain part of IS.

Full-blown end-user ownership. Business managers and key end users (who represent all the end users) must have the skills to initiate, participate in, and lead application development projects; in effect, they become managers of their information and systems technology. Training of new end-user project managers through courses and experience is required.

The role of the business manager is changing significantly. Training business managers in IS practices requires a new set of IS skills, from selling the ideas to interfacing closely on a daily basis with the business division personnel in joint development teams. Due to the large numbers of business managers to be trained in RAD techniques, a "train the trainer" approach is often the best choice.

Operations, Maintenance, and End-User Support

Traditionally, support and maintenance has been performed on a general, horizontal basis across all applications and then proceeds vertically by platform after the initial level of analysis. However, for distributed and client/server systems, operations and support functions may be based on particular applications (following the business logic) instead of on traditional computing functions. For example, a major securities house conducts application-centric management for its new client/server-based center in the United States, where staff roles align with the support needed for particular investment applications. This approach is more suited to the particular problems of the transactions chain involved in a single financial application.

Help Desks

In general, educating end users to work in distributed and client/server systems is made easier with the introduction of the intuitive presentations now available, such as the GUI screens that figure so prominently in many developments. In the words of one organization, "If they are not self-teaching, you have failed." If they are well designed, new applications and system tools should be far more user-friendly than the traditional command line of mainframe-style applications. However, operational end-user support becomes more complex as end users multiply, and application and system errors become more problematic.

The help desk organization becomes critical for supporting end users. Generally, it must be more competent and better equipped to test as well as diagnose a complex distributed system remotely, down to workstation level. The skills necessary for help desk personnel are specific and may be tied to the business process in question, not just the technical support. For example, to answer a question about why a budget extension feature in an electronic ordering system does not work means the help desk employee must know the assigned rights of the end user—his or her authority to use that function may be restricted.

Skills required by help desk staff are tiered:

Level 1. A front end to handle main queries; light technical knowledge, including screen manipulation, business process, and business logic [first resolution attempt, if unresolved after 20 minutes of effort the problem (or caller) gets bounced to the next level].

Level 2. A more technical background, with far deeper knowledge of the business logic; support from operating systems and networking/NOS technicians (between 1 and 4 hours, depending on application resolution before problem gets bounced to the next level).

Level 3. Technical application development staff and distributed system support staff (serious technical/business logic design problems taking many hours or perhaps days to resolve).

End-User Programming

End-user programming is of course common today, although it is sometimes not recognized or seen as presenting a difficulty. Traditionally, all companies have had some end users who are more skilled with the PCs and the server tools at their fingertips than the majority, and who have always "done their own thing." But end-user participation in standalone developments outside the RAD process has to be controlled. End users often have more access to data than expected, especially if they can write their own SQL queries.

As computer literacy spreads, through macro programming in Visual Basic for instance, the core data and programming implemented in daily operations by end users can be completely outside the framework of the IS department. They are, essentially, private additions to core applications. For example, in one of the top oil companies in the world, end-user programming is at the core of everyday operations, providing simple decision support tools that take data from the many major operational management information systems and integrate it into specific parameters on stock levels, the supply chain, yields, and cash flow. They provide a corporate dashboard starting at middle management levels and extending into top management. Such tools use database extracts that may not be regularly updated and are for the most part undocumented and unsupported; indeed, their very existence may be unknown. In fact, some are confidential, and no ordinary IS manager is likely to be given security clearance to go near them.

In this way, end-user programming can cause chaos and can be a major security problem when SQL code is not checked, because end-user creation of SQL queries often results in garbage in/garbage out, though both the input/output look reasonable and are thus very difficult to detect and correct. This has been the numbing experience of one local state administration, whose many end users

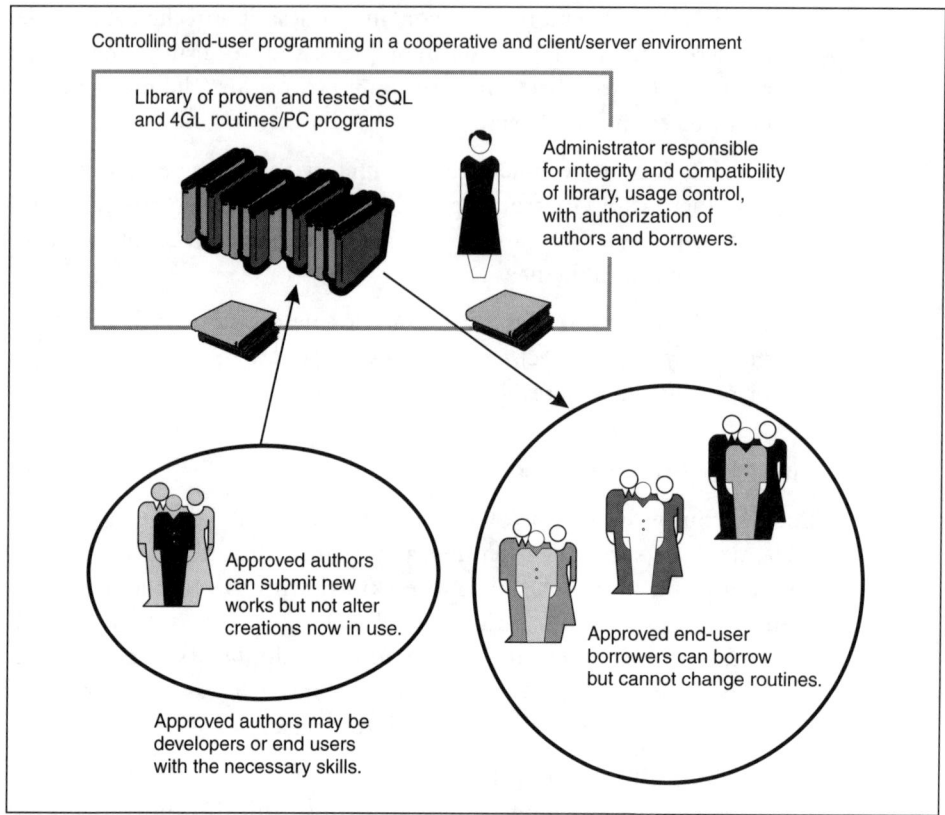

Figure 9.3 Library security and the borrower paradigm.

feel competent to do their own query formulation. A special control mechanism is the only viable solution, as illustrated by the library and borrower paradigm in Figure 9.3. With proper library security, end users can take out and reuse preset queries, but not write them. An extension of this security model applies to the development program at all levels; for example, approved services writers can enter routines, and approved application development borrowers can use them, but not change them.

Conclusions

In this chapter we have developed a strategy for introducing distributed systems to your company that comprises finding, using, and retaining a team with the right skill set. Often these skills must be sought in new pastures, such as Web technology and middleware. The chapter also pointed out how end-user involvement can become an integral part of the distributed environment strategy. The next chapter examines outsourcing, an option to consider when you are unable to find the right people resources you need within your company to build and manage a distributed system.

FOR FURTHER READING

Brooks, Frederick P. *The Mythical Man-Month.* (Reading, MA: Addison Wesley), 1995.

Forge, S. C. "Software Engineering Pitfalls in Distributed Systems," *Proceedings of Eurocon 84.* 6th European Conference on Electrotechnics, Computers in Communications and Control, Brighton, UK, 1984.

---

10 OUTSOURCING

"We have no choice," Milo informed him resignedly, "it's in the contract."

Catch-22, Joseph Heller, 1955

This chapter explores:

Reasons outsourcing has become a popular option.

Under what circumstances you should consider outsourcing.

The human resources issues of outsourcing.

Outsourcing contract negotiations.

Although outsourcing is becoming fashionable in the information systems world, it is not without its pitfalls. The most obvious are that moving to a distributed environment often requires far more skills, many of which are new; advanced technology; and for many corporations, greater risks than conventional systems. In the face of these issues, outsourcing can be tempting.

Another major pitfall of outsourcing is its expense: Making the transfer to outsourcing usually measures in millions to tens of millions of dollars, and raises questions of business strategy. Do it wrong and you're out millions; do it right, and you may *save* millions to hundreds of millions of dollars per year, depending on the size

257

of contracts and assets transferred. You may even get a one-time injection of major funds, for instance, from the sale of that real estate where those data centers you never really used properly are located.

Clearly, "giving away" assets to another company has to be considered from multiple points of view. Ask yourself these questions to help direct your thinking as you begin the process of making the outsourcing decision:

- What are our core competencies? Where will they be in five years?
- What should we retain because our core operations depend on it?
- Where do we add value in the chain that forms our firm's business? Will this be the same in five years' time?
- What role does IS play in establishing and maintaining a competitive advantage?
- How critical is IS to business success?

This chapter offers guidelines on best practice in the IS outsourcing process across all industries. They are drawn from research and counseling conducted during outsourcing experiences in the United States and Europe. To help you to implement these guidelines, we lay out a pragmatic approach to the process and alert you to the dangers of outsourcing, including contract negotiations and human resources issues.

When to Outsource

The outsourcing strategy must begin with the company deciding upon its key objectives for outsourcing, not just in the IS department, but at the CFO and business planning/development levels as well. These objectives may include:

- To economize on overhead expenses.
- To raise funds for core business.
- To obtain greater business flexibility, while increasing control.
- To improve IS performance.
- To reduce staff.
- To gain better support by access to external expertise (especially for scarce or rare skills or future technologies).

Another issue that comes to mind is politics; for example, one major company outsourced its data processing just to reduce the number of its data centers. This was done because management did not have the political strength to successfully imple-

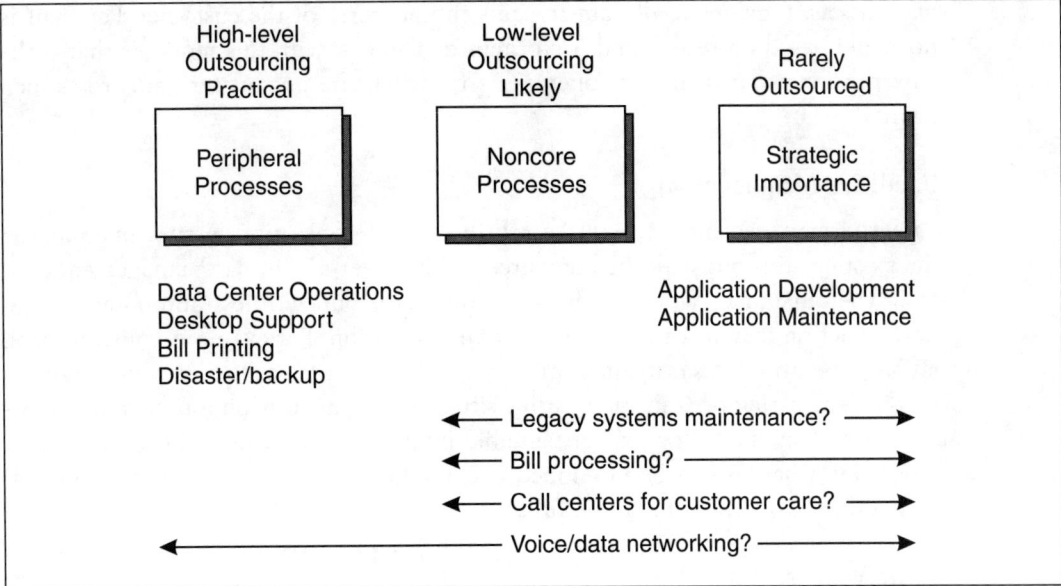

Figure 10.1 *Business priorities for outsourcing.*

ment a reduction as an internal operational decision over the objections of the end user departments and IS. Outsourcing allowed the reduction (in the absolute number of data centers) to be seen as a decision by an external organization.

What is considered "strategic" varies by industry and by company. Figure 10.1 shows one set of priorities (but note that, normally, the development of business-supporting applications is not outsourced).

Outsourcing Models

Before we go any further, let's define what we really mean by outsourcing. Although most IS leaders regard the splitting off of any part of the IS operations as outsourcing, in fact there are many specific and different models. The four main methods we consider as broadly defining the range of outsourcing options for any IS operation set include *conventional outsourcing*, *facilities management*, *joint venture*, and *management buyout*. We discuss each of these in the following subsections.

Conventional Outsourcing

So-called conventional outsourcing includes transfer of ownership (and possibly relocation) of hardware, software, network, staff, and application and system software assets. Obviously, all data remains the property of the customer. Payment is normally based on results and performance. The risk with this model is that if the enterprise runs an inefficient operations function, the outsourcer gains too much profit.

Facilities Management

Facilities management involves the takeover of the operation in situ, maintaining the existing staff but with the outsourcer taking over day-to-day management control. The outsourcer works onsite as a contractor but with less autonomous freedom of action than in an offsite outsourcing operation. For example, constraints on layout, operations, security, infrastructure, etc. can more easily be set and imposed by the contracting organization in this situation. Payment is on a time and materials basis. This model invokes a valuable interim stage during which better cost model information can be developed and inefficiencies can be removed, thus enabling the negotiation of a fairer, fuller contract.

Joint Venture

Using this model, the customer enters into a partnership with the outsourcer on a 49 percent or a 51 percent basis. The outsourcer partner would have prime responsibility for marketing operations. In terms of existing operations management, the outsourcer would also contribute to improvements of the existing operations and both partners would share the profits generated.

Management Buyout

In a management buyout, the current operations department is funded to become a commercially independent entity (to a greater or lesser degree). This approach is not suitable for inexperienced and commercially naive organizations (unless the company is looking for an inexpensive way to reduce staff). Usually, the new company formed by the management buyout will offer its services on the open market to other clients, as well as to its original parent, and so needs some marketing capability.

Model Responsibilities and Ownership

We can further classify these methods of outsourcing in terms of responsibilities and ownership (see Figure 10.2). But with all this information in hand, how do you choose which outsourcing model is best? The answer is, you don't choose just one; the option that will prove to be the best for your company will combine characteristics of one or more of them. You will choose model characteristics based on these factors:

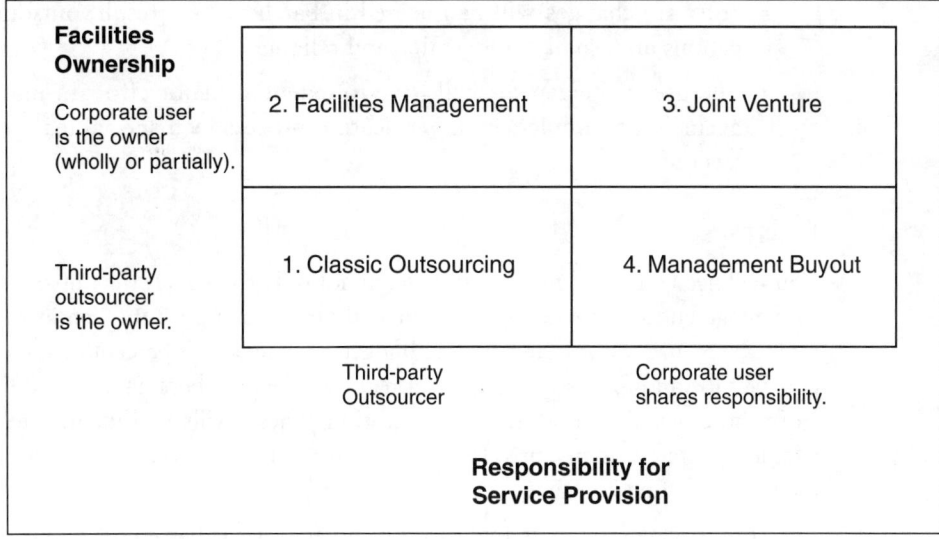

Figure 10.2 *Methods of outsourcing in terms of responsibilities and ownership.*

- Risk to core operations.
- Speed of implementation.
- Level of assistance needed.
- Preferred commercial control.

Operating with Outsourcing

Once the outsourcing approach has been defined, a fundamental cultural change affects IS and user departments. In short, outsourcing demands a new way of operating; what previously had been implicit in informal procedures becomes explicit, and a formal agreement.

Procedures and interfaces will have to be much more formally defined and in greater detail, since they will be individually priced. The first three steps are to define each process, measure each operation, and formalize cost models during an initial (or *baseline*) period.

Throughout this process, remember that, with outsourced services:

- End users must learn to accept a more formal relationship and formal change controls.

- Software changes will be released in batches. As a result, outsourced applications are usually more stable and reliable.

- End-user management will have to extend a major effort in interface management and implement a verification process by a special team to maintain level of service.

Costs

You will need a central management team not only to oversee the outsourcer, but also to manage end-user requirements, but without touching on the details of how these might be realized. For that purpose, budget 5 percent to 7 percent of the outsourcing contract for an in-house management team whose members have very different skills from those usually found in an IS operation. These skills will include account management, intercompany problem solving and coordination, negotiation, customer management, and contracts.

Transition costs can be high; for example, a major bank with a staff of 900 and three data centers could cost $100 million. Preparation—that is, measuring/costing operations and defining processes—and contract negotiation can be lengthy and require outside expertise on the technical, legal, and organizational sides.

The costs of new technology have to be planned with the outsourcer. These costs, however, can be reduced by using the outsourcer's expertise and purchasing power.

Implementation

The next issue to address is how to proceed with the outsourcing project. What are the major activities to be carried out? The rest of this chapter is devoted to this important topic. To begin, most outsourcing projects can be divided into the four activities shown in Figure 10.3.

We will look at each of these outsourcing processes, along with the issues associated with them, such as assets transfer. But before we do that, it's important to alert outsourcing managers to five common types of problems that can impact each of the four key processes. These problem types are shown in Figure 10.4. We look at the five problem types further as we consider each stage of the outsourcing project.

Staff Relations

Staff relations must be carefully considered if the outsourcing project is to succeed. Here, legal issues are always a paramount concern. For instance, if staff from your company are outsourced to another company, your company will have to provide the outsourcer with contractual indemnity to prevent the staff suing for changing their conditions of employment. If the contract is subsequently handed on to an-

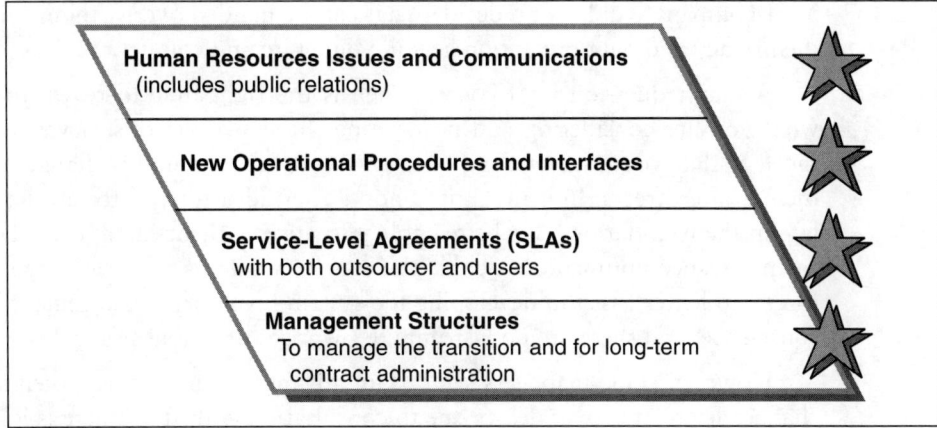

Figure 10.3 *Four outsourcing activities.*

other outsourcer this indemnity must also be handed on. Often, when staff are made redundant, the outsourcer will pass on the costs to the business client. Again, the actual legal situation must be carefully explored.

Obviously, if the outsourcer has to take on staff, their pertinent information—age, length of service, salary, skills, and so on—will have to be passed on.

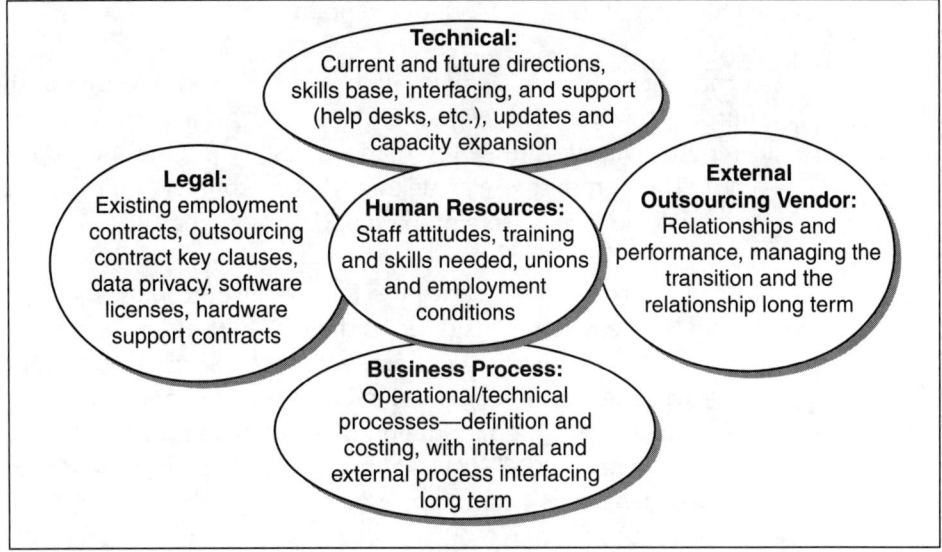

Figure 10.4 *Five outsourcing problem areas.*

Your company will have to decide what can be handed over without infringing on the privacy and data protection acts in your state and country.

A major question is of course when is the right time to reveal to your staff what you are considering and negotiating. In answering this, never lose sight of the fact that your outsourcing decisions will fundamentally change and impact their future careers. In general, it is not a good idea to wait to tell the workforce late in the negotiations. It's better policy to apprise them early. The advantages of early, advance notification include the company retains a better image; the workforce can better assist in developing the system inventory; management has a clear conscience; and there are no last-minute surprises or ambushes.

However, some managers see certain advantages in waiting to tell staff of the change: There are fewer delays due to consultation with staff; there is less opportunity for "spoiling tactics" by staff; and fewer key people leave since the delay is shorter.

If your company is unused to management by consensus, then you may need experienced support for a successful consultation exercise. It may be worth investi-

---

Surprise versus No Surprises Outsourcing

A chemicals group gave its staff no warning of the impending outsourcing change. One day they were just told they were working for another organization. They did not react well. Could your management keep such a secret this well? More to the point, should it?

In contrast, in a local administration, the staff were involved in the outsourcing transfer from day one. As a result, the outsourcer selection committee was vast (the "too many cooks" syndrome spoiled the planning). The committee was deluged by outsourcers' salespeople; staff were lost; the unions were mobilized; delays ensued.

If the corporation has to advertise for an outsourcer, as may happen in certain legal environments (such as the U.S. federal government and the European Community for contracts where costs exceed a certain threshold value), then the decision will become open. In another, but successful example, a state administration used human resources staff from the get-go to generate staff enthusiasm and commitment as well as to motivate user department commitment.

gating how your company outsourced any other of its services (cleaning, building management, food services) in the past and use this information as guidelines in consultation. And don't forget public relations: this is a major and time-consuming aspect of outsourcing. A sound case for outsourcing needs to presented to the outside world, as well as to the user departments and to the IS staff.

In most organizations, it is critical to involve the user departments in activities for planning outsourcing. End users have to see that there are benefits for them.

In some corporate cultures, the necessity of a more formal approach to implementing necessary changes in applications as a result of outsourcing can appear to actually be a reduction in levels of service delivered to the users. Users need to be reassured that necessary services will not be cut or reduced as a result of the change, or have it explained how any reductions will be compensated for in performance or other improvements. If the reliability of the current level of service does not appear to be too bad (i.e., it doesn't cause significant pain to the users), despite existing poor procedures, strong user resistance to any change may be expected.

Don't forget that outsourcers will be charging for all services. Most make their profits on the application modifications and changes required. Consequently, in the future, the end-user departments may have to make a business case for any changes they want. For example, one outsourcer and client agreed to set aside a fixed amount to fund small changes. Most contracts allow for x days of development support either in the price or in a fixed extra sum (for installation of new releases and so forth). This must be treated with some care; for example, in the case of a national taxation authority, the level of changes were significant, and the outsourcer did not satisfy the customer completely. From the point of view of the outsourcer, the monies allotted for system changes was inadequate, while the business client saw costs as shockingly high.

Outsourcing Assets

Existing company relationships with other suppliers can be a major stumbling block when implementing an outsourcing project. Your company may have exclusive contracts with hardware and software suppliers that will have to be renegotiated, and arrangements will have to be made to transfer or renegotiate these agreements.

Packaged applications software may also create a problem. Software vendors do not like third-party organizations running their software because they suspect it may be used in nonagreed-upon ways. In any case, all the current application licensing agreements have to be renegotiated package by package.

Probably, the current interfaces between the IS department and the rest of the organization are not as well defined as required for outsourcing; often, they are fairly informal. Consequently, these interfaces will have to be more explicitly defined and agreed on either by changing or putting in place for the first time new operations processes. For example, an outsourcing group in the United Kingdom took nine months to get an insurance company's documentation in order—and it was not considered to be in bad shape to start with. All software changes have to logged, although some software updates may be bundled into periodic releases of these accumulated changes. One favorable consequence of this is that software often becomes more stable.

An important question is what should you do with the manager responsible for high-level technical decisions and directions on systems, many of which impact the business? He or she should normally be brought in-house.

Next you need to decide how to plan and then carry out an outsourcing operation in IS. This can be divided into an eight-step process:

1. Decide on the Key Objectives

The outsourcing strategy must start with the company deciding what the *key objectives* are for outsourcing. Often the approach is to use a series of meetings with the top management team to define these objectives, with the option of including the outsourcers in discussions.

Most outsourcing projects can be divided into the aforementioned four key areas, and most projects start by considering the management of and appropriate staffing for the implementation in each area:

- Human resources and public relations handling.
- Developing new operational procedures and interfaces.
- Drawing up and negotiating the SLAs.
- Creating two management structures for the transition and for long-term contract administration.

2. Implement a Task Force and a Project Office

For management structures, you should use the following two powerful organizational tools:

- *An outsourcing task force to act as a steering committee.* This should be headed by human resources, not IS, since most problems and decisions can be expected to be in human relations. The task force could be headed by a senior VP to give it the power needed, as well as to provide a channel to top management.

- *An outsourcing project office to take care of the detail.* This should be led by a pair of managers, one with technical know-how of the functions, and the other with business-process know-how about the application areas being outsourced. Most important, they should report to a project office chief who is a real manager (a fixer and diplomat); she or he can make quick decisions and smooth over difficulties without creating new ones.

3. Take an Inventory

Early in the outsourcing project, you need to take an inventory of the following:

- Staff with professional resumes, salary, pension plans, and so on.
- Skills and their value to the company. Much intellectual capital and legacy knowledge may be lost if staff leave.
- Services performed, and their real costs.
- Business and operations processes.
- User interfaces and their management structures.
- Business practices and relevant company information.
- Buildings, data centers, office equipment, vehicles, and other physical property.
- Documentation.
- Internally developed applications and databases to be supported, and licenses for operation by an external concern.
- Third-party applications software and their licenses.
- Systems and utilities software and their licenses.
- Systems, data, and network management centers, tools, and facilities.
- Hardware equipment: systems, networks, and peripherals.
- Computer supplier agreements on supply, leasing, and take-back.
- Miscellaneous (such as high-speed printer supplies).

Accumulating an accurate inventory is often very difficult since few organizations really know how many printers or PCs they have, let alone what software is loaded on them.

4. Establish the True Costs of the Existing Service

As indicated, it is important to establish the true costs of the existing service as a basis for negotiations. Often these costs are not itemized in the detail you will need to successfully implement the outsourcing project. Without them you cannot assign value to what you are outsourcing and thus you will have no position from which to negotiate.

5. Understand Your Processes

Next you need to verify that you understand the processes of the operations to be outsourced and the contractual arrangements for service-level agreements. Even if the IS staff are reluctant to provide information on processes and their real costs, you will have to go forward. One option is to interview staff individually, using personnel (the outsourcing project team) who already have a good understanding of the area and can spot missing or inadequate information.

6. Approach the Outsourcers

The next step is to approach the outsourcers. The process for gathering bids from outsourcers begins with issuing a *request for information*. This should establish all relevant facts and approximate pricing. The aim should be to come up with a short list of two outsourcers to be issued with a *request for tender*. Multiple outsourcing contracts are rare, and usually are split between application maintenance and operations. There are major management problems in having three or more outsourcing vendors; and any subcontractors must be vetted, and responsibilities ensured. Often, though the main outsourcer will perform well, that vendor may seem powerless to enforce equal effort from any subcontractors.

7. Begin Negotiations

Following the creation of a short list, you are ready to begin negotiations. It may be sensible to involve the procurement department in this step to take advantage of their expertise in purchasing and contract negotiation. Most companies going through an outsourcing negotiation spend large sums on legal, financial, and technical/tactical advice (as much as 5 percent to 10 percent of the outsourcing value, often totaling more than $5 million).

> **TIP**
>
> It is inadvisable to accept contract terms from outsourcers without negotiation.

Certain additional actions may have to be taken before the contract can be signed. For example, all the contractual prerequisites on status of equipment, data centers, information, and so on, may have to be completed.

8. Begin the Transfer Process

Finally, the transfer process begins. This requires a special management team for the transfer, the *project office*, and for the ongoing contract management. We describe the outsourcing management team in more detail later in the section titled "Ongoing Management of the Contract." The outsourcing transfer for an IS operation the size of a large corporation can take at least 3 to 12 months to arrange and to prepare for handover. And following contract signature, it will take at least another 12 months before delivery of benefits.

During the detailed negotiations, the IS department should start putting its house in order. One approach is to enlist the assistance of the outsourcer on a time and materials basis. Such a "first contact" phase can also serve to form the initial relationship between existing IS staff and the outsourcer, and act as a test of understanding and coworking abilities, thus giving a clear indication of the viability of the relationship, preferably before final signatures are on the contract.

Contract Terms

It is wise to spend whatever time it takes to develop a good contract and anticipate problems. Many major corporations spend $1 to 10 million on contract negotiation alone. Organizations have to decide what sort of outsourcing vendor relationship they want, because the basis for the contract is this relationship.

Two major relationship models are *transactional,* customer and vendor; and *partnership,* where the outsourcer (in theory) fully understands your business and is a partner to you (many outsourcers today prefer this model as it affords greater leverage on fees and a greater hold over the client).

Major surveys report that the transactional model is overwhelmingly favored over the partnership model of outsourcing. The transaction model has been more successful because outsourcers are rarely able to deliver true partnerships.

The partnership model is marked by these characteristics:

- Different strategic alliances from standard outsourcing agreements; focuses more on cost efficiency.
- Contracts are based on shared risk and shared reward deals, and involve teams of internal and external staff working far more closely.
- Joint activity provides a competitive advantage for both partners (in theory).

Partnership deals, however, may result in unexpected fees and unacceptable service levels. The results of a study of 61 major transatlantic outsourcing contracts signed by 40 U.K. and U.S. corporations reveal that in nearly half the deals examined, long-term cost savings failed to materialize or were not clearly evident. Strategic partnerships rarely provide the expected cost savings. In summary, partnership deals are questionable if we accept the premise that outsourcing vendors and customers are fundamentally opposed.

The best advice is to go for short-term contracts. In the survey cited, 60 percent of long-term contracts failed to achieve objectives, whereas only 11 percent of short-term deals failed. (Note: Long-term refers to a 7- to 10-year contract; short-term refers to a 2- to 5-year contract.)

That said, successful IS outsourcing practitioners have gone for "win-win" agreements—long-term satisfaction of both sides. But if the outsourcer suffers too low a margin, the customer will eventually pay in poor service and disagreements on contract terms.

When negotiating, pay attention to the main contract conditions, which include:

- *Service-level agreements.* SLAs set quality of service for every important process and operation, in detail, such as parameters to measure user satisfaction.

- *Arbitration mechanism.* A tool for settling disputes.

- *Exit clauses.* A provision that enables you to switch contractors. Without this, your contract has no force (on price, service level, and so on).

- *Open-book operations.* Set costs and prices. The outsourcer agrees to show the customer the costs and revenues of the operation, and a reasonable profit level is agreed and guaranteed.

- *Good performance incentives.* Incentives give the outsourcing contractor reason to improve services.

- *Definition of roles.* You need formally defined roles of managers, on both sides.

The contract requires a well-prepared negotiation strategy. Weaknesses in contracts can cause you to lose control of costs; this is referred to as the *hidden cost* of outsourcing. Top management, the IS department, and any outside departments (such as procurement) participating in negotiations must have a close working relationship both inside and outside the negotiating sessions, and agree on a common position on all points. If this is not done, the outsourcers will win advantages by exploiting tension and lack of control.

The following are some guidelines for negotiating an outsourcing contract:

- Agree on common aims internally across the entire organization before negotiating. Conflicting aims in different parts of the organization, including among the end users, will weaken your negotiating position.

- Insist on making joint contract decisions that involve both the IS specialists and the senior managers, who decide corporate strategy and end-user needs.

- Ensure that the technicians managing the SLAs and the lawyers negotiating the contract cooperate to avoid ending up with a weak contract.

- Go for a win-win situation; build up confidence in the outsourcer.

- Ensure that each process is defined and that each operation is measured during an initial (baseline) period, then adjust or attribute costs.

- To prevent poor performance, negotiate a "balanced score card" for the SLAs; this will ensure that the end users are happy and that the outsourcer does not have an easy ride.

Defining Commercial Service-Level Agreements

Internal SLAs negotiated by the IS department with the end-user divisions are unlikely to be adequate as the basis for an outsourcing contract. A commercial contract needs SLAs that cover systems aspects unseen by the end users, such as tape loads, management of systems software, and so on. The end-user aspects are only the tip of the tasks to evaluate and costs in the outsourcing iceberg.

Furthermore, the outsourcing contract and the SLAs must be aligned. When the technicians managing the SLAs and the lawyers negotiating the contract diverge, a weak contract is the result.

Ongoing Management of the Contract

Your company has to develop a close working relationship with the outsourcer to ensure that the two cultures are compatible and can work together. Ask yourself if you would want to do business with the outsourcer. A risk-sharing and win-win agreement is likely to lead to greater long-term satisfaction. An open-book arrangement with the outsourcer will ease management concerns over profit gouging. (As noted, major management problems arise from having three or more outsourcing vendors, so stick to one if possible.)

The parameter to measure in an SLA is user satisfaction, the ultimate objective of the exercise. To avoid a skewed performance, the corporation must be very careful to negotiate a balanced score card to ensure that users are happy and that the outsourcer does not have an easy ride. The profit expectations of the out-sourcer should be 23 percent to 25 percent of gross margins and 10 percent of net profits.

The management demands of an outsourcing contract are quite high: A team of 20 and more is typical for a major IS department outsourcing. These managers

---

Two Outsourcing Examples

This first example of an outsourcing catastrophe occurred in a U.S. insurance firm, which negotiated a contract with a major systems outsourcer to transfer the main IS assets to a new data center. The insurance firm expected to close down its old computer center. An exhaustive tendering process was undertaken, which culminated in a month of negotiations conducted in a hotel.

Despite all this work, the outsourcing supplier overlooked the support of the development interface that comprised about 30 percent of the total contract cost. This was discovered at the last moment; as a result, the deal fell apart because the outsourcer refused to sign. By this time, key staff from the insurance firm had left (in anticipation of a transfer to the outsourcer), and there was no computer accommodation. Currently, this company is renting a center at the outsourcer and renegotiating.

In contrast is the example of a leading global oil exploration company that decided to outsource to cut overhead costs. It chose a rather novel approach, which involved contracting with multiple outsourcers to stimulate competition. To handle the resulting inevitable conflicts between the competing firms, only one firm was identified as prime contractor for a single geographic region. The remaining firms act as subcontractors to the prime. The expected competition has ensured, first, better pricing, and second, that the latest technology is always being introduced. Moreover, the company imposed short-term contracts (on the order of three years), and sees this as a prime reason for its successful experience in cutting costs and raising service levels. This case is, however, an exception, in that it is generally advisable to seek a single contractor for outsourcing. This company's success stems from its strong management team and from the clear delineation of responsibilities through the prime contractor relationship.

need different skills from those found in IS operations, including account management, problem solving, coordination, negotiation, customer management, and contracts.

Exit Arrangements

Generally, experience confirms the general belief that outsourcing is a one-way street. Once outsourced, the contract can only be transferred; that is, it cannot be taken back in-house. Consequently, exit arrangements must be carefully negotiated to avoid a deadly embrace of total dependency on one outsourcer.

Conclusions

In this chapter we looked at outsourcing as a possible option to consider when you are unable to build and maintain an effective distributed system in house. We covered some of the planning and contract negotiation concerns, and highlighted what can happen when an outsourcing arrangement is not properly planned. In the next chapter we introduce some theories about the future of distributed systems and how they can become living systems that will grow and change with your company.

FOR FURTHER READING

Lacity, Mary C. and Rudy Hirschheim. *Study of Outsourcing.* (Oxford, UK: Templeton College), 1995.

Lacity, Mary C. and Rudy Hirschheim. *Information Systems Outsourcing.* (New York: John Wiley & Sons, Inc.), 1993.

---

11 BUILDING EXTENSIBLE SYSTEMS

These success encourages: they can because they think they can.

Aeneid, Virgil, 70–19 BC

This chapter explains:

How to design and build extensible enterprise systems.

How to plan for the future of your distributed system.

The underlying principles that make distributed object computing work.

The benefits and pitfalls of using a component-based development model.

The eXtensible Markup Language (XML).

How the data-centric computing model eases development of distributed application in the enterprise.

In Chapter 4 we explained that executives must understand the principles of living systems and briefly defined the concept of a living system. Now we will explore living systems in more depth from a technical perspective. To determine whether you know the current state of your systems, select one of the following that best defines the state of your organization's application base:

1. We build each application ad hoc to fit the requirements of a single department, with little or no analysis of integration obstacles with existing systems.

2. We use middleware extensively to link disparate systems.

3. We design applications to reuse existing applications where possible, but lack of documentation often hinders the process.

4. We use a formal development methodology and design tools on each project, which enhances our ability to build systems in record time with minimal resources.

If you're in category 4, congratulations! You're among the exclusive 1 percent of businesses that can claim this optimal approach. If your answer was 2 or 3, changing your systems for competitive reasons is doable but likely to be painful. If you answered 1, the chance of gaining a competitive advantage by using the applications in your organization is slim.

Based upon the health of your existing applications, could you develop a new application today and drop it into the set of overall systems such that it could share data with any other application without additional programming? Probably not, but that's okay; it is highly unlikely that any organization has accomplished this feat. The point is, it *can* be accomplished, and living systems represent the embodiment of the concept as a deployed system. Because living systems mark a fundamental change in the way we think and design distributed applications and entire computer systems for the enterprise, we devote the rest of this chapter to walking you through the transitions necessary to create living systems.

Today, distributed application development relies heavily on object-oriented methodologies and connective middleware. The use of the processing resources of many different machines and programs to accomplish any given task stands as the central design goal for distributed applications. The time to move to the next phase of computing has arrived. In a living system, endpoints are applications that receive their data through a single input mechanism and push data through a single output mechanism. Between applications, data exists in a flexible self-describing state such that anyone or any service with proper access levels can view and manipulate it (see Figure 11.1). This dynamic data access leads to the development of a universal data repository.

Living systems concepts are being worked on by the leading software vendors today, including Microsoft, Sun Microsystems, Novell, Netscape, Sybase, DataChannel, webMethods, Poet Software, and many others. In the near future, the tools and technologies will be available to corporate developers to enable them to build living systems with ease. Since living systems rely heavily on an understanding

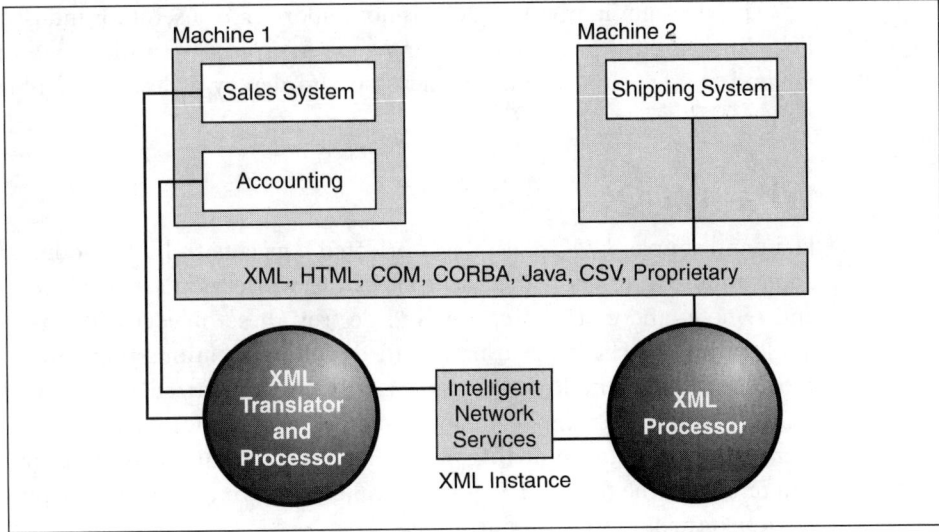

Figure 11.1 *An extensible system system.*

of the concepts of distributed object computing, to begin this discussion we will review some of these concepts.

Distributed Object Computing

Distributed object computing (DOC) is one of the hottest buzz terms of the corporate development community. It represents the holy grail of computing; it stands as the one area of computing where the "peacocks flaunt their feathers." It marks a battle engaged in by both the end user and vendor companies. Occasionally, when tempered with pragmatic developers, DOC pays off in success. For most companies managing DOC developers and projects, however, it is a time-consuming process that yields no significant added value to the company's systems. Alone, technologies do not solve problems; they require realistic implementation approaches. Unfortunately, due to its complexity, those attracted to DOC usually come from an academic and purist background with all too little grounding in practical, profitable implementation.

> **WARNING**
>
> Today, DOC may not be appropriate for meeting the real-world goals of enterprise systems.

This does not imply that DOC is not important or useful for industry solutions. Logical methods exist for determining on a project-by-project basis the correct method for deciding whether to develop and deploy a distributed object application.

What Is DOC?

Plain and simple: DOC uses object-oriented concepts to build modular distributed applications. In essence, the client views the world as a set of objects, both local and remote, and can create, use, and destroy these objects with ease. The object model allows a client programmer to design applications that mimic real-world processes. For example, DOC can present an "objectized" view of a mainframe COBOL accounting application. A Microsoft Windows client application would then create an instance of that object, load it with data, execute some processing, and terminate the object. The process, called *wrapping,* is widely employed to reuse existing, tested in-house applications.

Simply, DOC creates an illusion. The COBOL accounting application remains the same program it was when initially created, but it now appears as a programmable object. "Under the hood," most DOC implementations use some form of remote procedure call (RPC) to create the illusion of a programmable object.

Since DOC is central to this chapter, we have included some DOC terminology and definitions. We've already used two so far: RPC and IDL, which are important for building DOC. Page 279 shows a few more important terms and their definitions.

An Example: ACME Aircraft

This example provides a pragmatic introduction to distributed object computing. ACME Aircraft wants to model the manufacturing process for a single aircraft regardless of its model. ACME has an extensive database of parts, as well as a parts list for every model aircraft it offers. The company's goal is to synchronize all its internal systems to reflect the current status of any aircraft being built, which means that accounting, inventory, and sales data must be constantly updated. Since ACME does not want to spend hundreds of thousands of dollars building systems for each model it offers, it decides to use an object-oriented metaphor that would allow it to model its real-world manufacturing process.

ACME starts by objectizing all its systems. It makes accounting look like money objects, inventory look like parts objects, and sales look like customer objects. With these base sets of objects defined, building the system is a matter of defining the relationships between these objects and the behaviors of those relation-

DOC Terms and Definitions

Encapsulation. The process of binding context to an instance of data. Encapsulation is a feature of the object-oriented programming paradigm. Each object is really an allocation of memory for a particular set of variables defined within the context of a scope identified by an object type. Encapsulation provides the ability to create multiple instances of the same object, each with different data.

Inheritance. Another important feature of the object-oriented programming paradigm. It allows new object types to be defined by referencing preexisting object types. When an object is created through inheritance, it shares the same attributes with the parents, but may change behavior or extend the object for additional functionality.

Instance. A singular memory allocation of data associated with a particular set of functions, within the scope of an object.

Methods. Function calls that perform processing within the scope of an object. Methods can only see the attributes of the object within which it is defined.

Object Model. A definition of the standard way to create and interact with objects in a particular environment.

Polymorphism. The ability to make the correct method call on a particular instance of an object without knowing its exact type information. Mainly used in conjunction with inheritance, this feature allows groups of objects descending from the same inheritance tree to be treated identically, even though they may each be a different implementation.

Reference. A variable that represents a remote object. It is essentially a pointer to the stub.

Remote Method. A method call on a object that exists in a different process, usually on a different machine. Remote methods behave like methods on local objects to the client, but consume a great deal more resources.

Stub. A local proxy that represents a remote object locally. To the client application, the stub looks identical to the remote object so that the function call can succeed regardless of the location of the object. Stubs use RPCs to implement the remote method call.

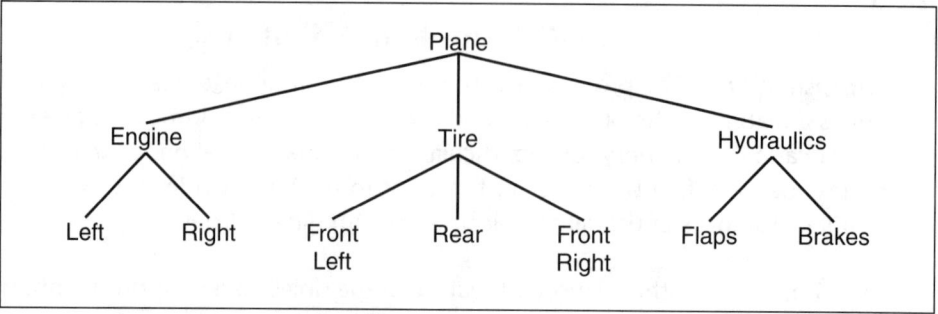

Figure 11.2 *Hierarchical representation of a plane object.*

ships; in fact, the relationships themselves are objects. For example, the aircraft object is nothing more than a collection of parts objects (see Figure 11.2). The method *assemble()* on the plane object removes a part object from inventory and adds it to the plane object. Notice that the part remains the same entity everywhere it goes in the system.

> **NOTE**
>
> One feature of a distributed object system is that objects can be transferred between other objects.

When ACME uses the *assemble()* method on the plane object, there is an interesting interaction between some large-scale system objects. After all, a part object is fairly small, and mostly data. But the warehouse object, which stores the inventory, and the plane object are very big objects, not the type you would consider passing around. Actually, the warehouse object is an objectized version of the inventory system. Instead of taking a part out of the inventory system, we call the warehouse object's *use()* method, which takes as parameters the part being removed from inventory and a *reference* to the plane for which it is being used—again, illustrating the *illusion* of passing the plane object to the warehouse object.

Some objects are just too large to consider moving from system to system for processing. In those instances, we create a proxy (reference) that is small and can be passed around; it is actually an *alias* to the original large object. Everything we do to the reference is actually committed on the large immovable object. Here is where the operational pieces come in: the remote method, stub, and RPCs.

Partitioning a process helps to better understand the task at hand. With small objects, partitioning is not necessary since the quantity of information that must be

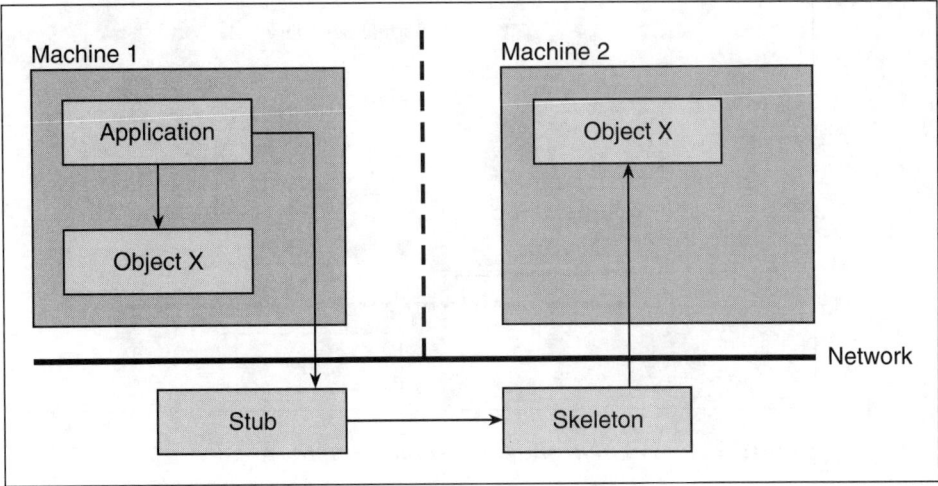

Figure 11.3 Interaction of stub with remote object.

moved between processes is relatively small. But we are now working with an extremely large immovable object, so we need to partition the object into a lightweight component and a fixed immovable component. The lightweight component we call the stub. To create an instance of the large immovable object, we instead create an instance of its stub. Once the stub is loaded in memory, its first duty is to alert the large immovable object that the stub is alive (see Figure 11.3).

The stub has the same set of methods on it as the large immovable component, but its implementation is designed to make remote method calls on its counterpart. That is, there is no real processing code built into the stub, merely networking commands to marshal the data from the client to the immovable piece, which we will now term the *object server*. It's really nothing more than a facade placed over the common client/server paradigm (see Figure 11.4). The only difference is that now this contextual entity exists that gives the illusion that we're in fact dealing with a real warehouse, instead of a database.

> **NOTE**
> Another major feature of distributed object computing is the provision of the object-oriented metaphor over client/server implementations.

The main difference between building *n*-tiered client/server systems and distributed object systems is found in the design. DOC systems require extensive planning

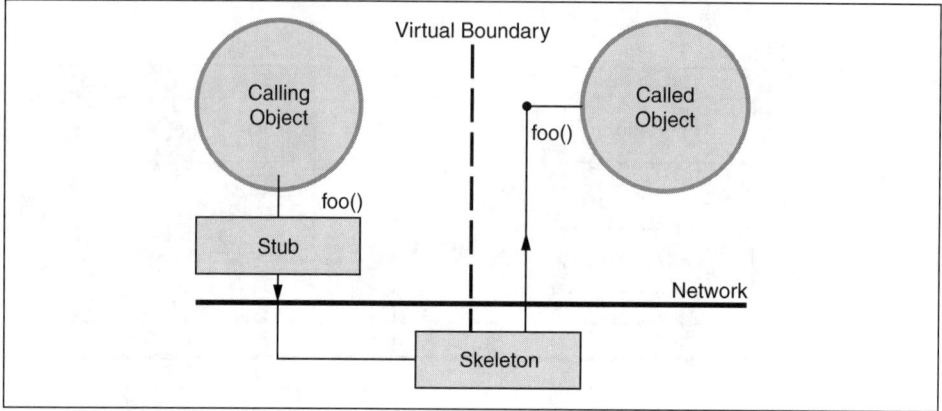

Figure 11.4 A client makes a remote method call.

on the front end to flesh out *all* core relationships required by the first phase of implementation. (Core relationships are those that include objects and interfaces that will be relied on and used by the rest of the system.) Overlooking core relationships could necessitate redesign of the total system after the implementation has started. With DOC systems, it can be as difficult to add a core relationship after implementation as it is to change the name of a heavily used field in a database. All code that references the changed object would have to be rewritten, even if only in some small way. However, a well-designed object-based system can add an unlimited number of noncore relationships and objects postimplementation with relative ease.

Large-scale distributed object systems may require six to nine months of up-front design, but they can then be implemented and be working properly in three months. In contrast, systems developed quickly, with little design, often malfunction and can still be incomplete a full year after deployment.

The Importance of Homogeneity

Communication represents one of the most essential functions in our lives, and as humans we require homogeneity of language to ensure coherence of our verbally conveyed ideas. That's why, in order to communicate in today's global environment, most people speak English as a primary or at least a secondary language. Computers also require language homogeneity. If computers had feelings, they might find it disconcerting to have their bytes ripped apart and reorganized to talk to another machine. Yet we repeatedly and continually rip apart and rearrange computer bytes; we call the resulting process *interoperability*.

To understand the capabilities of DOC, we must first understand the importance of homogeneity. One of the major problems of implementing distributed object computing today is dealing with the heterogeneity that plagues the industry. Vendors, such as Microsoft, and consortiums, such as the Object Management Group (OMG), have fought valiantly to provide solutions that tie these disparate platforms together to make them operate seamlessly. Unfortunately, their best solution attempt offers only 50 percent of what is required for robust distributed object computing. Data must still be massaged and converted as it moves among different operating systems and hardware environments.

Java

In 1996, Sun Microsystems introduced what appeared to be a better alternative for building distributed applications: Java. Java was introduced as a lightweight "virtual" machine able to run on top of all these other operating environments, making the application communications layer homogeneous. (A virtual machine is really a software-only version of a computer instruction processing entity. In software, it is very similar to hardware processors like the Intel x86 or Sun SPARC.)

The Java Virtual Machine defines a set of instructions that tells the software machine what to do. Then each virtual machine implementor makes the instructions perform a real operating system or hardware instruction. There is a level of translation for all instructions, changing Java instruction into real chip instructions; hence the term virtual. This level of indirection provides the homogenous layer essential for robust distributed computing.

The leading tools of the time, which include the Open Group's Distributed Computing Environment (DCE), Microsoft's Distributed Component Object Model (DCOM), and the OMG's Common Object Request Broker Architecture (CORBA), attempted to provide homogeneity by making all systems agree on a standard set of data types at the messaging layer (see Figure 11.5). In contrast, Java objects can be understood at the application layer, thereby allowing much richer type support and seamless integration. Some very important differences exist in these attempts to provide distributed application support, which are listed in Table 11.1, along with some of their characteristics.

When viewed from the application transport perspective, data communication appears as a stream of bytes with no meaningful information except who sent it and where it is going; that is, the application context is lost and requires a knowledgeable receiver to make sense of it. By moving data communications into the application layer, the context, such as class structure and references, can be preserved. Additionally, this homogeneous perspective can be driven all the way down into the

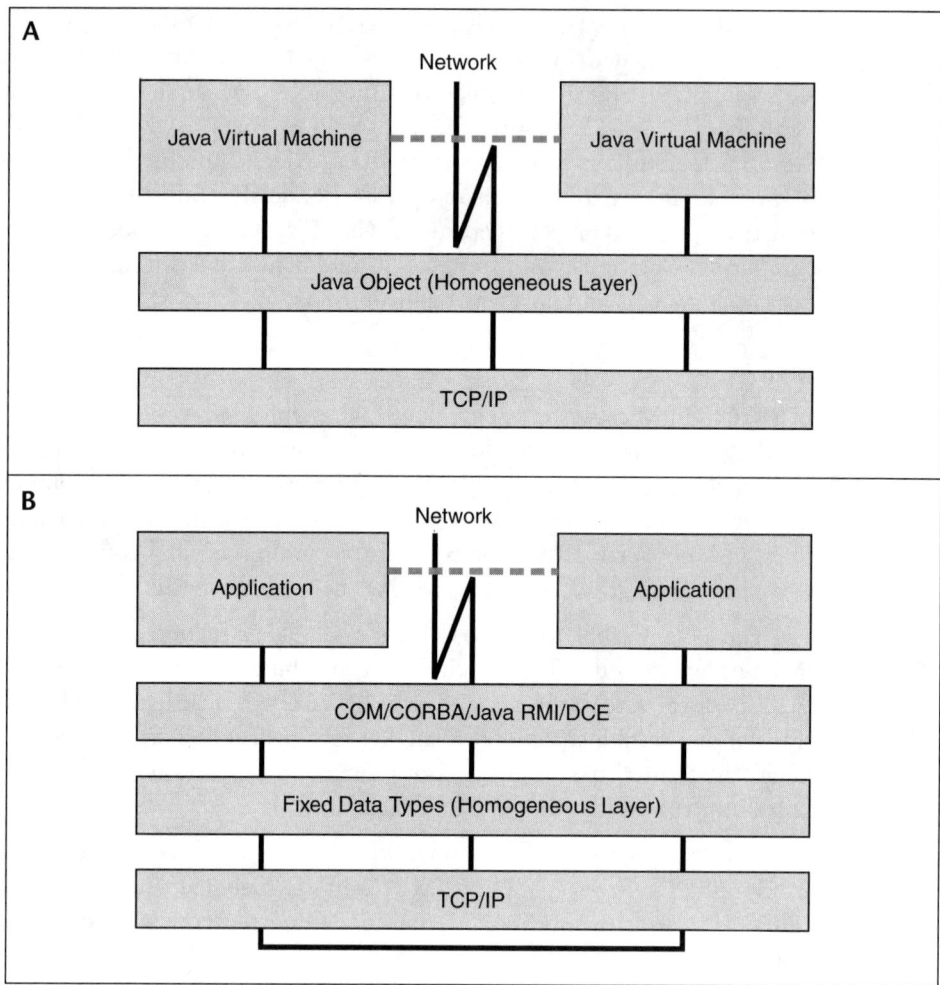

Figure 11.5 Homogeneity at the application versus the messaging layer.

Table 11.1 Distributed Application Support Offerings

	Messaging Layer	Application Layer
Programming Language Support	Neutral	Java
Operating System Support	Neutral	Neutral
Legacy Integration	Can be written in same programming language as legacy application	Works only over Java; needs middleware to communicate with legacy applications
Data Types Supported	Only defined types	All Java objects

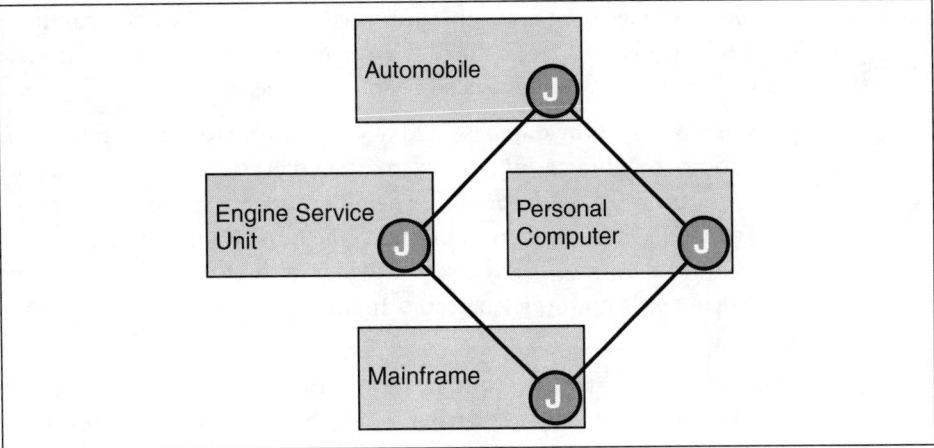

Figure 11.6 *A Java-connected universe.*

network services. Here, data being transmitted by an intelligent service—a service that can recognize the data it is transporting—allows the application to make certain assumptions that require only the address of the receiving application. For example, a Java-based router could examine the data and make decisions based upon a certain class, such as transferring all objects of type *accounting* to the accounting system. Why is homogeneity important? If we look at the benefits of Java, we see two trends emerging:

- Java creates a unified view of all machines (see Figure 11.6). This makes moving data between systems a much easier process.

- Universal representations of data that can exist both inside the enterprise and be exported to suppliers and customers allow us to easily provide a continuous flow of information regarding commercial transactions.

Java can satisfy many levels of deployment, but the one that will clearly rise above the rest involves the development of application servers. Application servers provide application-specific information to a network (via a messaging protocol), and can provide services via a networked programming interface, either Web- or RPC-based.

Today's most common application data access method uses a database with SQL (Structured Query Language) to retrieve datasets matching certain criteria. There are notable differences in approach between Java access methods and those used with SQL-database implementations. Databases represent primarily centralized mechanisms with data stored in a specific format that must be known in advance in order to generate a useful request. In contrast, application servers can respond to requests via a number of different approaches and can use multiple access mechanisms. Moreover, there is no requirement that internal data structures be known in advance with Java-based application servers.

In many ways, the database and SQL have provided a level of homogeneity for application communication. A key reason for the popularity of databases is that one application inputs information while another can access it. Of course, databases and SQL do have their limitations, the most significant being the requirement to break out data into a fixed set of fields that can be linked efficiently in a relational manner. If not done correctly, application and database performance will be diminished.

In an ideal system, communication with all applications would be seamless, and a common data representation would be used to move data inside as well as outside the organization. We've seen how Java can provide a homogeneous access layer on top of all operating systems and hardware platforms. A Java-based application server can also give users transparent access to an existing database. The Java-based application server provides seamless communications and preserves investments by removing the link between the application and the database.

Can Java satisfy the requirement for a common data representation? Yes, but with limitations, as outlined in the following points.

- Java supports *introspection,* a method of examining the structure of a Java object dynamically, without creating an instance of it. This feature allows the recipient of an unknown Java object to explore the attributes, methods (inclusive of parameter declarations), and class hierarchy.

- Java instructions can be executed by any properly written Java Virtual Machine. This feature allows applications to send code and data together to any receiving application. For example, an accounting application may not know anything about the attribute names or structures of a Java object it just received, but it knows to call the method *getMoney()* on all received objects. This allows you to pass any Java object representing a product sold to the accounting system as long as you supply the *getMoney()* method. The accounting system will be able to retrieve the data it needs. Requiring objects to support a fixed set of methods may not be the most flexible solution, but the alternative would require the accounting system to know about the money field in *every* product table. (Note, the ability to pass code includes the code for an entire class hierarchy for each object.)

With these Java features, we move closer to being able to represent data independently of any application that might create that data.

> **NOTE**
>
> Homogeneity at the application communications layer provides the greatest ability to make data independent of the application that created it, while maintaining universal coherence.

Java, however, gets us only part of the way to homogeneity. For data to be truly independent of the application that created it, data must be self-describing. Java objects are a form of self-describing data with introspection, but they require the use of a Java Virtual Machine in order to provide coherence. Since the current product offerings cannot guarantee 100 percent compatible implementations of the Java Virtual Machine, Java cannot be used with confidence as a universal representation across all operating systems and hardware. Using the PC as a gauge for industry standardization, it seems a fully cross-platform Java Virtual Machine may never be a reality (consider that an Intel Pentium computer from COMPAQ still behaves differently from one created by Gateway 2000).

Java's undoing may be its ownership by a single vendor. While Sun Microsystems continues to develop the Java platform to support operating system-level functionality, Microsoft has put to use only the parts of Java that enhance its NT operating systems. By not accepting the rest of Java as defined by Sun, Microsoft faces industry backlash.

Disagreement over Java components occurs because the language requires a particular subsystem as part of the base Java Virtual Machine implementation. Java by definition provides homogeneity, but cannot guarantee it in implementation. To achieve that, we need a tool that provides the power of Java for data representation, but without the implementation hurdles.

DOC *Reborn*

Theoretically, distributed object computing offers tremendous promise for application development. The concept of plug-and-play systems has attracted much attention over the past few years. Though some success stories have been reported, the current tools available for development of distributed object applications will not work for the largest base of application developers.

Distributed object computing is only a methodology—a different way of viewing the problem—so it cannot really be said to fail. It represents merely a facade that covers the mess of wiring—the implementation code—that lies just beneath the surface. Remove the cover and you'll discover that a system should not be judged by its objects. Too frequently, this apparently smooth-functioning object model hides a complex, convoluted, poorly thought out, idiosyncratic reflection of inflexible business processes.

> **TIP**
>
> Implementation is the key to success!

As developers discover this secret, tools that enable them to develop cleaner and higher-quality implementations will become more important than tools with which they can build poor, but connectable, applications. The rebirth of DOC will be initiated by programmers and vendors who understand that the perception of objects assists in design; but moving that design to implementation will require a very different architecture from the client/middleware/server one currently in wide deployment. Furthermore, the objects that stem from this revival will offer real plug-and-play capacity, leading directly to the development of living systems.

Why does DOC need to be reborn? With all the hours and effort expended in the development of frameworks or architectures like CORBA, COM, and Java, how could so many developers be so wrong? The response becomes obvious as the next generation of application architectures unrolls before our eyes.

First, it is important to understand that inventors and implementors of CORBA, COM, Java RMI, and DCE were not wrong. It is not an issue of right or wrong; these frameworks should be used to develop the underlying intelligent services that power the network, not given to the application developer. The group that should be implementing object request brokers and the like should be vendors shrink-wrapping their value-add service around the object request brokers and selling an out-of-the-box solution to corporations. (A more thorough discussion of intelligent services follows in the subsection entitled "Data-Centric Computing.")

Object-oriented programming initially became popular because people believed it would lead to easier code reuse, and eventually save millions on application development. With the creation and deployment of Microsoft's Visual Basic (VB) controls architecture, it soon became apparent that developers would not use each other's code directly, but would use a black box (component) implementation. Black box means the code is locked inside an executable entity with the specifics of the implementation hidden from the developer/user. Typically it also provides the developer with an easy-to-use programmable interface (see Fig-

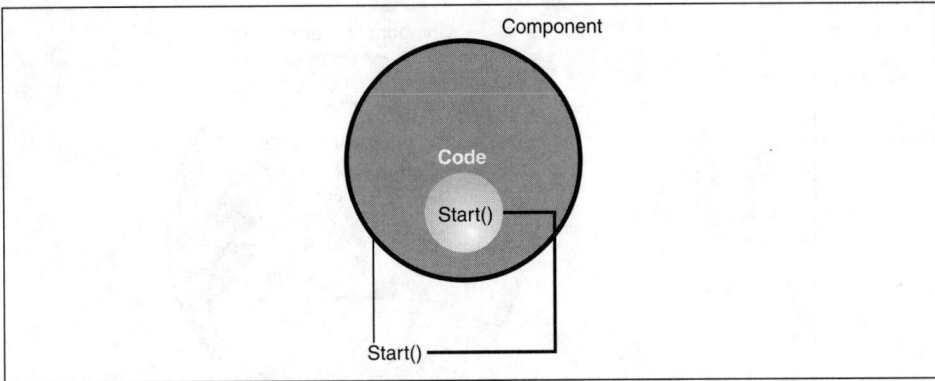

Figure 11.7 Black box implementation.

ure 11.7). VB controls architecture grew a multimillion dollar cottage industry because third-party vendors are supplying developers with these components.

A component object model defines a core subset of functionality that every object in the system must inherit. For example, the two most popular component object models, Microsoft's ActiveX and Sun's JavaBeans, define how their components will fire events, be made persistent, and manipulate property values. Since all objects inherit this behavior, it becomes very simple to treat all components identically.

Treating components identically is a very important concept. Imagine if every single object in the universe required learning a different set of methods in order to use it. This would soon become unwieldy for the implementor of object-based systems. In contrast, the component model allows us to build applications that make certain, consistent assumptions about the objects we're using. For example, Microsoft's Visual Basic makes extensive use of ActiveX's capabilities, therefore it can handle object creation, event handling, and persistence on behalf of the programmer. Moreover, it displays a list of properties the component offers to the programmer, allowing them to manipulate a large set of objects very easily (see Figure 11.8).

Because it is easy to manipulate a large set of objects with COM, component-based development has been deemed the wave of the future in application development. Unfortunately, few see the not-so-apparent bumps in the road, and component-based application development is very likely to fail. Along with it will go the "value-added" pipe dreams that objects once promised. (Note, DOC is just an extension of the component-based development methodology, where application components reside on separate machines in a network.)

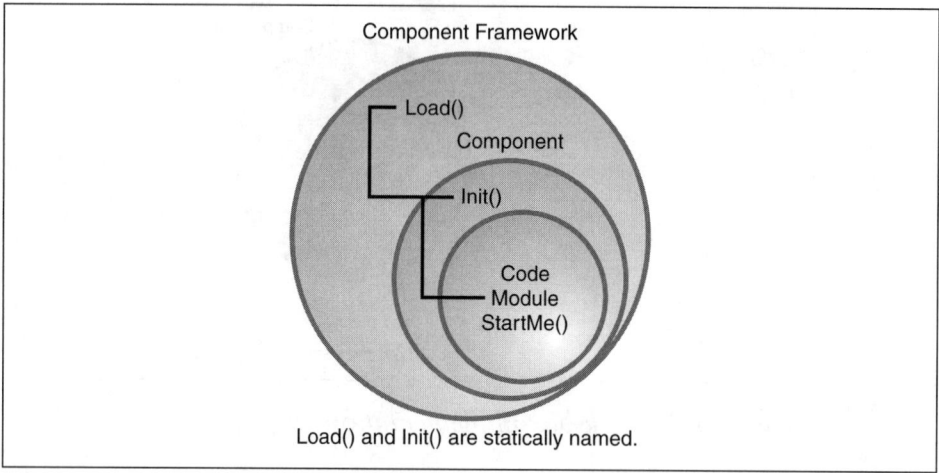

Figure 11.8 Interaction of code module with component and component framework.

Why will component-based application development eventually fail? We will examine the question from the following three key categories: human resources, application development costs, and indeterminable value-add.

Human Resources

The key to a successful component-based application requires putting all the application logic (business rules) into software components, which will then be brought to application developers through high-level programming and scripting languages. Application developers then have the responsibility to provide the presentation layer, linking these components under a certain context, such as for a sales entry form.

This development approach entails hiring a large base of component developers, who program in languages like C++ and Java. The development team must be well versed in both component development and business rules. The possibility of putting together a group like this with the severely limited resources available to the industry stands as a huge challenge. Figures of 200,000 openings for C++ programmers in 1999 have been put forth in the trade press. To meet this need, it seems more reasonable to build a team of application developers by teaching business managers Visual Basic.

Additionally, this model of development reduces the value of the application developer. In essence, they become drones pumping out user interfaces. The repetitive programming will cause many quality application developers to burn out.

Eventually, there will be a large void of resources in the application developer role. Those who recover from burnout will again command more money, fill the positions, and restart the cycle. The economics of supply and demand will forever cause component-based development methodology to suffer from an unstable pool of resources.

Development Costs

The average hourly wage for a Visual Basic programmer is between $35 and $65. The average hourly wage for component developers using C++ or Java is between $65 and $95. If component development were a one-time effort, it might be worth this expenditure; but in a global economy, no system is ever complete. Business rules will begin to change monthly instead of yearly. Companies that buy into component-based architectures will be trapped into constantly maintaining and writing new components using expensive resources.

Indeterminable Value-Add

Failure of component-based architectures will also be attributed, in part, to the industry's failure to recognize the real factors driving the ActiveX controls market. Third-party ActiveX controls work for two reasons: They are generic, and they are built for an operating system that guarantees their operation. It is because the controls are built specifically for Windows that they are guaranteed to work. They are generic because ActiveX controls have been designed to function in many RAD environments. People believe that components work because this very specific model has been successful, but in fact and in general there is no real documented proof of any value-added benefit actually accruing from components. However, because of this widespread belief, as well as accepted practice, it makes sense to build ActiveX components for Microsoft Windows if you're looking to resell functionality to other developers.

For corporations, developing a new application as a set of components may not be worth the cost of entry. How valuable is an application component that represents inventory when the requirements for retrieving inventory information change monthly? To develop systems that must compete in a global economy, this is an important consideration. For example, each time your company wants to enable electronic transactions with a new vendor, your system is faced with a unique set of requirements for interchange of data, including currency, language, and level of detail.

Or ask yourself, how valuable is it to create a reusable entity that represents an employee? It may be extremely useful if that entity is represented in all systems the employee interacts with, such as human resources, security, and accounting systems. However, this does not represent reality in today's large corporate computing environments. Most HR, accounting systems, and the like are purchased from outside vendors and offer little real opportunity for integration with existing object structures. At best, with some expensive consulting, the vendor may be able to write you a translation program.

How can an organization establish a stable development department of mixed skills if an in-house component-based model is a pipe dream? It is important to mention here that creating a dynamic development team is a key requirement for migrating to a component-based development methodology. Some organizations have claimed success with developing component-based applications in-house. Deeper investigation reveals the component development was not instituted for the company at large, but on a project-by-project basis, and with a majority of the team actually outside consultants. Since the team members have a single purpose and a short-lived goal, there is no real distinction between the consultant and a component vendor. Therefore, development of the application is analogous to one built using third-party purchased components.

Back to the topic at hand: DOC's rebirth is heavily influenced by the component movement. Because of their well-defined interfaces, components are easily integrated over the network by extending the launching and method invocation mechanisms to incorporate sending messages between the client and the object; sometimes this is accomplished through the use of middleware. However, the simplicity of accomplishing these tasks is misleading and ignores the intricacies of building distributed applications discussed in Chapter 3. For example, Visual Basic programmers building presentation layers for applications cannot, and should not, be using components that will be invoked on remote machines. Use of distributed components requires the same care and caution as any distributed application.

Over time, companies will reject the notion of building systems by gluing together disparate components, especially over a network using an RPC. This does not spell the end of distributed object computing, rather to its being implemented on top of the client/server architecture. In its place a distributed computing model will emerge that completely separates transport and partitioning from the application.

Goodbye N-Tiered Client/Server, Hello Data-Centric Computing

As we've tried to illustrate so far, building distributed applications (using today's tools and methodologies) requires that developers tightly integrate the application with distribution and partitioning technologies. For example, for an accounting application to be distributed, it must have inherent code to send electronic messages, initiate and commit a transaction to a database, and fire events to another process. The forced integration of these services into the application layer complicates the development of the application.

Instead, the application should focus on performing its special, single function, that is, accounting. Separation of application logic from the distribution and partitioning services marks a growing trend, with the emphasis on component-based development. The problem is that the key component-based solutions appearing on the market today end up based upon synchronous and asynchronous messaging backbones. That is, these new component designs operate by sending messages back and forth to each other. These message-based systems, while simpler to design, thus reducing development and deployment time, yield solutions neither extensible nor flexible since the messages are fixed and static representations of data. This makes them more expensive to maintain and support long term.

In addition, message-based systems still require developers to understand complex distributed computing concepts in order to build the application. Developers may link to a library file to connect to a distribution service, but the operation is still tied to the application. That means the developer becomes responsible for ensuring the application's quality and correctness. To fully remove this requirement, services and transport must be moved outside of the application space completely, and new partitioning methods and technologies need to be instituted. Removing services and transport from the application layer is the focus of XML-based distributed object computing.

Data-Centric Computing

Data-centric computing (DCC) was first defined in the January 1998 issue of the *NC.Focus Research Bulletin*. Today, three main application architectures are being built: standalone, *n*-tier client/server, and peer-based. All partition applications function in fundamentally the same way, forcing developers of distributed applications to understand how to move a byte from process A to process B when processes A and B are separated by a physical or logical barrier. There are major reasons why you do not want your business application developers to build applications with barrier-transcending requirements. The following two examples illustrate why:

A top-notch Visual Basic developer who uses ActiveX for component development has a problem. In the process of building a new application to perform a 3000-record ODBC (database middleware) query and cache the results in 10 record chunks to display in a list box, he exported code as an ActiveX component and attempted to change the application from a two-tier application to a three-tier application. When running two-tier, the execution performance was excellent, but when he moved the component to another server and used DCOM, the performance became intolerable. *The developer did not understand that the ODBC performance was optimized for the network, while the performance of the component over the network was not.*

Another programmer was charged with developing a two-tier client/server application with Visual Basic. He was able to easily access an Oracle database by its machine name from his own workstation, but when he moved the application to a workstation on the other end of a leased line, the application would hang while attempting to access the database. When asked to attempt to *ping* the server running the database from the remote machine, the developer's response was, "Huh? What's a ping?" *He had no concept of network protocols or how to debug the client/server application if it did not work due to networking problems.*

In both examples, the business application developers actually needed to solve partitioning and distribution problems, but they had no understanding of networking. A business application developer should not be expected to understand how to set up a network, anticipate potential connection problems, and implement procedures for all the networking protocols. Therefore, the network requirements (distribution and partitioning) must be removed to ensure the success of applications in the enterprise. Data-centric computing uses a very different partitioning method (from client/server) to build applications.

> **NOTE**
> The main goal of data-centric computing is to provide the application developer with a single view of distribution and application partitioning.

With data-centric computing, the application developer from the accounting example would not need to know how data is transferred from one machine to another or how it is stored in the database. Application development environments like PowerBuilder and Oracle2000 get the job done but force the application developer to understand how to access and manipulate databases. Instead, what we really want is to have the application developer focused on understanding how the company does business.

There are many ways to provide transparency of the network during development, but eventually they all require some understanding of how to link the program to the data transports. Examples of this include Unix Streams, which view the network as a normal file input and output, or remote procedure calls (RPC), which view the network as a series of function calls. Both provide minimal transparency since they operate differently from their local version cousins. For example, Unix Streams gives the illusion that the developer is reading from a file, when in fact, he or she is reading from the network. But normal file input and output do not require the developer to set time-outs and realize that the circuit may be broken in the middle of a read (which causes an exception). The same can be said for RPC.

The data-centric computing model was developed with the key goals of ensuring that the data's context was maintained as it moved between different applications; providing a singular channel for sending and receiving data for business applications that would not require networking experience; making provision for some mechanism to support extremely large datasets that would be unreasonable to move; and finally, defining a common programmatic interface that would allow access from all programming languages without restricting the functionality of the delivery services.

Implementation of the model requires the existence of an environment with some specific features that include:

- XML datagrams (objects).
- Intelligent services-based transport.
- Implicitly invoked behavior.
- Dynamic content.
- Platform independence.
- Peer-based architecture.
- Focus on building and transporting datasets.

It is this last feature, the focus on building and transporting datasets, that allows data-centric computing to finally reach its goal. COM, CORBA, and Java RMI provide function call-level transparency, and DCE provides operating system transparency. By nature, both call-level and operating system transparency force coherence at the application level. In addition, most of the middleware services (transaction processing, asynchronous messaging, and event notification) require integration with the application layer to be useful, even with the component development model.

Next we will define the features of data-centric computing and provide examples for development of systems.

Identifying Application Developer Roles

As illustrated in the previous section, there are developers who require the support of network services but have no idea how to use them effectively. Moreover, the learning curve for new technologies is typically between two and three years. But not all developers should need to understand application partitioning or distribution in order to build applications. Distribution and storage decisions should be made only by the group in your company that is focused on understanding scalability and reliability.

For purposes of clarity, we will define the specialization of the developer by identifying the following roles:

Business application developer. This person focuses on translating the rules of the business into programming logic. Most likely, he or she works in rapid application development environments, such as Microsoft Visual Basic, Borland Delphi, or Sybase PowerBuilder. Business application developers do not understand the requirements of distributed computing, but will provide methods of getting data into and out of their applications.

Integration developer. This person has responsibility for building the interfaces between the transport layers and the application layers. Preferably he or she works for a software vendor and businesses can purchase the results of their expertise as part of an overall application. In many cases of existing applications and in-house developed applications, this person is necessary to write application servers that will handle the distributed computing requirements. This person understands the implications of using distributed services, but does not have the architectural capabilities of a network services developer.

Network services developer. This person builds the software pipes over which the data will flow. He or she has a thorough understanding of building distributed applications.

Data-centric computing is about providing the business application developer with the ability to send, receive, store, and retrieve data without linking directly to any single facility that provides these services.

What Is XML?

The eXtensible Markup Language (XML) is the foundation of data-centric computing. First and foremost, XML defines a grammar—a way of expressing information that follows a succinct syntax. Each XML statement is parseable into atomic components. Functionally, XML is self-describing data, as seen in following example:

```
<Person Name="J. P. Morgenthal" E-Mail="jp@ncfocus.com"/>
```

This XML block can be parsed into an entity called Person that has two *child* attributes: Name and e-Mail. Notice the freedom and flexibility in describing the Person dataset. Any application that can parse XML format can extract the values of Name and e-Mail, regardless of the order or placement within an XML document. We could even add a new attribute called Phone, and it would not affect applications that assume only the existence of Name and e-Mail.

The following three analogies illustrate the distributed computing benefits XML provides.

Data Transport Example

In cut-price buying clubs and discount stores around the United States, cashiers take excess funds, load them into plastic canisters, and stick them into a tube that sucks them into the back office for secure storage. The cashier is concerned only with removing the excess funds, not with how to get them safely to the back office. If this process were modeled with today's distributed computing environments, developers would be required to first build the tube and then load it with the canister.

Tubes are all relatively similar, but in the computing world, each application has a custom "tube" designed for it. Imagine if for different amounts of excess funds, the cashier had to use a different tube; it would make the system totally unusable! In distributed computing terms, the tubes are services like transaction processing, asynchronous and synchronous delivery, persistence, and event notification.

XML allows development of a system with a single tube that is useable for any type of service. The XML document is the canister that holds the money, and the attributes and elements of the document are the money itself. We can now concern ourselves with building registers and back offices, or in software development terms, *applications*.

Data Format Example

Today's distributed computing environments are analogous to being forced to eat your soup with a soup spoon. While it represents the traditional method, it may not be the most comfortable and natural method. Perhaps you like to drink your soup from a cup or eat it with a tablespoon. Regardless, it's still soup. The same can be said of your data. No matter what format or structure it's in, the data is still the same and has the same elements. Still, many of today's development tools require specific knowledge of the entire dataset in order to manipulate it, like the soup spoon. XML gives you the power to "eat your soup" any way you like.

XML extracts attributes from name-value pairs, giving us the ability to access and display information however we choose. Moreover, we need only know the name of a particular attribute to retrieve its value, which is far simpler than requiring knowledge of the entire dataset, as do most of today's application development tools.

Data Structures Example

Let's say the owner of the deli around the corner accepts only $5 bills as payment for food. Most people would take their business elsewhere. Yet this is exactly what remote procedure (RPC) call-based mechanisms expect when passing data between components. For example, to pass the Person dataset just defined using the popular distributed computing methods such as DCE, CORBA, COM, and Java RMI, Person would need to have a fixed attribute set. Adding the new attribute of Phone and then passing it would break receiving processes. This occurs because RPC-based mechanisms only pass data of fixed sizes and structures; it works by assuming all incoming data fits these formats.

With XML, it is possible to send variable-sized and -formatted data structures between processes that require only inclusion of the expected name-value pairs for success. Moreover, XML Document Type Definitions (DTD) represent the set of name-value pairs and hierarchies that an XML document must support in order to be valid. That is, when an XML document is received, it can be compared against a DTD to ensure that all the attributes required for acceptance exist before initiating processing.

These three analogies illustrate the power of XML to overcome the problems associated with distributed computing environments today: lack of data extensibility, lack of flexibility in format and size, required use of static data structures, and the requirement for services to be customized on an application-by-application basis. Interoperability can be achieved in spite of these hurdles, but at a very high cost.

Transitioning from Client/Server to Data-Centric Computing

Before networking and multithreaded operating systems, applications were monolithic beasts with batch-processing methods. These monolithic applications were not only static in usage, they were also extremely expensive to create and run. In addition, the data generated by these applications was not easily

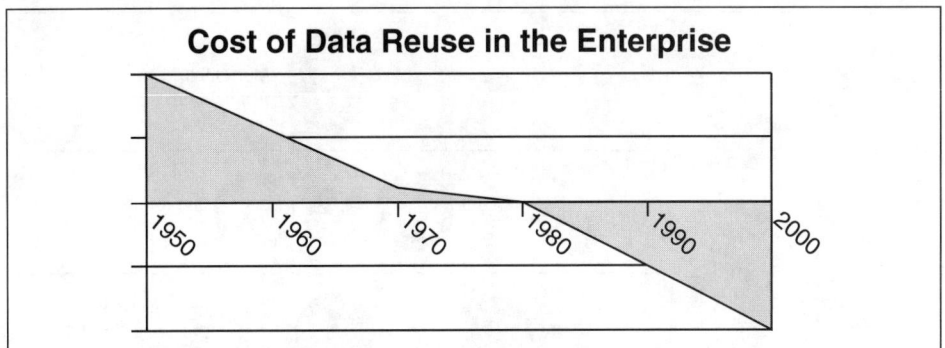

Figure 11.9 *The rising cost of not reusing data.*

reusable. Advances in technology allowed us to build responsive and interactive systems, but still with little data reuse (see Figure 11.9).

Most current client/server applications are database-driven, where the database acts as a central repository for data. Therefore, the partitioning of these applications breaks down into a database server, which controls storage and retrieval of large datasets, and presentation clients that facilitate access and editing. These applications provide organizations with tremendous flexibility in data reuse. That is, the data that was originally used only for a single batch-oriented task could now be used to provide a plethora of information regarding the company. However, centralized database architectures do not lend themselves to large-scale uses, and the database dictates the program interfaces for building new applications. Because it is centralized, the resource that runs the database has to handle all the requests coming in from the network. Each database accepts SQL queries, but each also has its own messaging scheme to get/send/receive the results.

As the popularity of client/server systems increased, differences in the database vendors' program interfaces created problems for heterogeneous database environments, and a new type of application arose to correct the problem: middleware. Middleware abstracts the client and server by placing a standard programmatic component between them. This abstraction can be continually extended to move from a three-tier architecture to an *n*-tier architecture (see Figure 11.10). But regardless of how many tiers are used, the main goal of distribution is to move data between the client and the server, hence demonstrating the flaw in using programmatic interfaces to facilitate the data transfer. Much like its monolithic parentage, the application is useful only for accomplishing a single task.

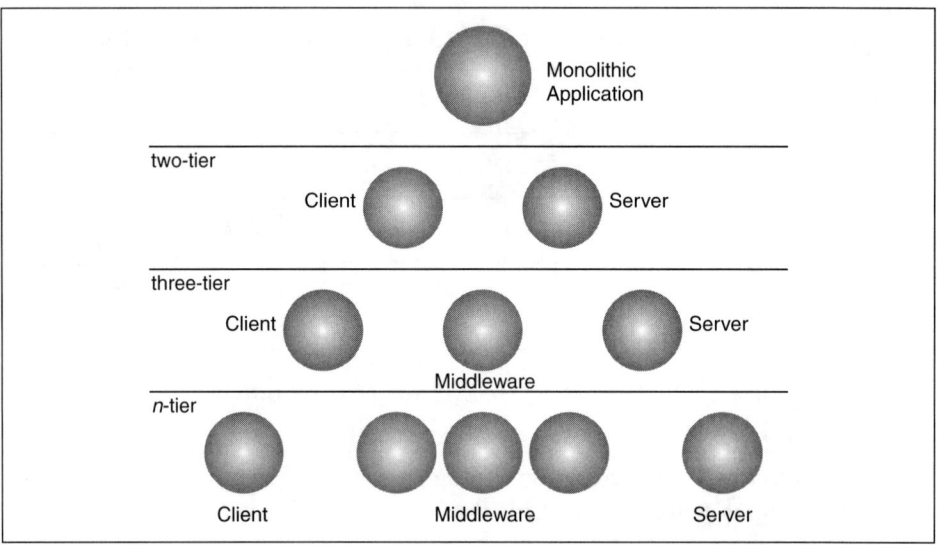

Figure 11.10 Middleware and client/server.

Today's applications must be more responsive to changes in direction and vision of the enterprise. The client/server applications of the late '80s and early '90s need to be replaced by a new architecture with freedom and flexibility not tied to any program interfaces. Companies attempting real intercorporate data sharing need this flexibility for tasks such as enterprise resource planning (ERP) and supply-chain integration. Client/server was about interoperability of applications, but data-centric computing is about sharing data. The hope for client/server computing was that application interoperability would give us data sharing capabilities; but it was not a pure solution.

Figure 11.11 illustrates the new development architecture: the data-centric computing model. Instead of partitioning a monolithic application into a presentation-based client and a process-heavy server, the application is broken down into three core component types: *viewers*, *processors*, and *translators*. Viewers present data to users graphically. They can be generic (such as trees or tables) or application-specific (such as a form). Processors process data (specifically XML instances) into the document object model (DOM) for access by an application. The DOM provides a standard program interface for setting and retrieving attributes from an XML document. Translators export data from proprietary data formats to XML instances. The organization boundary in Figure 11.11 represents the future maximum development responsibilities of the corporation in the data-centric model.

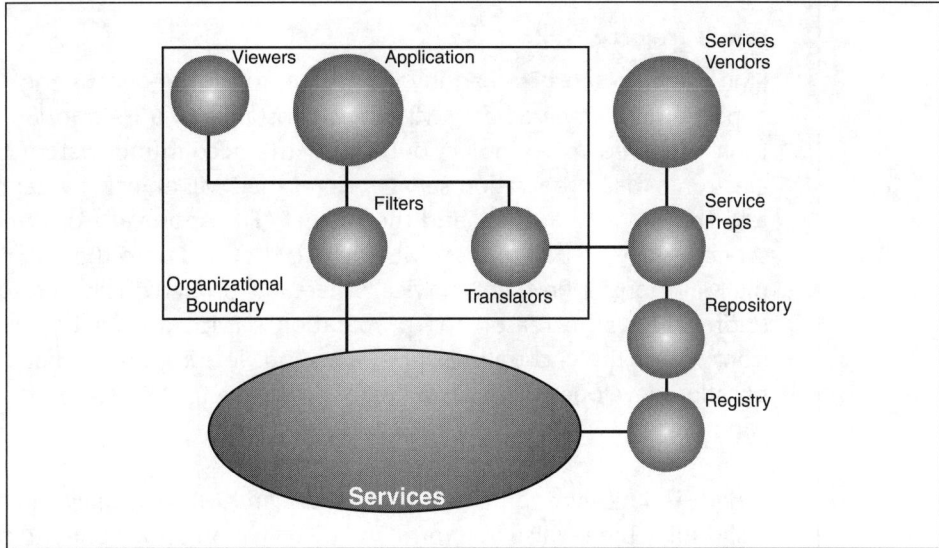

Figure 11.11 *Data-centric computing model.*

The three other data-centric computing component utilities include *service preparers*, *repositories*, and *registries*. These utilities should be purchased along with intelligent services from third-party vendors. In addition, they should be maintained and serviced by the network operations department, not application development teams. Service preparation utilities make XML documents ready for transfer over the services layer. For example, an electronic mail preparation utility would request addresses and a subject for use in delivery of the XML document over e-mail services. Repositories act as stores of additional information to which a single XML document links for additional information. Registries store the relationships between XML datasets, so that traversal of information allows a six-degree type of search (any data point can be reached as part of a traversal by following a set of corresponding relationships or links; e.g., hyperlinking).

These six components can then be used by the intelligent services layer to route and transfer data between applications. Moreover, the components can be distributed anywhere in the network, providing maximum flexibility and scalability in application partitioning. By changing the focus of development from distributing of process to distributing of data, we can encapsulate the process of sending and receiving away from the application. Hence, the application developer is left with a single view of transporting data between applications, both locally and over the network. The sidebar entitled "Jane's Invoice" clarifies the power of data-centric architecture.

Jane's Invoice

Jane wants to send Fred an invoice for approval. Her accounting system exports the invoice as an XML object (instance) via its translator. It is then prepared for shipping outside of the accounting system by the electronic mail preparation service. Here, the XML object is amended to add Fred's e-mail address and the subject "For Approval" for the e-mail service. Once prepared, the XML object is dropped onto the SMTP (Simple Mail Transfer Protocol) service, where it is properly delivered to Fred. (Note, there's no reason the preparation service cannot be launched from within the accounting application, but it is important that the application developer view it as an external service to the accounting application).

When Fred receives this e-mail, he can use an XML invoice viewer, which will display the invoice as a form and give Fred an opportunity to mark it with his approval. The approval is then added as a new attribute to the original XML object and delivered back, via another intelligent service, to the accounting application processor. The processor processes the returned XML instance to extract the necessary field values, and updates the permanent accounting record with the approval.

The concept here is to allow the company to buy the accounting system, intelligent services, and preparation tools, and only require the company to develop the XML invoice viewer and accounting system filter. Wouldn't it be a time-saver to provide your suppliers and customers with a method of electronically submitting and approving invoices?

Detail of Service Components

Client and network service components represent different responsibilities. Our discussion here focuses on the client's view, centered on dropping our data into a chute with the confidence that it will come out where we expect it to. To this end we give you the following discussion of the role of the registry and the repository in this architecture.

The Role of the Registry

The data-centric computing model works because the network is guaranteed to have certain supportive services. One of these services is a directory that locates and correlates information. Traditional directory services simply allow hierarchical organization of networked data in a distributed fashion, but do not fulfill the requirement for data correlation. For example, it is important to find Fred's phone number, but it is equally important to understand the relationship between the returned phone number and the possibility of reaching Fred, not his voice mail.

In the data-centric computing model, the registry would store the relationships and rules for locating Fred. Note that, this example, while possible, is less likely than other more mundane data associations; nevertheless, it illustrates the requirement best. For a more boring explanation, assume that a single data entity is composed of hundreds of other data entities. Some of those entities exist only in the context of the first entity, while others exist alone but are referenced inside of the first entity.

Managing a set of relationships is extremely complex; in fact, there will probably never be one single tool to do it. However, the registry acts as a common interface for other tools to manage singular relationships between two or more entities without affecting the relationships already established for any given entity.

The Role of the Repository

To reiterate, business application developers can envision dropping their data into a chute, knowing that when it comes out the other side it will be processed. Sometimes, however, the opening at the other end of the chute might be closed or blocked, in which case, the data must wait in the chute until the situation is corrected and the chute opens again. Of course, this would be simple if we were dealing with physical entities such as a piece of paper and a chute, but we are not. We are dealing with electronic entities that must be preserved when this scenario presents itself.

The repository primarily serves as a temporary storage facility used by the network services when they are unable to complete their task. Of course, there are granular controls provided to those managing the network that correspond to how long a message is kept, the type of message returned to the sender if a message cannot be delivered, and so on. Without the repository, business applications would be forced to remain connected to the network until a message was successfully delivered—a primary problem with distributed computing solutions today.

The fact that companies are turning in droves to asynchronous middleware indicates the enormity of the connection problem. But, like all forms of distributed computing middleware, products like IBM MQSeries and Microsoft's Message Queue require programming to be useful. In the future, such products are the most likely contenders for leadership—especially when they are shipped with generic data senders and receivers (filters and translators).

Using XML to Define Business Rules

Besides facilitating self-describing data, XML is also a meta-language, which means it can be used to create other language grammars. Data-centric computing means that no specific binary process is attached to the data, as is the case with distributed object technology.

How then can we access the process reuse provided by distributed objects today? Both DCOM and CORBA are built by defining the access functions in an interface definition language (IDL), which is then translated to generate specific platform and program language-specific skeletons. Skeletons must then be filled in with code to complete the server-side implementation of the object. The skeleton contains all the code necessary to invoke and communicate with that object from a remote client. The one thing that IDL does not provide is incorporation of business rules that can be used to generate a complete server-side language-specific object. Each platform and each programming language requires a developer to complete the code manually, *even for the same task*.

Data-centric computing aims to build business rules in an interim XML-based language. These business rules can then be used to generate platform- and language-specific code for manipulating an XML document. Generating language-specific code requires the following from XML:

- *A DTD (document type definition)*. This is a schema that defines the data elements that will be included with a particular XML dataset.

- *A grammar for representing business rules*. The Resource Definition Framework (RDF) under way at the World Wide Web Consortium (W3C) may provide a useful direction for this requirement, but it is not yet ready. This means possibly defining one for the company as well as the compilers that generate code for a particular programming language and platform. While an expensive operation, this offers the greatest preservation of business rules.

- *Business rules compilers*. These components read the business rules and the DTDs, and generate the platform and programming language-specific code to generate and parse an XML dataset. This code can be directly incorporated into an application for performing input and output operations.

Hopefully, over time, a standard will emerge for defining business rules in XML, which will spur a market opportunity for business rule development environments. Unfortunately, today much of this work must be done by individual companies. Unlike a vendor who wants to sell the package to mainstream developers, companies have the luxury of selecting the platforms and programming languages they will support.

XML and Objects

An XML object defines a new type of object that shares the core definition of an object as just described, but offers an added dimension over these entities. All of the previously mentioned object types have a fixed method of applying behavior; they have methods that act upon the attributes of the object.

In contrast, XML's behavior is implicit; it is defined by its attributes. For example,

```
<Person Name="J. P. Morgenthal"/>
```

in one XML parser might render a form with the field Name filled in. However, Name might also be aliased against a set of JavaScript statements located inside of an XML style sheet, thus, forcing some action upon it by the XML parser. Each attribute tag is a definition of behavior over the data it represents.

When discussing distributed object computing, we need a clear indication about the form of distribution being discussed. The two main types of objects are *process objects* and *data objects*. Distribution of process objects is usually associated with some form of RPC-based access capability. Data objects are primarily concerned with encapsulation of a dataset for transport between processes.

Those familiar with building distributed object systems today are well aware of the problems of sharing objects outside the enterprise, and sometimes within the enterprise as well. The key problem here is that different companies and different divisions have unique definitions of the attributes that should belong to an object. Many developers spend months designing sophisticated object applications that require multiple departments to come to an agreement on which attributes a particular object should have. This limits everyone's use of the system by forcing different systems to shoehorn their data into this interim medium.

Limited object attributes are not required with XML; the Person object provides an example. Assume that the Person record started as an entity in human resources and was sent to telecommunications to prepare a phone port for a new employee. Once configured, telecommunications can add the phone number to the Person object and pass it to another department. In essence, we build a dynamic object, in which attributes can be added or deleted during the object's lifetime, and the values of those attributes can be changed at any time. This is one of the great promises of XML.

Some people may argue that flexibility can be achieved with existing object environments. For example, CORBA has a service called the Property Service that will handle the addition and deletion of name-value pairs and allow those objects to be passed among CORBA objects. However, there is no way to detect the Property object without having that coherence programmed in advance, and there are no DTDs to describe the schema of the data. In addition, XML data is hierarchical, which means that entities can be contained within entities. For example, Person could belong to a larger dataset called Employees. Also, XML has referential linkage. This allows one entity to point to part of another entity. Best of all, any XML parser can recognize these features and organize them into the document object model for easy standardized access. All these features are missing from the simplistic CORBA Property Service.

> **NOTE**
>
> DCC does not obviate the need for distributed object computing architectures such as CORBA and COM; it just changes the model as to how it is incorporated into the overall application architecture. In addition, it changes who is purchasing and selling these technologies. In the future, for example, ORB vendors might make their money selling intelligent services built from their underlying CORBA services instead of selling raw ORBs, services, and development kits.

XML or Java?

To many application developers, Java holds promise for client application development because it offers platform independence, garbage collection, introspection, and remote method invocation. The concept of data-centric computing coupled with the power of XML offers the same capabilities, without the complexity of learning a powerful object-oriented language. (Note, we're not talking about replacing Java for its numerical processing or windowing capabilities. Again, data-centric computing focuses on building and transporting datasets; it is this capability of Java that can be accomplished with XML-based distributed object computing.)

Data-centric computing is not a one-for-one replacement of Java functionality either. Remember, data-centric computing provides a new and innovative way of solving distributed computing problems. Let's look more closely at what XML can do relative to Java:

Platform independence. Since XML is an ASCII representation of tagged data, it is immediately useable by all hardware platforms and operating systems.

Introspection. The ability to examine the construction of an object without having to query a specific instance. XML is self-describing data, which is pure introspection, especially once it is parsed into the document object model format.

Remote Method Invocation (RMI). This is one of Java's really interesting facilities, because it allows Java to download classes during runtime. This feature could be used to build dynamic objects, but RMI works by creating two proxies that pass the data between two Java objects. If these proxies are not generated at the same time, RMI cannot work. However, XML objects are truly dynamic. Changing them during their lifetime will not fatally affect running applications. Indeed, the worst-case scenario is that a required attribute is removed or goes missing, which will invalidate the entire dataset, preventing it from being processed.

This does not obviate the need for XML viewers, parsers, translators, and filters, which have to be developed using a programming language like C++, Java, or Visual Basic. But since the majority of client-based tasks are sharing, viewing, and updating information, the main focus of IS departments should be to create a dataset and deliver it to an application.

The key to a successful XML distributed object application lies in building application-specific viewers and filters. A filter utilizes an XML parser to parse an XML document into the XML document object model and then uses that object model to extract data. An application-specific viewer presents an XML document in a certain presentation format. Java can be useful in the presentation role, since components can then be deployed on any platform supporting a Java Virtual Machine. Because it uses only a small subset of Java functionality, XML components are more likely to be 100 percent compatible across Java Virtual Machines. Moreover, the combination of XML and Java allows for dynamic application configuration. That said, note that XML does not need Java to be useful, nor does it have any specific ties to the Java programming language or Java data types.

State of XML Technology

As with all emerging technologies, it is important to know which vendors are supporting XML and the anticipated changes. The core grammar that represents XML has reached the recommendation stage with the W3C. This group's work is recognized as a widely accepted standard among many Internet vendors and customers.

The XML grammar can be analogized to the Java Virtual Machine specification, which identifies how to build a Java interpreter (the machine instruction processor). Once complete, users could output Java class files from a number of different tools. Now that XML has reached the recommendation stage, vendors can supply tools and products that all conform to a single specification; this will ensure interoperability. The next two major advances that will build off of this momentum are the aforementioned Resource Definition Format (RDF), which defines a standard method of building relationships between entities in XML, and the Document Object Model for XML (DOM).

Unlike Java, XML is useful in its current state, whereas Java required Sun to define core libraries to make the VM useful. However, the DOM is important from a developer perspective since it will allow the development of a single interface for setting and retrieving information in an XML document from a programming language. RDF will provide some additional enhancements that will make the data more useful to clients, but its real impact will be seen in the repositories.

Data-Centric Computing Models' Living Systems

This chapter has taken many twists and turns, so to remind you of our goal, we want to build living systems. In order to develop any computer-based system, some form of modeling will be required to map the logical components to physical ones. This is the relationship of data-centric computing to living systems. DCC provides us with the ability to partition our business applications into a set of discrete components that can be plugged together in a consistent manner.

The following example illustrates the relationship between DCC and living systems by examining the roles that applications play within the Enterprise Resource Planning (ERP) system and their integration requirements. ERP systems allow companies to accurately determine their capability to fulfill a customer's order and to manage production schedules and inventory. Each application within the ERP system will be broken down into its DCC components and then integrated using DCC concepts. To emphasize the benefit of living systems, after completing the original design, we will add a new unplanned application to the ERP system.

The need for ERP is obvious for integration of the sales, customer, inventory, design and engineering (CAD), production management, and accounting systems. For purposes of this example, we will discuss the integration of the sales, manufacturing, and inventory systems. Once integrated using DCC modeling, we will attempt to add the accounting system.

By its very nature, ERP requires multiple interdepartmental systems to cooperate and be synchronized. Certainly, the systems will change individually over time, but the whole system must continue to operate in a consistent manner in spite of these changes. Companies with ERP success stories (not many to date) all share the common goal of managing enterprise requirements, while making individual systems fit.

One approach to building an ERP system is to use a centralized database. That is, the database acts as a central repository for a static set of fields that represent the ERP dataset. Basically, this model extracts all the data that sits at the crossroads of all the systems and builds the necessary database schemas and relations. Two problems with this model are:

- Adding a new system is not straightforward since there is no clean way to update the database schemas.

- Centralized repositories are very poor at scaling to large numbers of users. In addition, the planning stages of this system would require that multiple groups coordinate their efforts, which is a waste of valuable time.

Successful deployment of an ERP system in any enterprise depends on the availability of data represented in each atomic information system. Companies can try to extract data via brute force, but the effort will likely prove futile. A more effective way to proceed is to ask the group controlling the data to provide access. This allows both the ERP implementors and the individual system groups to remain autonomous, while working cooperatively.

For purposes of our example, we need to make some basic assumptions:

1. The systems are built but not currently integrated.

2. The systems are running on a variety of platforms, including mainframes, Unix, and Windows NT.

3. The intersection where two systems share data is handled by sending forms and reports via interoffice mail.

ACME Paper Bag Example

As a paper bag manufacturer, ACME Paper Bag Company supplies paper bags to restaurant chains like McDougal's. Using its current systems, McDougal's places an order for its internal East Coast warehouse, which supplies all East Coast restaurants (so we're looking at a very large order). ACME obviously cannot fill all orders at once, and therefore, must identify the ship dates and sizes that make up the order.

The paper order is currently filled by faxing an invoice to a sales representative, who enters the order into the sales system. The sales system generates a fulfillment request that goes to the warehouse for processing. At this point, the best the representative can do is to tell McDougal's that the order was received. Then, as information becomes available, he or she calls back with the shipping information.

The fulfillment request is received by a warehouse representative who checks inventory to see what is currently available, then creates a shipment for one-third of the order because current inventory cannot satisfy the order. At this point, the warehouse representative enters a request into the manufacturing system for the remaining two-thirds of the order and receives a completion date that he or she will enter manually into the shipping system under back orders. A shipping record and a back-order record are printed and sent to the sales representative, who then calls McDougal's and gives a status update. Any additional pieces of the order will generate a shipping record also to be delivered to the sales representative.

Are there really systems like this still out there? More than you can possibly imagine. Why? Because they have been processing orders the same way for the past 20 years and see no financial incentive to change. To some degree, this makes sense. As long as McDougal's or any other customers aren't complaining, why spend the money to update a working process? But now let's say a Korean bag manufacturer that McDougal's uses in Asia is looking to supply the United States as well. It allows McDougal's to order over the Web, using electronic data interchange (EDI) or over the phone. And once the order is accepted, an immediate automated response tells McDougal's when the warehouse will receive the order.

McDougal's recognizes the Web-based system as an opportunity to automate paper bag purchasing. It can monitor warehouse inventory and generate an order whenever a low-water mark is reached. The Asian supplier effectively eliminates the need for a human resource cost (the person who used to watch for low inventory) and makes the overall operation more efficient. "Gee, I have 200 bag lots left; I better go online and place an order." It's simple: You reorder after shipping a certain number of lots.

Now ACME has a reason to change. Will it choose to spend money to buy expensive middleware and the developers/consultants to implement it? Or, will it choose a data-centric computing model, which can be implemented by the company's current Visual Basic developer staff and externally purchased software? For our example, the manager will choose data-centric computing. Other companies like ACME, forced to upgrade to current technology in order to compete in a global market, must make similar decisions about how to allocate resources.

ACME requires integration of two standalone systems: sales and inventory. In addition, ACME doesn't have a year to 18 months for implementation, it needs this system in months in order to compete. The most important component of the system, and the pieces that need to be developed first, are the processors. The processors tie the standalone application to the distributed computing layer. Processors are bidirectional, meaning they transmit and receive XML objects from distributed services.

Since the sales system initiates the ordering process, or at least is the first point of contact for an order, we will design the sales system processor first. It is responsible for the following functions:

- Taking the fulfillment requisition from the sales system and preparing it for transit to the inventory system.

- Receiving the shipping detail from the inventory system and supplying it back to the sales system.

In data-centric computing, processors are named entities that can be communicated with using standard networking mechanisms, such as TCP/IP. In essence, processors are application servers highly specialized to handle input and output over a network on behalf of an application. To send and receive XML objects, the application must invoke the correct processor; this can be done implicitly or explicitly (see Figure 11.12).

Processors communicate with the generic network service provider interface on specific networks services. That is, the processor will choose a special type of service to deliver the data to the inventory system. DCC services share a common method of notifying a processor that data has arrived, so that any type of service could be used to deliver the data. To analogize, these services become the software

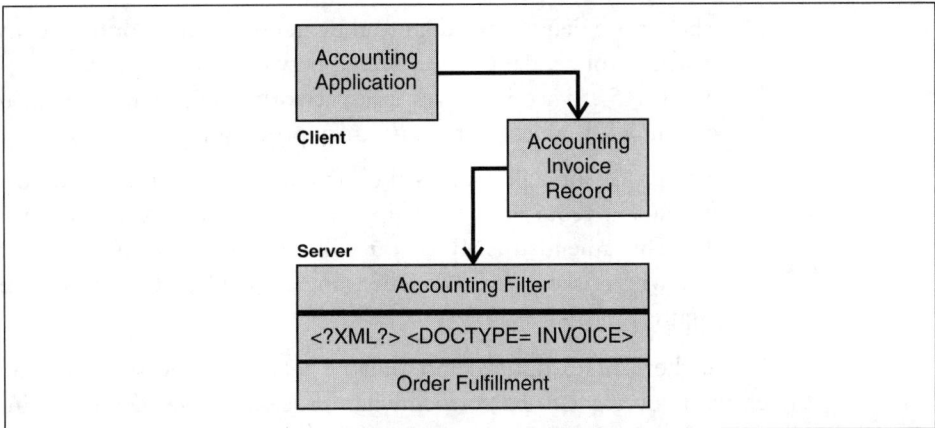

Figure 11.12 A processor as an application server.

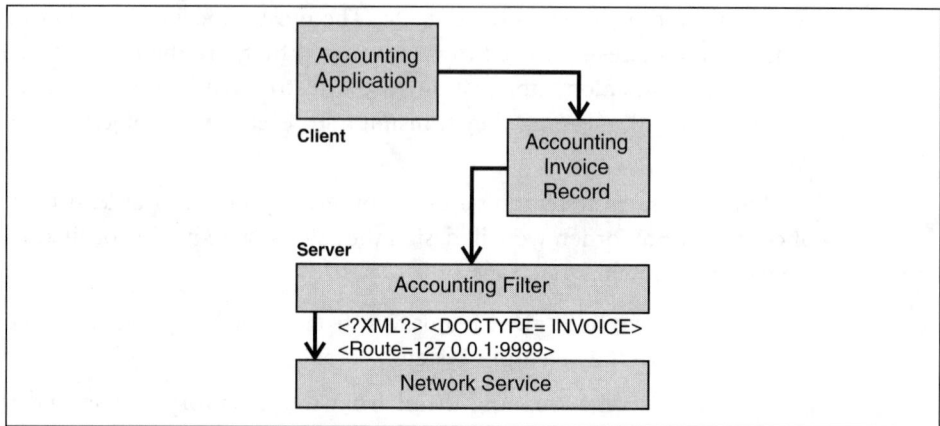

Figure 11.13 *A processor communicating with an intelligent network service.*

version of the router in a TCP/IP network. Their job becomes transferring packets between two endpoints using a certain processing logic (see Figure 11.13).

Once the processor hands off the XML object to the network service, several important things happen:

1. The processor marks the XML object as a dormant object and awaits a return status regarding its delivery. Some services will be able to respond immediately, such as synchronous services, while others will require some latency. Either way, the service and the processor now share a temporary relationship that will not be destroyed until either a positive or negative result has occurred (see Figure 11.14).

2. The service delivers the data to the intended processor on the inventory system. Notice, data is transferred between named processors (see Figure 11.15). Once it arrives, the network service will attempt to hand off the XML object to the inventory processor.

3. The processor will process the incoming XML object and add to the fulfillment requisition the shipping information for this particular order. This amended XML object will be returned to the sending processor, where it will be reconciled and applied to the sales system (see Figure 11.16).

Note, there is no natural integration between processors and applications; therefore, if you want to be notified when processors receive updates inside the application, the two need to be connected over an event system. However, this does not interfere with our goal of hiding the distribution and partitioning from the ap-

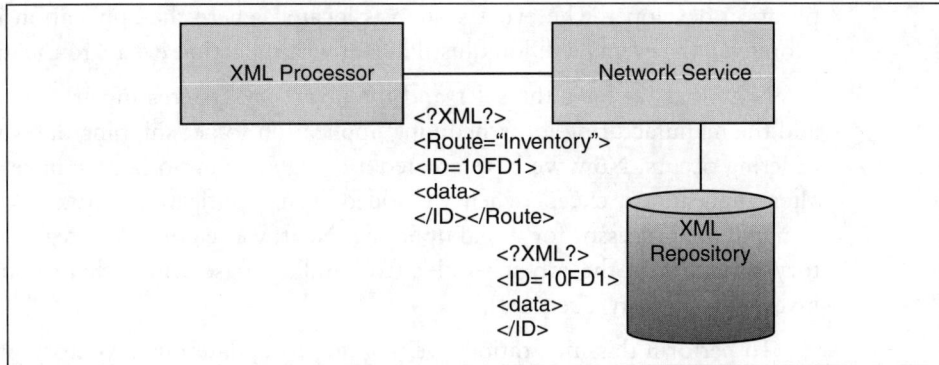

Figure 11.14 *Step 1.*

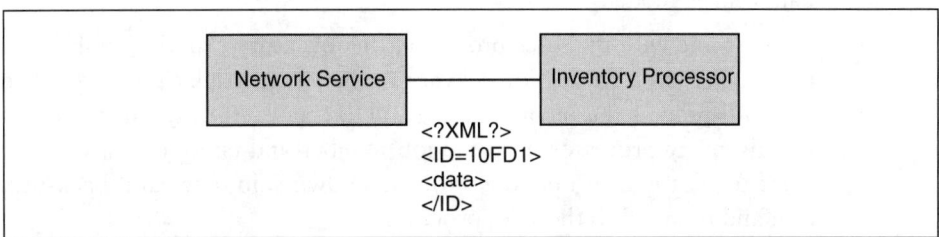

Figure 11.15 *Step 2.*

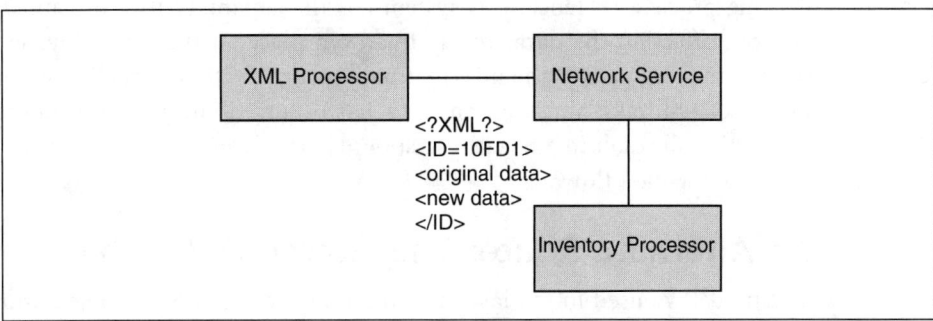

Figure 11.16 *Step 3.*

plication developer. The event system is located where the application is running. Moreover, the events will look just like native application events to the application.

Now that we have the sales and the inventory systems integrated, we need to add the manufacturing job scheduling application to get shipping dates when back ordering occurs. Now we have created a living system. So far, we have not had to alter applications, except when we added event notification between the application and the processor for visual updating. Next, we're going to integrate the inventory system with the job scheduler (to handle a case where there is not enough inventory to satisfy a request).

To perform this integration, we're going to update our inventory processor to handle out-of-stock scenarios. When there is not enough stock to fill an order, the inventory processor will make the XML object dormant and generate a request to the job scheduling system. Notice, the same XML object is now dormant in two locations: in the sales processor and in the inventory processor. This becomes an important point when attempting to apply transaction management over the data-centric model.

Just like with the sales processor, the inventory processor will hand the job request object to a service for delivery to the job scheduler processor. The job scheduler will process the incoming XML object and return the updated job request to the inventory processor with the job number and expected ship dates. The fulfillment request is then updated with the known ship dates and back-order information and returned to the sales processor.

Since we have not updated our sales processor, it has no back-order information yet, so it only processes the known shipping information. Since the job scheduler processor provided the inventory system with expected ship dates, the sales system sees the correct number of pieces as being shipped, and all is well.

We added completely new functionality and data without disrupting any of the existing processes. Hence, this system has the capability to grow and be extended without affecting the data flows already in place. If there is a bug in one of the processors, and part of the information is not correctly returned, then the receiving processor will take note that an error has occurred and not process the XML object. This will result in a negative response being propagated all the way back to the origin of the data flow.

An Alternate Route: The Shared Data Object

The model we used in the last section requires that an XML object move between processing centers. In addition, each time we need to perform a serial process that is subordinate to the original, the XML object is made dormant, and then activated when the results are available. This process works well for certain types of applications, where latency is acceptable. However, there is a class of applications where latency is disastrous and, therefore, not well suited to the regular XML model. In addition, we would not want to use the XML model once the dataset grows beyond a certain size. For larger applications not tolerant of latency, we use a shared data object model (SDO).

Shared data objects (SDO) rely on the same underlying transport mechanisms as mobile XML objects, but all changes are marked on a shared version. This requires some level of concurrency control and a formal naming system for locating living documents. In addition, SDOs rely on advanced caching algorithms that will allow an outline of a very large XML instance to be delivered to a user, and which expands dynamically as the instance is traversed.

With SDOs, applications write their XML objects into shared named workspaces. These workspaces are created by administrative personnel and have access controls placed on them; this controls read and write access. Of note, this can be accomplished explicitly or transparently. Explicit use would require a reference to a remote XML target, for example:

```
http://www.ncfocus.com/target?data.
```

Implicit use would be accomplished with caching facilities that would pull the elements over the network when actually processed. A comparison of the two models is made in Table 11.2.

In this table, listed as the controller for SDOs is the DOM pseudo-object. This is a programmable entity invoked from inside an application. Once a workspace is created, an application invokes the DOM pseudo-object locally to communicate with the shared document. The actual method of transport is unknown to the application; all the application knows is that it is reading and writing from a document that is *exactly the same in both remote and local instances*. That is, the user

Table 11.2 Comparison of XML and SDO

	SDO	REGULAR XML OBJECT
Controller	DOM pseudo-object	Application filters
Purpose	Immediate notification Large datasets Real-time changes	Application integration
View to Application Developer	DOM	DOM

does not have to understand different semantics or operational differences between using a shared and a local document.

Since a new application can be dropped into the SDO environment and start feeding and updating attributes to an already created shared document, it also meets the criteria for enabling a living system. Combined, the XML and SDO models offer an organization the ability to focus on its business application development and to outsource the development and maintenance of the network infrastructure, at least outside of the information systems department.

Conclusions

This chapter covered:

- The importance of designing for extensibility via data reuse, in contrast to process reuse.

- A new model for designing distributed systems that separates the application from the partitioning methodology.

- How the eXtensible Markup Language can be used to describe data between systems and business rules in a highly reusable form.

- A methodology for designing applications that are naturally interoperable.

The next chapter explains how to deliver enterprisewide network services using data-centric computing.

FOR FURTHER READING

Connolly, Dan. *XML: Principles, Tools, and Techniques.* (Cambridge, MA: O'Reilly), 1997.

Chappell, David. *Understanding ActiveX and OLE.* (Redmond, WA: Microsoft Press), 1996.

Holzner, Steven. *XML Complete.* (New York: McGraw-Hill Computing), 1997.

Light, Richards. *Presenting XML.* (Indianapolis, IN: SAMS), 1997.

Mowbray, et. al. *The Essential CORBA: Systems Integration Using Distributed Objects.* (New York: John Wiley & Sons, Inc.), 1995.

12 DELIVERING ENTERPRISEWIDE NETWORK SERVICES

"The necessities were going by default to save the luxuries until I hardly knew which were necessities and which luxuries."

Autobiography, Frank Lloyd Wright, 1945

This chapter explores:

What we mean by network services.

How to provide a network service ubiquitously through the enterprise.

How skills from traditional IS operations transfer well into supporting network services.

A justification for moving to data-centric computing over client/server.

A New Role for IS Operations

In Chapter 11 we learned about the data-centric computing model. This chapter introduces the infrastructure requirements for delivering support to that model throughout the enterprise. To build robust data-centric applications, the network must offer a plethora of capabilities that will perform a whole host of services on behalf of the application. For example, the network should automatically route, store, and deliver messages with one simple posting.

If we look at large companies today, the group most likely to build and support a robust network of services is the IS operations department. For many companies, IS operations is that place that no one goes to, where the aging mainframe is maintained. At one time, this same group had the ultimate say in enterprise computing. Because its members maintained the mainframe system, they decided what hardware and software to purchase, when patches could be implemented, who had access to the data, and what level of access would be granted.

But with the new tides of computing, PCs and local area networking became popular, and the IS operations department ignored the writing on the wall, treating new network platforms as toys. IS operations became known as the "glass house" to signify an elitist group of people working in secured super-cooled areas. The new IS development staff were outsiders looking in. It is not surprising that a rift developed between those configuring new client/server applications outside the glass house and those maintaining the data and applications running inside the glass house.

As the rift widened, and client/server became the dominant method for building new applications, the IS operations department did little to cooperate with those outside, to jointly implement new methods of data access to legacy data. Therefore, client/server developers were forced to use existing paths to retrieve mainframe data and store it in the new client/server systems. Some of these methods (illustrated in Figure 12.1) included:

- 3270 High-Level Language Application Programming Interface (HLLAPI), a protocol developed by IBM for communication between the mainframe and a "dumb" terminal. HLLAPI, along with special hardware, allowed the PC to act as a programmable 3270 terminal, which allowed developers to pull data screen by screen.

- Application-to-Application Protocol (APPC), also known as LU 6.2. This protocol gave developers the capability to execute mainframe commands from a personal computer application as if it were running on the mainframe itself. APPC allowed developers to use emerging programming languages, such as C and Pascal, to access legacy data.

Mainframes also had a file transfer protocol that allowed complete mainframe files to be transferred to a personal computer's hard drive using either LU 6.2 or 3270 protocols. Then developers could pull result sets from existing batch processes and integrate them into networked databases accessible from PCs.

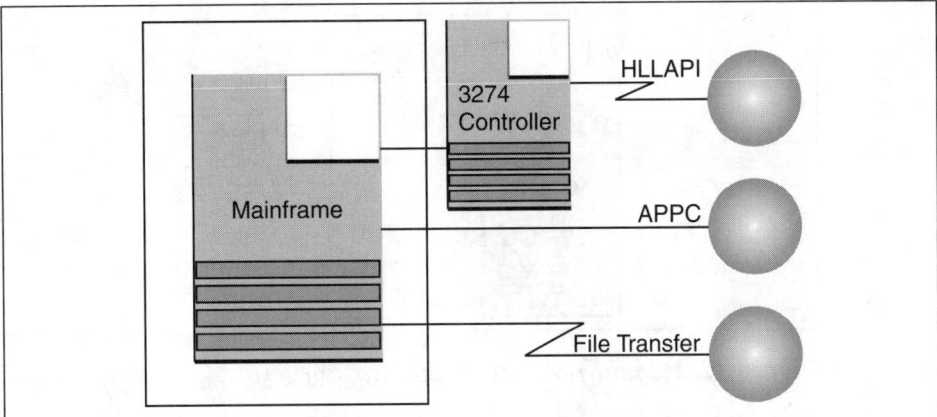

Figure 12.1 Access to mainframe data from outside the glass house.

To say the least, it was difficult to extract legacy data without the cooperation of the IS operations department. Irreconcilable differences continued to develop between the staff in IS development and IS operations, even as the technology wall between them started to crumble.

All that began to change once senior and executive management came to understand the importance of their data to the overall health of the corporation. In many organizations, the glass house has been prodded by management directives to ensure that certain nonmainframe applications get built. Management has also begun to take an active role in selecting the platform for these new applications, which usually incorporates some form of low-end or midrange server. This increased management involvement has diminished the power of the IS operations department, and in many companies IS operations have moved from a dominant position to that of an outsourced entity.

Deconstructing or reorganizing the IS operations department, however, can mean losing a valuable corporate commodity. Ironically, even as analysts predict the mainframe's demise, a recent surge is occurring in use of mainframes as application servers for Web serving, object request brokers, and proprietary application servers (see Figure 12.2). That means the IS operations department needs to survive in order to implement and support new core services. Mainframe *boxes* also still retain data required to run the enterprise. The question then arises: Why is control and care of the mainframe environment being outsourced or placed on the shoulders of a reduced workforce? The IS operations workers who do not make the transition to a new IS management model take with them a set of skills that is sorely missing from the newly emerged client/server staff.

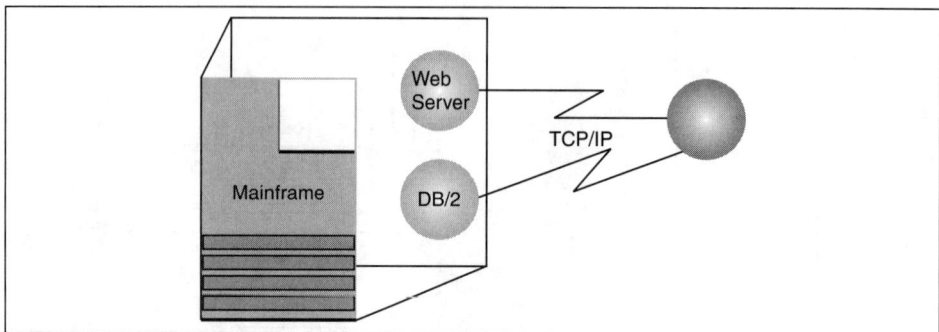

Figure 12.2 Mainframe as an application server.

PCs have given us "instant gratification" computing. For example, when a client/server developer sees a problem with a new system in production, he or she may fix it "hot," that is, after the application or system is already running. In contrast, traditional IS operations personnel are meticulous about designing and mapping out changes to their environment *before* the system goes live. They understand everything about the change and every system that might be affected by it. Furthermore, they institute the change after hours and test the environment before leaving the change in place. They also bring an understanding of security and control needed in today's client/server environments. This level of quality in production environments is desperately needed in today's client/server world.

We need not lose the skills of the "glass house" workers after dismantling it. With a little retraining, IS operations workers can become prime candidates for care and maintenance of the distributed computing environment. Of course, the transition will not be easy for many IS operations staff because they will have to acclimate themselves to a new culture (one that is less formal and disciplined).

> **NOTE**
> Combining the IS development and operations cultures will help make the distributed network as safe and secure as the mainframe.

When was the last time you read a quote like the following from Steven Bellovin, a leading network researcher from AT&T? "The Internet is not designed to resist certain kinds of malicious behavior ... I live in fear of someone noticing these accidents and saying, "Hey, I could do that." Some vulnerability of the Internet—a distributed environment—is due to the technology's limitations, but many

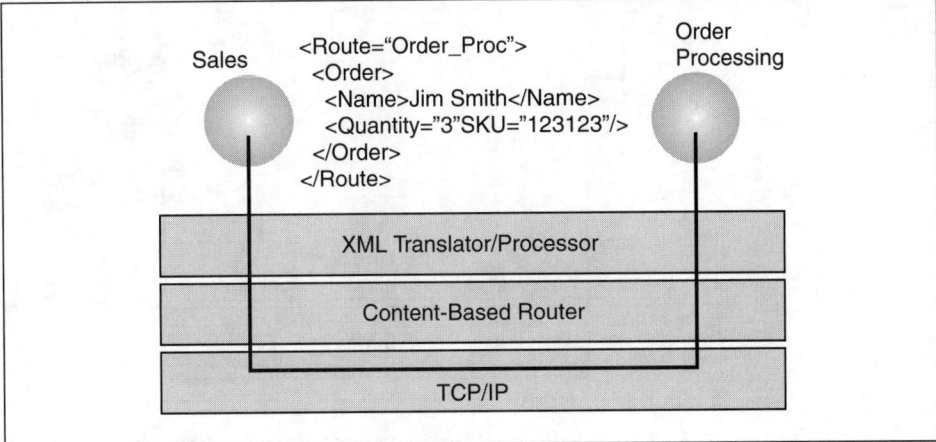

Figure 12.3 A distributed application designed using the data-centric model.

security risks are caused by the lack of controls over the Internet-based server environment. Many Internet-based servers are located in unlocked offices or on desktops in cubicles. Because of the connected nature of the Internet, any open access point could be used to invoke harm on the rest of the Net.

To utilize the skills of the IS operations workers effectively, and to give them an opportunity to transition successfully, we need to implement a network infrastructure that provides a hands-off approach to network services. Because of their tightly integrated nature to applications, this would be impossible in many cases today. For example, installation and maintenance of all CORBA ORBs in the enterprise could not be handed off to an IS operations facility; in fact, it requires a project-by-project deployment mentality, ultimately limiting its viability in the enterprise.

The data-centric computing model we discussed in the previous chapter was designed as an architecture that enables business application developers to focus on their job, and to know that when they need to move data between systems, there is a robust readily available set of services for them to use.

Figure 12.3 shows the architecture for a data-centric application. Figure 12.4 represents the same application developed with client/server technology. By moving to a data-centric model from a client/server model, there are many components that can be handed off to the IS operations staff for implementation and maintenance. For example, in Figure 12.2, all the deployment and maintenance of the services that represent the transport layer, inclusive of the registry and repository, can be handed off to IS operations.

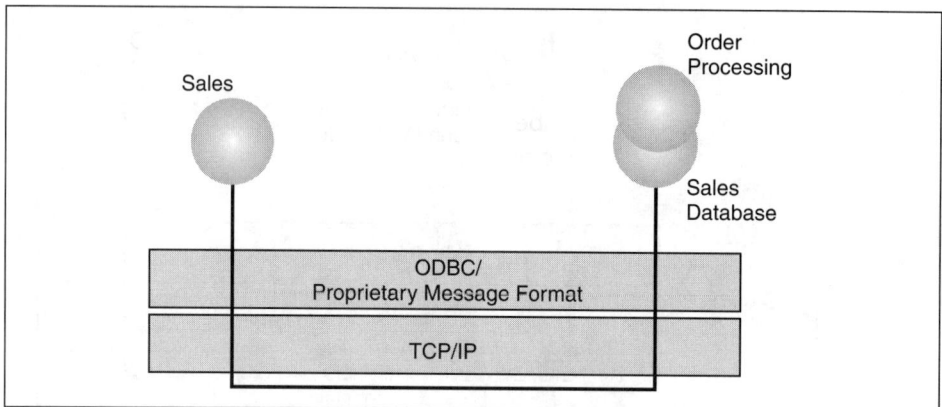

Figure 12.4 *A distributed application developed using the client/server model.*

Data-centric computing has sweeping implications for the way companies implement their network infrastructure. In some companies, the routers and cabling for networks is handled by the telecommunications department (the same group responsible for the phone system). Separating roles is problematic when network and distributed applications take center stage as the premier method of development. The ACME case study illustrates the importance of uniting the IS department for an effective distributed enterprise network.

Providing Ubiquitous Network Services

Earlier in this chapter and in Chapter 11, we discussed the concept of ubiquitous network services. Is it reasonable to believe that network services, such as publish and subscribe, asynchronous messaging, electronic mail, and transaction processing can become the software equivalent of network routers—each adding value by moving the data in a unique manner? This is an important question whose answer forms the foundation of the decision for moving forward with a data-centric computing model. But because of the manner in which these network services are delivered today, the answer is unclear. After all, vendors are selling network services to application developers to integrate them into applications via programming interfaces.

However, there are only two concerns from an application developer's point of view: getting data from another application, or pushing data out to another application. Moreover, application developers are not interested in *how* data transfer is accomplished; they would prefer a single method for programming both ends. Therefore, developers with the goal of delivering the application continue to mer-

ACME Case Study

If the ACME Bag Company enables its customers to place orders over the Web, it must be prepared to ensure a certain level of availability. Three main components are necessary for the new ordering system: the Web server, the sales system, and the program to link the two. Network connectivity will be used to satisfy the request coming in over the Web. The linking software is a middleware service, such as database, transaction processing, or asynchronous messaging.

McDougal's, a customer of ACME Bag Company, automates its internal process to order bags using the Web interface supplied by ACME. One day, McDougal's process fails because the ACME system is not operating properly. It turns out ACME's problem is tied to a communications error that occurs when connecting to the middleware. But ACME's real problem is that when they attempt to diagnose the problem, the telecommunications staff points to the application developers, who point to the Unix system administrators. It seems no one group is responsible for ensuring that the network, inclusive of the routers, cables, wires, and services, is up and running 24 hours a day, 7 days a week.

If ACME would move to a data-centric development model, the network services would become a ubiquitous component of the network. In this situation, it makes perfect sense to utilize the skills of the traditional IS operations staff to keep the system running and in check. ACME might need to shuffle some of its resources to ensure that the proper technical skills are available within the IS operations department. And ACME must assign accountability for each IS system to a specific person or group because it is becoming the lifeblood of the enterprise, and thus well worth the price.

rily integrate these services into their applications instead of looking to distance themselves from the plumbing issues.

The developer's concerns do not obviate the need for programming interfaces for network services; they are just an indication that the business application developers need a single method for putting the data into the service, routing information that can be understood by the service to deliver it to an endpoint, and to retrieve the data when it comes out at the other end. Picture the big tubes that move canisters with data from one location to another in a drive-through bank.

What routing and delivery capabilities are required to support a data-centric model of computing? First, a service cannot be required to have different configurations for each and every application that uses it. For example, object request brokers require each application to provide configuration information, such as which memory model or threading model to use. This makes implementing ORBs for the enterprise unwieldy.

Second, services must act as a conduit to deliver data between two endpoints in a generic fashion. While inside the service, value-added functions can occur—such as transformations, routing, caching, storage, and so on—but once it reaches an endpoint, it must be delivered through a single portal.

This reinforces the concept of network service exporting a "vanilla" set of a data from an application and moving it to another location where it will be processed (see Figure 12.5). Users can view this as analogous to a laundry chute capable of discerning colors from whites and performing separation functions, dropping colors in one basket and whites in another. We offered a solution to the data exchange problem from the application perspective in the previous chapter by creating an entity called a service preparation utility. Now we will examine this process from the network services perspective.

For purposes of this explanation, we will assume that we are using a publish-and-subscribe network service. Many of these services work by creating *subjects*, or named channels, that supply a specific set of information. Publish-and-subscribe services can route data using a number of flexible mechanisms, such as domain-based routing (over a fixed set of machines or addresses), content-based routing

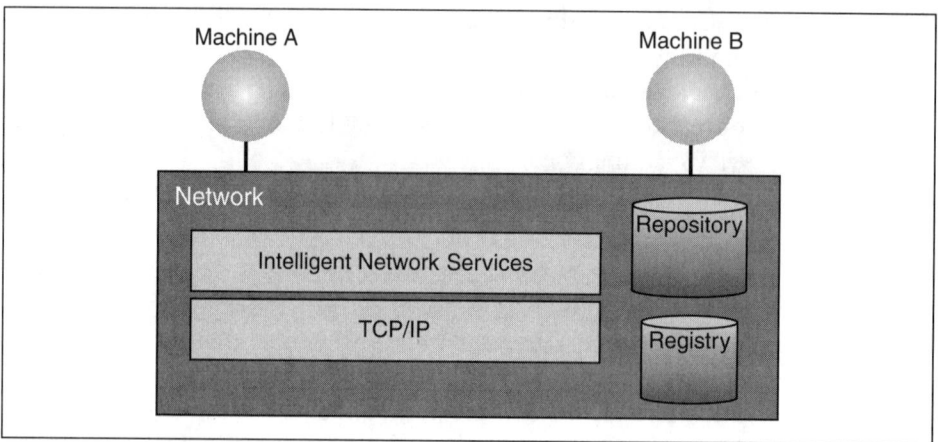

Figure 12.5 The network is the container.

(using the content of the message to make the decision), or direct addressing. These capabilities provide a good foundation for data-centric computing.

The mechanism that simplifies the data routing task best is content-based routing (CBR). CBR looks to the message itself to provide information about where the data should be routed. Very simply, routing information could be a set of keywords found in the message. However, CBR can quickly become a very sophisticated routing mechanism when written using the eXtensible Markup Language (XML).

As discussed in Chapter 11, XML is a method of tagging data for very specific meaning. These tags become increasingly useful when used to categorize and route data. It should be possible to configure a CBR-based publish-and-subscribe network to recognize certain tags as routing information. These tags could be as direct as:

```
<Route IP="127.0.0.1"/> or <Route Name="ncfocus.com"/>
```

or as indirect as is the case with CBR. A Subject tag could represent the recipients of this data. The tag information can be used by hardware routers as well as by publish-and-subscribe software. Cisco routers can be configured to utilize XML tags inside of TCP/IP data packets to define routes.

Again, publish-subscribe establishes a network pipe through which we can transmit data. We can now move a piece of data from system A to system B. Next, we need to get the data into the pipe from our application. That is, we need to take the data generated by the application and prepare it to be moved to another location. This can be handled by the service preparation tools as follows:

1. **Service preparation.** This is a special application used by the end user or by an application to prepare data for delivery to another location. An electronic mail package is an example of a service preparation tool. End users prepare the mail for delivery by providing name, subject, and mailing directions (urgent, return-receipt, etc.). The service preparation tool can be unaware of the value of the data; it simply knows how to take a packet of data, start to end, and add routing characteristics. Data routing transparency is an important feature of data-centric computing; an application needs no knowledge about sending and receiving data because the service preparation tool will handle these requirements.

2. **Processors.** At the receiving side, there is another component called a processor. Processors can be application servers that listen continuously for incoming data, or they can be activated entities like an e-mail

reader. The e-mail reader requires some facility for storing messages until they can be delivered; this is the role of the repository in the data-centric computing model. Because we want behavior of distributed network services to be consistent regardless of how they are implemented, there are certain components that must exist in the model.

The data repository may be made up of many different storage facilities and access mechanisms, but it is controlled through a single programmable interface. A single interface allows services to act in either a synchronous or an asynchronous manner, but not have to make the decision at design time. For example, assume that a message is intended to be delivered to an awaiting application server (processor), but that server is down. When the processor is restarted, it should be able to check the repository for missed messages and handle those before pulling new ones off the network.

Use of the repository is analogous to the concept of voice mail. How many companies today would be willing to run without voice mail? Voice mail is a backbone of business. This is the exact same mentality that should be applied to designing enterprisewide network services. When a message is sent out and the receiving application is down or unavailable, the message should be transferred to the repository the same way a call would be routed to voice mail. The repository can manage these messages, and even expire them if they get too old, as long as there's a consistent handling of nondelivered messages regardless of the delivery mechanisms.

The central aim is to provide homogeneous behavior of network services without forcing a particular type of implementation. [Note, this is what the Common Object Request Broker Architecture (CORBA) has promised for years, but never delivered.] The key reason for their lack of dominance in this area is that everything is designed as a programmatic interface (process first) instead of offering a data-centric (push/pull) capability. The network bus that CORBA attempts to supply is exactly the type of facility we want from data-centric computing; but the object infrastructure—the OMA—needs to be redefined to operate over XML-like objects and not fixed entities.

Once network services are implemented on the network, they have to be made readily available. This entails replication over servers and multiple-path delivery mechanisms. Designing a data-centric system may require the expertise of a telecommunications architect—the experts who build our phone and data communications networks and understand the requirements of dynamic switching (decide delivery paths at the time of next hop) and redundant paths (ensure that there is always a single path to a destination even if certain equipment is damaged or down).

Is Data-Centric Computing Worth the Effort and Expense?

You need to answer this question for your own company, but to guide you, Table 12.1 offers a simple comparison of a data-centric architecture versus continuing with client/server architectures.

Table 12.1 Data-Centric Computing Compared to Client/Server

LAYER	CLIENT/SERVER	DATA-CENTRIC COMPUTING
Infrastructure	Tied to network protocols (TCP/IP).	Network protocol-independent.
	Requires multiple programmatic interfaces.	Platform-independent.
	Platform-dependent (counts Java as a single platform).	Tied to a single programmable interface.
	Requires decision regarding asynchronous or synchronous at application design time.	Data transport is independent of application function.
	Network service change could require sweeping changes in application code. This has a ripple effect that impacts testing and deployment.	
Application	Requires expensive middleware for scalability.	Relies on (possibly expensive) intelligent network services.
	Application and network service tightly integrated.	Application and network services developed independently.
	Requires fixed data structures.	Data structures are dynamic, but need to maintain a minimum of support for a base set of data.
Hardware and Software Costs	Computed on a project-by-project basis.	Computed on an enterprisewide basis.
Reuse	Low to medium levels of code reuse.	High amount of code reuse.
	Medium level of data reuse.	High amount of data reuse.

Conclusions

This chapter has demonstrated how you can deliver available network services to the enterprise by utilizing concepts learned by combining data-centric computing requirements with distributed computing technologies.

FOR FURTHER READING

Baker, Sean. *CORBA Distributed Objects: Using Orbix.* (Reading, MA: Addison-Wesley), 1997.

Gilman, Leonard, Richard Schreider, and Len Gilman. *Distributed Computing with IBM MQSeries.* (New York: John Wiley & Sons, Inc.), 1996.

Ligon, Thomas. *Client/Server Communications Services: A Guide for the Applications Developer.* (New York: McGraw-Hill), 1997.

Lowe, Doug. *Client/Server Computing for Dummies.* (Foster City, CA: IDG Books Worldwide), 1996.

GLOSSARY

Applet An entity that represents a Java application and has specific functions for running inside of a Web browser.

Asynchronous communications Communications exchanges take place between two devices without regard for the sequence or timing of previous exchanges of information; transmission is controlled by start and stop elements at the beginning and end of each message.

Asynchronous message passing *See* asynchronous communications.

Backoffice The description for the department(s) responsible for the noninteractive processing of business data.

Balanced score card (contract) An evaluation matrix with a (usually flexible) rating system for product/technology features and functions that allows comparisons in a way that reflects usage.

Best-in-class performance Outstanding or above average activity when compared to all enterprises engaged in similar function, for example, software development.

Best-of-breed Outstanding or above average performance in the delivery of a service or performance of a function when compared to others performing the same task in the same industry.

Black box A device that produces an output based on processes performed on input data but with no explanation of the process taking place within the device.

Business object A binary entity that stores business-specific processing logic. Usually defined in an object-oriented manner.

Business process Any series of repetitive tasks performed to accomplish a business function, for example, order entry, design approval, billing.

Business process view A performance or functional view that reports on the state of the process taken as a whole rather than focusing on individual elements involved in the process, for example, reporting that order entry takes 2 hours instead of 10 minutes versus stating that the router for the sales database server has malfunctioned.

Business related view *See* business process view.

Business rule Formal definition of activities to implement a business function, for example, the sequence of signatures to authorize a design change.

CEA Chief Executive Architect; the person responsible for designing how data will flow between multiple departments.

Chargeback Method of accounting for services within an enterprise by tracking and charging the consumers of those services, for example, billing the Engineering department for the amount of disk space its files take up on the data storage system.

Cherished system Euphemism referring to a legacy application or business system that has been in existence for a long period of time, typically one implemented without using current design and implementation techniques.

Child class Derived classes (or subclasses) of objects which possess the basic attributes of the parent but usually with unique values or properties.

CIO Chief Information Officer; the person responsible for ensuring that the goals of the business are properly represented by the information systems.

Client The system, device, individual or element requesting services or activity in a client/server system; for example, a program requesting print services is the client of the print server.

COM Component Object Model. This is Microsoft's architecture for providing interoperability of applications for the Windows operating system.

CORBA The Common Object Request Broker Architecture is a standard for invoking object components, it defines a standard way for users to access self-contained objects. This standard is controlled by the Object Management Group (OMG).

CTO Chief Technology Officer; the person responsible for applying emerging technologies to enhance the goals of the business.

Data-Centric Computing Model An architecture developed by NC.Focus for building naturally interoperable applications in the enterprise.

Datagram services Data communications or information exchange services that send data in asynchronous, independent frames or packets, similar to a letter sent through land mail; also called connectionless services.

DCOM A version of Microsoft's COM (*See* COM) that operates over a network.

Development methodology A process or set of processes which define the standards for creating, record keeping, and testing a product, for example, the processes and standards within a software development team.

Distributed computing The term to define the separation of process over geographic or electronic boundaries.

DMTF Desktop Management Task Force.

Document objects Object code describing documents.

Dumb client A device requesting service that has no local intelligence or ability to interpret data or perform local information processing, for example, a simple terminal.

Electronic Data Interchange (EDI) A protocol for the exchange of commerce-based data between consumers and suppliers.

Event-driven management As it applies to distributed systems and network management, a management style marked by reaction to events reported to the administrator, one that concentrates on monitoring what happens in their environment, as opposed to, for example, a policy-based management focus.

Extensible The term used to define an entity capable of growth through extensions.

Extranet The term for networks that are publicly accessible by members outside of the company.

Fat client A distributed computing processing design which places a significant amount of intelligence and processing on the client; for example, data input at the client is processed and reduced using a locally resident application with just summary or significant information forwarded to a central processor.

Framework An architectural entity that describes how new entities can be added to it.

Groupware Applications or groups of applications that facilitate the exchange of information and cooperation within an organization.

Indeterminable state   The state of a distributed process when a response packet is not acknowledged.

Infrastructure   The term used to identify all the equipment and software necessary for distributed data and process.

Inheritance   A term used by the object–oriented paradigm to represent child entities that gain all of their parent's features.

Interface Definition Language (IDL)   The language used to define the formal specification of the functions and parameters exposed by or used by other system elements to interface to a distributed object module. This vendor-neutral language is used by the OMG to define content and interface specifications for objects.

Intranet   The term used to represent the network that is accessible only by members of a single organizations, be it departmental, enterprise, or domain.

IS   Information Services department.

JAD   Joint Application Development; an applications development process that calls for the active involvement of the end user of the application during design and development.

Jurisdictional management   Management implemented according to formal agreements describing acceptable levels of service, also known as Service Level Agreements. An explicit agreement between a service provider (e.g., a telephone company or IT organization which specifies agreed levels of payment based on the availability of and response time of the network).

Language bindings   The formal mapping from a neutral format to a specific programming language.

Living system   A system that is continuously changing to meet the needs of business. These changes come by adding, removing, and updating existing components.

Lower middleware   A term used to describe the pieces of "middleware" used to manage the interactions and transactions between applications on the different machines, including low-level shared services at the application level, such as printing and filing, and functions such as security and recovery.

Management framework   A distributed management implementation model which provides a standardized interface and can include a set of basic services such as event collection and forwarding, display capability, data storage, etc., essentially synonymous with management platform.

Management platform   *See* management framework.

Management service   A service implemented as part of an automated management solution, for example, event collection, report generation, etc.

Marshaled   The act of breaking down a data structure, packetizing for network delivery, and recombining it upon receipt.

Message queuing   The process of queuing messages for asynchronous delivery.

Metering (applications)   The process of embedding mechanisms for collecting and storing management and control information within an application.

Method (objects)   A function called within the context of a specific instance of an object.

Middleware   A term used to define the middle-tier software in an *n*-tiered client/server application. It provides the interfaces or "glue" to enable remote machines to work together, hides details of the underlying systems software and hardware of computers and networks from the applications, allowing applications to converse in standard ways across a network.

MoM   Manager-of-Managers, an application designed to coordinate the activities of other automated management tools and applications; also, Message-Oriented-Middleware—applications designed to act as message handlers (storage, routing, and forwarding) in interprocess (and application) communications.

NOS   Network Operating System.

NSAPI   Netscape Services Application Programming Interface.

Off budget resource   A resource (person, system, device) which is not accounted for in an operating budget.

OMG   Object Management Group; a consortium of vendors who have been working to define standards for object based technologies specifically CORBA and its constitute elements, the ORB (Object Request Broker), CORBAservices, and CORBAfacilities.

Open solution   Any solution based on de facto and de jure standards.

Operational model   A model of how a system, application, process, etc. operates.

Orange book   A definition of security procedures supplied by the U.S. government.

ORB   Object Request Broker; a standard promoted by the Object Management Group that describes requests for and provision of services in an object environment.

OSF   Open Software Foundation, now a part of the Open Group, previously an organization formed by vendors (HP, IBM, etc.) to counter the market momentum of AT&T and Sun in the area of UNIX and its user interface.

OSI reference model   Open Systems Interconnect reference model; describes the seven layers required for communications in a network. Starting with a basic description of physical connectors (pin voltage values and significance) and ending at the application interface level. These are described explicitly in the text.

Outsource   The process of contracting with external resources for services previously delivered by resources within an organization or enterprise.

Parent class   An object entity which defines a primary function, characteristic, or element in a modeled system with unique attributes and processing capabilities associated with them.

Partitioning   The act of splitting an application across a process boundary.

Persistence   The act of storing an in-memory object to permanent medium.

RAD   Rapid Application Development; a methodology for designing, testing, and implementation of software solutions which dramatically shortens the time lapsed from conception to availability.

Reuse   The act of using existing code and data in a new task.

Roll back   To return to the status prior to an attempted change; for example, having all users use Version n instead of Version $n+1$ of a file or application.

Roll out   To distribute or introduce a product, application or service to the user or consumer community.

Screen scraping   A technique for providing data and information display to a user that involves adding a GUI front end to a character-based user interface (CHUI).

Service Level Agreement (SLA)   An explicit statement that defines the expected services as well as metrics to evaluate the level of services between the provider of that service and the user or consumer of that service and typically linked to payment for the services.

Service registry   The facility for registering the location of service handlers.

Service repository   The facility for persistently storing data messages while in transit across asynchronous transports.

Shelfware   Software application that, while purchased, never gets installed and used but remains "on the shelf."

Smart device   A device with application "intelligence" embedded/implemented as part of itself.

State machine   A model for describing the possible logical states of an application.

Stub   A piece of code that proxies the actual processing logic.

Telco, Telecom   Acronyms referring to telecommunications industry, companies, and services.

Thin client   A distributed computing processing design which places a significant amount of intelligence and processing on the server rather than on the local device or processor; for example, data input from the client will be sent for processing at a remote server.

Total Cost of Ownership (TCO)   Refers to the effort to account for all costs and expenses associated with the acquisition, use, and maintenance of a device or service, typically used in relation to desktop computers.

Trouble ticket   A "job ticket" or order prepared in response to a system or device problem which is an authorization to repair or take corrective action, used to track problems reported to and requests made to Help desks.

Upper middleware   A term used to describe the pieces of "middleware" that handle the problems of interfacing to applications and users, including any changes in application-level formats and presentation formats.

VAR   Value Added Reseller; a systems distributor adds value to a system before reselling it to an end user. The added value can be combining and bundling of applications, "hardening" of the system to withstand environmental shocks, or the provision of any number of services that the consumers do not want to provide themselves.

Vendor   Used in our context to identify the manufacturer of an application or computing devices, for example, Bull, IBM, Sun Systems, Computer Associates, Tivoli, Hewlett-Packard, etc.

Virtual private network (VPN)   An extension of standard network firewall (access protection) capabilities to permit authenticated, encrypted communications between sites on the Internet.

Web server A computer processor dedicated to running applications that implement services for and provide access to the World Wide Web.

Wrapping A programming technique for integrating older systems and applications using a communications bridge to legacy functions and data. Wrappers provide a communications interface between the systems by turning the legacy systems into service objects. The legacy system code appears as an object that is a complete function (e.g., to handle a shipping order).

X.500 standards Standards defining the implementation of directory services for name-to-address resolution in networks; part of the OSI standards set.

XML eXtensible Markup Language; a derivative of the Standard Generalized Markup Language (SGML).

X-windows A GUI interface, developed initially at MIT for the Unix operating system; an early version called Motif exerted considerable influence over versions developed by the various vendors.

X-terminals Diskless terminals and "nonintelligent" terminals running versions of X-Windows using a vendor-supplied GUI.

INDEX